Second Edition

Introduction to
Early Childhood Education
Preschool through Primary Grades

Jo Ann Brewer

Salem State College

ALLYN AND BACON

Boston London Toronto Sydney Tokyo Singapore

Vice-President, Publisher: Nancy Forsyth
Editorial Assistant: Christine R. Nelson
Marketing Manager: Ellen Mann
Production Administrator: Annette Joseph
Editorial-Production Service: Communicáto, Ltd.
Text Designer: Karen Mason
Composition Buyer: Linda Cox
Manufacturing Buyer: Louise Richardson
Cover Administrator: Linda Knowles
Cover Designer: Susan Paradise

Copyright © 1995, 1992 by Allyn & Bacon
A Simon & Schuster Company
Needham Heights, Mass. 02194

This book is printed on
recycled, acid-free paper.

Library of Congress Cataloging-in-Publication Data
Brewer, Jo Ann.
    Introduction to early childhood education : preschool through
primary grades / Jo Ann Brewer. — 2nd ed.
       p.   cm.
    Includes bibliographical references and index.
    ISBN 0-205-15432-8
    1. Early childhood education—United States.   2. Early childhood
education—History.   3. Child development—United States.   I. Title.
LB1139.25.B74   1995
372.21'073—dc20

                                                              94-27444
                                                              CIP

Printed in the United States of America
10 9 8 7 6 5 4 3 2 1   99 98 97 96 95 94

PHOTO CREDITS: pp. xxii, 34, 64, 91, 104, 115, 138, 202, 212, 220, 244, 367, 415,
436, 451: © Jim Pickerell; pp. 4, 400: Deborah Kahn Kalas, © Stock, Boston; pp. 11,
232, 416, 425: © Robert Harbison; pp. 19, 59, 130, 181, 195, 282, 327, 403, 456, 468,
475: © Will Faller; p. 39: Ron Wood; pp. 76, 94, 164, 170, 187, 247, 272, 365, 380,
410, 488: © Stephen Marks; p. 122: Peter Simon, © Stock, Boston; pp. 143, 338:
Elizabeth Crews, © Stock, Boston; pp. 155, 443: Laimute Druskis, © Stock, Boston;
p. 235: George Malave, © Stock, Boston; pp. 299, 357: Gale Zucker © Stock,
Boston; p. 316: © Mary Ellen Lepionka; p. 352: Fredrik D. Bodin, © Stock, Boston;
p. 383: Bob Kramer, © Stock, Boston.

To my daughter Leslie—

a wonderful mother

and teacher of her young children

Brief Contents

••••••••
Contents

Chapter Four

PLANNING AND ASSESSING LEARNING ACTIVITIES 104

Chapter Five

PLAY: Learning at Its Best 138

Chapter Six

LANGUAGE: Celebrating the Magic　170

Chapter Seven

THE DEVELOPMENT OF LITERACY:
Reading and Writing   202

Chapter Eight

MANIPULATION AND DISCOVERY: Mathematics 244

Chapter Nine

MANIPULATION AND DISCOVERY: Science 282

Chapter Ten

ENCOURAGING THE CREATIVE ARTS 316

Chapter Eleven

LIVING TOGETHER: The Social Studies   352

Chapter Twelve

WELLNESS FOR THE YOUNG CHILD: Motor Development, Health, and Safety   380

Chapter Thirteen

GUIDING BEHAVIOR: Encouraging Self-Control   410

• • • • • •
Preface

In the Preface to the first edition of *Introduction to Early Childhood Education*, I said that teaching young children was a very complex undertaking. That statement is even more true now, three years later. Today, teachers of young children are expected to know and do more than ever before.

The challenges of early childhood education are enormous: teaching more children who are poor, who are homeless, who live in dysfunctional families, and who endure the social upheaval in American cities. But as the challenges increase, so do the rewards for helping children develop in a safe and supportive environment. This text is designed to help those teachers who choose the important work of teaching young children make the many decisions required daily.

This book defines *early childhood* as the period from birth through age eight and focuses on the school experiences of children in this age range. The early childhood years are more important than any other eight-year period in the life of a human being in terms of the learning that occurs, the attitudes about learning and school that develop, and the social skills that are acquired that will enable the individual to succeed in today's world. The problems of the future will only be solved by today's children if those children value learning, learn to cooperate with others, and value a democratic way of life. Teachers can help young children develop these attitudes and skills.

FEATURES OF THE TEXT

The changes in this edition reflect some of the changes in the profession of early childhood education and the needs of those who are or who want to be teachers of young children. The book has been reduced to fifteen chapters in order to emphasize those topics and issues that are most practical for beginning teachers or for those new to early childhood education.

The text begins with a brief overview of child development (Chapter One), especially as it relates to planning curriculum experiences. Chapter Two provides a "slice of life" look at three different ways of organizing experiences for young children. Chapters Three and Four focus on the decisions that teachers must make about organizing environments and planning and assessing activities for young learners. Chapter Five is devoted to the topic of play and its value in curricula for young children.

Chapter Six on language and Chapter Seven on emerging literacy were designed to provide fundamental knowledge about children's language and the extension of their oral language to its printed form. No other area of curriculum receives the scrutiny from parents and others that is aimed at instruction in literacy. The decisions teachers make about language and literacy are crucial.

The content chapters (Chapters Seven through Twelve) provide goals and activities for reading and writing, mathematics, science, the creative arts, the social studies, and physical education and wellness. Although the content areas are discussed in separate chapters, the focus is on integrating the curriculum. To demonstrate this focus, the theme of patterns is developed through "Integrating the Curriculum" boxes in these chapters. The purpose is to help teacher education students understand that any well-chosen theme can include all the content areas. Young children learn best when the experiences or activities planned for them are not divided into discrete subject-matter areas.

The last chapters in the book consider the decisions teachers must make about discipline and classroom management (Chapter Thirteen), assessment and reporting of students and programs (Chapter Fourteen), and working with parents and other adults in classroom settings (Chapter Fifteen). These chapters are included to help readers with decisions that are not directly related to planning curriculum experiences but are crucial to the success of any program for young children.

An Epilogue has been added to this edition to present information about the changing field of early childhood education and issues that will concern teachers and prospective teachers in the future.

In this edition, real effort has been made to help readers view *developmentally appropriate practice (DAP)* as the process of choosing learning experiences that are individually appropriate for each child, that recognize the strengths of each learner, and that involve children actively in their own learning. In each chapter, readers are presented with a "Developmentally Appropriate Practice" box that asks them to respond to questions or statements designed to help them build a strong understanding of DAP and what it means when implemented in classroom settings. Other comments about DAP appear throughout the text in relevant discussions.

Following the "Chapter Summary," each chapter includes several exercise sections that ask students of early childhood education to reflect on their own learning in responding to situations or questions common to practicing teachers. "What Would You Do?" sections pose real-life situations and issues and ask readers to consider how they would respond. "Theory into Practice" sections put students in touch with teachers and teaching materials and in actual classrooms, observing early childhood education firsthand. The questions or situations posed in these sections do not have "right" answers; rather, their purpose is to help students reflect on their own understanding and experience and apply them in real-world teaching situations.

The activities recommended in this text have been tried by real teachers in real classrooms. They are presented not as isolated units or events (something to do on Monday) but as applications of theory. When teachers understand theory, they can design their own learning activities and also can evaluate other activities presented in the many publications aimed at teachers of young children.

Every teacher makes important decisions every day. This book is designed to help teachers of young children make wise decisions that will benefit the children they teach and, therefore, all of us.

ACKNOWLEDGMENTS

When one of my students learned that this second edition was underway, she asked, "Have you learned enough that is new to write a second edition?" The answer is, "Yes, I have," and the reason is that I have been fortunate enough to be involved with many thoughtful teachers as they have struggled with important questions in their classrooms and with bright and energetic students who have taught me much more than I have ever taught them. My thanks to all those students and to the teachers who have allowed me to be part of their classrooms. I wish that I could list all their names, but Marilyn Herzog, Anne Thiebeaux, Marie Buckreis, and Sig Boloz are among the many who have helped.

This second edition would not have been possible without the success of the first edition, so I must acknowledge the help of Colleen Dyrud, who was so important to that book and continues to be supportive. I have also received feedback from many colleagues who used the first edition in their classes and offered constructive advice for making the second edition better. My thanks to all of them.

The editorial staff at Allyn and Bacon have provided support and encouragement at every stage of producing this book. I wish especially to thank Nancy Forsyth and Christine Nelson for their optimism that this project could be completed and for their interest and knowledge.

Several individuals reviewed the first edition and helped shape this new edition by making invaluable suggestions for improvements. I want to thank Donna M. Banas (Moraine Valley Community College, Illinois) and Joan Isenberg (George Mason University) for their reviewing help and also Julie K. Biddle (University of Dayton), Sheila M. Cole (Garden City Community College), Mary-Margaret Harrington (Peabody College of Vanderbilt University), Carol R. Foster (Georgia State University), Kathy Lake (Alverno College), Donna L. Legro (University of Houston), Betty Mason (Ohio University), Nancy Russell (Texas A & I University), Sandra L. Starkey (West Virginia Graduate College), Beverly Tucker (Valdosta State College), Betty Watson (Harding University), Deborah Webster (Mount Mary College), and Nancy Winter (Greenfield Community College), for their insightful answers to the questionnaires that helped shape this edition.

Many other people have helped make this book possible, but none is as important as my husband and colleague, Bill Harp. He always believes that I can do anything and provides humor, pep talks, serious discussions of issues, or whatever else is needed at the time to keep the work going.

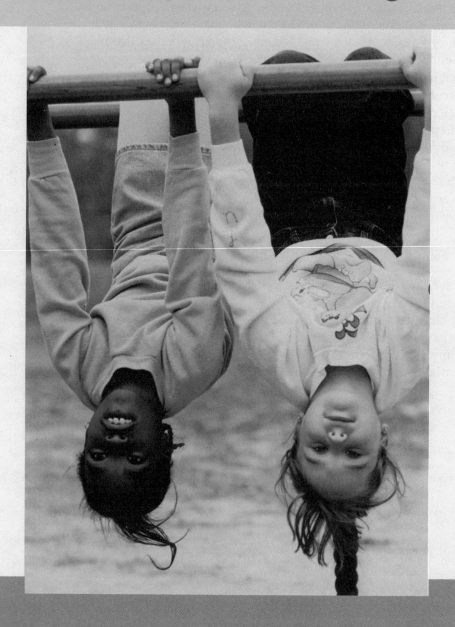

Chapter One

Young Children Growing, Thinking, and Learning

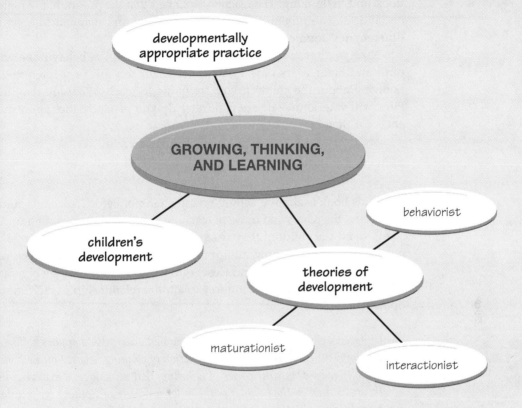

Since deciding that you want to be a teacher of young children, you have looked at children and their teachers and classrooms with different eyes. Your visit to observe a child-care center this afternoon was fascinating. You were looking for specific evidence of children's development at different ages. You made some observations about children's physical abilities—some were riding two-wheel bikes, some could use scissors easily, and some were skipping around the play yard. You also noticed children working cooperatively at the sand box and water table, and you saw some older children helping younger ones complete puzzles—both examples of social development. Some of the children you observed were demonstrating their intellectual development by organizing the play materials into categories and labeling the categories with signs they had written. In the very short time since infancy, these children have made great gains in controlling their bodies, in expressing their emotions, and in thinking. The teacher explained that the program, the materials, and the equipment were carefully selected and planned to meet the different developmental needs of the children.

Now you have more to think about: What is typical behavior between birth and eight years old? What is atypical? You are very interested in knowing about the children you are going to teach. What are they like? How will your knowledge of children help you plan activities and experiences for them?

· ·

This book is about teaching young children. Before teachers can discuss the whats and hows of teaching children, they must first understand the children they teach. Knowledge of child development is not sufficient for planning an appropriate program, but it is a necessary starting point. Bredekamp and Rosegrant (1992) use the analogy of a manufacturer of children's clothing to explain the relationship of child development and curriculum:

> Children's clothing is an entire industry that successfully applies child development knowledge. The construction of clothing is based on its own knowledge base, the intricacies of tailoring, that is analogous to curriculum theory; but when the product of the tailor is a piece of clothing for a child, knowledge of child development must be activated. First, the tailor must know what is age appropriate. The basic size dimensions of the typical client are determined by typical growth patterns. Similarly, the tailor must be aware of the client's other developmental needs. For example, the fine-motor development of toddlers prohibits zippers, just as their diapering needs dictate snaps along the legs. The range of options in children's clothing, similar to the breadth and depth of curriculum, is influenced by children's development in general. Occasionally a designer applies child development knowledge with brilliant results, such as using Velcro™ to fasten preschoolers' shoes.
>
> For clothing to actually sell and be functional, it must also be individually appropriate. Some children, despite the growth charts, are much larger or smaller than average. It is not sufficient to know a child's age to purchase appropriate clothing; one must also know the individual child's size, cultural background, and preferences. While overalls may be the most developmentally appropriate clothing design for active 3-year-olds, an individual 3-year-old may prefer dresses—and only dresses in lavender. Knowledge of

clothing construction and design as well as knowledge of child development are essential, but still inadequate. Knowledge of individual and cultural differences must be activated by the responsible person (usually the parent) if the clothing is to be worn, appreciated, and practical. Similar connections must be made between child development knowledge and curriculum if programs for young children are to reach their potential. (p. 6)

The National Association for the Education of Young Children defines *early childhood* as the period from birth to age eight (Bredekamp 1987). Some child-care programs serve infants and toddlers as well as preschoolers (three- and four-year-olds) or primary children (five-, six-, seven-, and eight-year-olds). Most of this chapter will discuss normal growth and development. Keep in mind that to determine the average age when a child is able to perform a task or behave in a certain way, half the children must perform that task earlier than the average and half, later than the average.

You will meet many children in your teaching career who have special needs, ranging from severe mental or physical challenges to slight delays in the development of language. You also will meet children who are gifted and talented in a variety of ways, who are suffering from attention deficits, and who are wise beyond their years in relating to people. Children come in all sizes, colors, and places on the developmental continuum. Our job, as teachers, is to recognize each child's abilities and growth and plan for the next steps as she grows physically, intellectually, socially, and emotionally.

DEVELOPMENTALLY APPROPRIATE PRACTICE

The term **developmentally appropriate practice (DAP)** will be used throughout this book to mean practice that is age and individually appropriate for each child in a program. Planning a developmentally appropriate curriculum means that teachers have to know each child—where he is developmentally and what his individual talents and interests are. DAP also requires that teachers think about children's basic needs for play and rest, that they focus on children's development in all areas, that they plan an inclusive program that honors the cultural differences each child brings to school, and that they work to support parents and families (Bredekamp 1987).

The chapters that follow will provide more detail about developmentally appropriate practice and ask you to reflect on what makes one choice developmentally appropriate and another, inappropriate. Please remember that although there are some basic guidelines that define DAP, in classrooms across the United States, it looks quite different. DAP requires that

Developmentally appropriate practice (DAP) Practice that is age and individually appropriate for each child in a program.

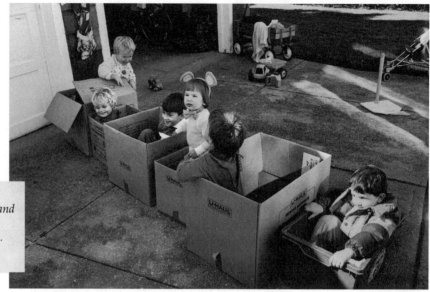

Play episodes often reflect children's growing social and physical development.

teachers and children work continuously to determine the best practice for a group of children at a given time. DAP is dynamic, not static. It cannot be the same for all children or all groups of children.

The purpose of this chapter is to describe briefly some theoretical lenses through which child development is viewed and to outline typical patterns of development. This knowledge is most useful when it can be consciously applied to selecting and organizing curriculum experiences. Often, teachers choose activities or organize those activities in ways that can be traced to the different theories of child growth and development, but they are unaware of these connections. As a teacher, you need to recognize why you choose one activity over another or one organizational scheme over another.

THEORIES OF DEVELOPMENT

Children's growth and development can be described from several theoretical points of view. Each of these points of view has its supporters among practitioners in early childhood education, and each offers explanations of human growth and development. These theoretical positions include behaviorism, maturationism, and interactionism. Throughout your career, as you read and think about children and about planning programs that will be beneficial to them, reflect upon the points of view expressed by authors of articles and reports and notice how their suggestions differ depending on what they believe about children's development.

Behaviorist Theory

John B. Watson (1878–1958), Edward Thorndike (1874–1949), and B. F. Skinner (1904–1990) are well-known **behaviorists.** Each of these theorists believed that behavior can be shaped by the response that follows any particular action. Skinner is the best known of the modern behaviorists. He wrote extensively about learning as controlled by a system of rewards and punishments. His name is synonymous with **stimulus-response theory** and operant conditioning (Hill 1977). The basic elements of stimulus-response theory include reinforcements, punishments, operant conditioning, and extinguishing behavior.

Behaviorists
Theorists who base their understanding of children on the belief that behavior can be shaped by rewards and punishments.

Stimulus-response theory
A theory that organisms will respond to given stimuli based on previous experience with the stimuli.

In classical conditioning, a learner is presented with a stimulus and a reward and learns to expect the reward whenever the stimulus is presented. This type of conditioning is exemplified by the classic Pavlovian experiment of ringing a bell and immediately presenting a dog with food until the dog salivates at the sound of the bell. Operant conditioning differs from classical conditioning in that the behavior precedes the reinforcement. For example, a pigeon may learn to push a lever to get a food pellet. Presenting a reward after a response provides positive reinforcement of the behavior. Negative reinforcement can also be used to elicit behavior. If the floor of the pigeon's cage were electrified and pushing the lever stopped the shock, the pigeon would learn to press the lever to avoid an unpleasant stimulus; that is negative reinforcement. Behavior can also be punished rather than reinforced. A pigeon might be punished by an electric shock for failing to push a lever on a set schedule.

In the classroom, reinforcements are often used to shape behaviors. Reinforcements in the classroom can be positive or negative. A positive reinforcement is something that is viewed by the learner as desirable. If a child completes a task or exhibits a behavior that is desirable, the teacher may positively reinforce that behavior by verbal praise, a token such as a sticker, or some other treat. Negative reinforcement involves allowing a child to avoid or escape from an undesirable consequence or situation if certain behaviors are exhibited. For example, the teacher might give a child the option of leaving the "time-out" chair more quickly if she does not talk at all for five minutes. Finally, punishment in the classroom need not necessarily be corporal (physical) punishment but can be "time outs," exclusion from the group, withdrawal of privileges, and so on.

Operant conditioning
A form of conditioning that rewards behavior that moves closer to target behavior.

In a classroom, **operant conditioning** might be used to shape children's performance on an academic task. For example, suppose a class of second-graders has been assigned the task of completing twenty arithmetic problems. Those children who complete the task promptly and correctly get a token, which can be redeemed for objects in the class store on Friday. With those children who do not complete the task either promptly or correctly, the teacher may take one of several approaches. If he knows that three of the children have never completed twenty problems, he may choose to reward their performance if they complete more than they have completed before. He may choose to provide neither positive nor negative reinforcement to children who complete the same number of problems they have completed in the past. If he believes that some children deliberately did not attempt the task for some reason, he might punish them by reducing their recess time.

Operant conditioning can be used to shape behavior by providing reinforcements when the learner's behavior moves closer to the target behavior. Shaping behavior involves the following components (Pellegrini 1987):

1. *targeting the desired behavior*
2. *fixing a behavioral baseline*
3. *selecting reinforcers*
4. *analyzing the task and sequencing the segments*
5. *systematically applying the reinforcers (p. 113)*

In the classroom example above, by rewarding a child who completes more problems than in previous assignments, the teacher is rewarding closer approximations to the target behavior of completing twenty problems. Teachers often use such techniques to help children gain control of their classroom behaviors. If a child is hitting other children, for example, the teacher will first collect baseline data through observations to determine how often the child is hitting and then provide rewards as the hitting behavior decreases.

Behaviors can be extinguished by failing to provide reinforcements for them. If a child is behaving in ways the teacher deems inappropriate, then the teacher can ignore the less desirable behaviors while consistently rewarding more desirable behaviors.

The goal of employing behavioristic techniques is for the desired behavior to become rewarding to the child so that the teacher or parent need not continue to provide extrinsic rewards. Most teachers, even those who believe strongly in other theories of development, employ some behavioristic strategies as they ignore some behaviors and praise others. Most teachers have had experience with children who prefer negative attention—that is, punishment—to no attention; the usual strategy for dealing with such children is to make every effort to ignore their misbehavior and to reward their appropriate behavior.

Behaviorist theory does not say much about physical development, since most authorities agree that physical development is genetically determined and thus does not affect a child's behavior, at least in an optimal environment that includes good nutrition, lack of disease, and safety. Behaviorists are more concerned with how children develop socially, emotionally, and intellectually.

Maturationist Theory

The roots of the **maturationist** point of view are found in the work of Jean-Jacques Rousseau (1712–1778), who believed that children should be allowed to "unfold." A child is like a seed that contains all the elements to produce a wonderful apple if given the proper amounts of nutrients from the soil and water along with sunshine and an ideal climate. The modern maturationist point of view is most often associated with the work of the Gesell Institute (Ilg and Ames 1955). The Gesellian literature describes growth and development in terms of children's maturity. Experience plays a much less important role in development in the maturationist point of view than it does in the behaviorist point of view. Maturationists believe that each child's physical, social, emotional, and intellectual development follows an individual schedule that is basically predetermined. They believe that a child will develop to his potential when placed in an optimal environment and that his development will be slowed or retarded if the environment is not optimal.

Maturationist theory
A theoretical belief that children will "unfold," or develop to their full potential, given optimal conditions.

Maturationists believe that a child's developmental level is the most important determiner of social and intellectual success, especially in school settings. They suggest that the child will have difficulty in school if he is "overplaced," that is, placed in settings where the requirements do not match his developmental level. Maturationists emphasize the child's own schedule of maturation rather than rewards and punishments, experiences, or interactions with the environment. Experience, in the maturationist point of view, is always filtered by a child's maturation level.

Even though this theoretical position has been criticized, many schools continue to screen children for entry into programs on the basis of developmental tests developed by the Gesell Institute (Meisels 1987).

Interactionist Theory

The **interactionist,** or developmentalist, point of view is founded in the work of Jean Piaget (1896–1980). Modern interactionists, such as Jerome Bruner, George Forman, and others, continue to refine the theories of Piaget and to clarify concepts about children's development.

Piaget believed that children create knowledge through interactions with the environment. Children are not passive receivers of knowledge; rather, they actively work at organizing their experience into more and more complex mental structures. Piaget and Inhelder's (1969) descriptions of children's thinking include the concepts of assimilation, accommodation, and equilibrium. *Assimilation* is fitting information into existing schemas or categories. If a child has developed a schema for "dog" and is presented with a new example of a dog, such as a St. Bernard, the new example can be assimilated, or included, in the existing schema. If presented with a cat, the child may create a new schema for furry pets that are not dogs. Creating a new category is the process of *accommodation*. Through a series of repeated assimilations and accommodations, the child eventually creates a mental structure that will account for all animals.

Equilibrium is the balance achieved whenever information or experience is fitted into a schema or a new schema is created for it. This balance is very short lived, as new experiences and information are constantly being encountered by the child. *Disequilibrium* describes the mental state in which there is an imbalance between assimilation and accommodation. Disequilibrium is motivating in that it drives the learner to achieve equilibrium. *Equilibration* is the process of moving from disequilibrium to equilibrium. Equilibration allows the learner to employ assimilation and accommodation as tools for achieving equilibrium (Piaget 1985). In the "dog" example, if the child is presented with a Basenji, a dog that rarely barks, disequilibrium may result as the child is confronted with a dog that does not exhibit one of the usual dog behaviors. The child must then assimilate this dog into her schema of dogs. Some researchers (for example, Flavell 1985) agree that equilibration is one process that contributes to cognitive growth but question the idea that one process can account for all cognitive development.

Piagetians categorize knowledge as physical, social, or logico-mathematical. Forman and Kuschner (1983) postulate a fourth kind of knowledge: knowing what one knows. The term used in the literature to describe this category of knowledge is **metaknowledge.** If a child knows about the number system, for instance, then his knowing that he knows the system is another type of knowledge that is not social, physical, or logico-mathematical.

Wadsworth (1989) describes the definition of *learning* in Piagetian terms as follows:

> *Two usages or meanings of the word* learning *are differentiated by Piagetians. The first usage can be called learning in the broad sense, and it is synonymous with development. It is appropriate to talk about the development of, or the learning of, physical knowledge, logical-mathematical knowledge, and social knowledge. The second usage of learning is narrower. It refers to the acquisition of specific information from the environment, learning that is assimilated into an existing schema. Most content learning is the second kind. Both forms of learning imply comprehension.*
>
> *Rote memory, or memorization, is not considered learning because it does not involve assimilation and comprehension. Some theories, such as behaviorism, consider rote memory as a form of learning and do not differentiate between it and the two kinds of learning defined here. For Piagetians, learning always involves construction and comprehension. (p. 156)*

Wadsworth goes on to explain that even though rote memory is not considered by Piagetians to be a kind of learning, it is valuable. Rote memory is certainly useful for knowing one's address or telephone number, for example, but comprehension is not necessarily a component of memorization. A child who comprehends place value is intellectually different from one who has simply memorized the algorithm for solving addition problems that require regrouping.

Theoretical Influences

The different theories provide points of view through which to interpret observations of children as they grow and develop (see Table 1.1 on page 10). Depending on one's theoretical orientation, one would look at examples of children's development differently. If a child were observed throwing a ball at a target, a behaviorist might point out the reinforcements that make the child seek closer approximations to the most effective throwing techniques. The maturationist observing the same child might focus on the child's physical maturity as indicated by her ability to grasp and release the ball appropriately. The interactionist would view repeated attempts to hit the target as evidence that the child was actively seeking information about velocity and angle of release in order to hit the target (although the child would not be expected to be able to verbalize these concepts).

A child develops as a whole. Development in one area certainly influences development in other areas. For example, when a child becomes

Table 1.1	General Overview of Different Theoretical Orientations		
	BEHAVIORIST	**MATURATIONIST**	**INTERACTIONIST**
Physical Development	No special attention	Indicator of readiness for social and intellectual tasks	Internally motivated; influences other areas of development
Intellectual Development	Learning is achieved through reinforcement and rewards; is incremental	Learning is unfolding of child's potential if in optimal environment	Learning is a continuous process of assimilation and accommodation; results in changes in thinking rather than incremental growth of facts
Social Development	Shaped by reinforcements	Dependent on optimal environment	Learned through process of testing hypotheses; same as learning in other areas
Emotional Development	Shaped by reinforcements	Dependent on optimal environment	Learned through internal process; developmental
Motivational Development	External; rewards and punishments	Internal; child follows own program	Internal; child is active in own development

mobile, he opens up many more possibilities for exploration and learning about the environment. Children who feel that they are learning successfully or who feel confident about physical abilities develop more positive self-esteem. Children who learn to control their impulsive behaviors may be able to sustain interactions with people and materials longer than children who do not, which affects their intellectual development. A child's social, physical, emotional, and intellectual development are always interrelated.

CHILDREN'S DEVELOPMENT

This section provides very brief overviews of patterns in children's physical, social, emotional, and intellectual development. Table 1.2 on pages 12 and 13 summarizes and gives examples of these patterns.

Physical Development

Patterns of Development

Physical development is orderly, not random. Infant development is marked by the change from undifferentiated mass activity to controlled

The rate of children's physical development is often related to influences in their environment and affects their development in other areas.

activity. It is easy to observe undifferentiated mass activity in an infant. If she is excited, her whole body moves and her arms and legs flail. Gradually, the baby becomes more capable of differentiated movements, such as deliberately reaching for and grasping a rattle. Movements that become controlled and deliberate also become organized into patterns, such as pulling oneself to a standing position, releasing the hands, and moving the legs and feet to walk. The patterns then become available to the child as possible responses to different situations. If the child wants a toy that is across the room, at first, the only option for getting there is scooting and rocking. As development progresses, crawling and finally walking and running become patterns of physical movement available to the child. The physical development of children in the infant stage proceeds very rapidly. The child learns to control head position, to grasp objects, and perhaps to stand and walk in the first year. As children grow, the development of their motor skills is not quite as rapid as it is in infancy, but it continues throughout childhood.

Observations of physical development reveal that growth is *cephalocaudal* (it proceeds from head to tail) and *proximodistal* (it proceeds from the center of the body outward) and that gross motor movements are developed before fine motor movements. Control of head and arm muscles is achieved before control of leg muscles. Similarly, children are able to control the muscles of their arms before they can control the fine muscles in their hands that are needed for tasks such as writing and cutting with scissors.

Table 1.2	Overview of Patterns in Children's Development			
	BIRTH TO THREE YEARS OLD	**THREE TO FOUR YEARS OLD**	**FIVE TO SIX YEARS OLD**	**SEVEN TO EIGHT YEARS OLD**
Physical Development	Physical skills develop rapidly Sits and crawls Walks and begins to run Fine motor skills develop; can stack and pick up small objects Manages spoon or fork for feeding Grasps and releases objects	Physical skills increase Rides a tricycle Walks up and down stairs, alternating feet Runs Jumps with both feet Walks balance beam Climbs on playground equipment Undresses and dresses self Catches ball with arms extended Walks backward and on tiptoe Holds crayon with fingers	Skips on alternate feet Rides two-wheel bike Skates Throws fairly accurately Catches ball with hands Turns somersaults Participates in games requiring physical skills Small muscle development increases; eye-hand coordination develops Fine muscle control increases; can use hammer, pencil, scissors, etc. Can copy geometric figures Cuts on lines Prints some letters Pastes and glues Begins to lose teeth Handedness is well established	Physical skills become important in self-concept Energy levels are high Rate of growth slows Fine muscle control is good; can form letters well Permanent teeth appear Body proportions, facial structure change
Social Development	Responds to others Enjoys company of other children Can maintain involvement with another for a very short period Is unable to share without coaxing Shows very little ability to postpone gratification Imitates actions of others Begins to engage in parallel play	Becomes more aware of self Develops more altruistic feelings Becomes aware of racial/ethnic and sexual differences Is able to take direction, follow some rules Has strong feelings toward home and family Shows a growing sense of self-reliance Parallel play is common; cooperative play begins Imaginary playmates are fairly common	Expresses rigid ideas about sex roles Has best friends but for short periods of time Quarrels often but anger is short lived Is able to share and take turns Is eager to participate in school experiences Considers teacher very important Wants to be first Becomes possessive	Is more competitive with peers Depends on parents for expansion of interests, activities Is influenced by peer opinions Plays with opposite sex less often Needs teacher approval Is able to share Wants to please Is more independent at work and play Forms more enduring friendships Peer groups begin to form

Table 1.2   Overview of Patterns in Children's Development *(continued)*

	BIRTH TO THREE YEARS OLD	THREE TO FOUR YEARS OLD	FIVE TO SIX YEARS OLD	SEVEN TO EIGHT YEARS OLD
Emotional Development	Cannot tolerate frustration Cries easily Is often unable to control impulses Begins to express affections Needs routines and security Begins to perceive emotions of others Expresses self, sometimes emphatically	Can tolerate some frustration Develops some self-control Appreciates surprises and novel events Begins to show sense of humor Needs overt expressions of affection Fears the dark, being abandoned, strange situations	Expresses and labels feelings Controls aggression better Expresses less concern when separated from parents Expresses sense of humor in jokes, nonsense words Learns right from wrong Develops a conscience	Expresses reactions to others Is sensitive to ridicule and criticism Expresses more worries: war, loss of parents Shows more persistence Expresses more empathy; is able to see others' viewpoints
Cognitive Development	Sensorimotor investigations of environment is predominate Development of concepts is rapid Develops a sense of object permanence Develops language May use some number and color words but may not understand them	Follows instructions of two commands Makes impulsive judgments and frequent mistakes Develops vocabulary rapidly Uses numbers without understanding Has difficulty differentiating fantasy and reality Begins to classify, especially by function Begins to use some functional abstract words "Why" questions are constant Thinking is very egocentric	Shows a growing attention span Is able to seriate objects Is able to group objects Is more deliberate, less impulsive in judgments Differentiates between fantasy and reality Uses language aggressively, in categorization Is aware that words and pictures represent real objects Becomes interested in numbers and letters Knows names of colors Does not spontaneously use rehearsal in memory tasks Follows three unrelated commands Some children begin to conserve number, length	Differences in reading and language abilities widen Transition to concrete operational thinking begins Talking and discussion are important Is able to plan Can sustain interest over long periods of time Begins to understand cause and effect Develops a growing understanding of time, money Uses slang and profanity Understands and uses more abstract terms Expresses more awareness of community, world

Sources: Association for Supervision and Curriculum Development 1975; Tudor 1981; Zigler and Finn-Stevenson 1987.

The rate of children's physical development is variable and is related to environmental features such as nutrition and the freedom to practice movements. Some behaviors, such as walking, tend to emerge at about the same time in children, even if they have been confined as infants; others, such as throwing, seem to depend more on practice opportunities. Most children are encouraged to practice their developing skills through interactions in daily life. The parent may encourage the child to progress from letting go of support, to standing alone, to walking a step or two, and finally to walking several steps across the room. Children give their caretakers clues about what to encourage at any given time by attempting the behaviors. Thus, for example, most caretakers would not attempt to encourage walking in children who are not yet showing they are ready to walk by pulling themselves to a standing position.

By the time they are three, most children can walk backward and on tiptoe and can run. They can throw a ball and catch it with their arms extended. They can also ride a tricycle and hold a crayon or pencil with their fingers rather than their fists. Four-year-olds continue to refine their skills; they can bounce a ball, hop on one foot, climb ladders, alternate feet while walking downstairs, and jump from a standing position. Some five-year-olds can skip, and some learn to jump rope. By the time children are six, most can throw fairly accurately, and many learn to ride a two-wheel bike.

Children seven and eight continue to refine the skills that they have acquired and learn new skills. They are physically active, running, skipping, hopping, and climbing—rarely just walking. Their fine motor abilities increase so that they can draw, write, and learn to play musical instruments. Practice in motor skills is important in this period, especially for newly acquired skills such as swimming. Age and practice have more effect on the development of motor skills in this period than does sex. Girls can run as fast and throw as far and as accurately as boys during this period.

Implications for the Curriculum

It is important during the preschool and early elementary school years for children to have many opportunities for engaging in physical activities. Three-year-olds are in a constant state of motion, and it is important that teachers and parents provide opportunities for safe physical activity and not expect motor control that is beyond what the child can achieve. Fours and fives still need much more movement in their programs than sitting, although they can sit still for short periods of time for such activities as story time.

Teachers and parents need to think carefully when planning activities for young children. For example, writing on a line requires excellent fine motor control, and most fives and sixes cannot perform this task without considerable difficulty. Children who engage in organized sports such as tee-ball and soccer when they are very young may face the same sort of difficulties. Some parents and coaches expect coordination beyond what five- to eight-year-olds are capable of. If children do participate in organized activities, parents and coaches need to be aware of the abilities that the activities require and to match their expectations to children's capabilities.

All young children need vigorous physical activity every day, and no child should be deprived of the opportunities for such activities because he must complete other tasks or because he is being punished. There is a growing concern that children in the United States are less physically fit than previous generations of children (Zigler and Finn-Stevenson 1987). This trend seems to reflect the time that children spend in passive activities, such as watching television and sitting quietly at desks, and the lack of vigorous exercise in their daily lives.

The following suggestions may help teachers plan activities that encourage the physical development of children:

- Provide outside play every day that it is possible. Equipment should encourage climbing, running, jumping, and so on.
- Make sure children have access to an inside play area that contains a tumbling mat, Velcro balls and targets, and other materials to encourage movement.
- For very young children, indoor equipment for physical development can include rocking boats, steps, and low slides and tunnels. As children mature, appropriate equipment includes more complex climbing apparatus, balance beams, and so on.
- Provide balls that are age appropriate. For very young children, balls should be large and made of soft materials such as foam and yarn. As children learn to catch and throw more easily, they can use balls made of soft rubber. Durable rubber balls should be provided for children of about five and six who are learning to kick a ball.
- Beginning around five years of age, children can use jump ropes and hula hoops for experimenting with movement and control.
- Many classroom activities help children gain fine muscle control: painting, cutting with scissors, manipulating clay, stringing beads, sewing cards, using pegs and pegboards, and so on. Teachers must encourage these activities as the children's development indicates.

ERIKSON'S STAGES OF PSYCHOLOGICAL DEVELOPMENT

Basic Trust versus Basic Mistrust (first year of life)

Experiences and sensations that give the infant a sense of familiarity and inner certainty provide him with a sense of self. He feels that the world is benevolent or at least reliable, and he likewise trusts himself and his own capacities. He has established basic trust. If the individual develops basic mistrust instead, he may tend to behave irrationally or to withdraw into schizoid or depressive states in later life.

Autonomy versus Shame and Doubt (second year of life)

During the second year of life, the infant develops muscular control; she moves about and begins toilet training. She needs firmness now, as a protection against the potential anarchy of her own impulses. The sense of self-control (autonomy) learned at this stage leads to a lasting sense of goodwill and personal pride. A failure to achieve well-guided autonomy can lead later in life to compulsive neurosis, a pervasive sense of shame before the world, and compulsive doubt of the self and others.

Initiative versus Guilt (the preschool years)

During the preschool years, the child has a boundless supply of energy, which permits him to learn all kinds of activities and ideas quickly and avidly. He concentrates on successes rather than failures and does things for the simple pleasure of the activity. Autonomy becomes more focused and effective. The child becomes "more himself." The danger in this period is that the child's exuberant and aggressive explorations and conquests may lead him into frustration. His new physical and mental strengths encourage ambitions that may turn out to be beyond his abilities—inevitably, he sometimes fails or is defeated. Unless he can

Social Development

Patterns of Development

As noted in the section on physical development, the child's first physical actions are not differentiated—she moves all over all at once when excited. The infant's social and emotional development is also undifferentiated, in the sense that responses to stimuli such as being cold or hungry evoke crying behaviors that are not specific to the stimuli. In a matter of weeks, the child's crying becomes differentiated so that the primary caregiver can distinguish between the cries that indicate that the child is hungry, bored, or in pain. By six weeks or two months, the infant is able to respond to an adult by smiling and begins to imitate behavior such as sticking out her tongue or closing her eyes. By eight months or so, the child has developed a strong attachment to the primary caregiver and is anxious about separation from him or her. Toddlers begin to develop attachments to their families. Two-year-old children are trying to establish their own identities, and "me do it" is one of their most frequent statements.

come to terms with these disappointments he may be overwhelmed by resignation, guilt, and anxiety.

Perhaps the best way to help the child at this age is to encourage him to play constructively, to do some chores around the house, or to help care for younger children. In this way, the conflict between initiative and guilt may be resolved by the establishment of a constructive moral sense; it can set the individual on the road to goals that are not only possible for him but also deeply satisfying. If the conflict remains unresolved, in adult life, the individual may be inhibited or impotent (socially as well as sexually), or he may overreact by compulsive showing off.

Industry versus Inferiority (middle childhood)

Building on the previously developed trust, autonomy, and initiative, the child can achieve a sense of industry. In school, she learns the basic tools of literacy and cooperation that will enable her to become a productive member of society, and a sense of achievement becomes important to her. She learns the satisfaction of persisting at a task until it is completed and of using her skills to perform according to her own and others' expectations. In a culture like that in the United States, in which achievement is often measured in terms of doing better than someone else, she also learns to compete and to measure her productivity in relation to that of others.

The dangers of this period are twofold. On one hand, the child may learn to value achievement in work above all else; she may alienate her peers by excessively competitive behavior. On the other hand, she may feel unable to perform the tasks required of her and develop a sense of inferiority that prevents her from trying. Experiences of failure may lead to the child's feeling that she is inadequate, that she cannot be successful as a worker. In extreme cases, this sense of inferiority can affect the child's attitude toward work for life.

Source: Adapted from Erikson 1963.

By the time they are three, children have established relationships with their families and with others outside their families. They have also developed some strategies for achieving what they want and some ideas about sex-role identification.

Development of Personality One element of social development is development of personality. Erik Erikson (1902–1994), a psychoanalytic theorist, concentrated on studying the development of the ego—a sense of self (Ambron 1978). His description of stages in ego development are especially useful to teachers. Erikson viewed the child's developing identity as a reflection of relationships with parents and family within the broader context of society.

Teachers who think about children's behavior in Erikson's terms will plan programs that provide many opportunities for children to build trust and to make choices and feel successful in the choices that they make. Buzzelli and File (1989) suggest that building friendships is important in building trust. Helping children recognize their own needs and the feelings and emotions of others are important steps in building trust. The child must feel that her ideas are good ideas and that others respect those ideas. If too much of the time spent in school or child care is directed by the teacher, children will begin to feel that their ideas are unacceptable. Older children need to be able to participate in activities in which their achievements are obvious and celebrated. For example, four- and five-year-olds need to know that if they suggest activities, the teacher will listen and help them carry out their ideas if possible. If the activity cannot be incorporated into the classroom, the teacher will still treat the idea with respect and perhaps help the child modify the idea or accomplish some part of the activity.

Development of Self-Esteem Another element of the social development of the young child is the development of self-esteem. The concept of self is developed gradually; the young child develops a concept of himself as a separate individual over a period of years. Through interactions first with the parents and family and then with peers and others outside the family, children gradually develop a concept of who they are and what they are like. In a classic study of children's self-esteem, Coopersmith (1967) found that children, especially boys, with high self-esteem had parents who were accepting, affectionate, and genuinely concerned about their child. The parents also enforced rules carefully and consistently and insisted on high standards of behavior but used noncoercive methods of discipline. They also demonstrated more democratic interactions with their children.

Teachers of young children often plan experiences in which improving self-esteem is the primary goal. However, such plans for activities often ignore the pervasive nature of the development of one's self-concept. Katz (1986) discusses the futility of planning an activity based on "me" (a booklet about my favorite food, my pet, my favorite dress, my best skill, and so on) as a means of improving self-esteem. Such an activity might contribute to the child's self-esteem if it is conducted in the context of a classroom environment in which children have choices and opportunities to participate in a variety of activities in which they can feel successful and in control. But if the classroom environment is generally structured so that children feel unable to be successful, then even a series of self-esteem lessons will not be effective.

Kostelnik, Stein, Whiren, and Soderman (1993) state that "fifteen-minute activities or the adult's gushing remarks will not infuse children with a sense of well-being or innoculate them against negative self-perceptions. Because esteem-influencing experiences pervade all aspects of children's lives and are ever-present, authentic esteem enhancing efforts must be pervasive too" (p. 78). Therefore, a teacher who wishes to build self-esteem in children will consider how children are treated all through the day. The kinds of experiences regularly provided for them are much more important in the process of building self-esteem than isolated lessons or activities designed to focus on positive feelings about oneself.

The Role of Play   Play experiences are very important in the social and emotional development of young children. Children can "play" various roles and behaviors and get feedback about the appropriateness of the behaviors in play. They can play "bully" or "baby" and find out what kinds of responses their behavior elicits in nonthreatening situations. They can also play various adult roles. Young children often play the roles of family members, and with experience, they begin to play roles of those outside the family. They might play "grocery clerk," "filling station attendant," "dentist," or "garbage worker" and explore the behavior patterns that they believe are appropriate for those individuals.

Because play is so important in the lives of children, an entire chapter will be devoted to the topic of play (see Chapter Five).

Social Skills and Social Relationships   Research continues to emphasize the importance of fostering children's social development in the early childhood years. Ullmann (1957) found that unpopular children were more likely to drop out of school; Roff, Sells, and Golden (1972) found that unpopular children were more likely to have emotional problems as adults; and Roff and Sells (1968) found that unpopular children were more likely

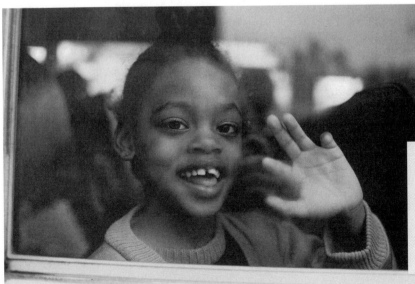

Teachers in developmentally appropriate classrooms are concerned with children's social and emotional development as well as their intellectual development.

to engage in delinquent behavior as adolescents. In a review of the research on unpopular children, Roopnarine and Honig (1985) reiterated the importance of helping young children gain social skills. Yespo and O'Connor (1989) also examined children's social abilities and concluded that the late-preschool years are critical for intervention in social development.

These studies underline the importance of helping children learn to participate in social relationships. Children who are unsuccessful in social relationships are not capable of analyzing the situation and determining which behaviors need to be altered. It is then the teacher's responsibility to help a child break an unsuccessful cycle and implement new behaviors that will lead to success in establishing social relationships.

Rogers and Ross (1986) describe *social skill* as the "ability to assess what is happening in a social situation; skill to perceive and correctly interpret the actions and needs of the children in the group at play; ability to imagine possible courses of action and select the most appropriate one" (pp. 14–15). Children who are popular and most successful socially demonstrate these abilities, but children who lack social skills may need direct instruction through modeling, role-playing, or the use of puppets to help them develop these abilities. Roopnarine and Honig (1985), in a review of research on the unpopular child, add that teachers can help children become more popular by helping their families focus on more positive discipline techniques and making sure that positive social development is a major program goal.

Teachers and parents are concerned with the development in young children of prosocial behaviors: helping, cooperating, and empathizing. Moore (1987) reports that prosocial behavior increases quite rapidly during the preschool years. In the classroom setting, teachers can help children develop these behaviors through modeling the desired behaviors, setting up situations that require cooperation, and suggesting specific ways that children can be cooperative or helpful. Some play equipment should be selected that can be used by more than one child, such as telephones, jump ropes, or board games. Teachers can model caring and empathy for each child and discuss with the children how some actions make others feel. Teachers can also demonstrate how to be cooperative by helping build a block construction or helping dig in the garden.

Honig (1982) found that prosocial behavior was most likely to develop under certain conditions, namely, when:

1. Children had consistent contacts with nurturing, individually attentive adults.
2. Children were able to identify feelings (their own and those of others).

3. Children were exposed to adults who modeled prosocial behavior.
4. Children had opportunities to respond to real situations in which prosocial behavior was appropriate.
5. Children were encouraged to think of possible alternatives to actions.

Pellegrini (1987) describes three skill areas that should be evaluated in assessing children's social development. These areas are *social role taking* (the ability to understand another's point of view), *social problem solving* (the management of interpersonal relationships), and *cooperation* (cooperative interaction with others). Teachers can observe children's behavior in these categories and provide instruction, modeling, or opportunities for interaction with peers that will help children develop these social abilities. When children are arguing over a toy, the teacher can help them understand each other's point of view and work out a way to solve the problem without fighting. Many tasks in the classroom, such as cleaning up after play or work time, require cooperative behaviors that teachers can model and discuss.

Aggression   Another aspect of social development that receives attention is aggression. Teachers and parents are concerned with children's aggressive behavior. The results of studies indicate that aggressive behavior in the classroom can be reduced by providing enough space and materials so that children do not have to compete with each other. These studies also suggest eliminating toys that lend themselves to aggressive themes and not allowing children to benefit from aggressive behavior by either controlling the victim or getting the teacher's attention. It is also important to model cooperative behavior and discuss and demonstrate solutions to problems other than aggression (Potts, Huston, and Wright 1986; Yarrow 1983).

Kostelnik et al. (1993) recommend the following strategies for helping reduce aggression:

reducing the frustration in children's lives, . . .
helping children feel more competent, . . .
teaching children prosocial behaviors, . . .
helping children recognize instances of accidental aggression, . . . and
rechanneling children's expressive aggression. (p. 253)

Although some authors believe that aggression with inanimate objects is not appropriate (Masselli et al. 1984; Gray 1981; Fagot and Hagan 1985), others, including Kostelnik and her co-authors, believe that channeling aggressive behavior (hitting, kicking, and so on) so that it is focused on inanimate objects and does not pose a threat to the safety of others is a useful strategy. These authors do caution against letting aggressive behavior get out of control under these conditions.

Sex-Role Identification   Sex-role identification is yet another important element of social development. Before they are three, children begin to identify themselves as boys or girls, and at around three years of age, they can identify others as boys or girls. They continue to develop their concepts of sexual identity and their attitudes about appropriate roles for males and females. In fact, preschoolers may be quite rigid about what is appropriate play or an appropriate task for males or females. After about age seven, children seem to grow less rigid in their ideas about sex roles, perhaps because they are more secure about their own sexual identities (Damon 1977). Teachers will want to structure the classroom and activities so that both boys and girls have equal opportunities and encouragement to participate. The literature selected for use in the classroom should contain models of behavior that is not stereotyped by sex, and teachers should avoid assigning tasks in a stereotypical manner (consistently having boys do heavy work and girls do verbal or artwork).

Implications for the Curriculum

Teachers do not usually plan activities whose sole purpose is social development; instead, they think about social development as one facet of children's participation in a variety of classroom experiences. Teachers who want to help children develop socially will be aware of children's social abilities and take advantage of the classroom routine to further their development. Activities should encourage children to cooperate, to develop their self-esteem, and to gain skill in interacting with other children. The following are only a few suggestions of ways to promote growth in social abilities:

- Provide dress-up corners where children can take on a variety of roles. Simple costumes such as aprons and hats can help children explore new roles. Threes and fours need more family-oriented props; older children need more props for roles found in the larger community. Sixes, sevens, and eights may respond to props that help them reenact stories from literature.
- Involve primary children in solving social problems in the classroom through role-play and discussions of how to find alternative solutions, how to disagree without being aggressive, and how to make changes in rules they believe are inappropriate or unfair.

- For threes, popular play materials should be plentiful so that fewer arguments arise and children do not have to wait long for a turn. As children mature, teachers may help children work out approaches to taking turns and sharing toys and equipment, such as using waiting lists, a timer, and so on.
- Use puppets to model appropriate techniques for entering a play group. For example, the teacher could use a puppet to demonstrate how a child might ask a group playing with blocks if she could play, too.
- Encourage children to make as many decisions as possible. In free play, allow children to choose activities and experiences. In more directed times of the day, such as music or story time, encourage children to choose songs or stories.
- Model empathy and caring behaviors, and encourage children to display these behaviors.
- Role-play solutions to problems in social interactions. For example, children might role-play how to make an introduction when a guest comes to the classroom or how to ask another child to share materials.

Emotional Development

Patterns of Development

Emotional development, like physical and social development, follows fairly predictable stages of growth (Zigler and Finn-Stevenson 1987). The infant responds to any emotion with undifferentiated crying. As the baby grows, this crying becomes differentiated to reflect various emotions. By the time the baby is a few months old, he may scream in anger but produce none of the tears that accompany crying caused by physical pain. Infants have almost no capacity to wait for someone to attend to their needs; their reactions to feelings are immediate. Some researchers (Thomas and Chess 1977) have found that children have distinct temperaments early in life and that temperament tends to be stable over time. Other researchers (DeVries and Sameroff 1984) believe that temperament is responsive to environmental influences. If a baby is difficult and irritable, for example, the parents may not handle the baby as much as they might have handled a more responsive or easy-going baby—and this in turn will further affect the baby's temperament.

Toddlers are very compulsive in their behaviors. They have little control of their impulses and are easily frustrated. By the time children reach three years of age, they have developed some tolerance for frustration. They can wait for short periods of time. If their mother explains that dinner will be ready very soon, they can manage to wait for it. They are also developing some self-control; they do not respond to every impulse. Three-year-olds have been observed talking themselves out of doing something that they would have done without thinking a year earlier.

Threes and fours like surprises and novel events. They need the security of knowing that there is structure to their day—that they are going to play, have a snack, and so on—but they respond well to some surprises in the day. When someone dressed as Mother Goose stops by the classroom to share some nursery rhymes, they can handle the change. Three- and four-year-olds are also beginning to develop a sense of humor. They often laugh when they hear a word that sounds funny to them or when they see something incongruous. They are not embarrassed when they laugh at inappropriate moments because they cannot analyze their own behavior in order to determine that it was inappropriate.

By the time children are in kindergarten and first grade, they are able to express and label a wide variety of emotions. They can describe their own sad, angry, or happy feelings and can describe situations that produce given emotions in others. These children become more capable of controlling their aggressive feelings and, with some guidance, can learn to work out their frustrations with other children using words rather than hitting. Five- and six-year-olds also begin to develop a conscience and a sense of right and wrong.

Fives and sixes express their sense of humor in jokes or nonsense words. They often tell jokes without punch lines and still laugh at their own stories. They repeat jokes they have heard, often without understanding them. "Knock-knock" jokes are favorites, and children frequently make up their own versions. They also have great fun creating nonsense words or making rhymes with other words. These tend to be especially funny if they are a little naughty.

Children in the primary years, seven- and eight-year-olds, continue to gain even more control of their emotional responses. They are much less impulsive than younger children. They have strong responses to other individuals and usually like or dislike them immediately. Children in this age group are quite sensitive to criticism or ridicule. They demonstrate embarrassment at their own behavior. They tend to have more worries than younger children as they become more aware of world conditions and attend more to news stories they see on television or hear being discussed by adults. They worry about war, about things happening to their parents (death or divorce), and about accidents.

Seven- and eight-year-olds demonstrate persistence in trying to achieve their goals. This often drives their parents mad, as the child asks to do something over and over after it has been denied. Children this age develop much more empathy for other people and feel badly when someone else is hurting, either physically or emotionally. They offer comfort to family or friends without being prompted to do so.

Implications for the Curriculum

Emotional growth can be encouraged through the typical classroom experiences if the teacher is aware of the child's level of development and what can be done to encourage development. The following are examples of classroom activities that can help children:

- Have children dramatize situations in which anger or frustration are handled appropriately.
- Use puppets to model appropriate responses to emotions. For example, with younger children, the teacher might use puppets to model the use of language rather than hitting to express anger. With older children, the teacher might model different responses to frustrations such as not winning a race or a game.
- Help children learn to acknowledge and label their feelings as they participate in classroom activities.
- Choose literature in which the characters respond to emotions appropriately, and discuss how they felt and how they acted.
- Provide empathy for children's fears and concerns. They are real to the child and should not be belittled.
- Allow children to share their humor; appreciate the growth in their sense of humor.
- Primary children may be helped to express their feelings through writing. Select examples from literature that illustrate how children have written about their frustrations or stresses and learned to cope more effectively with them through the writing process.

Intellectual Development

Patterns of Development

Cognitive development refers to the development of the child's thinking and reasoning abilities. Malkus, Feldman, and Gardner (1988) define *cognitive development* as "the growing capacity to convey and appreciate meanings in the several symbol systems which happen to be featured in a given cultural setting" (p. 29). These symbol systems include words, pictures, gestures, and numbers. The cognitive development of young children is described by different theorists in different terms. The behaviorist point of view is that children grow intellectually through accumulating more and more information. Most measures of intelligence are based on

Cognitive development
The development of the ability to think and reason.

PIAGET'S STAGES OF DEVELOPMENT

Sensorimotor Period (birth to two years)

The sensorimotor period is characterized by interactions with the environment based on the child's reception of sensory input and muscular reactions. The period begins with reflexive actions, which are gradually controlled by the child, and ends with the child's having developed a concept of separateness from others and the beginnings of symbolic thinking. The task of this period is to develop the concept of object permanence, the idea that objects exist even when they cannot be seen or heard.

Preoperational Period (two to seven years)

The beginning of the preoperational period is characterized by the emergence of the ability to represent objects and knowledge through imitation, symbolic play, drawing, mental images, and spoken language. One outstanding characteristic of preoperational thinking is lack of conservation. *Conservation* is defined as the knowledge that the number, mass, area, length, weight, and volume of objects are not changed by physically rearranging the objects.

Children whose thinking is preoperational are egocentric in that they cannot easily take the point of view of others. A preoperational child believes that everyone thinks as she does and that everyone thinks the same things she does. *Egocentrism* is not exclusive to the thinking of preoperational children but is most prominent then. Egocentrism is a factor in the child's reasoning at this stage because children do not question their own thinking and therefore do not change schemata readily.

Another characteristic of preoperational thinking is *centration.* The preoperational child tends to pay attention to one element of a problem at a time and cannot coordinate information from multiple sources. Centration is related to classification, seriation, and other such tasks. The following anecdote describes an example of centration:

A child was visiting with a family friend, and they were going out in a boat. The friend's boat was beside an identical boat at the dock. One boat was tied up about three feet further in the slip than the other one. The child walked up and down the pier several times, observing the two boats. After a few minutes he remarked, "Your boat is longer on this end, and that boat is longer on the other end."

A fourth characteristic of preoperational thinking is the difficulty a child has in trying to reverse thinking. *Reversibility* is defined as the ability to

this idea of accumulating knowledge. Another point of view is that of the interactionists, or developmentalists, who describe knowledge as being constructed from children's interactions with the environment. According to this viewpoint, intellectual development is influenced by both maturation and experience (Piaget 1969). Cognitive development is indicated by a growing ability to plan, to employ strategies for remembering, and to seek solutions to problems.

Piaget and Inhelder (1969) described the cognitive development of children as progressing in several stages, including the *sensorimotor stage,* the *preoperational stage,* and the *concrete operational stage.* The stages evolve with the child's growing maturity and experience. Although approximate ages have been attached to these stages, the rate at which individuals pass through these stages is variable; the sequence of stages, however, is invarifollow a line of reasoning back to the beginning point. In the problem of conserving number, a child is presented with two rows of eight plastic chips and observes that they are equal. When the space between the chips is lengthened, the pre-operational child believes that the number has been changed because the row is longer. When the child is able to reverse the reasoning process, she will be able to determine that moving the chips does not affect the number. A child may be able to reverse an operation physically before being able to reverse operations mentally.

Preoperational children have difficulty in reasoning logically about transformations. The child tends to concentrate on the elements of change and not on the transformations of objects or materials from one state to another. Piaget found that children had difficulty thinking about successive changes in states and about the relationship of one event to another. Piaget made this observation when walking with a child through the woods and drawing the child's attention to the snails that could be seen at various points along the path. The child could not determine if the snails were all the same snail or different snails. Children can observe the beginning point and the ending point of transformations, but they often have difficulty following all the points in between. If a child is asked to draw what happens to a pencil as it falls off a table, he can draw the pencil on the table and on the floor but not all the steps between the table and the floor.

Concrete Operational Period (seven to eleven or twelve years)

Children begin making the transition from preoperational thinking to operational thinking at various times. In most kindergarten classrooms, a few children will be beginning to think operationally. In the primary grades, more children will be operational thinkers, even though many may still be preoperational on some tasks. Piaget and Inhelder (1969) described the operational thinker as one who employs "identity or reversibility by inversion or reciprocity" (p. 99) in solving problems.

Concrete operational thinkers are able to solve problems of conservation and reversibility. They can decenter, or coordinate information from more than one source, in solving problems. They are not as egocentric in their thinking. Because they are aware that others may come to conclusions that differ from theirs, they are much more likely to examine their own conclusions.

Sources: Piaget 1969; Wadsworth 1989.

ant. In other words, a child must pass through each stage, but different children may pass through the stages at different ages. The transition time between stages is lengthy. Children do not move suddenly from one stage of thinking to another—changes may take months or years, as the child constructs and integrates knowledge. A child may be performing some tasks in ways that indicate preoperational thinking while performing other tasks in very stable operational ways.

More recently, early childhood educators have been influenced by two theories of intellectual development. One is that of Lev Vygotsky (1978), who stresses the importance of the social context in learning. In brief, Vygotsky believes that children can perform some tasks independently and some more complex tasks with adult assistance. He calls the band between these two stages the *zone of proximal development.* This zone is very important to teachers as they find out what knowledge and skills children already have and then assist them in learning more. For example, if a child can cut on a straight line with scissors, then the adult might help the child learn to cut on a curved line. Similarly, if a second-grader can spell a word with only one letter incorrect, the teacher might suggest a time to help the child learn the conventional spelling. Social context is important in children's learning as they learn to do those things that they observe others around them doing and for which they have some need in their own lives. Children would not usually learn to weave blankets if that were not part of their social context, but they would learn this skill if it were an important part of their daily life and their identification with their culture.

The other theory that has only recently begun to be applied to early childhood education is that of Howard Gardner (1983). Gardner believes that intellectual capacity does not develop as a whole but as different intelligences. So far, Gardner has identified six intelligences that meet the strict criteria for being labeled as such: linguistic, logical-mathematical, spatial, bodily-kinesthetic, musical, and personal. He does not believe that these are necessarily all the intelligences possible, but they are all that he has identified at this time.

Gardner's work is not a shallow or superficial examination of the development of intelligence; however, teachers must be aware that many other authors have used Gardner's work and developed rather shallow approaches to supposedly testing and teaching the intelligences. What is most significant about Gardner's theories to the early childhood educator is (1) the support for offering a variety of activities and experiences so that every child can learn and (2) the focus on the fact that every person possesses a unique combination of strengths in the intelligences. Every child has abilities that can be recognized and honored. If Gardner's work helps to change schools so that the focus is not solely on the acquisition of academic knowledge, he will have contributed greatly to the lives of young children.

Implications for the Curriculum

Planning for the intellectual growth of children is dependent on the knowledge of children's intellectual development. A child who is preoperational, for instance, would not be expected to solve problems in the same way that an older child would solve them. Also, children need chances to learn in ways that are active and that provide opportunities to learn in ways that suit their individual techniques for organizing and remembering information. One challenge for teachers is to avoid what Lilian Katz (1986) describes as "learned stupidity," which occurs when children are given tasks that they cannot do and, through failure at those tasks, learn to believe that they are stupid. No young child would have the life experience to evaluate an inappropriate task and determine that it was the task that was at fault, not the learner.

Young children learn best through manipulating objects and being reflective about those manipulations, not through passive experiences where they listen to someone tell them how something works. Young children need the stimulation of their peers in solving problems, and they need to be able to use what they already know in learning new information. Throughout this book, you will find suggestions for encouraging the intellectual growth of children; the following suggestions are merely a small sample of the endless possibilities:

- Provide old machines (toasters, TVs, radios, and so on) that children can dismantle and explore. (Be sure to remove the electrical connections and any springs that could be unsafe.)
- Set up problems to be presented to the class in ways that encourage divergent thinking and multiple right answers. For example, ask children how many different ways they can sort the blocks rather than ask them to sort the blocks by color.
- Give children the opportunity to choose as many of their own activities as possible. Children can learn to classify by playing with blocks, leaves, keys, items from the supermarket, and articles of clothing. When children are given a choice, they are more likely to learn.
- Provide materials that are open ended so that the challenge and complexity can be increased as the children grow. For example, given beads, children at different ages can string them, use them to create patterns, or use them to create models and designs.

DEVELOPMENTALLY APPROPRIATE PRACTICE

Knowing the child or the learner is absolutely necessary for planning a developmentally appropriate program. Several questions about DAP are directly related to children's development:

- Are the activities planned usually of interest to children of the age for which the activities are intended?
- Can most children complete the activities successfully?
- Will some children be allowed to choose more challenging activities?
- Will some children be allowed to choose activities that require less skill without being censured?
- Will expectations for performance reflect knowledge of child development?

- Encourage children to follow their interests. Jacque Wuertenburg (1993) calls it "leading through life." If a child is interested in spiders or snakes or computers, use that interest to help build skills and concepts.
- Assist children in understanding the application of what they are learning in school to real life. Learning without a purpose is difficult.

CHAPTER SUMMARY

- Development is described in different terms, depending on one's philosophical point of view. The major philosophical orientations are represented by the behaviorists, the maturationists, and the interactionists.
- Development is an orderly process of moving from undifferentiated movements and reactions to finely differentiated and controlled movements and specific responses.
- Physical development is most rapid in infancy but continues quite rapidly through the preschool years. Children in the primary grades continue to develop their physical abilities, but the rate is not as rapid as it is with younger children.
- Ideally, as their social development progresses, children become capable of successful interactions with others, develop prosocial behaviors such as helping and cooperating, learn to control aggression, and develop a positive concept of themselves.
- Emotional development is observed as children evolve from expressing undifferentiated responses to emotions to being able to express their emotions in socially acceptable ways and to control their impulses. Children grow more capable of understanding how others feel and develop a sense of right and wrong.
- Cognitive development describes the changes that take place in children's thinking and reasoning. Very young children learn best from handling objects; preschoolers need to manipulate objects and reflect on the outcomes of their manipulations; and elementary school children still need to use concrete materials in their reasoning processes. Young children do not employ adult logic in making sense of their environment, nor can they reason in abstract terms.
- The different stages of child development have implications for planning a curriculum for young children. Teachers need to think about children's physical abilities and the cognitive requirements of different tasks when they select learning experiences. They also need to plan activities that will help children develop social skills.

WHAT WOULD YOU DO?

Reflect on your reading and your own experiences with young children as you think about the following situations:

1. A parent asks why you do not send home papers that the children have completed. What would you tell him?
2. You are interviewed by the owner of a school for children from four to eight years of age. The owner tells you how much progress the children make each year in academic subjects, but you do not see any evidence of outdoor play equipment or play space. What would this suggest to you about the program?
3. You are expected to keep children quiet and encourage them to do their own work in a first-grade classroom. How would you feel about this expectation?
4. A child brings a toy gun to school. What would you do?

THEORY INTO PRACTICE

1. Observe in a preschool or a primary grade. Make a list of the activities or tasks you observe that are designed to stimulate a specific aspect of child development through either their content or their structure.
2. Discuss with your classmates the importance of understanding child development in planning curriculum experiences.
3. Compare two articles about cognitive development written from different philosophical perspectives. List the points of agreement and the points of disagreement in their descriptions of how children think.
4. Observe a group of three-year-olds and a group of eight-year-olds at play. Make a list of what you consider to be the most obvious changes in children between three and eight years old.

RECOMMENDED FOR FURTHER READING

Curry, Nancy E., and Carl N. Johnson. *Beyond Self-Esteem: Developing a Genuine Sense of Human Value.* Washington, DC: National Association for the Education of Young Children, 1990.

In this research monograph, Curry and Johnson discuss self-esteem and the development of self-esteem in children. They include a chapter on the growth of the self through infancy, toddlerhood, the preschool years, and kindergarten. Their suggestions for practitioners are practical. The chapter in which the work is summarized and policy suggestions are made is extremely valuable and will help teachers make decisions about classroom practice that will foster self-esteem.

Forman, George, and David S. Kuschner. *The Child's Construction of Knowledge: Piaget for Teaching Children.* Washington, DC: National Association for the Education of Young Children, 1983.

The authors provide excellent suggestions for adapting typical equipment and activities to help children "know what they know." The theoretical explanations are complex, but they will certainly generate thinking and questions.

Kostelnik, Marjorie, Laura Stein, Alice P. Whiren, and Anna K. Soderman. *Guiding Children's Social Development.* 2d ed. Albany, NY: Delmar, 1993.

This book is excellent for helping readers think more in depth about the social development of young children. The topics covered are valuable in today's world, such as helping children cope with stress and supporting children's growth in sensitive areas such as sexuality, ethnicity, and disabling conditions. Included are many suggestions for strategies that teachers can use.

Pellegrini, Anthony D. *Applied Child Study: A Developmental Approach.* Hillsdale, NJ: Lawrence Erlbaum Associates, 1987.

This is not a typical child development text, as it does not begin with infancy and cover all aspects of development through adolescence. It does provide a framework for studying children's development. The chapter on learning and cognition provides a good background to the different theoretical approaches to learning. Also included are good chapters on testing young children, language, play, and program evaluation.

Wadsworth, Barry J. *Piaget's Theory of Cognitive and Affective Development.* 4th ed. New York: Longman, 1989.

Wadsworth's descriptions of Piaget's stages of development are detailed and helpful to teachers yet not difficult to read. He includes chapters on each of the stages described by Piaget and discusses the implications of Piagetian theory for educators. He also includes articles on Piaget and mathematics, reading, and the computer.

Zigler, Edward F., and Matia Finn-Stevenson. *Children: Development and Social Issues.* Lexington, MA: D. C. Heath, 1987.

This is a comprehensive child development text that discusses development in all areas, from infancy to adolescence. The sections on social issues are especially interesting, as many political and economic decisions are very important in the lives of children and influence child growth and development. The book's presentations of such issues as support for families, nutrition programs, genetic engineering, and

children living in poverty are interesting and thought provoking.

REFERENCES

Ambron, Sueann R. *Child Development.* 2d ed. New York: Holt, Rinehart and Winston, 1978.

Association for Supervision and Curriculum Development. *Deve lopmental Characteristics of Children and Youth.* Alexandria, VA: ASCD, 1975.

Bredekamp, Sue, ed. *Developmentally Appropriate Practice in Early Childhood Programs Serving Children from Birth Through Age 8.* Expanded ed. Washington, DC: National Association for the Education of Young Children, 1987.

Bredekamp, Sue, and Teresa Rosegrant. *Reaching Potentials: Appropriate Curriculum and Assessment for Young Children.* Vol. 1. Washington, DC: National Association for the Education of Young Children, 1992.

Buzzelli, Cary A., and Nancy File. "Building Trust in Friends." *Young Children* 44 (March 1989): 70–75.

Coopersmith, Stanley. *The Antecedents of Self Esteem.* San Francisco: W. H. Freeman, 1967.

Damon, W. *The Social World of the Child.* San Francisco: Jossey-Bass, 1977.

DeVries, M. W., and A. J. Sameroff. "Culture and Temperament: Influences on Infant Temperament in Three East African Societies." *American Journal of Orthopsychiatry* 54 (1984): 83–96.

Erikson, Erik. *Childhood and Society.* 2d ed. New York: Norton, 1963.

Fagot, Beverly I., and Richard Hagan. "Aggression in Toddlers: Responses to the Assertive Acts of Boys and Girls." *Sex Roles* 12 (February 1985): 341–351.

Flavell, John H. *Cognitive Development.* 2d ed. Englewood Cliffs, NJ: Prentice-Hall, 1985.

Forman, George, and David S. Kuschner. *The Child's Construction of Knowledge: Piaget for Teaching Children.* Washington, DC: National Association for the Education of Young Children, 1983.

Gardner, Howard. *Frames of Mind: The Theory of Multiple Intelligences.* New York: HarperCollins, 1983.

Gray, Dianne E. *The Teacher's Role in Understanding Aggression and Dealing with It Effectively in the Preschool Environment.* ERIC Document Reproduction Service 200334. 1981.

Hill, Winfred F. *Learning: A Survey of Psychological Interpretations.* 3d ed. New York: Thomas Y. Crowell, 1977.

Honig, Alice S. "Research in Review: Prosocial Development in Children." *Young Children* 37 (July 1982): 51–62.

Ilg, Frances L., and Louise B. Ames. *The Gesell Institute's Child Behavior.* New York: Dell, 1955.

Katz, Lilian. *Curriculum for Preschool and Kindergarten.* National Association for the Education of Young Children. Videocassette.

Katz, Lilian. Keynote speech. Oregon Association of School Administrators conference of kindergarten teachers and elementary principals, Salem, Oregon, 1986.

Kostelnik, Marjorie, Laura Stein, Alice P. Whiren, and Anna K. Soderman. *Guiding Children's Social Development.* 2d ed. Albany, NY: Delmar, 1993.

Malkus, Ulla C., David Feldman, and Howard Gardner. "Dimensions of Mind in Early Childhood." In *Psychological Bases for Early Education,* edited by A. D. Pellegrini. New York: John Wiley and Sons, 1988.

Masselli, David et al. "Aggressive Behavior of the Preschool Child." *Education* 104 (Summer 1984): 385–388.

Meisels, Samuel J. "Uses and Abuses of Developmental Screening and School Readiness Testing." *Young Children* 42 (January 1987): 4–6, 68–73.

Moore, Shirley G. *Social Development of the Young Child: Two Theories, Two Stories.* ERIC Document Reproduction Service 297875. 1987.

Pellegrini, Anthony D. *Applied Child Study: A Developmental Approach.* Hillsdale, NJ: Lawrence Erlbaum Associates, 1987.

Piaget, Jean. *The Equilibration of Cognitive Structures: The Central Problem of Intellectual Development.* Chicago: University of Chicago Press, 1985.

Piaget, Jean, and Barbel Inhelder. *The Psychology of the Child.* Translated by Helen Weaver. New York: Basic Books, 1969.

Potts, R., A. C. Huston, and J. C. Wright. "The Effects of Television Form and Violent Content on Boys' Attention and Social Behavior." *Journal of Experimental Child Psychology* 41 (1986): 1–17.

Roff, Merrill, and S. B. Sells. "Juvenile Delinquency in Relation to Peer Acceptance-Rejection and Socioeconomic Status." *Psychology in the Schools* 5 (January 1968): 3–18.

Roff, Merrill, S. B. Sells, and M. M. Golden. *Social Adjustment and Personality Development in Children.* Minneapolis: University of Minnesota Press, 1972.

Rogers, Dwight L., and Dorene D. Ross. "Encouraging Positive Social Interaction Among Young Children." *Young Children* 41 (March 1986): 12–17.

Roopnarine, Jaipaul, and Alice S. Honig. "Research in Review: The Unpopular Child." *Young Children* 40 (September 1985): 59–64.

Thomas, A., and S. Chess. *Temperament and Development.* New York: Brunner/Mazel, 1977.

Tudor, Mary. *Child Development.* New York: McGraw-Hill, 1981.

Ullmann, Charles A. "Teachers, Peers, and Tests as Predictors of Adjustment." *Journal of Educational Psychology* 48 (May 1957): 257–267.

Vygotsky, Lev. *Mind in Society: The Development of Higher Psychological Functions.* Cambridge, MA: Harvard University Press, 1978.

Wadsworth, Barry J. *Piaget's Theory of Cognitive and Affective Development.* 4th ed. New York: Longman, 1989.

Wuertenburg, Jacque. Speech to Northern Arizona Reading Council, Flagstaff, Arizona, April 1993.

Yarrow, L. "Should Children Play with Guns?" *Parents* 58 (January 1983): 50–52.

Yespo, Jo Ellen, and Elizabeth O'Connor. *Social Sets and Social Status in Preschool Classrooms.* ERIC Document Reproduction Service 307065.

Zigler, Edward F., and Matia Finn-Stevenson. *Children: Development and Social Issues.* Lexington, MA: D. C. Heath, 1987.

Chapter Two

Schools for Young Children
Choices in Design

This morning when you and your classmates shared your observations from the school visits you made last week, you were certainly surprised at the variations in programs. You had expected that most of your classmates would have experiences very similar to your own. You did detect some common elements in the programs, but you also heard about distinct contrasts.

Some of your peers visited schools where the focus was on learning the ABCs and other academic facts; others visited schools where it seemed children were encouraged to play all day. What children could learn in some of the programs was really impressive—some two-year-olds were reading words from flashcards. In other programs, children seemed to be learning more about getting along together than about reading words.

You have many questions now: Why are the programs so different? Who makes the choices about the programs? Who decides what the focus of each program is going to be? How will a teacher determine which model is best for young children?

••

As an early childhood educator, you will be asked to make many decisions in your career. Many of those decisions will be about the programs and activities that you will provide for the children you teach. The decisions you make will reflect your own view of how children learn best and the most effective ways to teach them. You will want to know that early childhood education has a long history and that for many years, philosophers and teachers have been thinking about these same questions.

EARLY SCHOOLS FOR YOUNG CHILDREN

Early childhood programs today can trace their development back to early philosophers. For example, Martin Luther (1483–1546) believed that all boys should be educated (a radical thought in his day) and insisted that music and physical education should be an integral part of the curriculum (Frost and Kissinger 1976). A century later, John Comenius (1592–1670) suggested that all children should attend school, and he recommended an integrated, hands-on curriculum. He believed that children should learn to speak by speaking, to write by writing, and to reason by reasoning (Comenius 1642; reprinted 1969). Later educators, such as Dewey, Montessori, and Piaget, have echoed Comensius's call for active learning.

Two other philosophers, Jean-Jacques Rousseau (1712–1778) and Johann Pestalozzi (1746–1827), also made important contributions to early childhood education. Rousseau thought that educational decisions should be made on the basis of the child's nature. He also developed a stage theory of child development based on his belief that children from birth to age five learn best from physical activity and that children from five to twelve learn best by direct experience and exploration of the environment (Rousseau 1780; reprinted 1950). When educators advocate hands-on learning, they are agreeing with Rousseau. Pestalozzi wanted to rid the schools of cruel punishment and rote learning. He believed in having children participate in real, meaningful activities and in grouping children of various ages so that the older ones can help the younger ones (Pestalozzi 1885, 1894).

Friedrich Froebel (1782–1852)

Friedrich Froebel is credited with founding *kindergartens:* "children's gardens." He studied with Pestalozzi but believed that Pestalozzi did not go far enough in matching teaching to the nature of the child. Froebel began his school for young children in Blankenburg, Germany, in 1837. He believed that everything in the universe functions in relationship to God and that each person has a specific purpose to fulfill in this life. He wrote, "Education should lead and guide man to clearness concerning himself and in himself, to peace with nature, and to unity with God" (Froebel, 1826, ch. 5). The importance of the individual and the respect that must be accorded to each person is central to Froebelian thinking.

Froebel believed that play is the foundation for children's learning and envisioned the kindergarten as the child's bridge between home and school. He believed that appropriate play helps children think about the interactions between "life and self-activity, thought and action, representation and cognition, and ability and understanding" (Ransbury 1982, p. 104). Froebel believed that materials in forms found in nature—spheres, cubes, cylinders, squares, triangles, circles, and lines—help children explore the properties of matter and understand the relationships in the universe. He called these materials "gifts." He also designed sequences of activities that he called "occupations"; they included folding paper, drawing, and weaving. Froebel distinguished between what he called "thoughtless copying" and "deliberate imitation." He believed that when children perform the occupations, they restructure their own ideas and do not merely copy actions without thinking about them.

In Froebel's school, children often learned verses to accompany the occupations. Froebel encouraged these "Mother rhymes," which were what we would call *fingerplays* today. Children said the rhymes while they performed actions with the hands or body. Froebel believed that to teach young children, it was necessary to arouse and maintain interest and attention, use the child's curiosity, and plan for motivation to learn.

Although Froebel's structured approach to kindergarten instruction has been discarded, modern teachers of young children do employ fingerplays and play materials designed to encourage learning. Modern teachers also recognize the value of play as a mode of learning and the importance of recognizing the individual child. All these ideas can be traced to Froebel and his kindergarten.

CONTEMPORARY MODELS

Today, many models describe goals, materials, teacher roles, and appropriate instructional practices for early childhood education. Roopnarine and Johnson (1993) describe fourteen models, including home-based models, models for children with special needs, and center-based models. These authors also admit that models in early childhood education have never had the same impact as models in other areas of education.

Models can serve as guidelines for planning and organizing experiences, but they are rarely, if ever, implemented totally. Uncritical acceptance of any model certainly does not encourage the professional growth and development of teachers and curriculum planners. As teachers use models and theories, they construct their own understanding of the teaching-learning processes and should be able to incorporate their experiences into any model to make it a more cohesive or complete explanation of how children develop and learn.

Most knowledge of models in early childhood education grew out of work done in the late 1960s and early 1970s in Head Start programs. Financial support for developing and testing models has been much more difficult to obtain since that period; therefore, fewer models have been developed. Of the fourteen models described by Roopnarine and Johnson (1993), the center-based models fall roughly into three categories: Montessori models, behaviorist models, and interactionist models. In this chapter, we will describe each of these three basic approaches to early childhood education. Although some of the models have been extended to address both younger and older children, for the sake of comparison, each program in this chapter will be described as it applies to four- and five-year-olds; notes about applying programs to younger or older children will be included.

Each section will include a description of the theoretical foundation of the model and the beliefs about teaching and learning on which the model is based, the goals of the model, a typical day in a school based on the model, and a brief evaluation of the model.

The Montessori Model

Maria Montessori (1870–1952) opened her school in Italy for institutionalized children in 1907, and her successes with these children quickly

The influence of Montessori's work is apparent in providing children with child-sized equipment and having them perform real-life tasks.

attracted the attention of the educational community. Over the next few years, Montessori schools spread throughout Europe and the United States. Montessori schools, at both the preschool and elementary levels, are now common in most U.S. communities. Although most Montessori schools are private, some public school systems offer Montessori programs as alternative schools.

Montessori schools vary widely, depending on the philosophy of the teachers and how closely a school tries to maintain the original philosophy. However, all Montessori schools share some philosophy and approaches to learning that make them distinctively Montessori.

How Children Learn

Some key elements of Montessori philosophy include the ideas of the absorbent mind, the prepared environment, autoeducation, sensitive periods, and the principle of freedom for the child. Each of these elements is a factor in explanations of how children grow and develop.

The concept of the **absorbent mind** is important in Montessori philosophy. The prevailing idea in Montessori's time was that children do not do

Absorbent mind
A phrase describing Montessori's belief that the child is able to absorb information long before he can be taught certain concepts.

anything mentally during infancy. Montessori, however, believed that infants unconsciously absorb all that is around them and that gradually this process becomes conscious. As the child becomes conscious, he begins to organize experience and make generalizations. For example, after several experiences with cups of various kinds, the child comes to understand "cup" as a category that includes not only all existing cups but also all possible cups. Montessori philosophy also holds that the child's construction of a sense of self is accomplished if he is free to develop the pattern inherent in him (Standing 1962).

Prepared environment
A learning environment structured to promote the development of given concepts in a child's mind.

In a Montessori program, the teacher is responsible for the **prepared environment:** that is, for selecting and arranging the materials that make learning possible. Materials for learning must be carefully chosen and displayed to catch the child's interest. The tables and chairs must be child sized and lightweight so that a child can arrange them in the way that is most comfortable for her. The environment must be orderly so that the child develops a sense of order and control. It must also be attractive so that the child develops a respect for beauty. Most Montessori classrooms are decorated with plants and objects from nature as well as colorful displays and tasteful pieces of art.

The teacher is responsible for sequencing the child's experiences so that he builds concepts logically. The materials for instruction are arranged so that the child can select from among them the ones in which he is interested, but it is the teacher's role to bring out and demonstrate new materials at the optimal time in the development of each child. Once the teacher has demonstrated the procedures for using materials, the child can choose to work with them. It is within this carefully planned framework that **autoeducation**—the building of his own mental constructs by the individual child—takes place. Children learn to clarify their perceptions and organize their experiences through the activities. The teacher's role is not to present information through direct instruction but to demonstrate the materials and guide the child's selection of materials and activities.

Autoeducation
The child's ability to organize her own thinking when engaged in certain activities.

A basic premise of the Montessori philosophy is that the child copies reality rather than constructs it. From watching and then doing activities, the child organizes the world and her own thinking. One of the primary roles of a Montessori teacher is to demonstrate how materials are to be used and tasks are to be completed. These demonstrations are very specific in that there is an exact procedure for using each set of materials; children are not allowed free expression with the materials until they have mastered the exact procedures (Montessori 1914).

Most Montessori materials are self-correcting. They are designed so that the child gets feedback on the correctness of his actions from the materials. An example of self-correcting material is the Pink Tower, which is a set of cubes of graduated sizes. The child begins building the Tower by placing the largest cube on the bottom; each additional cube is placed on the Tower in order by decreasing size, such that the smallest cube is placed on the top. In demonstrating how to use the Tower, the teacher first shows how it is constructed; then he takes it apart and allows the child to construct it. The teacher does not supply information or cues to the child while she is attempting this construction. If the Tower is constructed correctly, each cube will be used and every cube placed on the Tower will be smaller than the preceding cube. If the child makes an error in construction, one or more cubes will be left over or will not fit properly. The purpose of the Pink Tower is to help the child develop abilities in seriation. Once the child has mastered the Tower, other materials are introduced in a careful sequence to aid her in transferring the ability to seriate from one situation to another and to further her thinking and reasoning abilities.

Montessori materials and exercises are basically divided into four categories that promote the development of daily-living skills and sensorial, academic, and cultural and artistic abilities. *Daily-living exercises* involve the physical care of oneself and the environment and include tasks such as washing a table or polishing shoes. The purpose of these tasks is not simply to develop a skill but also to aid the "inner construction of discipline, organization, independence, and self-esteem through concentration on a precise and completed cycle of activity" (Lillard 1972, p. 71).

Sensorial materials are designed to encourage the refinement of the senses for the purpose of aiding the child in developing intelligence. Montessori believed that intelligence is developed as the child organizes and categorizes perceptions into a mental order. An example of sensorial materials is a collection of seven different fabric samples: velvet, silk, wool, fine linen, coarse linen, fine cotton, and coarse cotton. The teacher is to take care that these samples are pure. The child is encouraged to play with the samples, to learn the names of the fabrics, and then to identify a given sample by touch.

Academic materials include the moveable alphabet, sandpaper letters, and plane geometric insets. After the child has learned to recognize the individual letters of the alphabet and to compose some words with help from the teacher, he is presented with the moveable alphabet. There are several duplicates of each letter, and the child is encouraged to compose words with them. The child is freed from the difficulty of forming letters by hand and so can progress more quickly in composing and recognizing words.

Artistic or cultural materials and exercises are designed to help children learn to love and appreciate music and learn to control movements of hands and feet in preparation for dance. Rhythm and then harmony and melody are introduced. Children are taught how to use musical instruments and to recognize musical sounds through the sensorial exercises. Although drawing is never taught directly, children are taught about line and color before painting is introduced.

Freedom
The principle that dictates that the child, not the teacher, should choose activities for learning.

Freedom to choose activities and when to change activities is very important in Montessori education. The teacher may guide the child by demonstrating new materials he thinks might interest or challenge the child, but the child must choose which materials to use. The choice of materials is the child's, but how the materials are used is clearly defined. If the child chooses to use materials in unacceptable ways, the teacher may remove the materials and ask the child to make another choice. Freedom of choice is related to the concept of autoeducation; the child must educate himself. Standing (1957) summarizes this concept in the following statements:

1. *The child must learn by his own activity.*
2. *He must be granted a mental freedom to take what he needs.*
3. *He must not be questioned in his choice—since the "teacher should answer the mental needs of the child, not dictate them." (p. 364)*

Sensitive periods
Times in a child's development when certain concepts are learned more easily.

Another important concept in Montessori education is that of **sensitive periods,** which are periods when a child is capable of and interested in learning specific things. This concept is much like that of *readiness.* For example, if a child is in a sensitive period in which she is fascinated with details, the teacher might supply materials that have many small parts to put together. Montessori teachers are trained to observe these sensitive periods and provide experiences appropriate for each period.

Montessori believed that young children want to be obedient and that they desire order in their environments. If a child becomes agitated or experiences "brainstorms" of activity, then he is to be removed quietly and gently from the environment and encouraged to rest quietly until he has quieted. Teachers in a Montessori school maintain discipline by expecting children to respect each other's work and workspaces and by removing children who lose control of their impulses.

Goals of Montessori Education

The most important goal of Montessori education is development of the individual. The facts a child learns are not as important as her mental or intellectual development. Therefore, the goals of Montessori programs emphasize development of general intellectual skills and general, rather than particular, subject-matter concepts. As stated by the American Montessori Society (1984), the goals of Montessori programs include development of:

- Concentration
- Observation skills
- An awareness of order and sequence
- Coordination
- Perceptual awareness and practical skills
- Mathematical concepts
- Language skills
- Writing and reading skills
- Familiarity with the creative arts
- Understanding of the world of nature
- Experience with and understanding of the social sciences
- Experience with critical thinking skills through problem-solving techniques

Montessori programs are concerned with children's development physically, socially, emotionally, and intellectually. The importance of physical development is reflected in an emphasis on outdoor play and participation in rhythmic activities. Social development is emphasized in discussions of appropriate behavior on the playground and in the focus on respecting the individual's work and space in the classroom. Intellectual development is achieved through activities designed to help children organize, classify, seriate, and heighten their perceptual awareness.

In the classroom described in the panel on pages 44 and 45, some children are developing perceptual abilities by matching pictures or completing puzzles. Others are learning the difference between lakes and islands by constructing models with clay. The outcomes expected from each of the experiences differ. Not all children share the same experiences, but all are guided to learn some concepts and to develop some abilities. Subject-matter concepts, such as the vocabulary to describe islands and lakes or the names of the letters of the alphabet, are conveyed through group or individual instruction. Content areas, such as science and social studies, are included in the program in the form of materials or equipment such as scales and maps. Math concepts are also developed through materials such as the Tower and beads. Literacy is promoted through materials such as alphabet letters of different textures and the moveable alphabet. Some activities, such as listening for syllables in names, are also designed to promote the development of literacy. Stories are read daily to encourage children's interest in books.

When children younger than three are accepted in Montessori programs, they usually attend two or three mornings each week and the programs are modified by having smaller groups and fewer choices for the

A TYPICAL DAY IN A MONTESSORI PRESCHOOL

9:00– 9:20	Arrival, group time
9:20–10:20	Choice time
10:20–10:45	Outdoor play
10:45–10:55	Group time, preparation for snack
10:55–11:10	Snack
11:10–11:30	Story time, one group in rhythms

In Susan's group, there are twenty-eight children, a head teacher, and two assistant teachers. The children in this group are between three and five years old. As Susan enters the light and airy classroom, she goes immediately to the area with open cupboards containing hooks and hangs up her coat while her mother signs her in for the day. Susan waves good-bye to her mother and joins the children who are gathered on the "blue line," a line of blue tape that forms a square in the middle of the largest room in the building. Susan is greeted by her teacher and says hello to her friend, who is already sitting on the line.

When all the children are gathered, the teacher sits at a small table containing a plastic mat, blue and brown clay, a rolling pin, and two identical trays about 5 by 8 inches in size. The teacher tells the children they are going to learn about the words *island* and *lake.* She tells them that an island is land surrounded by water and that a lake is water surrounded by land. She then asks about the colors of water and land, and the children respond "blue" and "brown." She makes a model of a lake by rolling out some of the blue clay and some of the brown clay and placing the brown clay around the blue clay on one of the trays. She repeats the process to make an island on the other tray. Then various children are called on to come up and point to the representations of the island and the lake. At the conclusion of the lesson, the teacher tells the children that this material will be available in the art room so that they can construct their own lakes and islands today.

The head teacher then tells the children that they may choose to work today in the solarium, the art room, or the large room. One of the teachers will be in each of these areas. The head teacher asks the children to go one at a time and choose their favorite things to work on and to get started working. All the children go immediately to an area and choose an activity.

One boy chooses a carpet square, places it on the floor, and selects from the shelves a tray containing a corkboard, a small hammer, and small wooden shapes, each with a hole drilled through it. Using the pegs on the tray, the child begins to attach each shape to the corkboard.

Susan takes a circular felt mat from a stack and places it on a nearby table. She then selects a basket containing a wooden board divided into six squares, with a picture of an animal on each square. She finds small squares with matching

children. The Montessori approach also includes elementary programs (and a limited number of secondary programs). Programs for children in the primary grades are fundamentally the same as preschool programs in that children are presented with materials and allowed to work with those they select. In the primary grades, there is much more emphasis on literacy, as children create words from the moveable alphabet. They begin writing by copying words and then move on to writing sentences and stories. Instruction in reading often emphasizes a phonetic approach. Many pictures and places one on each square. When she has completed this task, she places the pieces back in the basket, places the basket on the shelf, places the mat back on the stack, and chooses a carpet square, which she puts on the floor. She selects a puzzle from the shelf and begins to work on the carpet.

Meanwhile, some children have chosen to work in the solarium, where many science-oriented activities are available. Some children are working with the teacher using a scale to weigh various objects and find out whether they are heavier, lighter, or the same weight as other objects. Other children are filling containers with water from a tub; some are sorting objects based on the materials they are made of. In the art room, some children don painting smocks and paint at easels; one works with the clay to make islands and lakes; and other children choose paper and clay for drawing and molding experiences.

A few children in the large room are working with the teacher on recognizing letters. The teacher places white letters (upper- and lower-case) on a black background and tells the children the name of each letter and its sound. Then they look at a small set of pictures of objects whose names begin with that sound and name each one, emphasizing the sound. Another teacher moves around the room, working with individual children, for example, asking them the names of colors after they have matched color strips. Each child works with an activity as long as she chooses.

The children work with their activities for about an hour and are then instructed to put their materials away and get their coats for outdoor play. They play outside for about twenty minutes on swings, a climber/slide, and balance beams and also with some large outdoor toys. Susan walks the balance beam several times. One of the teachers holds her hand the first time, and then she walks with the teacher walking beside her but not touching her. Then Susan joins a group playing on the climber/slide and plays there until it is time to go inside.

As the children return to the room, they are instructed to wash their hands for snack and to sit on the blue line again. As the children are washing up, one of the assistant teachers beats the rhythm of a child's name on a drum, and then all the children clap the rhythm. Each child called on is asked what name to beat—some supply only their first names, some their full names. When all the children are on the line, the head teacher discusses a problem that occurred outdoors: Someone threw a rock. She asks the children to explain why they cannot throw rocks and concludes by having them think of things that they can throw outdoors. The children are dismissed to have their snack by getting up one by one as the teacher describes their clothing.

After the snack each day, one group stays in the large room for movement exercises. Susan goes with a small group to one of the small rooms for story reading. The small groups are selected on the basis of maturity and experience in listening to stories. The teachers read the stories and ask questions about them. They then read stories selected by the children, if there is more time.

By this time, parents are beginning to arrive. Susan's father signs her out, helps her collect her coat, and takes her home.

Montessori materials are available for helping children develop concepts in mathematics, social studies, and science.

The Behaviorist Model

The behaviorist model of schools for young children is based on the learning theories of Edward Thorndike and B. F. Skinner (described in Chapter

Direct instruction
Instruction in which the teacher presents information directly to the children.

One). Basically, these theories explain behavior in terms of a stimulus and a response and operant conditioning. Three other key components in the behaviorist model—also known as **direct instruction**—are reinforcement schedules, shaping of behavior, and extinction of behavior. A *reinforcement schedule* is established after a specific response has been achieved; after that point, the learner is rewarded on a schedule, rather than for every response. The learner might be rewarded for every two responses, then every four responses, and so on; eventually, the learner will not need a reward to continue the response. *Shaping of behavior* is changing behavior by controlling the rewards and punishments. If a child is disruptive to the group, the teacher might decide to change the child's behavior by ignoring all disruptive behavior and rewarding more appropriate behavior. Even calling the child's name when she is disruptive can be rewarding to a child seeking attention. Behaviors can be *extinguished* just as they can be encouraged. For instance, if a child throws a temper tantrum in order to get something that has been denied, the teacher can ignore that behavior until it is no longer exhibited. If a behavior does not result in the child's getting what she wants, she will try another behavior.

How Children Learn

In the behaviorist view, a child acquires knowledge as the result of repeated interactions with the environment. The consequences of the interactions—reward or punishment—determine whether the interaction will be repeated. The most effective teaching presents a carefully selected stimulus and then controls the rewards or punishments connected with the child's response to the stimulus. The behaviorist view is that a child accumulates knowledge through repeated exposures to stimuli and that the learning process is directed by the adult who controls the sequence of stimuli and the reward system. The best known behaviorist, or direct instruction, model is the program developed by Bereiter and Engelmann (1966) and marketed under the trade name DISTAR. This program was developed in the 1960s as one model for achieving school success with children who are disadvantaged. Another behaviorist model is the Behavior Analysis Model, developed by Don Bushell (Roopnarine and Johnson 1993).

In the direct instruction model, the focus is on achievement of academic goals, especially in reading, arithmetic, and language. The lessons presented to children are designed to be conducted in small groups, and lessons are carefully sequenced. Each lesson includes an activity designed to motivate students and attract their attention. Following this part of the lesson, new information is presented and responses are elicited from students. If their responses are correct, the students are rewarded. If their responses are incorrect, students repeat the lesson until the correct responses have been elicited and then rewarded.

The children's behavior is also controlled by a system of rewards and punishments. For example, when a child comes into the room in the morning and hangs up his coat without being reminded, the teacher might reward the child by giving him a token. Tokens can be redeemed later for extra play time or special activities or used to purchase items from a class store. Children who fail to follow the rules may receive no tokens or have tokens taken away.

Teachers who follow direct instruction models are expected to understand and be able to use reinforcement schedules, shaping of behavior, and extinction of behavior in achieving academic and behavioral goals. Bereiter and Engelmann describe the hallmarks of their methods as follows:

1. Fast pace. *During a twenty-minute period as many as 500 responses may be required of each child. Usually five or more different kinds of tasks are presented during a single period.*

2. Reduced task-irrelevant behavior. *The teacher controls the session relying only incidentally on spontaneous exchanges to dictate the direction of instruction. Efforts of both teacher and children are focused on the tasks being studied.*

3. Strong emphasis on verbal responses. *These are often produced in unison, so that each child's total output can be maximized.*

4. Carefully planned small-step instructional units with continual feedback. *The teacher is not receptive to irrelevant exchanges but is very sensitive to possible areas of difficulty, possible ambiguities that arise from her presentation. She quickly corrects mistakes. She tries to anticipate and avert them.*

5. Heavy work demands. *Children are required to pay attention and to work hard. They are rewarded for thinking; half-hearted or careless performance is not tolerated. (in Spodek 1973, pp. 177–178)*

With the direct instruction model, the classroom is simplified and the number of activities is limited. The rationale given by Bereiter and Engelmann (1966) for these limitations is that

an object-rich environment stimulates a culturally deprived child to attend to a glitter of superabundant stimuli. He darts from one object to another, treating each only in terms of sensory gratification. When the toy no longer "feels good," another one is selected. By minimizing the inducement of noise in the environment, the preschool can be far more effective in directing the child not to the vehicle of the concept but to the concept itself. Sterilizing the environment is a firm requirement of the work-oriented preschool. Toys should be limited to form boards, jigsaw puzzles (which are usually favorites with the children), books, drawing and tracing materials, Cuisenaire rods (to be handled during free time under the direction of the teacher), and a miniature house, barn and set of farm animals. Paper, crayons, and chalk (but no paint) should be available for expressive play. Motor toys, such as tricycles and wagons, and climbing equipment are not necessary for the program. (p. 72)

More recently, Neisworth and Buggey (1993) have summarized the basic procedures of the teacher in a behaviorist program:

- *Reward constructive behavior; ignore undesirable behavior. The best rewards are those that are natural or intrinsic to an activity. Add-on, contrived rewards (e.g., tokens, extra praise) should only be used when necessary, much as crutches should be used.*
- *Teach skills in simulated settings or in the actual circumstances in which the skills are expected.*
- *Practice what you teach. Children will imitate teacher behavior.*
- *Behaviorial teaching is by definition individualized. Plan developmentally appropriate sequences for each child.*
- *Choose rewards that are appropriate and motivating to the child. Children's preferences differ; not all children enjoy the same activities, rewards, or circumstances.*
- *Learning occurs when the child is interacting with the environment; maximize interaction.*
- *Plan for generalization; use shaping and stimulus-control. Evaluate acquired skills across settings, time, and persons.*
- *Make sure that children have opportunities to practice (and experience reinforcement for) learned skills periodically to maintain them. Optimally, what children learn at one time is used as part of more sophisticated behavior learned later. (p. 130)*

Goals of Behaviorist Models

The most important goals of behaviorist models are achievement of academic competencies in language, reading, and arithmetic. Children are also expected to learn to answer questions from the teacher articulately and in complete sentences and to perform on cue. The developers of direct instruction models believe that children who are academically capable will have improved self-concepts. Motor development is not among the primary goals of direct instruction models.

In the description on pages 50 and 51 of a typical day in a behaviorist preschool, the children are engaged in activities designed to teach content knowledge or facts and to help them develop the skills necessary for success in school settings, such as answering questions posed and responding to cues provided by the teacher. Other activities are included to accomplish specific academic goals, to complement the teacher's instruction, or to reward performance.

The behaviorist models focus primarily on *intellectual development,* which is defined as the learning of content and facts, not as the development of generalized intellectual abilities. Physical development is not a primary goal of this type of instruction, nor are social and emotional development. Behaviorists believe that children will achieve more positive self-esteem if they feel that they are successful learners. Children are assumed to develop emotionally as they learn to control their impulsive behaviors and respond appropriately in school settings.

Subject-matter content in language, mathematics, and reading is broken down into small discrete steps, which children must master before going on to the next step. These subject-matter areas are emphasized because they are considered basic to the children's success. The curriculum is tightly sequenced but not integrated. Children learn each subject without regard for what is being learned in other subjects. Science and social studies are rarely included in the curriculum, and the arts are included in a very limited fashion as part of the choice activities.

When implemented with older children, the fundamental behaviorist model remains intact. Basically, the changes for older children are found in the content of the lessons presented in subject-matter areas.

Many elements of the behaviorist models are evident in current elementary programs. Specification of limited objectives, emphasis on the sequence of materials or activities, and mastery of small steps as a method of achieving larger goals are all behavioristic in origin. In many elementary schools that do not claim to be behavioristic, tokens or stickers are used as reinforcers, and grades are often viewed as rewards or punishments.

The Interactionist Model

Several well-known models of instruction are interactionist, or constructionist, in philosophy. (The terms *constructionist* and *constructivist* are sometimes used as synonyms for *interactionist* and *developmentalist.*) Interactionist models are based on the learning theories of Jean Piaget (1896–1980). Examples of Piagetian programs include the High/Scope program, developed by David Weikart; Educating the Young Thinker, devel-

A TYPICAL DAY IN A BEHAVIORIST PRESCHOOL

9:00– 9:15	Arrival, group time
9:15– 10:00	Rotating instructional groups
10:00– 10:25	Outdoor play
10:25– 10:45	Snack
10:45– 11:10	Instructional groups
11:10– 11:25	Choice of activities
11:25– 11:30	Dismissal

The school Alan attends has separate classes for fours and fives. The classroom in which five-year-old Alan works each day is a large room with three smaller rooms that open off it. For Alan's group of thirty children, there is a teacher and two assistant teachers.

The teacher greets Alan at the door with a smile and tells him how glad she is that he is at school. As Alan hangs up his coat, the teacher slips him a red token, and he puts it into his pocket with a grin. Alan joins the other children sitting in a circle on the floor. In a few minutes, when all the children are present, the teacher joins the group and calls the roll. Alan responds to his name with "I am present." Then the teacher reviews the days of the week and the months of the year. Alan raises his hand to say the days of the week. He repeats the names successfully and receives another token. He also gets a smile and praise from the teacher. After a child is selected to pin the correct numeral on the calendar and move point-ers on the weather chart to indicate today's weather, Alan is instructed to go to the language room with his group. Alan's group membership is based on his ability level. There are high, middle, and low groups.

One of the assistant teachers conducts Alan's language lesson for twenty minutes. Alan and the other members of his group sit on small risers to be as close as possible to the teacher and to facilitate their choral responses. The first part of the lesson is a warm-up in which the teacher tells the children that when she taps her pencil three times, they should clap their hands. Some children do not clap on cue, and the exercise is repeated. The children are reminded that paying close attention and responding quickly are very important.

Today's lesson is on the use of pronouns: *I, he, she, we.* The teacher opens a paper bag and removes a comb. She says, "I comb my hair." The children are instructed to pretend combing their hair and to repeat, "I comb my hair." Each child

oped by Irving Sigel; the School for Constructive Play, developed by George Forman; and Piaget for Early Education, developed by Constance Kamii and Rheta DeVries. There are points of agreement among constructionist programs, as well as some differences. Among the points of agreement are the following:

1. *All contend that a basic objective to be drawn from Piaget's work is to foster structural change in children's reasoning in the direction of operational thought.*

2. *All emphasize the fundamental importance of the child's action for learning and development.*

who responds correctly is rewarded with a token. The teacher then goes through sentences using the pronouns *he, she,* and *we* with descriptions of other self-care actions, such as brushing the teeth, washing the face, and so on. When the lesson is completed, Alan and his group leave their room and walk with the teacher to the next room for their arithmetic lesson.

In this lesson, Alan's group is learning to recognize and complete simple addition equations. As the teacher holds up flashcards showing equations such as 3 + 1, the group responds, "Three plus one equals four." Today, the teacher repeats combinations whose sums do not exceed 6. When the children have reviewed these sums, they are given a worksheet, listing the same equations, and asked to complete it. Alan mumbles something to Brad, who is sitting beside him at the table. The teacher quickly reminds him that this is work time and that talking to friends is not appropriate now. She tells Alan that a token will be taken away if he talks again. Alan writes the answers to the problems and is rewarded when he does them correctly.

For the next twenty-minute period, Alan and his classmates play outside. The playground has swings, climber/slides, tire swings, and climbers. Alan chooses to swing and takes turns with Brad.

When the children return to the classroom, they are instructed to wash their hands before snack. The snack today consists of apples cut into fourths and crackers scored into fourths. The teachers introduce and reinforce the use of the fractional terms as the children eat their snacks.

After snack, Alan's group goes into a small room for the reading lesson. Again, the teacher gets the children's attention with a warm-up exercise, and when all have responded correctly, he begins the lesson. Today's lesson is on the sounds represented by the letters *b, m, l,* and *d.* The teacher presents a letter on a card and says, "This letter is *b* and its sound is 'buh.'" The children repeat the name and the sound several times. They already know the long vowel sounds, and today's letters are combined with each of the vowels in succession and pronounced.

When the reading lesson is finished, Alan and his group return to the large room, where all the children are gathered. They now have the opportunity to spend their tokens on some special activities. Alan chooses to spend three of his tokens for drawing with paper and markers. When he completes his drawing, he spends three more tokens to play with the jigsaw puzzles. Then he and the assistant teacher build some sets with the Cuisenaire rods. The teacher blinks the lights to indicate that it is time to put away all the materials and get ready to go home.

In a few minutes, the room is clean and orderly, and the children have put on their coats and are out the door.

3. All borrow ideas from the child-development tradition in early education for materials, equipment, and activities that permit children to be active (for example, painting and other art activities, blockbuilding, pretend play, singing, and sand and water play).

4. None of the . . . Piagetian programs is just "Piagetian." Each recognizes certain limitations in using Piaget's theory alone as a basis for educational practice. (DeVries and Kohlberg 1987, p. 51)

Programs differ in their definitions of action, the extent of emphasis on logic in language, the extent of reliance on child development traditions, and how cooperation and interest are fostered. Some developmentalists define *action* as physical action; some broaden the definition to include mental action. Some programs place more emphasis on children's being able to articulate their understanding; others place more emphasis on performance. Some programs allow more time for free play and free expression than others. Some programs rely on free-play activities to help children develop cooperative behaviors; others specifically plan for interventions in behavior cycles.

How Children Learn

Intrinsic motivation
Motivation that comes from within.

Recall from Chapter One that Piaget described learning as a process that is based on **intrinsic motivation.** He also described thinking as developing through stages in which the learner becomes more and more capable of thinking in abstract and logical terms. According to Piaget, knowledge is acquired differently, depending on the individual's stage of development and the type of knowledge to be acquired. For instance, knowledge of the physical characteristics inherent in objects is acquired only by experience with those objects; thus, children learn the concept "square" by exploring square objects and determining the characteristics they share. Learners develop social knowledge through experiences with mature members of their social group. Language and social customs, for example, are transmitted from one person to another; they cannot be learned by exploration because they have no direct relationship to real objects. Logico-mathematical learning requires action on objects accompanied by mental constructions. Putting objects in a series, from shortest to longest, requires creating a relationship among the objects. Numeration, seriation, and classification are included in the category of logico-mathematical learning.

Some basic approaches of a developmentalist program include promoting active manipulation of objects; stimulating intrinsic motivation; encouraging children's processes of assimilation, accommodation, and disequilibrium; and encouraging interaction with others. Children in these programs are expected to learn through active manipulation of objects and are guided to reflect on their actions by their teachers. Most learning experiences are discovery activities. For example, a teacher might choose to place an assortment of materials near the water table in order to let the children determine through play with these materials which ones float and which do not. The children might make some predictions about whether certain objects would float and later be guided to reflect on the results of their experimentation. Children who choose to participate in this activity might dictate or write about their findings.

Intrinsic motivation for learning is very important in a developmentalist program, and it is the teacher's responsibility to make available materials and activities that will interest children. Developmentalists believe that children want to learn and are, in fact, always learning.

Because each child must construct her own understanding, children receive very little group instruction. Children are helped to construct their knowledge by teachers who encourage them to reflect on their manipulation of objects; therefore, teachers are most often engaged with small groups or with individual children. A developmentalist teacher does not feel that a child should be supplied with all the answers to questions that arise during an experience and believes that some unanswered questions are important.

Another important component of learning is through interactions with other people. Children are encouraged to exchange viewpoints with others and to role-play various situations and reflect on the roles and interactions. Adults help children solve their own problems and find solutions that are acceptable without telling them the "right" answers.

Curricula are planned and learning experiences are selected to follow the child's interests or expose the child to new areas in which his interest might be aroused. The process of finding information, analyzing data, and reaching conclusions is considered more important than learning facts. An emphasis on process does not mean that content is lacking, however. Children learn a great many facts and concepts, but they are always embedded in meaningful contexts. For example, children who are learning about trees might "adopt" a tree and visit it on a regular basis in order to record changes over time. They might learn to identify and classify leaves of various trees and participate in experiments to discover the function of leaves. The children might examine the rings in a tree stump, draw conclusions about their observations, and so on. They might locate books about trees in the library, and the teacher might read to them about trees. In other words, the curriculum experiences would focus on children's learning how to find, analyze, and evaluate information, but facts would be presented in the process.

Developmentalists believe that it is important to select curriculum experiences containing content that can be acted on in various ways. Teachers must also consider the developmental stage of the learner and the complexity of the tasks required to be successful in learning the material.

Goals of Interactionist Programs

The goal of any developmental program is to stimulate children in all areas of development. Physical development, social and emotional development, and cognitive (intellectual) development are all important. Language development and an emphasis on the process of learning are also important. Programs attempt to keep a balance so that all areas of development are addressed and none are neglected. Encouraging children to become actively involved in their own learning and developing the child's desire to continue to learn are also important goals.

Kamii and DeVries (1977) state that education must be based on the long-term objective of developing the entire personality, with particular emphasis on intellectual and moral autonomy. Their emphasis on intellectual development is based on Piaget's own statements:

> *The principal goal of education is to create [people] who are capable of doing new things, not simply of repeating what other generations have done— [people] who are creative, inventive, and discoverers. The second goal of education is to form minds which can be critical, can verify, and not accept everything they are offered. The great danger today is of slogans, collective opinions, ready-made trends of thought. We have to be able to resist individually, to criticize, to distinguish between what is proven and what is not. So we need pupils who are active, who learn early to find out by themselves, partly by their own spontaneous activity and partly through material we set up for them; who learn early to tell what is verifiable and what is simply the first idea to come to them. (Piaget 1964, p. 5)*

In the short term, interactionist programs also strive to help children achieve the following socioemotional goals:

1. *To feel secure in a noncoercive relationship with adults*
2. *To respect the feelings and rights of others and begin to coordinate different points of view (decentering and cooperating)*
3. *To be independent, alert, and curious; to use initiative in pursuing curiosities; to have confidence in his ability to figure things out for himself, and to speak his mind with conviction. (Day and Parker 1977, p. 393)*

Finally, such programs encourage children to achieve cognitive objectives:

1. *To come up with interesting ideas, problems, and questions*
2. *To put things into relationships and notice similarities and differences. (Day and Parker 1977, p. 394)*

Despite their general similarities, the goals of different interactionist programs can vary. The descriptions that follow will help clarify some of the differences in programs based on Piagetian theory.

The School for Constructive Play   In George Forman's program, the goals are to help children develop cognitively through activities selected specifically to help them with the ideas of correspondences (identity and equivalence), transformations, functional relations, and changing perspectives. Forman (1992, pp. 143–144) recommends that teachers find ways to induce conflict in children's thinking. For example, in a game called Wedges and Wheels, the teacher plays with a set of wheels attached to a single axle and two wedges that form a ramp. When the child becomes interested in the game and wants to play, he is encouraged to do so. After a few experiences of rolling the wheels down the ramp, the teacher moves one of the wedges so that the wheels no longer fit on the wedges. She then watches to see how the child solves the problem of fitting the wheels on the wedges.

High/Scope   The High/Scope program, developed by David Weikart, is known for emphasizing careful and systematic observations of the child and for organizing the curriculum around key experiences. *Key experiences* have been identified in the categories of social and emotional development, movement and physical development, and cognitive development.

> *The key experiences in social and emotional developmental are making and expressing choices, plans, and decisions; recognizing and solving problems; expressing and understanding feelings; taking care of one's own needs; understanding routines and expectations; being sensitive to the feelings, interests, needs, and background of others; building relationships with children and adults; creating and experiencing collaborative play; and developing strategies for dealing with social conflict. Within cognitive development, representation key experiences include recognizing objects by sound, touch, taste, and smell; imitating actions and sounds; relating pictures, photographs, and models to real places and things; role playing and pretending; making models of clay or blocks, and drawing or painting. (Roopnarine and Johnson 1993, p. 201)*

Most activities lend themselves to several key experiences. For example, a child might choose to paint. Such a choice would give the teacher the opportunity to observe how the child was able to understand the routine of getting paper, paint smocks, and so on and then putting away the paper when he was finished. If the child needed instruction, it could be provided. Painting would also be an activity that allowed the teacher to observe how the child represented objects and related to other children involved in the same task.

Key experiences provide teachers with a basis for planning and organizing the curriculum so that activities are not random. Through observing individual students, teachers are also able to assess how children are growing in their abilities, as categorized by key experiences.

A TYPICAL DAY IN AN INTERACTIONIST PRESCHOOL

9:00– 10:00	Arrival, choice time
10:00– 10:15	Group time
10:15– 10:40	Outdoor play
10:40– 10:55	Snack time
10:55– 11:10	Group time for optional activities
11:10– 11:30	Story time and dismissal

Michelle bounces into her classroom, carrying a milk carton with a praying mantis in it. In Michelle's class of four-, five-, and six-year-olds, there are twenty-four children, a teacher, and an assistant teacher.

The classroom she enters has only one area large enough for all twenty-four children to sit down at once. The rest of the space is filled with areas arranged for different explorations or interactions. There is a large area for blocks; an area for dramatic play that contains dolls, child-sized kitchen equipment, dress-up clothes, and costumes; an area that contains easels and many kinds of art supplies; an area that contains a water table and sand table; an area that contains puzzles and games; an area for reading books that is furnished with two rocking chairs and some floor pillows; an area with many kinds of paper and writing utensils; an area that has baskets of math manipulative materials; an area that, at the moment, is filled with a large collection of old clocks and other small appliances; and another area where there is a table, which today is covered with paper and has some blocks and cardboard milk cartons on it.

Michelle's teacher notices her entry into the classroom and smiles a greeting. She notes that Michelle has signed in on the clipboard by the door and that she has hung her coat in the cubby labeled with her name. The teacher is helping two girls find a way to remove the levers and springs from an old toaster but turns her attention to Michelle and her box when Michelle approaches. The teacher listens while Michelle tells how she and her brother caught the praying mantis and made a container for it. She suggests that Michelle place the container on a display table near the door for other children to observe if they choose.

Michelle does so and then decides to spend some time in the block area. She selects a tagboard circle with her name on it and places it on one of the pegs beside a picture of blocks on a pegboard near the door. When she gets to the block area, she tells her friend Amy that she would like to build an apartment building. They decide to work on it together and find that it needs a strong base to support the ten stories that they want to add to it. The teacher observes their construction and offers them a pulley, a small box, and some cord so that they can make an elevator for their building.

After about thirty minutes of animated block building, the girls put away the blocks, and Michelle checks on her praying mantis. She finds three children at the table and tells them about catching the insect and making the milk carton container for it. She takes her name from the block peg and moves it to the art peg. She gets a friend to help her fasten her paint smock and attaches paper to an easel. She paints a picture of her praying mantis. When the teacher observes her painting, she suggests that perhaps Michelle would like to write about the insect. After Michelle has cleaned the painting area, she goes to a table where there are many kinds of paper, pencils, and markers. She finds her own journal in a basket and writes about the insect and draws pictures of it. The teacher helps her date her paper and her painting. The teachers have been moving from area to area in the classroom, asking questions, providing needed guidance, and suggesting activities to individual children.

The teacher rings a little bell, which is the signal for the children to finish their work and clean up the areas. After that has been done, the children meet on the rug, where the teacher is leading some fingerplays and songs. When all the children have gathered, the teacher asks them to think about some of the things they learned this morning. A few children tell about the parts they found in the appliances. Others tell about how they solved some problems in their play. The teacher says that she noticed that not everyone who wanted to do so could play in one of the areas where a new set of materials was available. She asks if they can think of some ways to solve the problem. The children finally decide to take a survey to determine who has already had a turn with the new materials and to make a sign-up sheet for those who have not yet had a turn. Some children make comments about the praying mantis and ask questions about it. The teacher asks how they could find out more about these insects. Two children decide that they could go to the library and ask the librarian for help in locating information. The teacher suggests a good time later in the morning for them to go.

Next, the children review the calendar, observing the patterns that they have been learning, such as the patterns created by sets of 5. Taped on the classroom wall is a strip of paper on which a count is kept of the days they have been in school; the children add the next numeral to the strip and review the patterns of 2's and 5's on the strip.

After these activities have been finished, the children go outside to play. They can choose riding toys, swings, climber/slides, climbers, and some large blocks and tunnels for play. Michelle and a small group of friends climb and swing, shouting joyfully most of the time.

After about twenty-five minutes, the teacher signals the children to return to the room. As the children enter, each is asked to choose a snack: apple juice, orange juice, apple slices, or orange slices. They wash their hands and begin helping serve the snack. When they have finished their snack, the children construct a graph of their snack choices with help from the teachers and discuss all the relationships that are illustrated on the graph.

After the graph has been finished, the children get their coats again, because today, they are going on a walk around the neighborhood. Each child has a clipboard and pencil and chooses something to look for. Some will observe the number and kinds of houses they pass; others will observe the number and kinds of businesses. A few children want to record the number and kinds of plants they see, and some will look for all the printed words that they can find. They know that tomorrow they will begin to transfer the information they collect to the map of their immediate neighborhood that they are building on the table.

When the class returns from the walk, the children gather on the rug again for singing and movement. Two children go off to the library to get praying mantis information; the others learn some new songs and review the lyrics to other songs that are printed on large charts. The children also use some little books in which they have illustrated a few of the songs.

The teacher then shares a story from a big book, with large illustrations and type so that all the children can see while the teacher reads. As the teacher reads the story a second time, some children join in on the words that they recognize. The teacher tells them that they will write their own stories tomorrow.

The two children return from the library with several books and some posters. The teacher places these books on the display table with the praying mantis. Several children are really interested in the insect, and the teacher promises that they will have time to observe it and read about it tomorrow.

As the children gather their coats and papers and get ready for dismissal, they review patterns and arrange themselves in line according to their coat colors. It takes some time, but they form a pattern of red, blue, green, and yellow coats; then they add the children who do not fit that particular pattern. Michelle has on a red jacket and gets in line to help complete the pattern. She has her painting in her hand and hurries to share it with her mother when the teacher dismisses the class.

Educating the Young Thinker   The goal of Irving Sigel's program is to develop representational competence. Sigel describes three principles that guide selection of materials and activities in his program:

1. *Children understand their world through representations of it.*
2. *Representational competence develops in an orderly sequence.*
3. *Representational competence develops fully only in response to interactions with the appropriate physical and social environments. (Roopnarine and Johnson 1993, p. 183)*

Overview of Interactionist Programs   Although the goals or emphases of these three interactionist programs are not identical, they are all concerned with the development of children's thinking and reasoning abilities and their abilities to represent experiences in meaningful ways. Each program depends on children's active involvement with materials and teachers' guidance in helping children reflect on their experiences.

In examining the activities of a typical day (see pages 56 and 57) in an interactionist classroom, we find that playing with blocks offers children opportunities to develop concepts in mathematics, such as length and equivalence. The addition of the pulley provides opportunities for developing concepts related to simple machines. Representation of experience is achieved through building the model of an apartment building. Several activities offer children opportunities to use their developing skills in literacy (signing in on arrival, recording comments about the painting, recording observations on the walk in the neighborhood) and to represent understandings. In exploring the numerical patterns in the room, the teacher attempts to aid children in the development of number concepts. Other activities require children to solve problems (taking apart the toaster, deciding who could play in the new area) using reasoning.

Interactionist programs focus on development of physical, social, emotional, and intellectual competence. The curriculum is based on children's interests and is integrated so that content is not arranged by subject-matter areas. Many activities and experiences are selected to help children think about solutions to social as well as cognitive problems. The interrelationship of all areas of development is important in developing the *whole child*. The content areas of science, social studies, mathematics, the arts, and health and safety are all integrated into themes of interest to the children. Literacy is taught in the context of children's other activities, as they extend their language to reading and writing. Interactionists assume that literacy skills are best learned within a context in which those skills can be applied.

Because the selection of materials and experiences is based on the child's developmental level, extending the program to younger or older children requires adapting materials and experiences; nonetheless, the

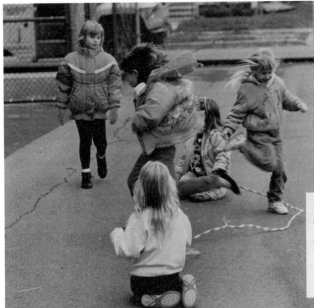

The experiences and activities offered to children reflect the philosophy and beliefs of the teachers and the school.

basic tenets of choice, intrinsic motivation in learning, and a balanced program remain constant. With younger children, the choices of activities are more limited and the guidance of the teacher is more apparent. Projects for older children are selected so that in-depth explorations of topics is possible. Teachers make conscious effort to teach subject-matter content in meaningful contexts and to select experiences in which children can apply skills being learned.

Summaries and Comparisons

The program models described in this chapter have some common goals, but each has a different view of what is the best and most appropriate learning environment for young children. One goal common to all three models—Montessori, behaviorist, and interactionist—is for children to learn. The models differ, however, on the means used to reach this goal. Those who follow Montessori philosophy believe that children learn best through interactions with materials in a prepared environment; there is little child-child interaction. Behaviorists believe that children learn best in a highly structured environment in which the information presented is carefully sequenced and the rewards are controlled. Those who hold a Piagetian (interactionist) view of learning also believe that children learn

DEVELOPMENTALLY
APPROPRIATE
PRACTICE

In Chapter One, we introduced the concept developmentally appropriate practice (DAP). *Although DAP may look very different in different situations, some basic criteria are critical to such practice, including choice, activities based on children's interests, and activities appropriate for individual children. Think about the critical elements of DAP as you respond to the following questions:*

- Are all the program models described in this chapter equally developmentally appropriate? Why?
- Some people argue that a kind and nurturing teacher is the most important element in any program. No one would suggest that teachers should be other than kind and nurturing, but is such behavior enough to counterbalance a lack of choice or a lack of individual appropriateness? Why?
- Must a program for young children give up academic goals in order to be developmentally appropriate? Why?
- Are the guidelines for developmentally appropriate practice a good yardstick for measuring programs? Why?

through interactions with objects and people but that children must reflect on their actions, as well.

Other goals of the programs also vary. An additional goal of Montessori programs is to develop the child's intellect and control. Piagetian programs focus on development in all areas: physical, social, emotional, and intellectual. Behaviorists generally focus on academic knowledge and place less emphasis on physical or social development. These differing views of how children learn (and the varied program goals based on these views) translate into very different experiences for children who attend these programs.

RESEARCH ON PROGRAM MODELS

Attempts to compare the effectiveness of different program models have been inconclusive. It is not an easy task to control all the variables that influence such research. For example, one could argue that it is invalid to compare the academic achievement of children who attend preschools based on the different program models described above because the focuses of some of the programs are much broader than academic achievement. Proponents of such broadly focused programs would argue that even if their children did not score as well on standardized tests as children from more academic programs, they learned other things that such tests do not measure. It is difficult to assess the academic achievement of young children accurately. It is also difficult to control for family involvement, teacher effectiveness, children's motivation, and so forth in studies that compare different program models.

Attempts to find differences between program models have produced mixed results. Children who show initial gains in skill levels as the result of a particular preschool experience may later show declines. Lilian Katz (1988) suggests that educators attend to the long-term, cumulative effects of programs, as evidenced by children's interest in learning. Not many long-term studies have been done, but one of the most significant research studies on the effects of preschool experience is the Perry Preschool High/Scope research, conducted by Schweinhart and associates (1986).

The High/Scope curriculum used at the Perry Preschool was based on a developmentalist approach. The research compared High/Scope to traditional and direct instruction (behaviorist) preschool experiences. When children were studied in 1988 at the age of fifteen, those who had either a High/Scope or a traditional nursery school experience reported engaging in about half as much delinquent behavior as children who had experience in a direct instruction program. This study also found that children from developmentalist and traditional programs exhibited much more prosocial use of time (holding offices in school, participating in sports) than those from the direct instruction group. Another long-term study (Karnes et al. 1983) compared five preschool curriculum models and found that students who had direct instruction did poorly on several measures of school success by the end of high school. None of these differences was statistically significant, although 70 percent of the nursery school students completed high school compared to only 47 percent of the direct instruction group.

The conclusion we can draw from research is that much remains to be learned about the development and learning of young children. Teachers and parents must think carefully about program choices and expectations for children. And researchers must continue to attempt to solve the complex problem of evaluating different approaches to instruction for young children.

CHAPTER SUMMARY

- Three models for early childhood programs were described in this chapter: Montessori, behaviorist, and interactionist.
- The key concepts in the Montessori program include the absorbent mind, the prepared environment, sensitive periods, autoeducation, and the importance of self-correcting, didactic materials. Montessori philosophy assumes that children need freedom to make choices and that they desire order and beauty in their lives.
- The behaviorist model of instruction is based on stimulus-response learning theory and operant

conditioning. The instruction is primarily teacher directed and academic in focus.
- The interactionist, or constructionist, model focuses on the child's development physically, socially, emotionally, and intellectually. Key elements include opportunities for the learner to construct knowledge and active manipulation of objects accompanied by reflection on that activity.
- The results of research that has attempted to compare the models of early childhood programs are very mixed. It is extremely difficult to control all the variables that impinge on children and their

school experiences in order to actually compare the programs. The long-term effects on children's interest in learning must be considered when examining research findings.

WHAT WOULD YOU DO?

Reflect on your reading and your own experiences with young children as you think about the following situations:

1. You are invited to teach in a program that is part of a national chain. The national headquarters provides each center with activity plans for each day. What would you think about this procedure?
2. A friend of yours has a three-year-old child. She knows that you are studying early childhood education and asks your advice about what to look for in selecting a preschool for her child. What would you tell her?
3. You have read about educators' concerns for children who are considered at risk of school failure. Some educators recommend skills programs that will help children succeed in school. What would you think about such programs?
4. You are on a committee that will develop the guidelines for a new preschool on campus. What would you recommend?

THEORY INTO PRACTICE

1. Interview a Montessori teacher and a teacher from another type of program about their educational backgrounds. What elements of their educational experiences influenced them to make the program choices that they made?
2. Visit at least two different programs that seem to have different emphases. (Check their advertisements in a newspaper or the Yellow Pages of the phone book, or call the principal of a public school.) Find as many common elements and as many differences as possible between the two programs.
3. Talk to the parents of children in your community who attend schools that follow different philosophies. How did the parents choose the schools for their children? What are their expectations of these educational experiences? How do they expect these experiences to influence their children's future educational experiences?
4. Visit a Montessori school or a school that follows a direct instruction model. Look for the influence of Montessori or behaviorist philosophy (respectively). Ask the teachers why they chose particular activities, materials, or reward systems.

RECOMMENDED FOR FURTHER READING

DeVries, Rheta, and Lawrence Kohlberg. *Programs of Early Education: The Constructivist View.* New York: Longman, 1987.

   This book contains a detailed explanation of the philosophy and program elements of three constructivist programs and compares educational approaches based on Piagetian theory with other approaches to teaching and learning.

Montessori, Maria. *The Discovery of the Child.* Translated by Mary A. Johnstone. Madras, India: Kalakshetra Publications, 1948 (distributed by Theosophical Publishing House, Wheaton, IL).

   There are many Montessori books from which to choose, but this is one of the most useful in terms of its review of the history of Montessori's work and its explanation of the philosophy. The book also contains detailed information on teaching methods and materials.

Roopnarine, Jaipaul, and James E. Johnson. *Approaches to Early Childhood Education.* 2d ed. New York: Merrill, 1993.

Roopnarine and Johnson collected descriptions of a variety of approaches to early childhood education for this textbook. It contains information on fourteen programs that are models for early childhood programs.

In addition, the book discusses evaluation of program models and public policy decisions that affect programs and their implementation.

REFERENCES

American Montessori Society. *Standards and Criteria for AMS School Accreditation*. ERIC Document Reproduction Service 2523040. New York: AMS, 1984.

Bereiter, Carl, and Siegfried Engelmann. *Teaching Disadvantaged Children in the Preschool*. Englewood Cliffs, NJ: Prentice-Hall, 1966.

Comenius, John Amos. *A Reformation of Schooles*. 1642. Reprint, London: Scolar Press, 1969.

Day, Mary Carol, and Ronald K. Parker. *The Preschool in Action: Exploring Early Childhood Programs*. 2d ed. Boston: Allyn and Bacon, 1977.

DeVries, Rheta, and Lawrence Kohlberg. *Programs of Early Education: The Constructivist View*. New York: Longman, 1987.

Forman, George. "The Constructivist Perspective to Early Education." In *Approaches to Early Childhood Education*, 2d ed., edited by Jaipaul Roopnarine and James E. Johnson. New York: Macmillan, 1993.

Froebel, Friedrich. *The Education of Man*. Translated by W. N. Hailmann. New York: D. Appleton, 1826.

Frost, Joe L., and Joan B. Kissinger. *The Young Child and the Educative Process*. New York: Holt, Rinehart and Winston, 1976.

Kamii, Constance, and Rheta DeVries. "Piaget for Early Education." In *The Preschool in Action: Exploring Early Childhood Programs*, 2d ed., edited by Mary Carol Day and Ronald K. Parker, 365–420. Boston: Allyn and Bacon, 1977.

Karnes, M. B., A. M. Schwedel, and M. B. Williams. "A Comparison of Five Approaches for Educating Young Children from Low-Income Homes." In *As the Twig Is Bent . . . Lasting Effects of Preschool Programs*, edited by Consortium for Longitudinal Studies. Hillsdale, NJ: Lawrence Erlbaum Associates, 1983.

Katz, Lilian. "Engaging Children's Minds: The Implications of Research for Early Childhood Education." In *A Resource Guide to Public School Early Childhood Programs*, edited by Cynthia Warger. Alexandria, VA: Association for Supervision and Curriculum Development, 1988.

Lillard, Paula P. *Montessori: A Modern Approach*. New York: Schocken Books, 1972.

Montessori, Maria. *Dr. Montessori's Own Handbook*. New York: Frederick A. Stokes, 1914.

Neisworth, John T., and Thomas J. Buggey. "Behavior Analysis and Principles in Early Childhood Education." In *Approaches to Early Childhood Education*, 2d ed., edited by Jaipaul Roopnarine and James E. Johnson. New York: Macmillan, 1993.

Pestalozzi, Johann Heinrich. *How Gertrude Teaches Her Children*. Translated by Lucy E. Holland and Francis C. Turner. Syracuse, NY: C. W. Bardeen, 1894.

Pestalozzi, Johann Heinrich. *Leonard and Gertrude*. Translated and abridged by Eva Channing. Boston: D. C. Heath, 1885.

Piaget, Jean. "Development and Learning." In *Piaget Rediscovered*, edited by R. Ripple and V. Rockcastle. Ithaca, NY: Cornell University Press, 1964.

Ransbury, Molly Kayes. "Friedrich Froebel 1782–1982: A Reexamination of Froebel's Principles of Childhood Learning." *Childhood Education* 59 (November–December 1982): 101–105.

Roopnarine, Jaipaul, and James E. Johnson, eds. *Approaches to Early Childhood Education*. 2d ed. New York: Macmillan, 1993.

Rousseau, Jean-Jacques. *Emile*. Translated by Barbara Foxley. 1780. Reprint. New York: E. P. Dutton, 1950.

Schweinhart, L. J., D. P. Weikart, and M. B. Larner. "Consequences of Three Preschool Curriculum Models through Age 15." *Early Childhood Research Quarterly* 1 (1986): 15–46.

Spodek, Bernard. *Early Childhood Education*. Englewood Cliffs, NJ: Prentice-Hall, 1973.

Standing, E. M. *Maria Montessori: Her Life and Work*. New York: Academy Guild Press, 1957.

Standing, E. M. *The Montessori Method: A Revolution in Education*. Fresno, CA: Academy Library Guild, 1962.

Chapter Three

Creating an Environment for Learning

Your observations this week focused on the physical arrangements of the classroom and the materials available for the children. You observed a second-grade classroom in which the tables for individual children were grouped into pods of four. One of your classmates observed another second-grade classroom in which the children worked at tables but did not have assigned places to sit. Each child had a cubby for storing his personal belongings, but the work areas were used as community property. Other classmates observed classrooms with desks for primary children, and some even found desks in kindergarten classrooms. The materials and equipment also varied a great deal from room to room. In some classrooms, children had access to many materials for art and construction, for reading and writing, and for working out problems in mathematics. In other rooms, the only materials readily available were books. In these rooms, each child kept his crayons, pencils, and paper in his own desk.

When you compare notes with your classmates, you find that classrooms vary considerably in the furniture available, in the arrangement of the furniture, and in the materials available to children. You are eager to know how the teachers made their decisions and how these decisions affect the children and their learning.

• •

Some planning decisions can be made before the children arrive. Teachers can decide on the basic learning areas to be set up, the basic materials to be used, and the initial room arrangement. Other planning decisions must be made after the teacher and children become acquainted. Planning is never just done. It is a continual cycle of making and implementing plans, observing, evaluating the effectiveness of your plans, and using that information for more planning.

Room arrangements
The arrangement of furniture and materials to meet the needs of the children and teacher.

Instructional materials
Materials selected to help children develop specific skills or learn specific concepts.

The decisions you make about **room arrangements** and **instructional materials** and equipment will reflect your goals and expectations for the children. It is fairly common during an interview for a principal to ask a prospective teacher of young children to sketch a room arrangement that she would use. Much of what a principal wants to know about a candidate's curriculum priorities is reflected in how the prospective teacher chooses to arrange the room. If your program goals include encouraging children's exploration of a variety of materials and investigation of the phenomena around them, then you will not choose to set up your room with a desk for each child and the teacher's desk as the focal point of the classroom.

GOALS AND OBJECTIVES

Environmental decisions reflect the philosophy and goals of the teacher. You will find contrasts among the instructional materials and room arrangements designed to accomplish various sets of objectives. For example, assume that one of Teacher A's beliefs is that children become more literate in the context of each of their school experiences. This teacher's beliefs about how specific skills are learned will affect the long-term goal of preparing children to read critically, to read for pleasure, and to write appropriately to meet their needs. Given these long-term goals, Teacher A would make sure that the classroom had a comfortable library area, that the environment was print rich, that books and charts were part of the children's experience in science, social studies, art, and so on. On the other hand, Teacher B might view the learning of specific skills as a primary objective. He might select a commercial reading program designed to teach the children letter and sound relationships and arrange the physical setting so that there was a location for group instruction on letter and sound relationships.

The general goals of many programs include helping children to:

1. Learn that they are capable learners, that they can make choices, and that their ideas are respected
2. Learn and apply skills in a meaningful context
3. Explore a variety of materials
4. Become able to communicate their needs and feelings
5. Learn to use and appreciate many sources of information—people, printed materials, visual materials
6. Become able to express themselves creatively

In order to meet these goals, teachers have many decisions to make. Be aware that decisions you make about the learning environment can either foster or hinder the achievement of these goals.

STRUCTURING THE PHYSICAL ENVIRONMENT

Often, many of the physical characteristics of the classroom in an early childhood program are not the choices of the teacher—the room may be too small for the number of children, have a sink that the children cannot reach, have a bathroom down the hall, have chalkboards on every wall, or have only one electric outlet. However, teachers can make other decisions about the physical environment, including how the furniture is arranged. Although teachers may not be able to choose the furnishings for the room at the outset of a program, they may be able to make changes over time.

The furniture selected must be of appropriate size for children and should be easy to rearrange to meet changing classroom needs. The most flexible furniture includes tables and chairs and shelf units on wheels. Rarely will every child need to sit at a table at once, so there need not be places at tables for everyone. Every child does need a space for her own things; this could be a cubby or a portable tub of some kind. Figure 3.1 on page 68 shows one design for storage cubbies.

FIGURE 3.1   Storage Cubbies

Room Arrangement

Room arrangement is one way of communicating to children how they are expected to behave in the classroom. An open, stimulating arrangement invites children to participate and explore. A sterile, restricted environment says that the most important considerations in the classroom are obedience and order. "A stimulating environment provides the teacher with many opportunities to observe where a child's interests lie as well as those areas the child may be tentative in exploring" (Greabell and Forseth 1981, p. 71).

Furniture (or the lack of it) gives all of us information about how we are to act in a given setting (Heyman 1978). Think of the furniture in a bank lobby, a college classroom, or a living room. Arrangements of furniture and materials are effective predictors of the quality of early childhood programs. Prescott, Jones, and Kritchevsky (1967) determined that one element of program quality was the physical environment. They found that as the quality of the physical environment (amount of empty space, complexity of play areas, and so on) decreased, the amount of teacher restriction and control increased, the teacher's manner became less friendly, the children became less interested and involved, the number of rules increased, and the amount of conflict among the children increased.

Weinstein (1979) found that the research on classroom environments was not definitive with regard to the effect of environment on achievement but that it clearly showed that nonachievement factors (attitudes, behaviors) are related to environmental factors. Classrooms that are aesthetically pleasing and comfortable make those who live in them for hours each day feel better, regardless of their effect on achievement (Hill 1989). In summarizing the importance of the physical environment, Taylor and Vlastos (1983) state that "the physical setting of the learning environment does make a difference in, and directly contributes to, a child's behavior and learning" (p. 25). Vergeront (1987) recommends "softer" spaces that convey the message that "this place is for people." Softness can be achieved through the use of fabrics, cushions, color, curves, and surface textures.

In choosing how to arrange furniture in the classroom, the first consideration—beyond the locations of doors and windows—is the locations of electrical outlets. In new schools, outlets are usually plentiful; outlets are often in short supply in older buildings, however. Areas that require electricity obviously must be located next to outlets. Usually, this means that record players, tape recorders, aquariums, and other items that use electricity must be placed in the classroom first. Teachers should keep in mind these general guidelines for room arrangements:

1. Space must accommodate multiple uses. Few classrooms and centers have enough space for each activity to have its own area; therefore, areas must serve more than one purpose. For example, blocks can be placed in a corner that is also used for story time during another part of the day.
2. Areas in which water is used should be as close to the water supply as possible. These include art, science, and water table areas.
3. Quiet areas should be close together so that children who want to work quietly can do so. *Quiet* does not mean that children cannot talk, but activities in such areas as the library, the writing table, and a listening station are quieter by nature than activities in some other areas.
4. Noisy areas, such as the blocks and dramatic play areas, should be grouped on the other side of the room from quiet areas.

Figures 3.2 and 3.3 (pages 70 and 71, respectively) show examples of room arrangements for preschool and kindergarten classrooms proposed

FIGURE 3.2 Room Arrangement for Kindergarten/Early Primary Grades

Source: Reprinted with the permission of Macmillan College Publishing Company from *Early Childhood Education*, 3/e by Barbara Day. Copyright © 1988 by Macmillan College Publishing Company, Inc.

FIGURE 3.3 Room Arrangement for Preschool/Kindergarten Grades

Outdoor Equipment
Swings
Slides
Sandbox
Climbing apparatus
Large motor toys

Farm area for animals and gardening equipment

Garden Area

Storage shed for outdoor and play equipment

Raised platform for dramatic play

Sand and water play

Concrete play area outdoors with overhang

Scale play house enclosed

Easels

Block and Carpentry Center

Art Center

Music Center Social and Environmental Center

KEY:
Bookshelves
* Homebase
Storage
Bulletin Board
Sink

Science and Math Center

Display and interest area

Creative writing

Quiet reading area

Language Arts Center

Teacher area and child study area

Storage and material work area

Cubbies

Cubbies

Hallway

Listening Center

Display area

Source: Reprinted with the permission of Macmillan College Publishing Company from *Early Childhood Education*, 3/e by Barbara Day. Copyright © 1988 by Macmillan College Publishing Company, Inc.

by Day (1988); Figure 3.4 (page 72) is an example of a room arrangement for a primary classroom proposed by Pappas, Kiefer, and Levstik (1990). Evaluate these plans in terms of use of space, how well they would accommodate your objectives, and what traffic patterns you think would develop.

FIGURE 3.4   Room Arrangement for Older Primary Grades

Source: From *An Integrated Language Perspective in the Elementary School: Theory into Action* by Christine C. Pappas, Barbara Z. Kiefer, and Linda S. Levstik. Copyright © 1990 by Longman Publishing Group. Reprinted with permission.

Assessing the Environment

One method of assessing the learning environment is to examine activity areas in terms of their simplicity or complexity (Kritchevsky and Prescott 1969). A *simple unit* for play or activity has one obvious use and does not have subparts for children to manipulate or improvise with; examples include

Table 3.1 Analysis of Play Spaces		
NUMBER OF PLAY UNITS	TYPES OF UNIT	NUMBER OF PLAY SPACES
12 vehicles	Simple	12
1 rocking boat	Simple	1
1 tumble tub	Simple	1
1 jungle gym with boxes and boards	Complex	4
1 dirt area plus scoop trucks	Complex	4
1 equipped sand table with water	Super Unit	8
		Total Play Spaces = 30

Source: Kritchevsky and Prescott 1969, p. 13.

rocking horses, swings, and vehicles. A *complex unit* has subparts made of two essentially different play materials that children can manipulate or improvise with; a sand table with tools is a complex unit. Art activity tables with paint or clay and tables with books are also classified as complex. A *super unit* has three or more play materials juxtaposed. Examples include a tunnel with movable boards and boxes, a sand table with tools and water, and a block area with hollow blocks, unit blocks, and block accessories. A super unit is about eight times as effective in holding children's attention as a simple unit; a complex unit is about four times as effective.

In analyzing your own room plans, count the variety of possible activities and the amount of things to do per child. Table 3.1 may help you analyze your own space. It shows Kritchevsky and Prescott's (1969, p. 13) analysis, in which the number of play spaces represents the number of children who can comfortably play in a given unit. Divide the total play spaces by the number of children to find the ratio of play spaces to children. If there are at least two play spaces for each child, children will be much more likely to find play spaces for themselves without teacher help than if the ratio is smaller. If the number of play spaces is less than the number of children, children will have difficulty finding something to do, other than grabbing something from someone else. An analysis of your room will provide information about whether there are adequate activities for the number of children and how you might rearrange the environment to make it more complex if you need to add play spaces.

Harms (1970) suggests that, in addition to assessing the environment for the complexity of play spaces, teachers should consider the following questions:

- *Can quiet and noisy activities go on without children's disturbing one another? Is there an appropriate place for each?*
- *Is a variety of materials available on open shelves for the children to use when they are interested? Are materials on shelves well spaced for clarity?*
- *Are materials stored in individual units so that children can use them alone without being forced to share with a group?*
- *Are activity centers defined so that children know where to use the materials?*
- *Are tables or rug areas provided for convenient use of materials in each activity center?*
- *Is self-help encouraged by having materials in good condition and always stored in the same place?*
- *Are cushioning materials used to cut down extraneous noise—rug under blocks, pads under knock-out bench?*
- *Are setup and cleanup simple? Are these expected parts of the child's activity?*
- *Is the children's work displayed attractively at the child's eye level?*
- *Do the children feel in control of and responsible for the physical environment? (pp. 305–306)**

In assessing the environment for a primary classroom, the teacher must think about adequate space and materials for completion of projects such as a study of animals or birds. Some questions to ask about a primary environment include:

1. Can a child or small group get materials (paper, markers, scissors, and so on) and find a space to work comfortably?
2. Is it possible to move around the room without disturbing the work of others?
3. Is there a quiet place for a child or small group to read or think quietly?
4. Is the furniture arrangement flexible enough to allow moving from large group to small group to individual instruction without major disruptions and loss of time?
5. Are necessary items (such as a pencil sharpener) placed in the room so that a child needing to use them can do so without disturbing others?
6. Have the children been involved in solving the problems they encounter in getting their work done?

---

* From Thelma Harms, "Evaluating Settings for Learning," *Young Children* 25 (May 1970): 304–309. Used with permission of NAEYC.

INSTRUCTIONAL MATERIALS

Materials for the classroom can be quite expensive. In addition to purchasing materials, most teachers ask for contributions from parents, go to garage sales, and scrounge materials from community sources. For example, some teachers get boxes and scrap paper from businesses that generate numerous computer printouts or wood scraps from local construction sites or cabinet shops.

The following guidelines will be helpful when you are selecting materials for the classroom:

1. Choose materials that can be used for more than one experience. Single-use materials like windup toys do not invite children to use them over and over, each time in a new or creative manner.
2. Select materials sturdy enough to withstand use by many active children.
3. Select materials that serve many instructional purposes, such as small blocks, which can be used for constructing, for counting, for sorting by color, for arranging into patterns, and so on.
4. Select materials that can be used by children of varying ages and abilities. Sand, for example, can be used by very young children, who like to feel it and pour it from container to container. Older preschoolers can use sand to compare quantities and to measure. Primary-age children will be more sophisticated in their sand play. Barbour, Webster, and Drosdeck (1987) report observing one group of second-graders creating a desert environment after listening to their teacher read *The Desert Is Theirs* (Baylor 1970).
5. Choose safe materials; those with broken parts or rough edges should be discarded.

Learning Areas

One common technique for organizing instructional materials in classrooms is to place materials into learning centers or **learning areas.** Use of the phrase *learning centers* is sometimes criticized because it seems to imply that learning only takes place in those specific centers. The assumption underlying this discussion is that learning takes place all over and outside the classroom.

Learning areas
Areas in a classroom where certain activities can take place and certain materials are stored.

The phrase *learning area* will be used to indicate a specific location where related materials are arranged in a classroom. The basic learning

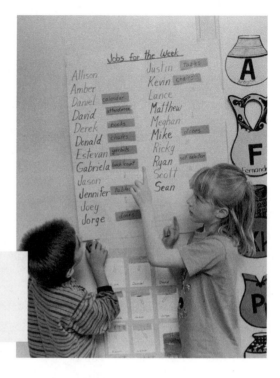

Children can be encouraged to take responsibility for their learning environment.

areas in early childhood classrooms include areas for art, music, library/listening/writing activities, blocks, dramatic play, science/discovery activities, manipulatives/mathematics/games, woodworking, sand and water tables, and quiet activities. If space and equipment allow, an area for physical education is also important. These areas should reflect the children's ages, development, growing abilities, and changing interests; learning areas are not static.

Art

Teachers who want to encourage growth in art will think carefully about the materials and classroom environments that encourage participation in art activities. If the goals of an art program are to be achieved, materials for many art experiences must be readily available to children. In choosing a place in the classroom for art, consider sources of light and access to water. An area with a sink is ideal, so children can clean up easily, but a container of warm water will serve if no sink is available. Low shelves for storage of materials, easels for painting, and tables for working with other materials are also important. Traffic patterns must be considered when deciding where the art area will be located. If the area cannot be in a corner, other pieces of furniture can be used to isolate the space so that children do not walk through it to get from one part of the classroom to another.

Teachers can be creative in designing storage for supplies. Lasky and Mukerji (1980) report some creative storage solutions they have observed:

- *Label cardboard or plastic shoe boxes and arrange them on bookshelves, windowsills, or counter tops that children can reach. Simple pictures can be labels for young children.*
- *Make adjustable shelves with cinder blocks to support lumber or heavy corrugated board (Tri-Wall).*
- *Place plastic dishpans or attractively covered cartons on top of children's coatracks for storing teachers' supplies.*
- *Cover a wall area with pegboard and suspend heavy shopping bags or see-through plastic bags from hooks inserted in the board. Hang smocks in the same fashion.*
- *Screw metal coat hooks into wooden moldings for suspending storage bags or smocks.*
- *Use the back of the piano or bookcase for hanging a shoe bag. Its pockets can hold many small items.*
- *Pierce an inverted small cardboard box or egg carton for use as a handy scissor or brush rack.*
- *Attach a roll of burlap, felt, or strip of cork to a vertical surface which children can reach. Keep a supply of needles threaded with yarn inserted in this oversize pincushion.*
- *Use divided frozen food trays or a revolving lazy Susan to hold miscellaneous small items.*
- *Make excellent containers for crayons or chalk out of discarded berry baskets or margarine cups. A label or clip clothespin painted the color of the contents helps children locate colors.*
- *Use small detergent or cosmetic bottles as dispensers for paint or glue purchased in quantity. (p. 30)**

Setting up an art area also includes deciding on smocks and floor coverings that will help children be most comfortable as they explore art materials. Smocks can be made from plastic or from old shirts. The point is to protect the children's clothing so that they are free from the worry of getting their clothes dirty. Floor coverings should be tile, if possible, so that floors can be cleaned easily. Floors can be covered with newspapers to aid

* From Lila Lasky and Rose Mukerji, *Art: Basic for Young Children* (Washington, DC: National Association for the Education of Young Children, 1969). Used with permission of NAEYC.

MATERIALS AND EQUIPMENT FOR EARLY CHILDHOOD CLASSROOMS

Some materials will not be appropriate for all age groups. The teacher must select those most appropriate for his group of students.

Basic furniture in any classroom should include tables and chairs of appropriate size, shelf units, storage units, an adult-sized rocking chair, sofas, child-sized rocking chairs, floor pillows, and a full-length mirror. The following lists include additional materials that teachers in preschool and primary grades have found to be useful. Teachers will also want to provide other materials to enhance the presentations of specific topics or themes.

Dramatic Play

- Child-sized kitchen equipment (with pots and pans)
- Dishes and silverware
- Tables and chairs
- Telephones
- Child-sized ironing board and iron
- Child-sized cleaning equipment (brooms, mops, dustpan, and so on)
- Assorted dolls
- Doll clothes
- Doll bed, carriage
- Doll house, furniture
- Assorted tubs, buckets, dishpans
- Assorted dress-up clothing and costumes

Blocks

- Blocks (unit and hollow)
- Block accessories (people, cars, safety signs, and so on)
- Small blocks (sets of cubes, small colored blocks)
- Sturdy wooden vehicles (cars, trucks, boats, planes, tractors, fire engines, buses, helicopters)

Art

- Adjustable easels
- Brushes (half-inch to one-inch widths)
- Liquid tempera paint (in a variety of colors)
- Painting smocks (purchased or homemade)
- Crayons
- Colored chalk
- Clay
- Scissors
- Glue, paste
- Paper (glazed for finger painting, newsprint, white drawing paper, construction paper in a variety of colors, tissue paper)
- Drying rack for paintings
- Miscellaneous supplies (fabric scraps, rickrack, yarn, ribbon, glitter, buttons, natural materials)

in cleanup. Materials for cleanup—water, sponges, a small broom and dustpan—should also be readily available to the children.

In selecting materials for art experiences, teachers must think about developmental appropriateness and possibilities for multiple uses. Chalk, markers, and crayons should be easy to grasp and should not break easily. Children should be allowed to use materials in a variety of ways. For example, some teachers only allow children to use crayons as they would pencils. But the wrappers can be removed from crayons so they can be rubbed across the surface of a paper on their sides. The fewer rules that are attached to materials, the more children will be encouraged to think for themselves and be creative.

Library/Listening/Writing

- Computer and printer
- Typewriter
- Paper (various colors, sizes, shapes) and writing instruments (pencils, markers)
- Tape recorder, tapes, books with tapes
- Record player
- Flannel board with stand and flannel pieces
- Books (professional and published by classroom authors)
- Magazines

Manipulatives/Games

- Hand puppets
- Puzzles
- Games (Lotto, checkers, chess, dominoes, Candyland, Chutes and Ladders, Hi-Ho Cherry O, and so on)
- Beads and strings
- Sewing cards
- Manipulative materials (ranging from stacking rings to very complex materials)
- Tinkertoys (regular size and large size)
- Lego blocks, bristle blocks

Science/Discovery

- Aquarium
- Terrarium
- Magnets of various kinds
- Magnifying glasses
- Prism

- Metric measuring equipment, test tubes, slides, petri dishes
- Pattern blocks
- Pegs and pegboards
- Geoboards
- Geoblocks
- Base 10 blocks
- Unifix cubes
- Scales (balance and other types)
- Rhythm instruments
- Sandbox
- Water table with top
- Workbench with equipment

Physical Education

- Balance beam
- Tumbling mat
- Rocking boat
- Steps
- Walking boards
- Jungle gym
- Fabric tunnel
- Sawhorses (sturdy metal)
- Climbing ladder, climbing rope
- Balls of various sizes
- Ropes
- Hula hoops
- Bowling set
- Outdoor equipment (wheeled toys, gardening tools, sandbox)

Just because art materials are arranged in one place in the classroom does not mean that art experiences cannot take place in other areas. Be open to a variety of places and possibilities for art activities. In nice weather, children might be offered the chance to do art outside; for example, they might do rubbings on outside surfaces. They might also choose to draw in other places in the classroom. On the other hand, even though art activities are not limited to one area of the room, it is convenient for all the supplies to be stored together in the art area so that children always know where to find what they need. Figure 3.5 on page 80 is a sketch of an art area that illustrates some of the suggestions in the preceding paragraphs.

FIGURE 3.5 Art Area

Music

A piano is often the center of the music area. If you are lucky enough to have a piano and can play a simple tune, you can use it in many different ways to encourage children's music skills. Although a piano is still very valuable in an early childhood classroom, many teachers today use guitars or autoharps. These instruments are much easier to play and allow the teacher to face the children while playing. Still, many teachers like to have record players or tape recorders in the music area, to be used in group music experiences or by individual students.

Exploration of music can be encouraged by making a limited number of musical instruments available to the children. If the classroom is equipped with a piano, a low shelf area near the piano is adequate for storing other selected instruments. A listening center with headphones gives children opportunities to listen to records and tapes without disturbing the rest of the class. Teachers should be aware that many children starting school today have no experience with records. They only know about compact discs and cassette tapes—a sign of the changing times!

The teacher might also keep a file of songs that children know, as well as charts of the lyrics. When these materials are made available, children can select songs for group singing or can review songs they especially like.

Usually, the space used for movement experiences is used for other purposes during other parts of the day. If possible, a space can be provided for movement during the time children choose their own activities. A shelf with scarves, hula hoops, large circles made of elastic (often known as *Chinese jump ropes*), a small drum, and ankle bells will encourage explorations of movement.

Library/Listening/Writing

An area for language arts activities should be located in a quiet part of the classroom and should have open shelves for storing books and a table for writing activities. Children may or may not need chairs for the listening center; sometimes the unit can be placed so that children sit on the floor to use it. It is better to display books standing up, with their covers showing, than to store them stacked on a shelf. Storing books standing up takes more space than stacking them, but children are much more likely to be enticed to choose a book if they can see the front cover. Since the number of books that can be displayed at once in this manner is limited, the books on display will need to be rotated frequently and selected to support topics of study.

In addition to a table for writing, a storage area for different writing papers and writing instruments is necessary. Pencils, pens, markers, and so on should be stored in small baskets or cans to make it easy for children to choose the ones they need. Paper in different colors and sizes should be available and can easily be stored in open boxes. Dictionaries should also be kept in this area. Picture dictionaries are especially useful for young writers. Children's personal dictionaries can also be kept in a basket in the writing area.

Typewriters and computers can also be housed in the library/listening/writing area. Children working with such equipment need the same supplies (word lists, dictionaries, and the like) that other writers need, so it is sensible to locate such equipment in this area. Use of typewriters and computers can generate quite a lot of talking and interaction, so they should be placed where students using them will disturb those in the quiet reading area as little as possible.

Blocks

Blocks require storage shelves and a large floor area for construction. A smooth carpet can help reduce the noise in this area and will not interfere

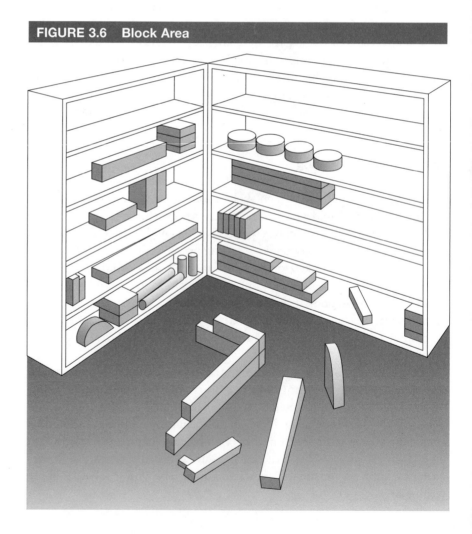

FIGURE 3.6   Block Area

with balancing the blocks. Larger blocks, such as hollow blocks, can be stored directly on the floor rather than on shelves. As Hirsch (1984) reminds us, the block storage area should be neither too neat nor too messy. If it's too neat, children will be intimidated and worry about cluttering the area when they use the materials; if it's too messy, children will find it difficult to locate the exact blocks they need, which is frustrating. Unit blocks should not be stored in carts or boxes. Such storage makes finding the needed block almost impossible and encourages children to toss the blocks back into the box, thereby denting them and reducing their useful life.

You will have to decide if you want to mark the block shelves (for example, with silhouettes of the blocks to be stored on each shelf) or if you want the children to determine the storage. Children do learn to recognize the shapes of the blocks and match them to the silhouettes, but they learn more about size relationships and classification when they are responsible for making storage decisions. Figure 3.6 illustrates a block area.

Dramatic Play

The dramatic play area is often called the *housekeeping corner* or the *doll corner.* It is an area that will reflect the development and changing interests of the children as they grow. For example, threes and fours may need child-sized kitchen equipment, dishes and pans, dolls and doll beds, and other materials for acting out the roles in a family. As children grow and develop, they are able to assume the roles of people outside the family. Although they may still enjoy the kitchen equipment, they will often use the dramatic play area to act out roles of people in such locations as a grocery store, a gas station, a beauty or barber shop, a doctor's office, a hospital, an airport, or other areas that are part of their experience.

The teacher will need to be flexible in providing the materials and assistance to support children's ideas. Primary-grade children often use this area for dramatizing characters in stories they have heard or read. They will need a variety of costumes, dress-up clothes, and props to support their play as their knowledge expands. If the dramatic play area stays the same throughout the year, then the teacher will need to take special steps to encourage children to develop and expand their interests.

Science/Discovery

Science activities do not take place only in the science or discovery area, of course, but the tools for investigations are kept on shelves in this area. Most teachers also like to have a table where interesting displays can be arranged and where children can explore materials—plants, soils, rocks, shells, leaves, or whatever. The area should be equipped with shelves that contain magnets, magnifying glasses, measurement containers, and other materials for investigating scientific topics. Teachers often include an invention corner in this area, where old appliances such as television sets, radios, toys, clocks, and toasters can be dismantled and reassembled, perhaps even using the parts to create new objects.

Manipulatives/Mathematics/Games

The math area is another area that will need to change to meet the needs and interests of children. This area should be the storage place for puzzles, beads, sewing cards, and other materials designed to help younger children develop fine motor skills. Older children will still be interested in puzzles and manipulative games and will also begin using pattern blocks, Unifix cubes, base 10 blocks, and other manipulatives used in mathematics. All ages will need construction toys and tabletop blocks. Games designed for individuals or small groups are often stored in this area. Playing cards, dice, and other game materials should also be available here; children will not only play with them but will use them for inventing games. This area needs shelves for storage and a table on which to work with the materials.

Woodworking

Woodworking areas require a workbench, storage areas for wood scraps, and shelves or a pegboard for holding tools. Young children who have not had much experience with woodworking are often satisfied with a sturdy log or other large piece of wood into which they can hammer nails. Children do not necessarily need to be able to make something until they have had more experience. Tools should be real tools designed to a small scale and sturdy enough to work well. Saws should really cut wood, and hammers should really drive nails.

Sand and Water Tables

Good-quality sand and water tables are available from supply catalogs, but they are expensive. A sand table can be constructed by adding a frame to the edge of a low table. Sometimes teachers substitute rice or cornmeal for sand in order to make cleanup easier. However, in addition to the fact that some teachers may be reluctant to use food in activities that render it inedible, neither of these materials has the same qualities that sand offers. For example, children cannot add water to these materials and mold them.

Many sand and water tables are equipped with covers so they can be used for other purposes when not being used for sand and water play. Accessories for sand and water tables depend on the developmental level of the children using them. Younger children may only pour and scoop, so precise measuring equipment is not needed. Older children will need materials to make measuring, comparing, and other investigations possible. Storage for accessories is often in boxes under the tables.

Water tables are more difficult to make than sand tables. The newest models of water tables are made of clear plastic and are often round with drains in the bottom that allow for easy draining and cleaning. Teachers often substitute a tub or a child's wading pool for a water table. These substitutes are better than not having water tables, but because children lean over them rather than stand around them and could easily fall in, even more supervision is required. Water in water tables should be replaced daily, so draining and filling conditions should be considered when purchasing a table. Water play accessories should include objects for filling and pouring, tubes and connectors, and materials that sink and float. Specific materials can be added to sand and water tables to help children explore topics in the curriculum.

Physical Education

An area where children can use a tumbling mat and engage in other physical activities is important. Some teachers like to place equipment that encourages gross motor development around the room, rather than in one area, because it takes up so much space. For example, balance beams or tunnels can be placed so that children can use them to get from one area of the room to another. Physical development is enhanced with bean bags, Velcro darts, Nerf balls, tunnels, bowling pins and balls, and so on. These materials should be stored on shelves or in a closet near an area large enough for children to use them without disturbing the work of others.

Quiet Area

Every classroom needs a small area where a child can go to be alone for a time. This area needs no special equipment—perhaps just a chair or a floor pillow. Some teachers like to make the quiet area inviting with flowers (nothing elaborate, just one or two), a piece of sculpture, or a drape of fabric. A child should be able to take a game or a book to this quiet area whenever she needs to.

Specialized Learning Areas

Some learning areas are set up for specific purposes and are not designed to be part of the classroom all year. Such specialized centers might be used for activities such as following up on stories, sorting and classifying objects, or demonstrating skills.

Activities to follow up on stories include placing pictures from the story in correct sequence, listening to a tape recording of the story while following along in the book, drawing a picture of a favorite part of the story, and so on. Sorting and classifying or problem-solving centers might offer collections to be sorted and explained (shells, keys, leaves, and so on) or materials to be grouped (paper and pencils, stamps and envelopes, keys and locks). Skill activities might be finding pictures of sets of objects whose names rhyme or finding the matching cylinders in a sound game. (Canisters from 35 mm film containing beans, rice, nails, stones, or other materials and having the lids taped on work well for this activity.)

Many magazines for teachers describe learning activities such as these. Teachers have to decide how they fit the program goals, if they suit the individual needs of children, and if so, where to locate the activities in the room.

Storage Areas

Each classroom needs an area in which materials not currently in use can be stored. A closet lined with shelves is ideal. If no storage facilities are built into the classroom, perhaps a storage unit can be purchased from a school supply firm. If the room contains no closet and a unit cannot be purchased, the teacher may have to improvise a storage area in one corner. Fabric can be used to cover the fronts of shelf units so that the contents are out of sight.

Beginning the Year

Teachers can begin the year by arranging materials in basic areas, knowing that they will make changes as soon as the children actually begin to work

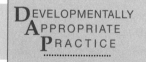

DEVELOPMENTALLY APPROPRIATE PRACTICE

Reflect on different classroom environments you have observed in terms of what you now know about planning a learning environment:

- Do any elements of the classroom environment indicate developmentally appropriate practice? Why?
- Can a classroom environment be developmentally appropriate when the desks are arranged in rows, with each child facing the teacher's desk in the front of the room? Why?

- Could a more flexible furniture arrangement fail to be developmentally appropriate? Why?
- In addition to furniture arrangement, what else in the environment would indicate DAP? Why?

in the classroom. Teachers should try to simplify areas so that only the very basic materials and equipment are available for the first few days or weeks of the schoolyear. Materials that are easy to put away should be used until the children learn the routines of cleaning up work areas. Some materials should also be kept back initially and brought out later to add interest and novelty throughout the year; for example, large blocks and a few unit blocks can be put out in the block center right away, but other unit blocks and accessories can remain put away for use later.

For the first few days of school, activities in the art center should be limited to the use of crayons, paper, and clay. Unless classroom assistance is available—such as a parent volunteer or paraprofessional who can help children learn where to find paint smocks and paint, where to place their paintings until they dry, and how to clean up the art area—paint and easels should be brought out only after children have learned to handle the materials in other areas. Similarly, such areas as music, water tables, and carpentry can be set up when the teacher knows the children better and feels they do not require such close supervision.

Managing Learning Areas

More often than not, children will distribute themselves among learning areas without any problems of overcrowding. If new materials are added, the teacher may have to help children solve the problem of who has a turn first. If some areas do not attract children, the teacher's responsibility is to determine what the area needs and why it is not interesting to the children. The youngest children will need teacher guidance in choosing areas for play; older preschoolers may be able to plan their activities more independently, with the help of a few guidelines for managing the learning areas; and primary-grade children can take most of the responsibility for distributing themselves.

Many teachers have an activity time when children first arrive for the day; this allows children to choose an area and begin their activities without waiting for everyone else to arrive. Other teachers begin activity time after a group meeting, during which they have reviewed the calendar or completed other discussions with the group. To avoid having everyone trying to get to an area at once, many teachers use some scheme for deciding who chooses first and how choices are made during the play period. Some teachers group children randomly into two or three groups and rotate the group that gets to choose first. For example, the groups might be labeled red, yellow, and blue; if the red group has first choice today, the yellow group will have first choice tomorrow, and the blue group, the day after.

FIGURE 3.7   Pegboard

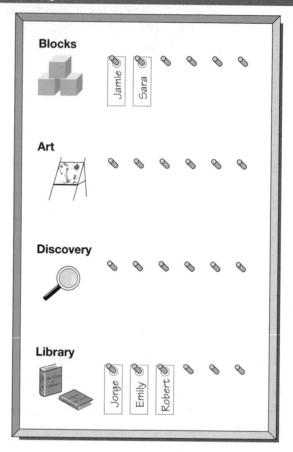

Teachers of very young children should try to allow them to play where they choose. When their choices cannot be honored, then the teacher should suggest another area and perhaps play there with the children for a few minutes. Some teachers of older preschoolers manage the number of children in each area by posting a number that defines how many can be in that area at a time. A child is free to join others in that area if the number of children allowed will not be exceeded. For example, if the block area will hold six children comfortably, a "6" is posted on one of the shelves. A child coming to the block area must decide if she can play with the blocks, given the number of children already in the area.

Other teachers like to use a pegboard system (see Figure 3.7). A pegboard is prepared, such that the learning areas are displayed down the left side. Pictures representing learning areas are added to aid the children in identifying each area. The number of pegs for each area is determined by the number of children that area can accommodate easily; pegs are placed in the row beside each picture to indicate how many children can use that area at one time. Again, if six children can use the block area, there will be six pegs beside the picture of blocks. Each child will have a tag with his name on it; he will place his tag on a peg when he wants to play with the blocks. If there are no empty pegs for the block area, he will have to make another choice. There should be more total pegs than there are children in order to give children as many choices as possible. And when an area is not available for some reason, the pegs for that area can be removed for the day.

Such a pegboard system also allows some subtle guidance in helping children make new choices. For example, if a child always chooses the art area and the teacher feels that she has developed enough confidence to work in another area, the teacher might limit the number of art pegs so that the child will have to make another choice. The teacher should make sure that choices are available that will interest the child and perhaps go there with her to play for a few minutes.

Teachers may want to involve primary-age children in more formal planning. One way to do this is to provide each child with a planning sheet

FIGURE 3.8   Planning Sheet

Name:_____

- ❑ Independent Reading/Writing
- ❑ Writing Conference with Teacher
- ❑ Reading Conference with Teacher
- ❑ Buddy Reading
- ❑ Special Activity
- ❑ Math Activity
- ❑ Outdoor Play
- ❑ Work on Project with Group
- ❑ Library
- ❑ Listening Center
- ❑ Games Center
- ❑ Special Lesson

on which the scheduled events for the day are listed (see Figure 3.8). After reviewing the events, each child can check what he plans to do that day.

CHILDREN WITH SPECIAL NEEDS

Some areas and materials may need to be adapted for children with special needs, for instance, to make them wheelchair accessible or to add visual or auditory information to help all children work as independently as possible. Teachers should analyze the room arrangement and material storage areas in terms of the needs of all children in the class. Some spaces may need to be enlarged or more clearly defined to facilitate children's movement, some materials may need to be placed on more accessible shelves so they are within children's reach, or some materials may need to be organized so that children who have trouble hearing receive the maximum visual information.

Clutter may be distracting for children with perceptual difficulties. Some common supplies may need to be stored in several locations throughout the room so that children who have problems moving around have easy access to them. Room arrangements, materials, and schedules must be adapted for each group and for each individual child.

COMPUTERS IN EARLY CHILDHOOD PROGRAMS

The debate over the value of computers in early childhood programs has not yet been settled. If one believes television advertisements, children will be behind their peers if they do not have a computer by at least age three. Critics of computer use see this technology as inappropriate for young children because the learning it promotes is too abstract; also, computer activities take time from other more concrete activities. The most reasonable approach seems to be to treat computers as a learning tool, in the same category with paper and pencils.

Computers are part of our world. It is obvious that they are not going away and that they will in fact become more common. We can only guess what computers will be like when the children who are now in early childhood programs are adults. The technology is changing rapidly, including the software available. The quality of software is a major factor in determining whether computer activities are appropriate for young children. Let us look at the issues involved in deciding whether to use computers in programs for young children.

Planning for the developmentally appropriate use of computers with young children is important.

One question is: What will the children learn from using computers? Computers will not take the place of real, hands-on experience with concrete materials; thus, playing with computers will not substitute for playing with blocks, sand, water, and all the other materials in the classroom.

The outcomes of computer experiences must also be appropriate in terms of what children should be learning. For example, several software programs on the market teach children to recognize the letters of the alphabet and match the letters with the sounds they represent. Some teachers believe that these skills must be developed within the context of meaningful reading and writing tasks, not as isolated knowledge; these teachers would not view using computers as an appropriate approach to teaching letter and sound concepts. Other software programs give children arithmetic problems to solve. Before a teacher can ask a child to complete such problems, the child should have a sound concept of number and know that arithmetic is one process used for solving real problems. In other words, the child's overall learning must include much more than the drill and practice offered by computer software. The teacher must not expect that learning to recognize letters or work arithmetic problems by using a computer will be equivalent to real literacy or learning to solve real mathematical problems.

Educators interested in using computers with young children are confident that the availability of quality software will improve drastically in the next few years. Much of it will be interactive, allowing children to do things such as add sounds and illustrations to their writing with the touch of a button. Advances like this should certainly be watched by teachers of young children, and new software should be evaluated carefully. Char (1990) believes that teachers and parents must take a more active role in determining how technology might enhance young children's learning.

Another question is: What is required for children to use given software programs? Most software for young children requires them to push only one or two buttons, touch a box on a screen, or touch a pad; keyboard knowledge is not required. It is likely that much more software will be developed that does not require typing skills; instead, software will be voice activated or operated by touching symbols. Primary children are often asked to use programs that require typing, especially word-processing types of programs that enable them to write and edit their stories, poems, and reports. Several studies have found that typing is a source of motivation for many children (Borgh and Dickson 1986; Lipinski et al. 1986; Muller and Perlmutter 1985; Swigger and Campbell 1981). An understanding of writing as real communication can result from computer use. Children can write without having to struggle with the motor control needed to form letters by hand.

Another issue to consider in deciding whether to use computers with young children is the amount of money involved. A lot of other materials and supplies could be obtained with the money allotted to purchase, maintain, and buy computer software and hardware. If money can be made available for computers without taking away funds for other essential materials and supplies, then allocation is not a problem. But if a program does not have adequate money to purchase enough blocks, physical education equipment, art supplies, books, games, or science equipment, teachers will have to balance the value of what children could learn having adequate supplies against the value of having computers.

If, after examining the costs, teachers decide to purchase computers, they will have to deal with the issues of equity and social abilities in how children use computers. Some research indicates that boys are more likely to have access to computers at home and more likely to use them at school (Lieberman 1985; Picard and Giuli 1985). Teachers need to be very aware of how computers are used and to make sure that all children have equal access to them.

When computers were first introduced into classrooms, there was some fear that children would become social isolates, just working away by themselves at computers. Although research has not found this to be the case—children do talk to each other, help each other, and work together at computers—teachers must make sure that computer use is structured in such a way as to encourage social interactions (Binder and Ledger 1985; Rosengren et al. 1985). A ratio of one computer to ten children seems to overcome problems of negative social interactions and to promote equal use by boys and girls (Clements 1987).

Swick (1989) suggests the following guidelines for introducing computers into the classroom:

1. *Integrate the computer into the environment so that children use it as a natural medium for learning.*
2. *Provide extensions of the classroom computer environment in another part of the center [or school] where special projects and parent-child computer experiences can occur.*
3. *Use the computer as part of the total curriculum, relating its content to the context of other activities in the program.*
4. *Select software that promotes children's active exploration of the environment; programs such as Logo are excellent in promoting children's thinking and analytic skills.*
5. *Experiment with different uses of the computer so that the program avoids the "mechanical" flavor often associated with commercial learning tools. (p. 9)*

Children's initial experiences with computers should be playful (Silvern et al. 1988), and children should be involved in solving the problems of taking turns, establishing rules for use, determining how disks are to be stored, and so on. Swick (1989) states that "in developmentally appropriate programs, the computer is used not only as a way of introducing children to technology but also as a means of strengthening their social skills, stimulating their inventiveness, and encouraging them to explore new ways of thinking" (p. 9).

PLANNING THE OUTDOOR ENVIRONMENT

Outdoor environments, like indoor environments, require planning if they are to achieve the best results for the children. Ideally, outdoor play areas should be adjacent to indoor areas, with easy access to toilet facilities. Outdoor areas should be securely fenced and should have covered areas

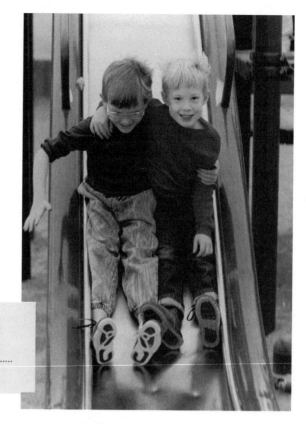

Successful outdoor play requires careful planning by teachers.

for play on rainy or very hot days. Outdoor areas should include different surface areas: grass, concrete, areas for digging, and sand. Play areas should include different terrain when possible; hills and inclines provide interesting terrain for riding toys, rolling downhill, and so on, as well as visual interest. Paved paths and large areas are ideal for wheel toys or riding toys. In addition to the physical exertion required by riding toys, they offer children many opportunities for dramatic play.

Apparatus for swinging, climbing, sliding, and crawling should also be provided in the outdoor environment. Some apparatus should have higher bars for swinging while hanging by the hands and lower bars for hanging by the knees or elbows. Studies have shown that children develop more upper-body strength when they play on playgrounds equipped with overhead ladders (Gabbard 1979). In selecting apparatus, the teacher should think about providing a balance of equipment so that children will use all the large muscles as they play. The hull of a rowboat or the body of an old car can stimulate dramatic play and offer something to climb on. Boards for walking or balance beams are also useful pieces of equipment.

Many playgrounds leave nothing for children to use in planning, arranging, or creating. Jones (1989) recommends that play areas have "loose parts" that children can move around and with which they can build and be creative. With movable equipment, children can construct their own play environment; boxes, boards, barrels, sawhorses, and short ladders work well. Tires and tubes are also useful for rolling around and stacking.

An outdoor play space should include a gardening area, a sandbox, a water play area or water table, a storage area for tools and toys, and tables or easels. (If need be, portable easels can be moved from the classroom for outside use.)

Having a gardening area does not mean that the entire area must be used for planting. At least some of the space should be reserved for impromptu digging. When children dig, they learn about the composition of soil, the differences between dry and damp soil, the insects and worms that live in the soil, and the pieces of organic matter that decompose to produce soil. A garden that includes an area for planting and caring for the plants, in addition to a digging area, can extend many classroom experiences.

An outside sandbox has advantages that an indoor sand table cannot offer. Children can climb into a sandbox, sit in the sand while playing in it, and create play areas on a much larger scale. An outdoor sandbox should have a cover to keep the sand clean, preferably one that folds back in sections to make handling easier. In many areas of the United States, a sandbox also should have some kind of roof so that the sand does not get too hot or stay wet all the time. Baker (1966) observed that the sandbox was frequently the place children started playing while they watched the more vigorous play around them. When they gained enough confidence, they joined the more active play.

Opportunities for water play outdoors can be provided with a small wading pool or a water table. Pools of water must be carefully supervised. Children can use the water outside much as they do in the classroom—pouring, measuring, and comparing. The differences are that outside, much more splashing is acceptable, and water can be carried all over the play area. Practically everything outdoors can be "painted" with water. A few large paintbrushes and some buckets are essential water play accessories outdoors.

Finally, many fine arts activities can be provided outdoors if portable easels or tables are available for painting, creating collages, or other art activities. When the weather is pleasant outdoors, art experiences can be

FIGURE 3.9   Playground Design

Source: Reprinted by permission from *Children's Play and Playgrounds* by Joe L. Frost and Barry L. Klein (1979, p. 193; designed by Nan Simpson).

especially satisfying because children do not have to be as concerned about paint spills or drips. Cleanup is simple.

A shed for storing outdoor materials is a must. It can hold garden and digging tools, sandbox and water toys, riding toys, balls, and other materials used outdoors. Teachers tend to be much more relaxed about allowing children to dig in sand and mud when they know that the tools do not have to be clean enough to take back indoors when the play ends. A shed will also protect the toys and tools from exposure to the elements and prolong the life of materials.

FIGURE 3.10 Playground Design

EXISTING STORAGE METAL BUILDING

TIRE SWING HUNG ON SWING FRAME

TRACTOR TIRE MOUNTAIN

SAND

CURVE AHEAD SIGN

VINES PLANTED TO KEEP METAL PIPE COOL IN SUMMER

4' WIDE TRIKE PATH

CARGO NET CLIMB OVER SWING SET

METAL POLE

5' METAL PIPE TUNNEL

GARDENING AREA

TIRE SWIVEL SWING

TIRE SWIVEL SWING

SAND

LOG CLIMBING STRUCTURE

6' GEODESIC DOME

QUIET WORK AREA W/PICNIC TABLE

PAINTED TRIKE PATH

RAMP LADDER

TIRE LADDER

4'x8' PEG BOARD

4'x8' BLACKBOARD

CLIMBING STRUCTURE

STORAGE

WATCH FOR PEDESTRIAN SIGN

LADDER

TIRE

EXISTING STRUCTURE

12" x 12" CONC. PAVING STONES

2' SPOOL

PLANK

12' GATE

CONSTRUCTION AREA

METAL DRUM

CRATE

TRACTOR TIRE CUT HORIZONTALLY AND FILLED FOR WATER PLAY

3'-0" WIDE SLIDE

4' SPOOL

BALANCE BOARD

GAMES AREA

LANDSCAPE TIMBER EDGE

SAND BOX EDGED W/ LANDSCAPE TIMBERS

HOLLOW VW

4' HIGH CHAIN FENCE

GARDENING AREA

PLAY HOUSE STRUCTURE

Source: Reprinted by permission from *Children's Play and Playgrounds* by Joe L. Frost and Barry L. Klein (1979, pp. 94–95).

Figures 3.9 and 3.10 are illustrations of playground designs (Frost and Klein 1979). Analyze these playgrounds, employing the same criteria that you used earlier for analyzing room arrangements. How well is the space used? What objectives will be met by each design? What traffic patterns do you predict?

PLANNING FOR SAFETY INSIDE AND OUT

In choosing any room arrangement or collection of instructional materials, one of the critical criteria is safety. Teachers must make every effort to provide a safe learning environment, both inside the classroom and on the playground. In addition to the safety considerations already mentioned for individual pieces of equipment, the following list will help you analyze the environment for safety:

A Safety Checklist

1. Check the environment, both inside and outside, for any hazards. Check electrical outlets and cords; make sure children cannot pull over any equipment (television sets, projectors, and so on); remove dangerous plants; cover sharp edges; make sure fences are sturdy and exit gates are childproof; and eliminate any other hazards to children's safety.

2. Practice emergency procedures on a regular basis. Children's and teachers' responses to fire drills (and in some areas, tornado and earthquake procedures) must become automatic.

3. Make sure that the classroom contains a fire extinguisher and that all staff (and children who are old enough) know how to use it.

4. All teachers and staff members should be trained in first aid and cardiopulmonary resuscitation (CPR). At minimum, one person with such training should be present at all times. Staff should be required to have special training for CPR with infants, if the program accepts children that young.

5. Post a list of the names of all children and a map of fire exit routes near each exit.

6. Keep a first aid kit adequately stocked at all times. Keep it in a specific place, so that any staff member can locate it quickly.

7. Keep an up-to-date list of emergency phone numbers (parents, relatives, doctors, and hospitals) for each child.

8. Keep the number for the nearest poison control center posted near the telephone.

9. Post a list of children's allergies (including reactions to wasp or bee stings), so that it can be checked before planning any food experiences or outdoor activities.

10. Keep a list by the door of the adults authorized to pick up each child. Do not release a child to any unauthorized person.

11. Make all posted information readily available to substitute teachers.

Teachers must consider a number of factors in assessing playground safety. Frost and Wortham (1988) devised the following checklist, which you may find helpful:

- *A fence (minimum four feet high) protects children from potentially hazardous areas (e.g., streets, water).*
- *Eight to twelve inches of noncompacted sand, pea gravel, shredded wood, or equivalent material is in place under and around all climbing and moving equipment.*
- *Resilient surface is properly maintained (e.g., in place, noncompacted, free of debris).*
- *The equipment is sized to the age group served, with climbing heights limited to the reaching height of children standing erect.*
- *There are no openings that can entrap a child's head (approximately four to eight inches).*
- *Swing seats are constructed of lightweight material with no protruding elements.*
- *Moving parts are free of defects (no pinch, shearing, or crush points; bearings are not excessively worn).*
- *Equipment is free of sharp edges, protruding elements, broken parts, and toxic substances.*
- *Fixed equipment is structurally sound—no bending, warping, breaking, or sinking.*
- *Large equipment is secured in the ground, and concrete footings are recessed in the ground.*
- *All safety equipment (e.g., guard rails, padded areas, protective covers) is in good repair.*
- *The area is free of electrical hazards (e.g., unfenced air conditioners and switchboxes).*
- *The area is free of debris (e.g., sanitary hazards, broken glass, and rocks). (p. 24)**

* From Joe L. Frost and Sue C. Wortham, "The Evolution of American Playgrounds," *Young Children* 43 (July 1988): 19–28. Used with permission of NAEYC.

CHAPTER SUMMARY

- Program goals and objectives are reflected in room arrangements and choices of materials and equipment.
- Basic learning areas in early childhood classrooms include art, music, library/listening/writing, blocks, dramatic play, science/discovery, manipulatives/mathematics/games, woodworking, sand and water, physical education, and quiet areas. These areas are designed to help children develop their interests; each should include storage areas for materials.
- Specialized learning centers are designed to help children master one activity or task. They are designed for temporary use in the classroom.
- Learning areas can be streamlined for the beginning of the schoolyear. Teachers must decide which areas and materials will be most important for children at the beginning of the year and which can be added later.
- Room arrangements help communicate to children what is expected of them and are related to attitudes and behaviors of the children.

- In planning room arrangements, teachers should consider multiple uses of space, the need for water, the need for quieter areas, and the need for areas where more noisy activities can take place.
- Environments can be analyzed in terms of the number of play spaces per child. This type of analysis will help teachers determine the complexity of the environment and what, if anything, should be done to change it.
- Teachers should try to select instructional materials that can be used for multiple experiences, can contribute to many instructional uses, are sturdy, and can be used by children of varying ages and abilities.
- Computers are increasingly likely to be included in programs for young children. Above all, teachers must think of computers as a tool for learning. Accordingly, software should be evaluated in terms of its appropriateness for the children and in terms of what is required of the learner in using it.

WHAT WOULD YOU DO?

Reflect on your reading and your own experiences as you think about how you would respond in the following situations:

1. Your new classroom is dominated by a large teacher's desk. The principal tells you there is nowhere to store it if you have it taken out of your classroom. What would you say to her?
2. Your second-grade classroom is furnished with a desk for each child and very little else. How would you plan an appropriate environment?

3. Your classroom has only two electrical outlets, one at each end of the room. How would you arrange the spaces in the classroom?
4. A parent suggests that you have individual children keep their own supplies, such as crayons, so that they will learn to be responsible for their belongings. How would you respond to this suggestion?

THEORY INTO PRACTICE

1. Visit a local classroom. Measure the room and make a sketch of it, marking the doors, windows, electrical outlets, and water sources. Design a room arrangement for this classroom that you think would be workable.

2. Assume that you have the basic furniture for your classroom and that you have been given $1,000 to buy other materials and equipment for it. Check the prices in catalogs from supply houses that sell early childhood equipment.

Make a list of what you would buy with your money. Compare your list with those of others in your group. How are your lists similar and different? Discuss reasons for your choices.

3. Conduct a complexity analysis of an early childhood classroom, as described in the text. Find the number of play spaces per child. Plan two or three ways that you could increase the complexity without buying any more equipment.

4. Observe for at least an hour in an early childhood classroom in which there is a computer.

How many children used the computer? What did they do with it (games, drill and practice, problem-solving programs, graphics)? How did the teacher handle who could use it? Did equal numbers of boys and girls use it? What kind of social interactions did you observe centered around the computer? From your observations, would you recommend that a center buy a computer? Why?

RECOMMENDED FOR FURTHER READING

Hill, Dorothy M. *Mud, Sand, and Water*. Washington, DC: National Association for the Education of Young Children, 1977.

Not very many centers or schools will have the space or the freedom to carry out the ideas included in this book, but it is worth reading to help you think about the educational possibilities in simple, unstructured materials. Some of the ideas can be scaled down to fit most classrooms. Every teacher should have a vision of what children can do, given materials and freedom.

Hirsch, Elisabeth S., ed. *The Block Book*. Rev. ed. Washington, DC: National Association for the Education of Young Children, 1984.

This book is included because blocks are such basic materials and their arrangement in the classroom can contribute so much to the children's play with them. The book has excellent chapters on the use of blocks in the content areas of science, social studies, and math. An important chapter covers the use of blocks in the elementary school. Also included are suggestions for the equipment needed for block play.

Kritchevsky, Sybil, and Elizabeth Prescott. *Planning Environments for Young Children: Physical Space*. Washington, DC: National Association for the Education of Young Children, 1969.

Although this booklet is older than other readings recommended here, it has many timely and relevant ideas. Included are ideas for planning and evaluating indoor space as well as outdoor space. Several diagrams help teachers visualize pathways and well-marked areas.

Loughlin, Catherine E., and Joseph H. Suina. *The Learning Environment: An Instructional Strategy*. New York: Teachers College Press, 1982.

A few sections of this book describe environmental arrangements for older learners, but most of the information applies directly to early childhood classrooms. Excellent suggestions are offered for finding useful spaces for children's work (including taking another look at the space used by the teacher) and for defining spaces. The book is filled with illustrations that clarify the text.

Taylor, Anne P., and George Vlastos. *School Zone: Learning Environments for Children*. New York: Van Nostrand Reinhold, 1975.

Basically, this book is an examination of an open-school environment. It is most helpful to teachers of young children to encourage their thinking about different shapes, colors, and levels in classrooms. The book is filled with photographs, which help illustrate the concepts discussed.

Vergeront, Jeanne. *Places and Spaces for Preschool and Primary (Indoors)*. Washington, DC: National Association for the Education of Young Children, 1987.

This booklet contains many practical ideas for room arrangements and storage. In addition to providing a sound rationale for the ideas proposed, it describes do-it-yourself ideas that are relatively inexpensive to implement.

REFERENCES

Baker, Katherine Read. *Let's Play Outdoors.* Washington, DC: National Association for the Education of Young Children, 1966.

Barbour, Nita, Tupper Dooly Webster, and Stephen Drosdeck. "Sand: A Resource for the Language Arts." *Young Children* 42 (January 1987): 20–25.

Baylor, Byrd. *The Desert Is Theirs.* New York: Charles Scribner and Sons, 1970.

Binder, S. L., and B. Ledger. *Preschool Computer Project Report.* Oakville, Ontario, Canada: Sheridan College, 1985.

Borgh, Karin, and W. Patrick Dickson. "The Effects on Children's Writing of Adding Speech Synthesis to a Word Processor." Paper presented at the annual conference of the American Educational Research Association, San Francisco, 1986.

Char, Cynthia A. *Interactive Technology and the Young Child: Insights from Research and Design.* ERIC Document Reproduction Service 335152. 1990.

Clements, Douglas H. "Computers and Young Children: A Review of Research." *Young Children* 43 (November 1987): 34–44.

Day, Barbara. *Early Childhood Education.* 3d ed. New York: Macmillan, 1988.

Frost, Joe L., and Barry L. Klein. *Children's Play and Playgrounds.* Boston: Allyn and Bacon, 1979.

Frost, Joe L., and Sue C. Wortham. "The Evolution of American Playgrounds." *Young Children* 43 (July 1988): 19–28.

Gabbard, Carl. *Playground Apparatus Experiences and Muscular Endurance Among Children 4–6.* ERIC Document Reproduction Service 288190. College Station, TX: Texas A&M University, 1979.

Greabell, Leon C., and Sonia D. Forseth. "Creating a Stimulating Environment." *Kappa Delta Pi Record* 17 (February 1981): 70–73, 75.

Harms, Thelma. "Evaluating Settings for Learning." *Young Children* 25 (May 1970): 304–309.

Heyman, Mark. *Places and Spaces: Environmental Psychology in Education.* Fastback no. 112. Bloomington, IN: Phi Delta Kappa Educational Foundation, 1978.

Hill, Carol B. *Creating a Learning Climate for the Early Childhood Years.* Fastback no. 292. Bloomington, IN: Phi Delta Kappa Educational Foundation, 1989.

Hirsch, Elisabeth S., ed. *The Block Book.* Rev. ed. Washington, DC: National Association for the Education of Young Children, 1984.

Jones, Elizabeth. "Inviting Children into the Fun: Providing Enough Activity Choices Outdoors." *Child Care Information Exchange* 70 (December 1989): 15–19.

Kritchevsky, Sybil, and Elizabeth Prescott. *Planning Environments for Young Children: Physical Space.* Washington, DC: National Association for the Education of Young Children, 1969.

Lasky, Lila, and Rose Mukerji. *Art: Basic for Young Children.* Washington, DC: National Association for the Education of Young Children, 1980.

Lieberman, D. "Research on Children and Microcomputers: A Review of Utilization and Effects Studies." In *Children and Microcomputers: Research on the Newest Medium,* edited by M. Chen and W. Paisley, 59–83. Beverly Hills, CA: Sage, 1985.

Lipinski, Judith M., R. E. Nida, Daniel D. Shade, and J. A. Watson. "The Effects of Microcomputers on Young Children: An Examination of Free-Play Choices, Sex Differences, and Social Interactions." *Journal of Educational Computing Research* 2 (1986): 121–125.

Muller, Alexandra A., and Marion Perlmutter. "Preschool Children's Problem-Solving Interactions at Computers and Jigsaw Puzzles." *Journal of Applied Developmental Psychology* 6 (1985): 173–186.

Pappas, Christine C., Barbara Z. Kiefer, and Linda S. Levstik. *An Integrated Language Perspective in the Elementary School.* New York: Longman, 1990.

Picard, A. J., and C. Giuli. *Computers as a Free-Time Activity in Grades K–4: A Two-Year Study of Attitudes and Usage.* Honolulu: University of Hawaii, 1985.

Prescott, Elizabeth, Elizabeth Jones, and Sybil Kritchevsky. *Group Day Care as a Child-Reading Environment.* Washington, DC: Children's Bureau, Social Security Administration, Department of Health, Education and Welfare, 1967.

Rosengren, K. S., D. Gross, A. F. Abrams, and M. Perlmutter. "An Observational Study of Preschool Children's Computing Activity." Paper presented at conference on Perspectives on the Young Child and the Computer, University of Texas, Austin, September 1985.

Silvern, Steven B., Peter A. Williamson, and Terry M. Countermine. "Young Children's Interaction with a Microcomputer." *Early Child Development and Care* 32 (January 1988): 23–35.

Swick, Kevin J. "Appropriate Uses of Computers with Young Children." *Educational Technology* (January 1989): 7–13.

Swigger, Kathleen, and James Campbell. "Computers and the Nursery School." In *Proceedings of the National Educational Computing Conference,* edited by D. Harris and L. Nelson-Heern. Iowa City, IA: National Educational Computing Conference, 1981.

Taylor, Anne P., and George Vlastos. *School Zone: Learning Environments for Children.* New York: Van Nostrand Reinhold, 1983.

Vergeront, Jeanne. *Places and Spaces for Preschool and Primary (Indoors).* Washington, DC: National Association for the Education of Young Children, 1987.

Weinstein, Carol S. "The Physical Environment of the School: A Review of the Research." *Review of Educational Research* 49 (Fall 1979): 577–610.

Chapter Four

Planning and Assessing Learning Activities

You observed in a kindergarten this week. You were amazed at the variety of activities the children had to choose from during most of the morning. You noticed that the teacher encouraged children to choose a project that interested them and that some children continued to work on the same activity for the entire time. One child built an elaborate block structure to represent the harbor the class had visited last week. She labeled all the parts with signs. She smiled happily when the teacher photographed her construction, asked the teacher for a blank book in which to mount the photograph, and told you that tomorrow she would write about the construction in the book. You wondered how building this block structure fit in with the teacher's goals and objectives for the class. Other children were involved in such activities as creating animals from cardboard boxes, painting at easels, observing and recording the behavior of a large frog, and following the directions in a book for making an appropriate home for a box turtle.

The teacher showed you his plan book, and you found lesson plans that did not follow the outline you learned in your first education class. How do teachers select learning activities? What does a lesson plan that includes many different activities look like? How does a teacher evaluate a program?

. . . .

Curriculum
A written plan for learning experiences.

In planning a **curriculum** for young children, the teacher must select objectives, select and organize content, choose the appropriate learning experiences, determine the most appropriate sequence for the learning activities, and determine how to assess both children's growth and the program itself. *Curriculum* is a term that has many definitions: It can mean all experiences that happen at school; a written plan for learning; a syllabus that lists learning topics and the order in which they will be presented; or a program, such as a drug abuse prevention program, that specifies a sequence of activities.

CURRICULUM PLANNING

In this chapter, *curriculum* is defined as a written plan for learning experiences in which children will be involved. A curriculum plan usually specifies *scope* (what will be learned) and *sequence* (the order in which the learning will take place). For example, a plan might specify that children will learn to recognize similarities and differences among given objects. It would make sense to provide experiences in recognizing these traits before expecting children to classify objects. Schwartz and Robison (1982) explain that art design and curriculum design have many steps in common, including:

1. *defining the purpose*
2. *analyzing the options*
3. *selecting the design features*
4. *producing the design*
5. *evaluating the design—does it measure up to your intentions? (p. 3)*

In designing a curriculum, the teacher must begin by selecting feasible objectives. These objectives must reflect the purpose of the curriculum: Is the goal content knowledge? social skills? physical skills? problem-solving skills? a balance of all these? The objectives should not be so broad that they provide no guidance for choosing learning activities or so narrow that they limit the possibilities for teachers and children too much. An example of an objective that is too broad is "Children will love reading"; an objective that is too narrow is "Children will be able to count to ten." Most teachers do well to limit the number of objectives they plan to achieve.

Once objectives have been selected, the teacher must make decisions about the selection and organization of content (analyze the options). For example, an objective might be "Children will develop increased skill in classification." The teacher must then choose how to achieve the objective by selecting which content will be learned and how it will be organized. This rather broad objective could be achieved by providing materials such as leaves, keys, or pictures of inside and outside activities for children to classify. If the children are already somewhat skilled in classifying objects, the teacher might decide to help them apply classification skills in classifying animals. (The content for classification might just as well be plants, rocks, or insects.) "Animals" is probably still too broad a category for meaningful learning; therefore, depending on the children's level of development and previous experiences, a teacher might choose one category of animals, such as "reptiles," and teach the children the characteristics of reptiles that determine their classification.

How the content of learning about reptiles is organized is also an important professional decision. The teacher could choose to bring a different reptile to class every week for several weeks, discuss it in group time, and allow the children to observe it during activity time. Another choice would be to make reptiles the theme of every class activity for a period of time.

After choosing the content (knowledge of reptiles) to promote an objective (improved skill in classification), the teacher must still select from many possible learning activities (select the design features). The children could take a field trip to a local zoo to visit the reptile displays; the teacher could have a pet shop owner visit the class to talk about care and feeding of reptile pets; children could create reptiles in the art center, demonstrate reptile movements, compare reptiles to amphibians on a chart, and so on. The teacher must select from among a multitude of possible learning activities those that she predicts will be most appropriate for the group and for individuals in the group.

Once the objectives and possible activities have been selected, the teacher must make decisions about sequence (produce the design). One obviously would not begin by asking children to classify a set of model animals as reptiles. One might begin by asking the children to recall what they know about another group of animals. After observing several reptiles for a few days, the children might be asked to compare what they have observed about reptiles with their knowledge of other animals so that they discover the characteristics that define reptiles. (Of course, a teacher who plans activities that include observing must be sure that children have had experience in observing—as opposed to just looking.) Some activities might be presented simultaneously, but others will need to be ordered so that the children can use information and skills from one experience in order to benefit from another experience.

Finally, the teacher must determine how to assess the experiences of the children (evaluate the design). Assessment must be appropriate to the age and development of the learners and to the activity being assessed. For example, if the activity has been a field trip to the local zoo, assessment might include observing the children's responses after the trip. Did they want to build replicas of the reptile house with the blocks? Did they use any knowledge of reptiles in their art or writing? Did they want more information about reptiles from the library? Did they apply their classification abilities with models of reptiles and mammals during play activities?

In short, when planning the curriculum, the teacher is responsible for selecting the objectives and the content, determining how it is organized, selecting the learning activities, and then assessing the activities. The teacher must also consider the interests of the children when selecting curriculum experiences. If the teacher who selects reptiles as content finds, after a day or two, that the children have absolutely no interest in reptiles, she should select another topic. Suppose the children had expressed interest in the caterpillars they found on the playground. Caterpillars and other insects could be just as useful in helping children understand and apply classification abilities as reptiles. Children should also be encouraged to choose from the many learning activities possible those they would like to do and to make some choices about what they would like to learn about any given topic.

Although the sequence of planning a curriculum has been presented as a linear process, in reality, it is usually more recursive than linear: Teachers plan content and activities, adapt them for individual children, select other activities, evaluate, and plan again. All the steps are there, but the process is rarely a completely linear one.

CURRICULUM ORGANIZATION

When designing curriculum, teachers have several options for choosing how to organize the learning experiences. The most common approaches to organizing curriculum for young children are a facts approach and a skills approach. With a *facts approach*, experiences are arranged so that children learn a given set of factual information, such as the days of the week, the letters of the alphabet, or the names of colors. With a *skills approach*, experiences are selected and arranged so that children learn to cut on a line, to share, or to find information that they want in a selection of reference books.

In elementary schools, the most common organization has been the *subject-matter approach*, whereby children learn reading or math or social studies. Another approach is *thematic organization*, in which skills, facts, and subject-matter knowledge are integrated around a unifying theme, such as a study of whales. In the 1960s, Jerome Bruner (1960) and other curriculum leaders attempted to help designers of curriculum organize experiences around the key concepts of the various disciplines. In some curriculum guides, you might find key concepts and ideas in such objectives as "Children will recognize change as basic to understanding the social studies." The broadest organizers are the basic human needs shared by all people: friends, social responsibility as a citizen, and so on. The various types of curriculum organizers are summarized in Table 4.1 on page 110.

THE DEVELOPMENTALLY APPROPRIATE CURRICULUM

The definition of a *developmentally appropriate curriculum* is provided in two documents from the National Association for the Education of Young Children (NAEYC). In *Developmentally Appropriate Practice in Early Childhood Programs Serving Children from Birth Through Age 8* (Bredekamp 1986), NAEYC defines developmentally appropriate practice in terms of parent relationships, staffing patterns, and curriculum. The guidelines for curriculum include ensuring age appropriateness and individual appropriateness, providing play activities, teaching content and skills in a meaningful context, increasing the difficulty and challenge of activities based on observation of the children, choosing content based on children's interests, and focusing on multicultural issues. These guidelines are not necessarily new; rather, they are a compilation of what good teachers already do in early childhood classrooms across the United States.

The curriculum framework has been expanded in a second NAEYC document, *Reaching Potentials: Appropriate Curriculum and Assessment for Young Children*, Volume 1 (Bredekamp and Rosegrant 1992). The following principles are intended to help teachers as they make curriculum decisions:

Table 4.1	Types of Curriculum Organizers
KNOWLEDGE SOURCES	**CONTENT**
Facts	Colors and shapes; number names in order; names of months and days of week; weather observations; stories of Columbus, the Pilgrims, George Washington, and Abraham Lincoln.
Skills	**Academic:** counting in sequence; letter recognition; phonics; number writing **Coping:** personal cleanliness; clothing management; eating; classroom cleanup **Social:** making friends; sharing; taking turns; using conventional rules of politeness **Process:** information seeking; problem setting; pursuing personal areas of curiosity; learning how to learn
Subjects Formal integration of subjects is referred to as an *integrated curriculum.*	Reading; social studies; math and science; language arts; music; arithmetic; health education; physical education
Themes A combination of subjects and skills is also referred to as an *integrated curriculum.*	**Historical and Current Events:** Columbus Day; Washington's birthday; Halloween; Spring; Circus **Topics:** transportation; community services; communication; families; nutrition
Structure of disciplines, key concepts	**Math:** sets, subsets, geometric shape, equivalent sets, greater than-less than, congruent length, longer, shorter **Physical Science:** force, energy, motion **Life Science:** adaptation if a factor in all plant and animal life **Economics:** key prices are determined in the marketplace largely by supply and demand
Holistic	Friendship: belonging and acceptance, approval, and respect; a sense of competence, independence, and autonomy; social responsibilities in the class, at home, and in the community; a healthful, nonpolluted environment; maintenance of personal well-being; survival skills

Source: Sidney Schwartz and Helen F. Robison, *Designing Curriculum for Early Childhood* (Boston: Allyn and Bacon, 1982), p. 35. Used with permission.

   1. *The curriculum has an articulated description of its theoretical base that is consistent with prevailing professional opinion and research on how children learn.*

   2. *Curriculum content is designed to achieve long-range goals for children in all domains—social, emotional, cognitive, and physical—and to prepare children to function as fully contributing members of a democratic society.*

   3. *Curriculum addresses the development of knowledge and understanding, processes and skills, dispositions and attitudes.*

   4. *Curriculum addresses a broad range of content that is relevant, engaging, and meaningful to children.*

5. *Curriculum goals are realistic and attainable for most children in the designated age range for which they were designed.*

6. *Curriculum content reflects and is generated by the needs and interest of individual children within the group. Curriculum incorporates a wide variety of learning experiences, materials and equipment, and instructional strategies, to accommodate a broad range of children's individual differences in prior experience, maturation rates, styles of learning, needs, and interests.*

7. *Curriculum respects and supports individual, cultural, and linguistic diversity. Curriculum supports and encourages positive relationships with children's families.*

8. *Curriculum builds upon what children already know and are able to do (activating prior knowledge) to consolidate their learning and to foster their acquisition of new concepts and skills.*

9. *The curriculum provides conceptual frameworks for children so that their mental constructions based on prior knowledge and experience become more complex over time.*

10. *Curriculum allows for focus on a particular topic or content while allowing for integration across traditional subject-matter divisions by planning around themes and/or learning experiences that provide opportunities for rich conceptual development.*

11. *The curriculum content has intellectual integrity; content meets the recognized standards of the relevant subject-matter disciplines.*

12. *The content of the curriculum is worth knowing; curriculum respects children's intelligence and does not waste their time.*

13. *Curriculum engages children actively, not passively, in the learning process. Children have opportunities to make meaningful choices.*

14. *Curriculum values children's constructive errors and does not prematurely limit exploration and experimentation for the sake of ensuring "right" answers.*

15. *Curriculum emphasizes the development of children's thinking, reasoning, decision-making, and problem-solving abilities.*

16. *Curriculum emphasizes the value of social interactions to learning in all domains and provides opportunities to learn from peers.*

17. *Curriculum is supportive of children's psychological needs for activity, sensory stimulation, fresh air, rest, hygiene, and nourishment/ elimination.*

18. *Curriculum protects children's psychological safety, that is, children feel happy, relaxed, and comfortable rather than disengaged, frightened, worried, or stressed.*

19. *The curriculum strengthens children's sense of competence and enjoyment of learning by providing experiences for children to succeed from their point of view.*

20. *The curriculum is flexible so that teachers can adapt to individual children or groups. (pp. 19–22)**

Thematic approach
The organization of curriculum and learning experiences around a chosen topic.

These guidelines clearly emphasize that an integrated, **thematic approach** to curriculum is most productive in helping teachers design a developmentally appropriate curriculum.

Rationale for an Integrated Curriculum

The idea of integrating curriculum is not a new one. At the turn of the century, John Dewey (1859–1952) (1902) advocated the organization of curriculum around projects that would interest and involve children. The most common approach to curriculum organization in schools in the United States, however, continues to be subject-matter organization, in which learning is segmented into math or science or language arts (Jacobs 1989).

You probably remember that in elementary school, you had reading first thing in the morning, math right before lunch, and science in the afternoon. Yet when children learn outside of school, they learn in wholes. For example, a child visiting tide pools could learn about many things at once: language arts (learning vocabulary for the animals and plants of the tide pools); physical skills (staying on top of the slippery rocks); classification (noticing which animals are related); the environment (noticing pollution or litter); family stories (hearing parents tell about when they visited these tide pools as children); and so on. A child's learning experiences outside school are not divisible into subject-matter areas.

An integrated curriculum can help a child make sense of the world more easily. If a child is learning the names of the letters of the alphabet, that knowledge must be placed in a context that makes sense to him. When the child learns the names of the letters by hearing the teacher read alphabet books and by exploring the forms of the letters in writing, he knows that the names of the letters communicate information about the printed form of language. He recognizes that this information is personally useful, not something learned to please an adult but that has no other utility for him.

An integrated curriculum provides opportunities for:

1. in-depth exploration of a topic and learning that is more than just superficial coverage

2. more choices and therefore more motivation to learn and greater satisfaction with the results
3. more active learning
4. an opportunity for the teacher to learn along with the children and model lifelong learning
5. a more effective use of student and teacher time

Organizing learning experiences around a theme can be productive, but if thematic teaching is to be successful, the theme must be carefully selected, activities carefully planned, and evaluation of the theme and of individual children's progress carefully monitored.

Selecting a Theme

In choosing a theme, there are several important considerations. Katz and Chard (1989) list the following criteria: relevance, the opportunity for application of skills, the availability of resources, teacher interest, and the time of year.

Relevance is defined as the applicability of a topic of study to a child's life. In other words, does what is learned have meaning for the child other than the fact that her learning it pleases the teacher? In considering the *opportunities for application of skills,* teachers must think about whether children will have opportunities to engage in reading, writing, and computation activities that have real meaning for them. Will the skills help children answer their own questions and solve their own problems? *Availability of resources* must be considered because theme studies require many resources—a textbook and a workbook are not sufficient. Are community resources (people and places to visit) available that will contribute to the topic? Can real objects be acquired to illustrate the topic? Is there adequate support from the library—posters, media, reference material? *Teacher interest* is a consideration because teachers will want to model interest and guide the children's explorations and investigations. There are too many appropriate themes to choose one that does not appeal to the teacher. *Time of year* is important not only because the teacher will want to be aware of seasonal topics (in the fall, for example, materials for study such as seed pods can be collected; in the spring, leaves are available to feed silkworm larvae) but also because the teacher must take into consideration that he will know the children much better later in the year. The first themes of the year should not be unfamiliar to children but should be topics that the teacher knows have been part of their previous personal experiences and that will interest them.

Katz and Chard (1989) group topics of study in the following way:

1. The children themselves: *homes, babies, families, food, school bus, TV shows, toys, games*
2. The local community: *people, hospital, shops, building site, transport services, waterworks, fish market*
3. Local events and current affairs: *annual carnival or county fair, important anniversary, Independence Day, royal wedding, visit by a famous person*
4. Place: *neighborhood, roads, directions, landmarks, rivers, hills, woods, transport*
5. Time: *clocks, seasons, calendar, festivals, holidays, historical objects, historical events*
6. Natural phenomena: *weather, water, wind and air, plants, animals, mini-beasts, rocks, the sea, dinosaurs*
7. Content-free concepts: *opposites, pattern, color, symmetry*
8. General knowledge: *deserts, ships and other vehicles, inventions, space travel, rivers*
9. Miscellaneous: *hats, black holes, puppets, math or book week (pp. 65–66)*

There are other ways of grouping topics, of course. The point is that many different kinds of topics are available for study, and teachers will want to balance the program by offering a variety of topics. Some teachers choose topics that are more scientific to alternate with topics that are focused more heavily on social studies. For example, studying plants or animals would involve more science (although social studies would not be excluded), and a study of festivals would involve more concepts in social studies.

One of the major reasons for selecting a thematic organization is to offer children the opportunity for in-depth rather than superficial study of various topics. Therefore, the theme selected must be one for which the activities are worthwhile. Thematic organization alone does not guarantee a well-planned, thoughtful curriculum. There are trivial approaches to thematic organization as well as to other types of curriculum organization. A teacher could decide to focus on mice as a theme and provide meaningful activities in which children learned about nutrition, training, building mazes, genetics, and so on. Or the teacher could choose mice as a theme and focus on it simplistically: covering the container where the children place their work with paper to represent cheese, decorating the bookmarks children use to mark their places in the reader with mice, using pictures of mice to enliven math worksheets, and having children make paper mice in art. A theme cannot be implemented solely by classroom decorations.

Teachers must make decisions about how to schedule activities and experiences for children.

Implementing the Theme

Once a topic has been selected, the teacher (and the children, if they are old enough) will brainstorm areas of interest related to that particular topic. Older children will be able to see more relationships than younger ones. Figure 4.1 (page 116) and Figure 4.2 (page 117) illustrate webs of younger and older children's responses to the topic "school bus." Notice the differences.

After ideas have been generated, they can be grouped together, and some subtopics can be combined into larger topics. Figure 4.3 (page 118) returns to the example of a study of reptiles and illustrates how ideas might be grouped around that topic.

After a topic and related subtopics have been chosen, the next step is to select activities that will help children learn content and apply their skills in meaningful contexts. What can be learned on a field trip? What can resource people share with the children? What play experiences can be facilitated? Are there construction possibilities? What skills can be applied in this study? What curriculum goals can be met through the study of this topic?

FIGURE 4.1 School Bus Web for a Class of Younger Children

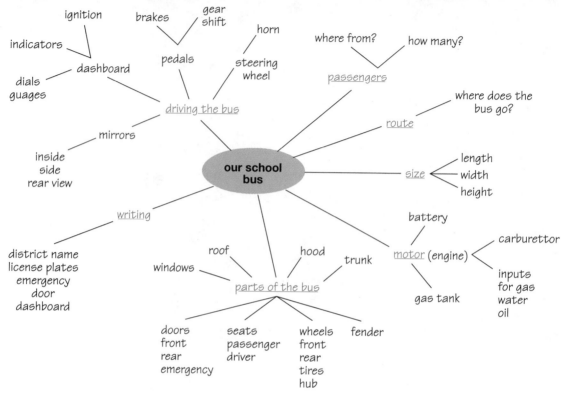

Source: From Lillian G. Katz and Sylvia C. Chard, *Engaging Children's Minds: The Project Approach* (Norwood, NJ: Ablex, 1989), p. 161. Reprinted with the permission of Ablex Publishing Corporation.

Let's assume that one of the teacher's curriculum goals is to help children become familiar with a variety of reading materials (narrative, poetry, expository writing, and so on). In the study of reptiles, children could read (or listen to the teacher read) information books about reptiles, narratives in which reptiles are important to the story, poetry about reptiles, and reference books about reptiles. Another curriculum goal might be to help children recognize how animals adapt to their environments. The study of reptiles would lead children to recognize how reptiles survive in their environments. Similarly, the curriculum would probably specify that children should participate in the writing process. While studying reptiles, children could write descriptions, narratives, or poetry that focused on reptiles and would thereby have opportunities to be involved in the process of writing on a daily basis.

FIGURE 4.2   School Bus Web for a Class of Older Children

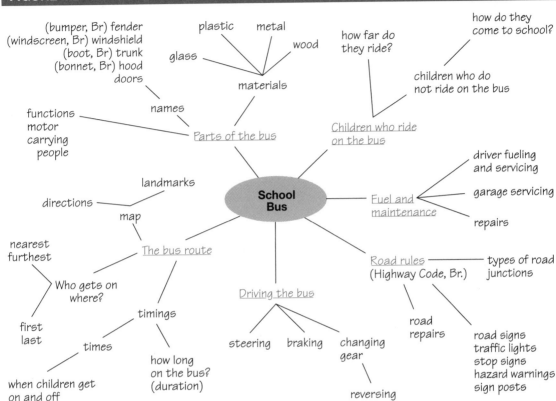

Source: From Lillian G. Katz and Sylvia C. Chard, *Engaging Children's Minds: The Project Approach* (Norwood, NJ: Ablex, 1989), p. 161. Reprinted with the permission of Ablex Publishing Corporation.

Once curriculum goals have been reviewed, the teacher (and children) can determine activities that will be possible in this study. Not every child will participate in every activity; choices will be available to the children. The teacher must think about the objectives of each activity and the relationship of the objectives to the curriculum goals. If an activity cannot contribute to the curriculum goals, it should be eliminated as a choice.

Next, the teacher must decide how to introduce the theme and activities. A theme of reptiles might be introduced by arranging for several reptiles to be housed in the classroom for several weeks. If their interest in the reptiles was high, the children themselves would generate many ideas for activities. Other themes could be introduced through field trips, literature selections, or media presentations.

FIGURE 4.3   Ideas for a Reptile Theme

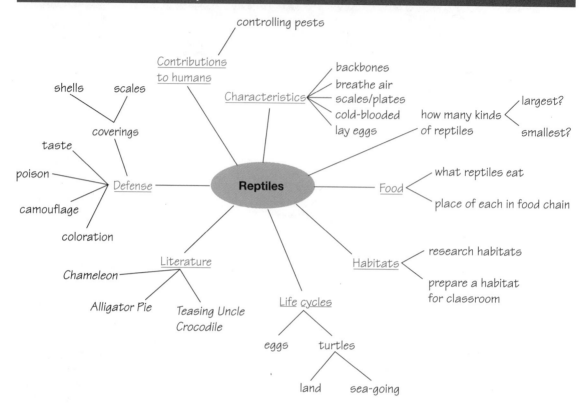

Often, the learning areas in a classroom can be made to focus on a particular theme. For example, materials could be placed in the art center for painting or drawing reptiles; the library center could display books on reptiles; perhaps a filmstrip would be available in a listening area; and children could observe reptiles in the science area. This does not imply that children would be assigned tasks in the areas; rather, materials would be available to help them complete their investigations or follow up on their interests.

What follows is a list of possible activities related to reptiles. Evaluate each activity in terms of its appropriateness for primary children:

1. Create a web about reptiles with the children. Determine what they already know.
2. Invite a pet shop owner to bring a selection of reptile pets to the classroom, and talk about their care.

3. Visit the reptile house at the zoo. Observe the different habitats and food of the different animals (if possible).

4. Create a chart of care rules for reptiles that are visiting the classroom. Include food, water, temperature, and so on.

5. Use a reference book to locate information about reptiles that are found in the local area. Note which ones might be poisonous or dangerous.

6. Interview two local gardeners to determine how reptiles are helpful in growing a successful garden.

7. Create a chart comparing the characteristics of reptiles and other animal groups that the children know about (amphibians, mammals, and so on).

8. Construct an appropriate habitat for a given reptile.

9. Create a class book describing local reptiles. One possible model might be *Desert Voices* (Baylor 1981).

10. Write a description of one of the classroom reptiles.

11. Read *Why Mosquitoes Buzz in People's Ears* (Aardema 1975). Dramatize the story. (The story begins with an iguana and a python.)

12. View a film about reptiles. Create a chart summarizing the facts presented in the film.

13. Create a booklet describing the life cycle of a given reptile. Include observations about hatching, shedding skin, and so on.

14. Compare the information about a given reptile in two or more sources.

15. Measure and record the food given to each classroom reptile.

Evaluation

Teachers must use some method of recording each child's progress and the goals met by the activities focusing on a given theme. One method is to construct a record sheet for each child, with a list of curriculum goals down the side and columns across for each theme of study. As children complete activities, their work can be recorded on the list. Figure 4.4 (page 120) illustrates this format. (Note that in most state or district curriculum guides, goals are generally grouped by subject-matter content; that is, all the literacy goals, social studies goals, science goals, and so on are listed together. Thus, a teacher might have to use a checklist with a subject-matter organization scheme even if her classroom activities are organized thematically.)

In evaluating the children's progress, the teacher might use several different assessments, such as observations of the children's behavior, a

FIGURE 4.4   Evaluation Checklist

CHILD'S NAME ___Jamie___

	REPTILES	INSECTS	
Reads a variety of materials: reference materials, narrative stories, poetry	10/6	11/5 11/20	
Participates in writing process: personal writing, letter writing, narratives, expository writing	10/8	11/10 12/1	
Recognizes adaptation as a factor in all plant and animal life (habitat, camouflage, food chain)	10/12 10/15 10/16	11/20 11/23 11/24	
Uses computation to solve problems			
Uses the scientific process to solve problems			

checklist to record skill achievement, or a narrative that describes the child's growth. (Assessment possibilities are described in Chapter Fourteen.) In evaluating the theme, the teacher would observe the children's interest and record the contributions of the theme to overall goals.

Although a teacher may choose to repeat a theme another year, rarely can a theme be repeated in the same form. The interests and experiences of different groups of children vary considerably, and some themes that work well with one group are not at all interesting to other groups. Even if topics are repeated, the activities chosen by the children are likely to vary so much that one year's implementation of the theme will not be the same as a previous year's. When a teacher simply applies a theme to the children, it becomes mechanical, and the classroom routine fails to reflect children's interests and experiences. Theme studies require considerable investments of time and energy by the teacher, but the result—meaningful experiences for the children through which they gain not only knowledge and skills but the disposition to learn—is well worth the effort.

As you read the chapters in this book about language, literature, literacy, math, science, social studies, the arts, and health and physical education, remember that although these content areas are presented in discrete chapters, the underlying assumption is that knowledge of each subject-matter area will help you to integrate curriculum. You do need to understand the goals and objectives in each area in order to plan appropriately, but you should use this knowledge to plan meaningful and conceptually important themes. Throughout the content chapters of this book (Chapters Seven through Twelve), a theme of patterns will be the focus. So even though the discussion in each chapter will be about a discrete subject (math, science, music, and so on), the emphasis will be on an integrated curriculum.

However curriculum is organized, teachers are responsible for developing the plans for learning experiences in their classrooms. The following section provides some advice on creating those plans.

LEARNING PLANS

A **learning plan** differs from a lesson plan in that often a lesson plan outlines only one lesson. In early childhood programs, however, learning experiences are not usually confined to single lessons. As Elkind (1982) reminds us, "Clearly children learn in many different ways and what mode of learning is employed depends very much upon what is to be learned" (p. 7). Learning plans involve long-term planning, unit or theme planning, and short-term goals. Each day's activities should contribute to the unit or theme goals, and each unit or theme should contribute to the overall goals of the program.

Learning plan
A comprehensive plan of learning experiences children will participate in.

As the teacher of the program, you may not have much control over the program goals. They are often established by the administration of the center or school, hopefully, with the collaboration of the teachers. These are the kinds of goals that centers advertise on their consumer brochures or that are printed in the curriculum guides of school districts. However, goal statements do not define how goals are to be achieved. The "how" is up to the teacher and should reflect knowledge of children's development, the children's abilities and interests, and the teacher's own interests.

A daily learning plan may indicate the materials to be placed in the learning areas, include notes about guiding specific children's learning, and suggest plans for evaluation of activities. If one of the daily goals is learning to use the concept "line" in talking about art, the learning plan would note the pieces of art to be displayed, specify that strings and strips of paper should be made available in the art area, and call for an emphasis on line in movement experiences. Teachers would work with individual children as they participated in art or movement to emphasize the concept of line and would talk with those who were looking at the art examples about how the artists had used lines. This plan would fit into the larger theme of lines and space being explored in a variety of areas and support the overall goals of increasing children's ability to communicate effectively and to explore a variety of materials.

Several daily learning plans for preschool and primary children are presented in boxes in this section. Take some time to review them, and as you do, keep this in mind: Learning plans should always be as complete as possible but should never be so rigid that **incidental learning** cannot be included in the day's schedule. For instance, if a child brings a pet rabbit to school, obviously time must be allotted to observing and discussing the rabbit. If the children are really interested in the rabbit, then the teacher might make some plans for additional experiences with rabbits in a few weeks. The point is to take advantage of what the children want to know

Incidental learning
Learning that occurs in addition to what is written into the learning plan.

Incidental learning is important in any program for children.

LEARNING PLAN (THREE- TO FOUR-YEAR-OLDS)

Program Goals:

Improved problem-solving skills, increased language development, increased fine motor development

Theme: Plants

Objectives:

- Children will be able to distinguish plants from nonplants.
- Children will learn the following vocabulary: *seed, stem, leaf, flower.*
- Children will learn the basic requirements for plant life (light, water, soil).

Activity Time:

- *Discovery:* Make available bean and pumpkin seeds for planting (have cups, soil, watering can in learning area).
- *Art:* Use leaves collected from local trees for printing (cover leaf with paint and press paper over it; Mr. Gonzales to help supervise here).
- *Library:* Put out information books about plants.

Small Groups:

Take a walk around the school to observe different kinds of plants. Gather plant materials for use in the collage. Provide each child with a small paper bag for collecting.

Cooking:

Mrs. Turner (parent volunteer) will help the children shell and cook green peas.

Read:

The Carrot Seed (Kraus 1945)

Movement:

Pretend to be trees swaying in the wind.

Evaluation:

The teacher will observe children's responses to the planting activity and will record evidence of plant knowledge on the walk (anecdotal records).

---

now as you keep the overall goals in mind. When Alice came to the Cheshire Cat and asked which road to take, he told her that it did not make any difference, since she did not know where she was going. Teachers of young children need to know where they are going—and they need to plan which road to take but be prepared to take another one, if it presents itself.

Although learning plans are more appropriate in terms of planning for instruction than isolated lesson plans, lesson plans may sometimes be designed to teach specific elements of a broader learning plan. For example, the learning plan on plants suggests that children use leaves for printing. A lesson plan for that activity might look like that in Figure 4.5 (page 124).

Some plans will provide for whole-class activities, others for small groups, and still others for individual children. For example, from the learning plan for six- to seven-year-olds, the whole class might listen to the teacher read *Everybody Needs a Rock* (Baylor 1974), small groups might work together in examining the rocks and making a chart of the information, and individuals might create collages from rocks or pebbles. In every

FIGURE 4.5 Sample Lesson Plan for Activity on Plants

Objective: Children will participate in a printing activity.

Materials:
- Leaves gathered from local area
- Tempera paint
- Brushes or sponges
- Newspapers
- Paper towels
- White construction paper

Procedure:
1. Cover the work surface with newspaper.
2. Allow each child to select the leaves he wishes to use.
3. Arrange the leaves on a paper towel with the veined side up.
4. Cover the leaves with a light coat of tempera paint, using a brush or sponge.
5. Place white paper over the towel and painted leaves; then press all over.
6. Lift off the paper.
7. Repeat as the child desires.
8. Place the finished paper on a drying rack, and help the child clean up (hang up smock, wash hands, and so on).

Alternative: The child may wish to paint the leaf and then pick it up by the stem and place it on the white paper. Allow experimentation.

Evaluation: Observe the child's interest and participation. Also observe the child's language. (Does he talk about leaves and perhaps even what kind of leaf he is choosing?)

learning plan, there should be a good balance of whole-group, small-group, and individual activities.

Mandated Lessons or Goals

Mandated goals
Goals set by a school director or written into the school curriculum.

If the school district has **mandated goals** and corresponding materials to be used, the professional teacher must decide if the materials are appropriate for his particular group of children and if not, how the children could achieve the mandated goals in a more appropriate manner. For example, in one school district, kindergarten teachers were told that all kindergarten children should have mastered eighteen basic sight words from the adopted basal reader by the end of kindergarten. A professional teacher would be accountable for teaching the sight-word vocabulary to all the children for whom this goal was reasonable, but given his knowledge

LEARNING PLAN (SIX- TO SEVEN-YEAR-OLDS)

Program Goals:

Increased ability to communicate, increased literacy, increased skill in computation and problem solving.

Theme: Rocks and stones

Objectives:

- Children will be able to classify rocks by hardness.
- Children will be able to describe rocks employing appropriate adjectives.
- Children will contribute to an ABC book of rocks.

Activity Time:

- *Science:* Sort a collection of rocks (numbered with marker), nails, pennies, and a piece of glass (edges taped). Have children use the instruction card (rebus pictures for less independent readers). Read the instructions aloud before children begin. Have children make a chart for recording information. Classify a collection of rocks and defend groupings.
- *Art:* Use a collection of stones or rocks for a collage, creating stone animals, painting on rocks.

- *Mathematics:* Compare the weights of various rocks. Find the heaviest rock in the collection. Seriate several stones by weight.
- *Language Arts:* Make a collection of words or phrases that include the word *stone* or *rock.* Choose one rock, and write as many descriptive words as possible about it. After hearing a reading of *Everybody Needs a Rock* (Baylor 1974), write your own rules for selecting a rock. Find stories that involve rocks or stones (*Stone Soup* [Brown 1947]; "David and Goliath," *Nanny Goat and the Seven Little Kids* [Kimmell 1990]). Find information books about rocks and stones in the library.
- *Social Studies:* Discuss famous rocks (Plymouth Rock, the Rock of Gibraltar, Mount Rushmore, Stonehenge).

Movement:

Walk as if carrying a heavy rock; walk as if on deep gravel; walk as if on slippery rocks.

Evaluation:

The teacher will evaluate whether children's entries in the ABC book demonstrate knowledge and skills.

---

of emerging literacy, he would choose a meaningful context for helping children learn to recognize the sight words. These basic words (*boy, girl, I, ran, look,* and so forth) are common in children's writing and in the stories and poems that a teacher would use in the classroom. The teacher would use the words as they occurred naturally and help children recognize them in these contexts. Keeping good records of the children's work helps the teacher discuss the learning that is taking place and the reasons why the choice of instructional materials is important to the children's success.

The professional teacher of young children depends on assessment of program goals and the growth of individual children to make decisions about what instruction is most appropriate for them. Materials and programs must be carefully evaluated in terms of children's needs before they are used for instruction. Most goals can be reached by many routes; the teacher must choose the one that suits the children best.

DEVELOPMENTALLY
APPROPRIATE
PRACTICE

Reflect on plans for learning experiences for children. Review the framework for developmentally appropriate curriculum as you think about these questions:

- Can a teacher of young children purchase a curriculum that is developmentally appropriate? Why?
- Given what you know about developmentally appropriate practice, can a teacher plan the topics of study for the year before meeting the children? Why?
- Can a teacher incorporate the topics/goals of the school curriculum guide into a developmentally appropriate curriculum? Why?

- If a first-grade teacher wanted to study transportation with her students, would that be developmentally appropriate? If your answer is "no," under what conditions would the topic be appropriate? If "yes," explain why the topic is appropriate.
- What qualities make any topic of study developmentally appropriate?

SCHEDULING

One professional chore that helps the teacher manage the activities of the class in an appropriate manner is setting up the daily class schedule. Like room arrangements, furniture, and choices of areas, the schedule can be planned before the teacher knows the children, but plans should be made with the knowledge that the schedule will change to reflect the needs of the group and of individuals.

A schedule must allow children to move around and select materials and activities as easily as possible. In planning a schedule, the teacher should begin by noting any fixed times, such as the time the class can use the outdoor play area, lunchtime, or time with specialists (music, physical education, or art). The teacher should try to arrange for a large block of the time that is left to be a period in which children have a choice of activities and materials. Other activities that the teacher wants to include can then be added: a story time, a music time, a group time, and a snack time.

The time allotted for these activities will depend on the children's ages. Threes and fours need much shorter story and music times than older children and probably do not need group time at all. Fives and sixes can benefit from longer story and music times and from group time, as well. Teachers in primary grades experience more intrusions in their schedules (fixed recess periods, visits from various specialists, and so on), but they still have long periods of time during which they can schedule activities. One source of tension in planning any schedule for young children is attempting to balance large-group times and times for self-selected activities.

One purpose of a schedule is to provide routine and structure for children so that they know basically what to expect each day (Lund and Bos

1981). Another purpose is to provide balance in the day. For instance, activities in which children are relatively passive should not be scheduled back to back so that children have to sit quietly for long periods of time.

Table 4.2 shows samples of schedules for younger children and older children on half-day programs, a full-day program for kindergarten children, and a full-day schedule for primary-grade children. Note that none

Table 4.2	Schedules for Various Programs	
PROGRAM	TIMES	ACTIVITIES
Half-Day Program for Younger Children	9:00–10:00	Activity Time
	10:00–10:10	Music Time
	10:10–10:40	Outdoor Play
	10:40–11:00	Snack Time
	11:00–11:10	Quiet Time
	11:10–11:20	Movement Activities
	11:20–11:30	Story Time
Half-Day Program for Older Preschoolers	9:00–10:00	Activity Time
	10:00–10:20	Music and Movement
	10:20–10:40	Group Time (calendar, weather, discussions)
	10:40–11:00	Outdoor Play
	11:00–11:10	Snack
	11:10–11:30	Story, Poetry
Full-Day Kindergarten	9:00– 9:15	Opening, Singing, Planning for the Day
	9:15–10:15	Activity Time
	10:15–10:45	Snack
	10:45–11:15	Outdoor Play (gross motor play indoors in bad weather)
	11:15–11:45	Story Time, Literature Study
	11:45–12:30	Lunch and Recess
	12:30– 1:30	Rest Period
	1:30– 1:40	Group Time (discussions, planning for afternoon)
	1:40– 2:15	Activity Time
	2:15– 2:45	Library Music, Art, or Physical Education
	2:45– 3:00	Evaluations of Activities, Dismissal
Primary Children	9:00– 9:15	Opening, Singing, Planning for the Day
	9:15–10:30	Activity Time (theme activities)
	10:30–11:00	Physical Education
	11:00–11:30	Math Activities
	11:30–12:30	Lunch and Recess
	12:30– 1:00	Literature Activities (read aloud, drama)
	1:00– 2:00	Activity Time (theme studies)
	2:00– 2:20	Recess
	2:20– 2:45	Library (alternating with art or music specialists)
	2:45– 3:00	Sharing Events of Day, Discussions, Plans for Next Day, Dismissal

of these schedules includes time for cleanup or toileting. Teachers should involve children as much as possible in cleaning up the room and putting away materials before moving to other activities. Ideally, all rooms for early childhood programs should have bathrooms attached so that children can just go to the bathroom when they need to. Teachers in some older buildings (where this arrangement is often not the case) may have to arrange to take the class to the restrooms in groups. If possible, the teacher should send a few children at a time with an aide or volunteer while other children continue working.

Details of the Schedule

Activity Time

Experiences that are appropriate for children will be discussed in more detail in the content-area chapters (Chapters Seven through Twelve). Children usually participate in these experiences during activity times. For example, if the theme were a study of insects, children would work puzzles depicting insects in the manipulatives area; observe insects on display in the science area using a magnifying glass and record their observations; read (or look at pictures in) books about insects in the library; sort pictures of insects; examine sequence boards showing the life cycles of insects in the language arts area; and play with puppets and flannel board cutouts of insects in the language arts area. Children might paint or draw insects or build insect homes in the art area. Whatever the theme, it would be incorporated into as many content areas as possible and reasonable. Activity times are scheduled so that children can participate in small-group and individual activities.

Group Time

Some traditional group time experiences are not especially meaningful to children. As noted earlier, threes and fours probably do not need group time at all. Trying to get them to learn about the calendar is not the best use of their time. Fives and sixes can review the calendar and daily weather, but these should be *brief* reviews, not extended drills. Other activities appropriate for group time for fives and sixes include planning and evaluating their experiences during activity time, participating in some short group experiences (such as viewing a videotape that relates to a theme topic), listening to a resource person, discussing a problem in the room, having specific instruction in fire safety rules, and so on. Whole-group instruction is not an appropriate teaching strategy for content areas; lecturing on a topic to children of this age is of little value.

Group time with primary children may be used for some of the same activities as those suggested for fives and sixes. It may also be used to help children recognize the choices they can make for their theme studies and to do more formal planning of their day. Some limited group instruction with primary children is useful. For example, the teacher may teach the whole group to recognize story structure or to recognize particular strategies that an author has used in a story the children are reading. Group discussions of books the children are reading are also important. Likewise, having children present work they have completed can be a valuable component of group time in the primary grades.

Show-and-tell, or sharing, is often a regular part of group time, especially with five- to eight-year-olds. Show-and-tell often becomes "bring-and-brag," as children bring their newest toy to show off. The teacher usually controls the audience for the speaker and directs the children while they speak or ask questions. If sharing time is to achieve the goal of promoting more effective communication, however, teachers must structure the time so that children do the talking and organizing, rather than the teacher.

One technique is to have the sharing focus on the children's work, rather than on objects brought from home. Children may also need to share something especially meaningful to them from time to time, but not every child needs to share something every day. Another technique is to organize sharing time into small groups so that children share with three or four others and do not have to sit while twenty-five children share, one at a time. It is important to evaluate sharing experiences on the basis of what the children are actually learning, rather than simply to state that sharing is an important means of children learning to communicate more effectively.

Snack Time

Very young children need a snack during the morning or afternoon. Snack time should be considered a teaching time, as children learn about new foods, learn to carry on conversations, and learn how to help prepare and serve the snack. Snacks should always be nutritious and help children learn about good nutrition.

Snack time for fives and sixes can be quite time consuming in a half-day program when time is so limited. By the time all the children have washed their hands, been served, eaten their snacks, and cleaned up, twenty to thirty minutes out of a two-and-a-half-hour day have been used up. Therefore, some teachers prefer to have snacks available on a table, so that two or three children can serve themselves and then go back to their activities. Other teachers prefer to incorporate snack time into the activity time by making food preparation one of the activities. In this way, the activity time can be extended.

Transitions

Transitions
Periods of time between activities in the classroom.

Transitions from one activity to another are the most likely times for behavior problems or disruptions in any program. What can the teacher do when one or two children are ready to begin a new activity and the others are still cleaning up their work areas? Or what can the teacher do when the class is ready to go the cafeteria for lunch and the principal asks her to hold her class for exactly two more minutes? The teacher can have children who have completed their cleanup help others finish. Those who have finished can then sit in the group area and listen to a tape recording of nursery rhymes, folk songs, or fingerplays; others will join as they finish. With older children, one child can begin a rhyme, the second can say the next line, and so on; the last child can begin another rhyme.

When moving children from one area to another, the teacher should try having them move in groups by color or kind of clothing (all children wearing yellow, all children wearing sandals, and so on). Playing rhythms

Transition times present management challenges to teachers.

on a drum or piano also helps in moving children from one area to another; they can march around the room and then out the door to go outside or to the lunchroom. There are many memory games that children can play in line, such as Going on the Train, in which the first player takes something beginning with *a*, the second something beginning with *b*, and on through the alphabet. Children can also play guessing games, such as Twenty Questions or Who's in My Family? or they can listen to tapes of jokes or short pieces of poetry (Alger 1984).

The teacher should involve the children in solving transition problems. If it is time to go outdoors, the children might be asked to think of ways they can all get their coats without bumping into anyone or crowding. It is also helpful to have the activity that follows cleanup be something the children are anxious to do; dawdlers are not encouraged to finish their tasks when what they are going to do next is not exciting to them (Alger 1984).

Simplifying Routines

The routines of checking attendance, counting the children who will purchase milk, and so on can take up quite a lot of time. Some teachers choose to make these routines learning experiences for the children and as simple as possible for themselves. One way to check attendance is to have the children sign their names on a paper attached to a clipboard by the door. The teacher can see from the child's signature what he knows and is learning about writing.

Another technique is to divide a board in half, labeling one half "Present" and the other half "Absent." Nails or pegs are added below the label on each half, enough for all the children in the class. Each child is given a nametag with a hole in it, which he will hang on the board. As the children come in every day, they move their nametags from the "Absent" side to the "Present" side of the board. In preparation for the next day, the teacher reverses the "Present" and "Absent" headings.

Taking a count for milk can be accomplished by having each child who is purchasing milk place a marker with her name on it in a pocket marked "Milk." The same technique works for lunch counts.

Adapting the Schedule

For the first two weeks or so of school, the schedule may be adapted to help children make a more comfortable adjustment to school. Some schools have only half of the children assigned to each classroom come each day for the first week; the other half of the class comes to school the second week. This way, children have a chance to learn about school routines and get more attention from the teacher while they adjust. Some schools for younger children divide groups in half and ask each half to attend for half of each day for the first two or three weeks; other schools begin the year on a staggered schedule, so that there are five children the first two days, ten the next two days, and fifteen on the fifth day. Teachers should work with the administration and parents to make the beginning of school successful for all involved; sometimes, parents are willing to help more at the beginning to assure a good start for all children.

Teachers may also have to adapt schedules to fit the children's developing abilities. Children may not be able to sustain their play for as long as the teacher predicted at the beginning of school and may need two short play periods, rather than one long one. Children may need more rest than was predicted. They also may be able to engage in activities of their choice for longer than might have been predicted. Teachers, with input from the children, may need to adapt schedules to fit the individuals' needs.

Kindergarten: Half-Day, Full-Day, or Alternate-Day Programs

This section applies specifically to kindergarten because there is so much debate about the values of different schedules for kindergarten children. The schedule for threes and fours is generally either a morning or an afternoon session of about two-and-a-half or three hours, whereas schedules for primary grades are usually set to match the full-day elementary school schedule. Some schools have two sessions of kindergarten each day. Because of transportation problems and the need for full-day child care, some schools have adopted an alternate-day schedule, so that kindergartners attend for a full day but only on alternate days. Other schools provide full-day programs for some kindergartners, especially those deemed at risk of academic failure. What does the research say about these different schedule patterns?

The research yields no conclusive results. Jalongo (1986) explains how difficult it is to control all the factors when trying to determine what is best for young children. Obviously, no child can attend a half-day program and an alternate-day program at the same time, so the effects of different schedules on the same population of children cannot be studied. Other factors involved in assessing what type of schedule works best include the skills of the teacher and the maturation and self-esteem of the children. To find that a group attending a half-day program scored more highly on an achievement test than a group attending an alternate-day program would not be especially useful because of all the confounding factors. One study (Gullo et al. 1986) did attempt to control for all the variables and found that children in all-day programs scored higher on achievement tests than children from half-day or alternate-day programs. The only significant difference in the social behaviors of children in these groups, according to teachers, was that children who attended alternate-day programs showed fewer negative behaviors. These findings are certainly not conclusive.

When evaluating schedules, the best approach is to determine what is best for the children involved, to plan for excellent experiences no matter when the children are in school, and to evaluate continuously. A full-day program that involves children in inappropriate activities is not beneficial to children, even though they are there longer than children in half- or alternate-day programs. Decisions should not be made on the basis of convenience; rather, the guideline should be to provide optimal environments for children.

Other Scheduling Issues

An ongoing problem for kindergarten and primary teachers is *pull-out programs,* in which children are removed from class at certain times for special lessons or activities, such as speech therapy. Removing children from the group makes it difficult to schedule large-group activities and also complicates having all children participate in small-group or individual activities.

One solution to the problem, which is being used in an ever-increasing number of schools, is to have the special teachers come to the regular classroom to work with individual students, rather than have the students go to the teachers. In schools in which this solution has not yet been implemented, the regular classroom teachers might approach the special teachers with the idea and agree to help solve any problems that arise. If this solution is not applied and pull-out programs remain a fact of life, regular classroom teachers should try to arrange activity time for that part of the day when the most children will be in the room. Classroom teachers should also try to work with the schedules of the special teachers in order to achieve a more reasonable day for the class. Regardless, there does not seem to be an easy solution to the problem of pull-out programs.

PROGRAM ASSESSMENT

When teachers evaluate an early childhood program, they are looking for evidence that the program is appropriate for the children enrolled and that it is effective in bringing about their growth. The following questions will help teachers evaluate their programs:

1. Would you like to be a child in your classroom?
2. Is there a balance of small-group, whole-group, and individual activities?
3. Do children spend more time in self-selected activities than in teacher-directed activities?
4. Do the children's interests influence activities and learning experiences?
5. Does every child find success and challenge every day?
6. Is there a balance of emphasis on intellectual, social, emotional, and physical growth?
7. Are skills taught in a meaningful context?
8. Can children withdraw from activities without penalty?
9. Are activities and experiences selected on the basis of their relationship to the goals of the program?
10. When planning activities, is the information from observations and assessments used to guide planning?
11. Do individual children show evidence of growth?
12. Are interactions with parents supportive of children's growth?

Answers to these questions will be derived from evaluating the schedule, the lesson plans, and the instructional materials and observations of interpersonal relationships in the classroom. A teacher who respects children's interests will not determine a list of topics to be studied before getting to know the children. (This is not to imply that a teacher cannot make tentative plans for topics he predicts will be of interest to the children.) Further, in a good program, materials will be readily available to help children learn a variety of facts and skills in a playful manner. Finally, other evidence that the program is a good one is found in the attitudes of the children. If they see themselves as active learners who seek support for their own learning, rather than waiting for the teacher to tell them everything to do, the program is effective.

If you are interested in reviewing a much more detailed evaluation of a program, consult the *Accreditation Criteria and Procedures of the National Academy of Early Childhood Programs* (NAEYC 1984).

CHAPTER SUMMARY

- *Curriculum* can be defined in many ways: as a program, as a written plan for learning experiences, as a syllabus listing topics and sequences of topics, or as everything that happens at school. In this chapter, *curriculum* was defined as the written plan for learning experiences.
- The steps in planning a curriculum include determining the purpose of the curriculum, analyzing the options that are available, selecting the features to be included, producing the design, and evaluating the design.
- Teachers developing a curriculum must select content and sequence activities so that children can use the information they have already learned to learn new information.
- Assessment of a curriculum must be appropriate for the age and level of development of the children and for the activity.
- A curriculum can be organized around facts, skills, subjects, themes, key concepts, or common human needs.
- A thematic organization of a curriculum provides learning opportunities that are not divided into segments and that better match children's learning experiences outside the school setting.
- In selecting a theme, the teacher must consider relevance, opportunities for application of skills, availability of resources, his own interests, and the time of year.

- Evaluation of themes and experiences is necessary. One technique is to record on charts the curriculum goals met by a theme and the goals met by the activities in which each child actually participated.
- A learning plan differs from a typical lesson plan in that a learning plan encompasses much more than one lesson. It may specify a variety of activities, long-term goals, theme goals, and short-term goals.
- When teachers are faced with mandated goals, they must use their professional judgment in meeting those goals and must document children's progress very carefully.
- A schedule is designed to offer children the security of routine and to add structure to the day. Teachers must create schedules that contribute to meeting the goals of the program.
- Findings of research on the effects of half-day, alternate-day, or full-day kindergarten programs have not been conclusive. Much depends on the goals and objectives of the program and the actual experiences of the children while at school.
- Teachers must evaluate the progress of individual children; they must also evaluate the program itself. Important areas for evaluation include teacher-child relationships, the opportunities for children to make choices, and the balance of activities provided for the children.

WHAT WOULD YOU DO?

Reflect on your reading and your own experiences as you think about how you would respond in the following situations:

1. Your principal is used to seeing lesson plan books, with the days of the week in rows down the page and the subject areas in columns across the page. You want to produce learning plans instead. How would you explain this choice to your principal?
2. A friend of yours tells you how much she enjoys teaching the theme "teddy bears" each year.

    Would you agree that "teddy bears" is an appropriate thematic choice?
3. All the children seem really interested in the topic "plants" except Noah. He wants to learn about the chemistry of mixing sparklers. What would you ask Noah to do?
4. You find that other teachers in your school believe that every child ought to learn exactly

the same facts and that it is unfair to let some children learn different information. How would you feel about every child learning the same information?

5. A paper-and-pencil activity is described as "active learning" by one of your peers. If you disagreed, what criteria would you use for evaluating activities in terms of active learning?

THEORY INTO PRACTICE

1. Examine a brochure for a preschool or a curriculum guide for a primary grade. Determine the long-term goals of the program. Choose one of the goals, and list two or three content topics that might help to meet those goals.

2. Develop a list of possible themes for a given age group that meet the criteria listed in this chapter.

Compare your list with those of others in your group.

3. Write a learning plan for a given group of children.

4. As a group, develop a theme around one of the topics on Katz and Chard's list (1989, pp. 65–66; see p. 114 in this book).

RECOMMENDED FOR FURTHER READING

Brown, Janet F., ed. *Curriculum Planning for Young Children.* Washington, DC: National Association for the Education of Young Children, 1982.

This is a collection of articles that deal with curriculum topics for young children. Sections focus on the value of play, communication, and the child's explorations of the world. The selections are easy to read and have practical implications for beginning or inexperienced teachers.

Katz, Lilian G., and Sylvia C. Chard. *Engaging Children's Minds: The Project Approach.* Norwood, NJ: Ablex, 1989.

In describing the project approach, Katz and Chard offer enough detail for the novice teacher or the experi-

enced teacher eager to try a more wholistic curriculum organization in implementing projects. They provide examples of suitable projects, steps for getting started in the project method, and ideas for evaluating progress.

Schwartz, Sydney L., and Helen F. Robison. *Designing Curriculum for Early Childhood.* Boston: Allyn and Bacon, 1982.

The authors of this text discuss the influences of philosophy on the design of curriculum and include prototypes of curricula in science and math, music and art, and language and beginning reading. The discussions of the advantages and disadvantages of organizing the curriculum in various ways are especially useful.

REFERENCES

Aardema, Verna. *Why Mosquitoes Buzz in People's Ears.* New York: Scholastic, 1975.

Alger, Harriet A. "Transitions: Alternatives to Manipulative Management Techniques." *Young Children* 39 (September 1984): 16–26.

Baylor, Byrd. *Everybody Needs a Rock.* New York: Atheneum, 1974.

Baylor, Byrd. *Desert Voices.* New York: Charles Scribner's Sons, 1981.

Bredekamp, Sue, ed. *Developmentally Appropriate Practice in Early Childhood Programs Serving Children*

From Birth Through Age 8. Washington, DC: National Association for the Education of Young Children, 1986.

Bredekamp, Sue, and Teresa Rosegrant. *Reaching Potentials: Appropriate Curriculum and Assessment for Young Children,* Vol. 1. Washington, DC: National Association for the Education of Young Children, 1992.

Brown, Marcia. *Stone Soup.* New York: Macmillan, 1947.

Bruner, Jerome. *The Process of Education.* New York: Vintage Books, 1960.

Dewey, John. *The Child and the Curriculum.* Chicago: University of Chicago Press, 1902.

Elkind, David. "Child Development and Early Childhood Education: Where Do We Stand Today?" In *Curriculum Planning for Young Children,* edited by Janet Brown, 4–11. Washington, DC: National Association for the Education of Young Children, 1982.

Gullo, Dominic F., Carol U. Bersani, Douglas H. Clements, and Kathleen M. Ramsey. "A Comparative Study of 'All-Day,' 'Alternate-Day,' and 'Half-Day' Kindergarten Schedules: Effects on Achievement and Classroom Social Behaviors." *Journal of Research in Childhood Education* 1 (1986): 87–94.

Jacobs, Heidi Hayes, ed. *Interdisciplinary Curriculum: Design and Implementation.* Washington, DC: Association for Supervision and Curriculum Development, 1989.

Jalongo, Mary Renck. "What Is Happening to Kindergarten?" *Childhood Education* (January 1986): 154–160.

Katz, Lilian G., and Sylvia C. Chard. *Engaging Children's Minds: The Project Approach.* Norwood, NJ: Ablex, 1989.

Kimmell, Eric A. *Nanny Goat and the Seven Little Kids.* New York: Holiday House, 1990.

Kraus, Ruth. *The Carrot Seed.* New York: Harper and Row, 1945.

Lund, Kathryn A., and Candace S. Bos. "Orchestrating the Preschool Classroom: The Daily Schedule." *Teaching Exceptional Children* 14 (December 1981): 120–125.

National Association for the Education of Young Children. *Accreditation Criteria and Procedures of the National Academy of Early Childhood Programs.* Washington, DC: NAEYC, 1984.

Schwartz, Sydney, and Helen F. Robison. *Designing Curriculum for Early Childhood.* Boston: Allyn and Bacon, 1982.

Chapter Five

Play

Learning at Its Best

This morning, you are on your way to visit a local kindergarten to observe young children in a classroom setting. When you get there, you find that it is a warm and welcoming place and that the teacher is glad to have you visit. As you begin your observation, you see several children putting on costumes and pretending they are grown-ups. One child is playing the father, one the mother, and several pretend to be children in the family. When another child wants to join the group, she is asked to be the doctor for the sick child. You notice that several children have constructed a block structure in another part of the room. Another child is building a smaller structure without displaying much interest in the group structure. At a nearby table, three children are working with puzzles. Each child has a puzzle, and although the children are talking to each other about a variety of topics, each is completing his puzzle individually.

When the children go outside, there is more rough-and-tumble play than you expected. Many of the children spend most of their time in "chase" and "war" play. A few children dig in the garden and play in the sandbox, which is what you had expected to see.

You have many questions about the activities you have observed: Why does the teacher encourage play in the classroom? What are the children learning as they play? What is the purpose of play activities in the children's development? How are these play activities related to academic curriculum goals? You also wonder how the parents feel about their children "just playing" at school. The purpose of this chapter is to answer some of these questions and to help you make informed decisions about play in the school settings for which you will be responsible.

• •

Teachers, parents, and administrators need continued support in their efforts to include play in the curriculum and to defend its use to those not as knowledgeable in early childhood education. Almy (1984) has published statements in several sources about the child's right to play. She writes that the distinguishing characteristics of play make it essential to the child's development. She believes that adults must provide opportunities for children to play and to learn from observations and actions as well as from being told things.

In a position paper approved by the Association for Childhood Education International (ACEI), Isenberg and Quisenberry (1988) state that "play—a dynamic, active and constructive behavior—is a necessary and integral part of childhood, infancy through adolescence." The ACEI also asserts that teachers must take the lead in articulating the need for play in children's lives, including as part of the school curriculum.

DEFINING AND DESCRIBING PLAY

Play in a school setting can be described on a continuum that runs from free play to guided play to directed play. *Free play* can be defined as play in which children have as many choices of materials as possible and in which they can choose how to use the materials (within bounds, of course; for example, they cannot hit others with the blocks). *Guided play* is defined as play in which the teacher has selected materials from which the children may choose in order to discover specific concepts. If the goal is to learn to classify objects as large or small, then the teacher will provide several sets of objects to play with that could be classified as such. *Directed play* is play in which the teacher instructs the children how to accomplish a specific task. Singing songs, engaging in fingerplays, and playing circle games are examples of directed play (Bergen 1988).

Levels of Play

Social Play

Teachers who observe children playing will notice several different levels of involvement with other children in play episodes. In her classic study, Parten (1932) describes these levels as *solitary, onlooker, parallel, associative,* and *cooperative* play. Table 5.1 summarizes Parten's descriptions of levels of social play.

Table 5.1	Levels of Social Play
LEVEL	**DESCRIPTION**
Solitary Play	Play in which children play without regard for what other children around them are doing. A child may be constructing a tower with blocks and be completely oblivious to what other children in the room are doing.
Onlooker Play	Play in which the child who is playing individually is simultaneously observing those playing in the same area. The child may be talking to peers. Children who watch other children play may alter their own play behavior after watching. Children engaged in onlooker play may seem to be sitting passively while children around them are playing, but they are very alert to the action around them.
Parallel Play	Play in which several children are playing with the same materials, but each is playing independently. What one child does is not dependent on what others do. Children working puzzles are usually engaged in parallel play. They usually talk to each other, but if one leaves the table, the others continue playing.
Associative Play	Play in which several children play together but in a loosely organized fashion. Several children might decide to play "monsters," for example, and run around the playground, chasing each other. But there are no definite roles, and if one child does not run and chase, the others can continue to play.
Cooperative Play	Play in which each child accepts a designated role and is dependent on the others for achieving the goals of the play. When children want to play "store," for instance, one child must accept the role of store clerk and others must be shoppers. If a child refuses to play unless she can be the storekeeper, the play episode will end.

Source: Based on Parten 1932.

Children of different ages exhibit different levels of social play. Very young children are not cognitively capable of assuming different roles and playing cooperatively. They do not possess enough information about roles or enough social skills to work together for a single purpose. Older children do not engage in cooperative play exclusively. They may engage in any of the levels of play; they simply have a much broader repertoire of possible play behaviors.

Play with Objects

Practice play
Play in which the player explores the nature of objects or materials with no other play goals.

There are levels of play with objects as well as levels of social play. Piaget (1962) and Piaget and Inhelder (1969) have described different types of play with objects, including practice play, symbolic play, games with rules, and games of construction. **Practice play,** or functional play, is play in which children explore the possibilities of materials. For instance, children using dominoes in practice play would stack them and stand them on end. After playing with the dominoes for some time, children might begin to use them *symbolically.* They would use a domino to represent something else. Perhaps they would make a corral of blocks and pretend that the dominoes were cattle in the corral.

In a *game with rules,* children might play according to rules they have made up themselves or according to the rules that are generally agreed on for playing the game. If the children were playing with dominoes, for example, they might decide that the rules were to match all the ends but not play the doubles across; if they know the conventional rules for playing dominoes and keeping score, they might follow those rules instead. Anyone who has ever tried to play a game with rules (such as Candyland or Concentration) with a three- or four-year-old knows that a child this age will usually play the way she wants to and that following the rules is almost impossible.

Games of construction are described by Piaget as growing out of symbolic play "but tend later to constitute genuine adaptations (mechanical constructions, etc.) or solutions to problems and intelligent creations" (Piaget and Inhelder 1969, p. 59). Levels of object play depend on the children's maturity and experience. Even adults often participate in practice play when presented with novel objects. As children mature, they become more capable of using materials symbolically and of playing a game with accepted rules.

Sociodramatic Play

Sociodramatic play
Play in which children assume roles and act out episodes, such as putting a baby to bed.

Sociodramatic play is of particular interest to researchers. Smilansky (1971) has studied sociodramatic play and methods for facilitating such play and observed that it has the following elements:

1. Imitative role play. *The child undertakes a make-believe role and expresses it in imitative action and/or verbalization.*
2. Make-believe in regard to objects. *Movements or verbal declarations are substituted for real objects.*
3. Make-believe in regard to actions and situations. *Verbal descriptions are substituted for actions and situations.*
4. Persistence. *The child persists in a play episode for at least ten minutes.*
5. Interaction. *There are at least two players interacting in the framework of the play episode.*
6. Verbal communication. *There is some verbal interaction related to the play episode. (pp. 41–42)*

Sociodramatic play is especially important in the development of creativity, intellectual growth, and social skills. Not all children will have had experience with sociodramatic play. Therefore, teachers may need to assume more responsibility in fostering such play with these children. Teachers can look carefully for the elements of sociodramatic play and encourage it by intervening and helping children achieve any missing elements.

The ability to take on the role of another person and to shift perspective are important basic skills for academic learning. For some children, sociodramatic play occurs if time is allowed for it; for others, the teacher may have to be much more involved to get children to participate. This can be accomplished by providing time and often props to get children started in sociodramatic play. The dramatic play area or housekeeping center are often settings that encourage sociodramatic play by providing costumes, furniture, and other props. If children have ideas about play themes, the teacher can help them carry out these ideas by providing needed props.

Teachers might consider asking parents to help them collect materials that could be used for any number of play situations. Materials for given situations might then be stored in individual boxes so that they are available when the children's interests dictate use. Such boxes might include materials for playing "repair person," "beauty shop," "office," and so on. Myhre (1993) suggests prop boxes containing materials to recreate a bakery, a flower shop, and a beach party, as well as a jewelry and accessory box and "dentist," "police," and "firefighter" boxes.

In addition to providing time and props, the teacher might have to model appropriate play behavior for children with little or no experience in sociodramatic play. He may have to assume a role and play it for a few minutes, at least long enough to demonstrate the behavior so that children will understand and be able to perform the behavior themselves. The teacher might also suggest roles others could play or ask questions to get the children started on a play episode. The line between assisting children and dominating play is a fine one. Teachers must develop skills in listening to and responding to children, following their lead, rather than imposing their ideas about what children should be playing.

Finally, teachers should look for opportunities to encourage sociodramatic play that stems from real events in children's lives. For example, suppose one of the children has been in the hospital. When she returns to school and tells of her experience, the children will likely be anxious to play "being in the hospital." The teacher might ask some questions to help the children think about what they need to play "hospital" and then help them find appropriate props, such as clipboards to use for patient charts, stethoscopes, boxes for furniture, and so on.

Roles in Play

Role of the Child

Children in free-play situations choose to become involved in the play, are active in their involvement, can suspend reality, have no extrinsic goals for their activities, and bring their own meaning to the play (Spodek, Saracho, and Davis 1987).

Play Is Personally Motivated   In order for an activity to be called *play*, the player must choose to participate. If a child chooses an activity, it is usually play, although what is being done may appear to be work. For example, a child may load up a wheelbarrow with sand, move it across the playground to a new sandbox, and dump it. Similarly, children often "work" for hours gathering materials and building forts. The difference between play and work is that a play activity is self-chosen: The child controls how long she will participate and defines the goals of the activity. If an adult assigns the task, he has control of the goals and the time frame; therefore, even if the child has fun doing it, the task is not play. Play is always pleasurable to the participants. The feelings may be satisfaction with achieving internal goals or the pure joy of running freely. The player experiences pleasure in play.

Play Is Active   All play experiences require some active involvement on the part of the player. Play is *not* a passive activity, such as watching television, although play does not require active physical involvement. Children are playing when they participate in a "tea party" or investigate the hardness of rocks. Children playing are engaged in thinking, organizing, planning, and interacting with the environment. If the involvement is passive, then the activity is probably not play.

Play Is Often Nonliteral   Children at play can suspend reality, usually with the magic words "let's pretend." Time, setting, and characters involved in play can be negotiated at the moment and are not tied to reality. They need not even be possible; children might pretend to fly, to be from outer space, or to be monsters.

Play Has No Extrinsic Goals   Suppose a child is arranging and re-arranging a set of letters on a magnetic board. If this task has been assigned for the purpose of helping her learn alphabetical order, it is not play. If the child is arranging the letters to suit goals that are her own, then it is play. In playing, the process, or means, not the end result, is most important. The *outcome* of play is not as important as the *participation* in it.

Players Supply Meaning to Play   Children sometimes explore or use materials in ways specified by others, but when they play, they provide their own interpretations for materials. A child might use base 10 blocks to build models of numbers if directed to do so by an adult. But if allowed to use the materials freely during another portion of the day, the child might use the blocks to build houses or roads.

Play Has No Extrinsic Rules   If an activity is to be considered play, the players must be able to alter the rules of the activity as needed. In a game of tag, for example, the players negotiate where the "safe" areas will be. Similarly, children playing with blocks may establish rules about spaces for building, but these rules are negotiated by the players.

Role of the Teacher

The role of the teacher in play within the classroom setting is very important. The teacher must be an observer, an elaborator, a model, an evaluator, and a planner of play (Bjorkland 1978).

In *observing*, the teacher should watch children's interactions with other children and with objects. He should observe the length of time that children can maintain play episodes, and he should look for any children who have trouble playing or joining play groups. These observations should then be used in planning additional play experiences, in making decisions about whether to enter play situations, and in making assessments of the play of individual children. In a review of studies concerning the effects of the physical environment on children's behavior in preschool settings, Phyfe-Perkins (1980) concludes that if a setting is to provide support for developmentally appropriate activities, the teacher must engage in systematic observation of children at play.

Another aspect of the teacher's role is that of *elaborator*. If the children are playing "going to the hairdresser," the teacher might help them collect items that could be used to represent those found at a hairdresser's shop. She might find photographs or magazine illustrations that would help the children construct a beauty salon. The teacher might even join in the play briefly and ask questions that would guide the children in thinking through their roles or their conceptions of a trip to the hairdresser. If older children were involved in a study of insects, the teacher might supply a film or videotape of insects so that the children could recreate insect movement or sounds in their play.

Teachers who value play will often *model* appropriate behaviors in play situations. For instance, a teacher may choose to sit in the block area for a brief time and join children in building in order to model ways in which the blocks might be used. Or she might choose to join dramatic play in order to model behaviors that are useful in entering a play group and responses that are useful for helping play continue. Sometimes, the teacher might model play behaviors that will get a play episode started or back on track if it has gone in a direction she considers negative. For example, children playing characters from a television program might begin to chase and catch each other rather aimlessly. The teacher might ask some questions about the purposes of the characters and demonstrate how a character might handle interactions without running and chasing inside the room.

As an *evaluator* of play, the teacher has to be a careful observer and diagnostician to determine how different play incidents serve the needs of individual children and what learning is taking place as children participate in play. It is the teacher's job to recognize the academic, social, cognitive, and physical growth that takes place during play and to be able to communicate these changes to parents and administrators. Evaluation means that materials, environments, and activities must be carefully considered in light of the curriculum goals, and changes must be made if needed.

Finally, the teacher has to serve as a *planner*. Planning involves all the learning that results from observing, elaborating, and evaluating. The teacher must plan for new experiences that will encourage or extend children's interests in topics. For example, a parent who was a shoe clerk could come to the classroom to share her occupation. She might measure the children's feet and demonstrate that part of her job is to show the customers several choices of shoes in the proper sizes and to help them try on shoes. In planning to continue the children's obvious interest, the teacher might do several things: gather a collection of many kinds of shoes, find a rack suitable for storing them, borrow several of the instruments used for measuring feet, and so on. The teacher's careful planning will result in days of active play involvement by the children, as they arrange chairs to make a shoe store, write up sales, and bag shoes to send home with the "customers." The teacher can encourage the children to talk about the different kinds of shoes and who wears them, to draw shoes, to create signs for their shoe store, and even to write stories about shoes. When the children tire of the shoes and no longer demonstrate interest in playing with them, the shoes should be removed. By that time, the teacher will have already planned other experiences that will pique the interest of the children and can be extended in play.

DEVELOPMENT OF PLAY BEHAVIORS

The play of infants is *sensorimotor:* They explore objects and people and investigate the effects of their actions on these objects and people. At about the end of the first year, children begin to exhibit play behaviors such as pretending to eat or sleep (Rubin, Fein, and Vanderberg 1983). They are also able to begin playful interactions with others, such as playing peek-a-boo.

Preschoolers engage in practice play, but as they mature, the time spent in exploring new objects decreases drastically (Ellis 1979). Only about 15 percent of the play of six-year-olds is practice play. Most of the play of older preschoolers can be labeled *constructive play:* play involving building or making something (Rubin, Fein, and Vanderberg 1983). Children may build things at any of the levels of social play. The objects are usually used in symbolic games or games with rules.

The play of preschoolers is very vigorous. They like to chase each other, especially in "superhero" play. (See Kostelnik, Whiren, and Stein 1986 for some specific strategies for managing "superhero" play.) As children mature, they are able to play without materials that resemble the real objects; older preschoolers can pretend that they have whatever they need. Children also grow more able to assume the roles of characters outside their families. Three-year-olds can play family roles; older preschoolers begin to play characters from the larger community. Pretend play for five-year-olds is very intense and may incorporate children's knowledge of story characters or employ their developing literacy skills (Garvey 1977).

As children move into the elementary years, sociodramatic play decreases considerably. Games with rules tend to dominate the play of children moving into the concrete operational years (six or seven to ten or twelve), and pretend play becomes less acceptable, except in more formalized versions such as theater. Play becomes more competitive and based on language or academic skills.

PURPOSES OF PLAY

Play contributes to cognitive growth, aids social and emotional development, and is essential to physical development. Many of the abilities required to succeed in school settings are gained through play experiences. Eheart and Leavitt (1985) state that play offers young children opportunities "to master many fundamental physical, social, and intellectual skills and concepts" (p. 18). Other researchers have come to similar conclusions about both younger and primary-age children (Garvey 1977; Sylva, Bruner, and Genova 1976).

Intellectual Development

Both exploratory play—play in which the child has no objective other than exploration—and rule-governed play—play in which the child has objectives such as finding solutions to problems or determining cause and effect—contribute to cognitive growth. *Cognitive growth* is defined as an increase in the child's basic store of knowledge (Lunzer 1959); it occurs as a result of experiences with objects and people (Piaget 1952). Many studies support the positive relationship between play experiences and the development of children's cognitive abilities. Cognitive abilities include identifying, classifying, sequencing, observing, discriminating, making predictions, drawing conclusions, comparing, and determining cause-and-effect relationships. These intellectual abilities underlie children's success in all academic areas.

Play helps children develop organizing and problem-solving abilities. Children playing must think about organizing materials in order to meet their play goals. For example, a child who wants to play "visiting the doctor" must decide where the doctor's office and the waiting room will be, what will be used for a stethoscope, and so on. Children must also organize tasks, deciding how to move and arrange materials so that they can play. Some of these organization tasks require very fine discriminations, such as sorting by size, shape, or color. Children playing must also think about the other players involved. Older children playing the roles of characters in books they have read must think about the roles being assumed by other players and take those into consideration when creating their own roles.

Children playing are often engaged in problem-solving behavior. They might experiment with adding water to sand to make it the proper consistency for holding its shape when molded, or they might search the room to find suitable materials for something needed in play. Children playing "going on the bus," for example, might look for things to use for seats and

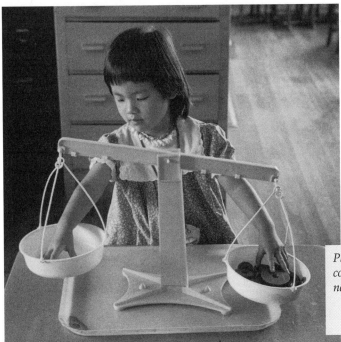

Play helps children develop the concept knowledge and skills necessary for academic success.

perhaps something to be the steering wheel of the bus. They might also look for props to serve as tickets and baggage. They might find old purses in the dress-up area to be suitcases or a pie pan to be the steering wheel.

Because they will also need people to participate as passengers, the children playing "going on the bus" will have to solve the problem of how to persuade enough other children to join the play. Sylva, Bruner, and Genova (1976) found that children who played with materials were as capable of solving a problem as children for whom the solution had been demonstrated. Children who play with materials are more likely to assume that there are many possible solutions to a problem and to continue trying to solve a problem longer than children for whom a solution has been demonstrated. Older children as well as younger ones are actively engaged in problem solving when they attempt to create a structure to match the image they plan. For example, children learning about triangles might build structures supported with triangles and test their strength; children learning about hexagons might build dodecahedrons from Popsicle sticks.

Children at play certainly demonstrate creative thinking and creative problem solving. During play, children must put together information from previous experience, from the real world, and from other play participants. Frank (1968) concludes that play "is a way of learning by trial and error to cope with the actual world" (p. 436).

Social and Emotional Development

Egocentric thought patterns
Thought patterns in which the individual fails to consider the viewpoints of others.

In the Piagetian view, play pushes children out of **egocentric thought patterns** (Piaget 1962). That is, children in play situations are forced to consider the viewpoints of their playmates and therefore become less egocentric. If Susan and Juan are pretending to cook dinner, each may have definite ideas about how the task should be done. They will each have to accommodate the other's thinking in order to continue their play. Children learn to cooperate to achieve some group goals during play. They also have opportunities during play to learn to delay their own gratification for a few minutes—for instance, while someone else finishes playing with a drum.

Children often play out their fears and concerns. One study reports the reactions of a group of children after they witnessed an accident on their playground and describes how they worked out stress through their play (Brown, Curry, and Tittnich 1971). Children in different age groups (threes, fours, and fives) incorporated the accident into their play differently, but each group revealed some fear and tried to relieve it through "hospital" play or other play involving someone being injured. In another instance, children who had experienced a tornado played various forms of "hiding from the tornado" or "the tornado is coming" for a long time after the experience. Barnett (1984) found that children who were anxious showed reduced anxiety after enacting their fears in play episodes.

Although most teachers are not trained to be play therapists, they can be aware of how children explore different emotions (anger, sadness, and so on) and different social roles in their play. For example, children might "try on" the role of "bully" in a play situation; after they get feedback about how other people react to them in that role, they can alter their behavior.

Physical Development

Children achieve both fine and gross motor control through their play. They can practice all the gross motor skills of running, jumping, and hopping while playing. Children at play can be encouraged to lift, carry, and walk or hop, spin, and move in response to rhythms. They can also practice fine motor skills as they string beads, fit together puzzles, hammer nails into wood, or paint at easels.

Not only young children need active play; older children should participate in this type play, too. They can throw, catch, kick, bat, balance on two-wheel bikes, and skate. Today's children often spend a great deal of time in passive behavior, such as watching television or videos. These children especially need to have the chance to climb, swing, pull, push, run, hop, jump, and walk in order to gain control of their bodies.

PLAY IN THE SCHOOL SETTING

Play at school usually differs from play at home in several ways. Generally, there are larger numbers of children in play groups at school than in play groups at home. The materials at school are often different from those at home; only a few children would have access to unit blocks or easels for painting at home. Toys and play materials also differ in the degree to which they must be shared. In a large group, children must learn to work cooperatively with others.

Play is often more restricted at school than at home. Play activities at school tend to be more guided and more closely observed. Teachers are more likely to plan specific ways of enhancing play than are most parents. For example, if the teacher observes a group of children attempting to build a space rocket, he may collect materials from around the room, such as boxes or paints, that will assist the children in achieving their goals. He may also find books in the library, pictures of spacecraft, or filmstrips or videotapes to extend the play to other activities.

Teachers will select play experiences that match the goals of the program. If program goals emphasize discovery, then free play is most appropriate. If objectives require children to explore concepts, then guided play is most appropriate. Finally, directed play experiences are best if the teacher wants children to demonstrate specific skills. In learning concepts about sound, a child in a free-play situation might discover that he can produce sound by striking a surface. The alert teacher would help the child verbalize his discovery and continue to explore sounds, if he still showed interest. Guided play would be appropriate for teaching children the concept that the pitch of sound varies with the length and size of the string that is vibrated. The teacher might display cigar boxes with rubber bands of various lengths and thicknesses stretched over them. Whenever a child expressed interest in these materials, he would be encouraged to discover the differences in sounds produced by the various rubber bands. In directed play, the teacher might have the children listen to sounds produced by various instruments and indicate with hand movements the changes in pitch.

Van Hoorn et al. (1993) describe play at school as instrumental or illicit. *Instrumental play* is that which the teacher plans and encourages, such as the sociodramatic scenarios of playing "hospital" and "shoe store," described earlier. *Illicit play* is not sanctioned and may even be expressly forbidden by the teacher. Examples of illicit play include children creating guns from Tinker Toys or passing secret notes behind the teacher's back. Although such play may make the teacher uncomfortable, Sutton-Smith (1988) reminds us that it also contributes to a child's developing social skills.

Should illicit play be banned from early childhood classrooms? There are no clear-cut answers to this question. Teachers who try to ban play with weapons, such as "war," realize that children find ways to engage in these activities anyway, which creates more tension and management problems. On the other hand, some educators believe that "war" play stimulates children to believe that violence is an acceptable means of solving problems. "Sociopoliticalists argue that war play and war toys glamorize fighting and killing, promote excessive materialism, and foster unnecessary aggression" (Isenberg and Jalongo 1993, p. 246).

Some teachers recommend redirecting "war" play or "superhero" play to focus on the positive things that soldiers or heroes can do, such as saving people who are trapped by natural disasters or building hospitals to help people who are hurt. Teachers must also help children learn to solve their everyday conflicts peacefully (Rogers and Sharapan 1991). Parents should be involved in making decisions about how to handle "war" toys and other types of violent play in the classroom so that teachers will have their understanding and support.

Play in the Primary Classroom

Most teachers are aware that play is much more acceptable in classrooms of preschoolers and kindergartners than it is in classrooms of primary-grade children. The expectation that only serious learning should take place in primary classrooms is prevalent among parents and also among some teachers. Others believe, however, that play can be serious learning for primary-grade children. Granted, the play of first- and second-graders does not look that like of preschoolers and kindergartners; nonetheless, many play experiences are appropriate for primary-age children.

For example, children in the primary grades enjoy exploring and building with various materials, creating new machines from old parts, inventing toys, building robots and models, and working out basic physics problems (such as dropping different materials from different heights and measuring the speeds with which they fall). Activities for primary-grade children usually must be based on the children's special interests in order to generate enthusiastic participation, which is not so much the case with preschoolers.

Wasserman (1992) tells stories of the Wright brothers and Frank Lloyd Wright and their early play experiences, "messing about." Sadly, these ingenious and productive individuals, who contributed so much to our knowledge and our lives, often had to stay out of school in order to indulge their curiosities and play. Wasserman asserts that "messing about" is essential for developing children's creative-thinking and problem-solving skills. Teachers should encourage children to discover and explore what really fascinates them.

Primary children are also interested in games with rules and enjoy learning to play a variety of board games. Although this type of play may not provide as many opportunities for exploring problems and creating solutions as "messing about," playing board games can help children develop social and communication skills.

Benefits of Play at School

Play that aids children in their development can be achieved at school if teachers provide time, space, materials, and sanction for play activities. Obviously, children need time to plan and carry out play episodes if they are to develop knowledge and skills in play. No child can get organized and complete a satisfying block construction in the ten minutes allotted to play in some classrooms. Christie, Johnson, and Peckover (1988) and Christie and Wardle (1992) found that the play patterns of children in longer play periods were more mature than those of children in shorter play periods. Space and materials are also prerequisites for productive play. Materials such as sand, water, blocks, and paint take up large amounts of space. Teachers may have to arrange the classroom so that the same space is used for different activities during the day.

Sanctioning play is important, as children will pick up subtle hints from the teacher that play is important or not important. One way for the teacher to make sure the children feel that play is important is to join in the play. It is a real art to know when and how to join in without disrupting the play or changing it to meet adult definitions of appropriate play. Other ways a teacher might indicate that play is important are to talk about play when children evaluate their day and to share the products of play. Often,

DEVELOPMENTALLY
APPROPRIATE
PRACTICE

Reflect on the importance of play in a developmentally appropriate classroom:

- How does play contribute to a developmentally appropriate program?
- Would it be possible to have a DAP classroom without play? Why?
- Would it be possible to have a play session that was not developmentally appropriate? Why?
- If play is important in developmentally appropriate practice, what are the most effective

means of facilitating it?
- Does all play contribute to DAP? What about rough-and-tumble play? solitary play? Explain your answers.
- What aspects of play that are developmentally appropriate for eight-year-olds that would not be appropriate for four-year-olds? Why?

teachers share and display only the products of work activities, such as drawings or pieces of writing; as a result, children come to believe that play is unimportant in comparison. To validate the importance of play, a teacher might take photographs of block constructions or of children discovering the attributes of water and share these along with artwork and stories.

As children gain experience and maturity, play in the classroom should reflect changes in the children. Children of different ages and different developmental levels use materials in different ways, so teachers must be alert in providing materials that will challenge the children to develop more in their play. For example, if the housekeeping center for five-year-olds is exactly the same as that for four-year-olds, play in that area by five-year-olds may stagnate. It is the responsibility of the teacher to add materials that will stimulate new play or allow children to play out their fantasies.

Selecting Materials for Play

Teachers have many choices when selecting materials for play. *Open-ended materials*—those that allow multiple outcomes and unique uses in each encounter—are the most useful. Such materials may be fluid materials that have no inherent structure, such as sand and water, or structured materials, such as various forms of blocks. Blocks, sand, and water do not have built-in functions that limit the possible outcomes of playing with them. Therefore, they are conducive to creative thinking and problem solving in children.

Children playing with blocks can create structures that represent their own understandings of the real world or that represent their fantasy worlds. Players can reproduce known structures or design totally new ones; they can control the outcomes and determine when the structure is

Providing time and materials for children's play is an important responsibility of the teacher.

complete without fear that it will be criticized or rejected. Players with blocks are free to make discoveries about the relationships among the block shapes and sizes and about the physics of stacking blocks. These children can experience the aesthetic pleasure of the feel of blocks and the symmetry of their constructions.

Children playing with sand and water are free to explore the properties of the materials and to learn how the materials respond under different conditions. They are in charge of the outcomes and derive satisfaction from playing to meet their own goals. Sand and water allow for individual experimentation and also group interactions. Children using sand and water establish their own goals and feel satisfaction when those goals are met.

Materials that allow children to make play choices and allow multiple outcomes are necessary for the best play environments. Many materials can be considered open ended if it is possible for children to use them in different ways. For example, teachers might supply rollers, boxes, balls, and targets that will help children develop concepts in physical science (Kamii and DeVries 1978). These materials are open ended to the extent that children have choices in exploring the arrangements and outcomes that can be achieved with them. Many commercial materials, on the other hand, are limited in terms of what children are able to do with them, providing only one or two options. When dollars for purchasing materials are limited, open-ended materials are the best investment.

Play as a Teaching Strategy

Teachers have a choice when deciding how to present information or new concepts to children. Some information must be presented in a teacher-directed format. For example, safety rules, such as those about fire, cannot be explored; they must be stated firmly. But generally speaking, telling is the least successful strategy for presenting information to young children. Even the young child can repeat words or phrases, but verbal responses only indicate that she has learned the words; such responses do not measure the child's understanding at all.

Teaching strategies
Methods of presenting instruction, such as demonstrations, lectures, or simulations.

Play is one of the **teaching strategies** available to teachers as they plan for children's learning. The following examples illustrate goals that could readily be achieved through play:

- To encourage children to learn about appropriate clothes for the weather, provide many different pieces of clothing in the dress-up area.
- To encourage children to learn how to create secondary colors, provide paints in primary colors.
- To encourage children to demonstrate the ability to classify, provide leaves, shells, keys, buttons, and models of farm and zoo animals.
- To encourage children to learn the characteristics of three-dimensional shapes, provide the shapes in boxes, geoblocks, and regular building blocks.
- To encourage children to learn about water erosion on land forms, provide water in containers (so that the flow can be varied) in the sandbox or gardening area.

Using play experiences as teaching strategies requires that the teacher observe how children use materials and that he ask questions to guide children's thinking and reflections. Sutton-Smith (1986) reminds us that "although we use play in various ways in the classroom for our own purposes, we need to remember that the children have purposes of their own, and need to deal with purposes largely by themselves (even if under distant supervision), making use of this vital and universal kind of communication [play]" (p. 13). Teachers can make plans for play experiences, but children's needs must be honored and they must be allowed to use play for their own learning.

Teachers have many opportunities to plan environments and materials so that learning goals can be achieved in playful activities. Observations of children at play will help teachers choose other play materials that will help children learn concepts and clarify and extend their understandings. Selecting guided play as a teaching strategy does not imply that play is assigned; it means that careful thought is put into the selection of materials and intervention in children's play. A teacher might put out an assortment of materials that she expects will invite children to explore a new concept. If children do not learn the concept from interacting with the materials, then the teacher must choose other materials or select a different approach. Assigning a child to complete a task means that he no longer has a choice and that the teacher has chosen a strategy other than play.

Communicating the Benefits of Play

Teachers have an obligation to explain to parents and administrators the benefits of the time children spend playing during the schoolday. Teachers are and should be accountable for children's learning. Part of that responsibility is to be able to provide specific information about individual children and their play experiences. The following section applies specifically to assessment of play; a more comprehensive discussion of assessment is included in Chapter Fourteen.

One form of data to be shared is the *anecdotal record*. With this type of record keeping, the teacher or another adult records the child's behavior and verbalizations for a brief period of time. Judgments about the child's intentions or motivations should be clearly labeled as such in the record and distinguished from descriptions of the child's overt behaviors. At the end of the day, these notes are placed in the child's file. Over a period of time, the notes should reveal some patterns that will help the teacher talk to others about the child's growth through play. For example, the teacher might have noted that Jennifer played alone with the blocks and made horizontal patterns with them. A few weeks later, an observer might note that Jennifer had started to use vertical patterns along with the horizontal ones. Later, Jennifer might be seen building a vertical structure with a friend. Still later, she might build a vertical and symmetrical structure. An observer might note that Jennifer had talked about her building before she began the construction and completed a structure that matched her plans. These records would clearly reveal Jennifer's growth in building more complex structures and in planning her activities.

Another technique for recording play is to record where the children are in the classroom at given time intervals. For example, every ten minutes, the teacher or an adult records on a grid which children are playing with blocks, in dramatic play, in art, or in reading. Over time, these records reveal children's patterns of choice and, in combination with anecdotal records, can be very useful in planning other activities. Figure 5.1 is an example of such a record.

A third technique is to keep several records scattered through the room. As an adult observes a child engaged in particular behavior, he notes it on the record. For example, the following behaviors might be listed across the top of the form: "Completes puzzles with ten pieces," "Strings beads in a pattern," "Plays cooperatively with at least two other children," and so on. The children's names are listed down the side of the form. Whenever a child is observed completing a puzzle with ten pieces, the date

---

FIGURE 5.1   Time-Activity Record

Date ___4/17___

	9:00	9:10	9:20
Unit blocks	Sara Carlos Hillary Jason	Sara Hillary Brian Michael	Sara Michael Brad Gretchen
Easels	Cheri Karen Phil Juanita	Dolores Cheri Juanita Jason	
Clay			
Dress-up			

is recorded on the form. Such records are helpful because they offer flexibility in selecting what to look for in observations and make it quick and easy to record information. Figure 5.2 is an example of such a record.

Finally, teachers can keep samples of products from some play activities. Selected paintings, for instance, can be kept in a file for comparison with previous artwork. Obviously, it is impossible to keep samples of block constructions or sand play. Some efforts of these activities can be recorded in photographs, but most will have to be described in anecdotal records. As children talk about their experiences each day, the teacher can record some of their own evaluations. The teacher will also want to add to the child's file her own insights and interpretations of the child's play.

Before a teacher can share what children are learning in play experiences, he must be actively involved while the children are playing. If the teacher is busy doing other tasks while the children are playing, he will

FIGURE 5.2   Sample Record of Behavior

	Completes puzzles with 10 pieces	Strings beads in a pattern	Plays cooperatively/ at least 2 others	
Geoffrey				
Judith				
Leslie				
Michael				

miss chances for observations and insights. One cannot share what one hasn't seen or heard; therefore, play time is a very busy time for the teacher of young children.

PLAY AND ACADEMIC LEARNING

Sometimes observers of young children think that children will not learn academic skills if they spend their time playing. The truth is that play contributes to the development of academic ability. Children who are ordering objects by length or size in free-play situations, learning rhymes and chants in directed play, or exploring rhythms or constructing with Legos in guided play are all involved in activities that contribute to reading ability. Reading is a complex process that involves eye coordination, visual and auditory discrimination, and the cognitive ability to work with parts of wholes. Play is an important means of developing such abilities. Collier (1983) found that play assists the development of representational skills and the formation of the symbolic foundations that are necessary for reading.

One of the most important goals in reading instruction for young children is oral language development. During play, children have a chance to talk, argue, explain, and persuade as well as to use language in imaginative ways. Also, children engaging in pretend play grow more able to take on the perspectives of others. They practice visual discrimination skills as they sort, classify, and compare objects in the classroom. They practice auditory discrimination as they listen to others, explore sounds made by a variety of materials, and engage in musical play. Some children will want to create stories at the puppet stage, others will want to make books related to their play, and still others will want to create signs or messages as part of their play. Pellegrini (1980) found that children's play was a better predictor of success in some aspects of reading and language achievement than IQ or socioeconomic status.

The development of beginning science skills is easy to observe in play situations. Children are observing, making predictions, gathering data, and testing hypotheses. For example, children constructing with blocks are learning about physics as they experience practical applications of stress, mass, and weight. They can also explore ramps and gears and the operation of simple machines. They learn about earth science as they play in the sand and observe the weather. They learn about biology as they observe classroom animals and their life cycles. They learn about chemistry as they mix colors in water and observe the melting of snow and the effects of salt on ice. Children working at easels are engaged in scientific investigation as they experiment with various consistencies of paint and the results obtained with different paints and papers.

Abilities in mathematics are also developed when children play. Children may use two half-unit blocks to fill a space left by removing one unit block from their construction. They learn about set theory as they group objects such as wooden cubes or buttons. They learn about geometry as they explore various shapes in planes or in three-dimensional forms. They learn about topology as they construct with blocks. Children playing have many opportunities to sort, group, and classify. They also learn to use mathematics to solve problems: How many places should be set at the table? How many forks are needed if we need one for each plate? Children engaged in play have opportunities to explore the mathematical relationships in their environment. Curiosity, divergent thinking, and motivation to learn are vital for success in math and science, and these traits are best fostered through play (Henniger 1987).

Writing requires fine motor development; therefore, any activity that contributes to developing control of the fine muscles is useful in writing. Children can paint, cut, work puzzles, build with Legos, manipulate clay, and use various kinds of pens, crayons, and pencils for developing the control needed to make letters. Writing itself can be a part of many play activities, as children write notes to each other, make signs to enhance their buildings, and write menus or tickets as part of play. These examples illustrate the support for academic learning that is provided by play. Many of the activities contribute to learning in several different subject-matter areas. For example, sorting and seriating contribute to abilities in reading, mathematics, and science. Play has multiple outcomes.

Primary-age children engaged in project work can be involved in play experiences that will help them consolidate their learning and explore possibilities in given topics. Children learning about seeds can sort, group, and classify seeds; pretend to be sprouting seeds; create board games with facts about seeds; create models of seeds from clay or other materials; paint seeds; use seeds in counting and other mathematics activities; and so forth. Play should not be limited to the preschool years, as it is also an important tool for teaching children in the primary grades.

OUTDOOR PLAY

Outdoor play offers children the same opportunities for growth as indoor play. And to be productive, outdoor play requires the same planning, observation, and evaluation as indoor play.

Outdoor and indoor play offer similar benefits to children in terms of physical activity; an added bonus of outdoor play is that it includes large muscle activity, which is usually restricted indoors. Gross motor activities such as running, jumping, rolling, pushing, and hopping should not only be available to children but encouraged. To encourage outdoor play, the teacher may need to use some of the same strategies that she would use to encourage any kind of indoor play. Recording and celebrating outdoor play activities, perhaps through photographs or video recordings, may be one means of promoting them. For instance, the first time a child is able to hang by her knees on the bars is certainly an event worth celebrating. Providing props that encourage dramatic play outdoors, such as old boats or cars on playgrounds, is another effective means of encouraging children to play outside.

A definitive advantage of outdoor play over indoor play is that the rules for voice levels and physical exuberance can be relaxed. When playing outdoors, children can shout without being reprimanded and they can run, dance, and climb without damaging equipment or endangering others. Of course, rules that ensure children's safety and provide for cooperation among them are still needed for outdoor play. In most settings, children are allowed to play outdoors only in groups, and outdoor play times are set by the teacher.

Careful observation of children engaging in outdoor play will reveal many examples of problem solving. Children planting seeds might try to determine how deep is "shallow" or "3 inches deep." The child riding a tricycle down a slope might try to determine what speed is fast enough to raise her level of excitement but not so fast that the tricycle will go out of control. A group of children might try to persuade several more children to play Treasure Island. Children playing "race car" might try several methods before they successfully attach a steering wheel so that it can turn. None of these problem-solving skills is enhanced solely by outdoor play, but it is important to be aware that outdoor play is more than children just running off excess energy. Curriculum areas enhanced by outdoor play are summarized in Table 5.2 (Frost and Wortham 1988).

Children's social skills can be observed in play outdoors as well as indoors. Teachers will find it interesting to observe which children are able to organize peers to play games or participate in other activities. Children's developing roles as leaders and followers may be evident in these situations. Some children may need the teacher's guidance in learning and applying strategies for joining groups at play and for learning to share equipment outdoors.

Many indoor activities can be brought outdoors, given the right materials. For example, children might set up easels and paint pictures outdoors, or they might use water to "paint" buildings and sidewalks, using big brushes that encourage large, sweeping strokes. Children might enjoy block building outdoors when provided with large plastic or weatherproof

Table 5.2	Play and Curriculum			
COMMUNICATION	COGNITIVE DEVELOPMENT	MOTOR DEVELOPMENT	FINE ARTS	SOCIAL/EMOTIONAL DEVELOPMENT
PVC pipe telephone system	Sand play	Wheeled vehicles	Chalkboard	Sharing materials
Cooperative planning	Water play	Super-structure with many motor options	Clay	Planning activities
Group dramatic play	Gardening	Sliding	Fingerpaint	Testing abilities
Organized games	Building with tools	Swinging	Musical games	Playing out frustrations
	Weather awareness	Running	Musical instruments	
		Balancing	Textures	
			Dramatization	

Source: Joe L. Frost and Sue C. Wortham, "The Evolution of American Playgrounds," *Young Children* 43 (July 1988): 25. Used with permission of NAEYC.

blocks, ramps, ladders, and other equipment. Such materials lend themselves to building structures that are large enough to get inside.

Although teachers of young children often discourage or forbid rough-and-tumble play because they believe it turns into negative or aggressive behavior, research reveals that such play is age related. Specifically, the incidence of rough-and-tumble play increases as children move from preschool into kindergarten and the primary years and then decreases as children reach middle childhood (Kostelnik, Stein, Whiren, and Soderman 1993). Other research shows that children who are typically rejected by their peers are more likely to misinterpret rough-and-tumble play and to participate aggressively. Popular children, on the other hand, are more likely to participate in a playful, unaggressive manner (Pellegrini and Boyd 1993). Teachers should be aware that rough-and-tumble play is developmental in children's play lives. When such play becomes aggressive, teachers should intervene and help children modify inappropriate behavior.

Ideally, children should be able to play either indoors or out. However, lack of supervision and the fact that few schools have outdoor play areas connected to classrooms make such choices difficult.

CHILDREN WITH SPECIAL NEEDS

Planning play experiences for children with special needs may mean structuring the physical environment so that participation is possible. For example, a child in a wheelchair cannot use blocks if the blocks are on the floor. A child who is visually impaired might need more tactile clues attached to play materials; a child who is hearing impaired might need help communicating in some play situations. These adaptations of the physical environment are relatively easy to make. Planning play experiences for other children may require much more than physically rearranging or adjusting the materials to be used.

The play of children with developmental delays may be more similar to that of younger children than to that of age peers. Some children with developmental delays may not be able to participate in cooperative play or to negotiate the rules of a play situation with other children. Some children

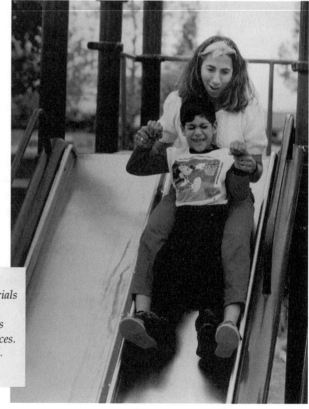

Some adaptations in the environment and in materials may be necessary to help children with special needs benefit from play experiences.

need specific guidance in play skills. For example, they may lack the social skills necessary for joining a play group or for sharing materials (Combs and Arezzo-Slaby 1977).

However, children can be taught specific play skills (Peck et al. 1978). Cole (1986) compared the effects of direct verbal instruction, modeling, and withdrawal of intervention in promoting play skills in children with and without disabilities. He found that withdrawal of intervention was the most effective approach to promoting play skills in children with and without disabilities. He also found that withdrawal of intervention was most effective in promoting play skills and that persistent teacher intervention had negative effects. In other words, letting children teach each other seems to be more effective than intervening. Some researchers have found that motor development can also be fostered through play programs (Roswal and Frith 1980).

Gunsberg (1989) reports that contingency play that is structured by a simple, repetitive format is very effective with young children who have been abused or neglected. With this approach, the teacher responds to the child's actions so that the child can become attached to an adult and trust the adult to respond. For example, if the child covers her head, the adult plays peek-a-boo; if the child claps her hands, the adult plays pat-a-cake. These are the kinds of play routines that most children normally experience with caregivers. In addition to fostering feelings of attachment, the goals of contingency play include helping children control their impulses, helping them feel more effective in relationships, and motivating them to initiate and sustain play.

Children who are gifted also need special planning to make their play experiences appropriate. These children may be more socially advanced and more physically active than their age peers (Barnett and Fiscella 1985). They need play experiences that help them relate to their age peers and give up some of their need for perfection (Roeper 1987). Helping children who are gifted use some of the products of their play for other learning experiences is one way for the teacher to indicate that play is respected. For example, a child who invents a vehicle from odds and ends on the junk table might be challenged to think of ways to use the vehicle or to write about it.

Teachers who appreciate the benefits of play for children will strive to involve children with special needs in play by making whatever adjustments seem necessary in the play environment and by planning specific instruction in play skills for those who need guidance.

CHAPTER SUMMARY

- Play in the school setting can be defined on a continuum that runs from free play to guided play to directed play. *Free play* is defined as behavior that is personally motivated, active, and pleasurable and that has no extrinsic goals or rules that cannot be negotiated by the players; free play is often nonliteral, and players bring their own meaning to the play experience. *Guided play* is play in which the teacher has selected materials from which the children may choose in order to discover specific concepts. *Directed play* is play in which the teacher instructs the children in how to accomplish specific tasks.
- Play contributes to the development of gross and fine motor skills, to cognitive growth, and to social and emotional development. In playing, children strengthen many problem-solving abilities, learn to express emotions in socially acceptable ways, and learn the social skills necessary for success in groups.
- Play can be described in terms of how the player interacts with other people. Play can be solitary play, onlooker play, parallel play, associative play, and cooperative play.
- Observers of children's play have noted developmental trends in play behaviors. Younger children exhibit much more exploratory play, preschoolers engage in sociodramatic play and constructive play, and elementary-age children

- are most likely to be involved in games with rules.
- Play in a school setting and play at home usually differ in terms of the guidance offered, materials available, and number of children involved in the play situations.
- Play contributes to academic achievement. Teachers who are concerned with academic success do not have to force children to give up play in order to gain abilities in math, science, and reading.
- Teachers have a very complex role in children's play. Teachers must observe, plan, and evaluate play experiences. They must also plan learning experiences that are best achieved through play. Finally, they must learn to communicate the benefits of children's play to parents and administrators.
- Carefully planned outdoor play experiences can provide many of the same benefits of indoor play and often allow more freedom for children than play indoors.
- Planning play experiences for children with special needs may include adapting the physical environment; special instruction in play skills may also be necessary. Children who are developmentally delayed may exhibit play behaviors that are typical of much younger children.

WHAT WOULD YOU DO?

Reflect on your reading and your own experiences with young children as you think about how you would respond in the following situations:

1. A child brings a toy to school that is a model of a violent movie character; it speaks lines from the movie, which are followed by shooting sounds. What would you say or do?
2. Your second-graders seem to lose all control when you allow time for play. How would you handle their play?

3. One child in your class of four-year-olds never plays. What would you do to involve her in play?
4. A parent tells you that her child has plenty of time to play at home and that she does not want him playing at school. How would you respond to the parent?

THEORY INTO PRACTICE

1. Observe the play of three-year-olds, five-year-olds, and seven-year-olds. Record the play behaviors in the categories that Parten used (1932; see Table 5.1 in this book). Among the different age groups, do you observe differences in the number of categories of play and the amount of time spent in each category? Explain your answer.

2. Construct a chart for recording where children play in a classroom at different times of the day. Record the number and sexes of the children in each area at five-minute intervals for a thirty-minute period. How might you use this information to change the physical environment or the materials available for play?

3. Observe one preschool child for a thirty-minute play period. Make a list of the intellectual, social, emotional, and physical developments that you observe (for example, learning a concept, learning to share, learning to assume the role of another person, and so on).

4. Plan a play experience that would help children learn a specific concept.

5. Observe children playing outdoors. What are the most common activities you observe? Can you identify differences in outdoor play and indoor play? If so, what? Do the playground and the equipment and materials available limit or encourage the play? How?

RECOMMENDED FOR FURTHER READING

Bergen, Doris, ed. *Play as a Medium for Learning and Development: A Handbook of Theory and Practice.* Portsmouth, NH: Heinemann, 1987.

This is a fine collection of essays and articles by well-known play researchers. One of the sections, "Play as a Curricular Tool," is especially useful for those wanting more information about implementing theory in the classroom. There are also excellent chapters on planning play environments for infants and toddlers, preschoolers, and children in elementary school.

Caplan, Frank, and Theresa Caplan. *The Power of Play.* Garden City, NY: Anchor Press/Doubleday, 1973.

In this book, the authors discuss play as a source of learning, physical development, and personality development. They include information about the contributions of toy manufacturers and pioneers in the study of play.

Fein, Greta, and Mary Rivkin, eds. *The Young Child at Play: Reviews of Research.* Vol. 4. Washington, DC: National Association for the Education of Young Children, 1986.

This book, a collection of essays and research studies on the play of young children, was written for the practicing teacher and is very readable. Topics include the effects of play on language development, play environments, and the play of boys and girls.

Frost, Joe L., and Barry L. Klein. *Children's Play and Playgrounds.* Boston: Allyn and Bacon, 1979.

The authors discuss children's play and the contributions of play to children's development. There are descriptions of various types of playgrounds and discussions of playground designs. The chapter on playgrounds for children with disabilities is especially interesting. Many photographs illustrate the various elements of playgrounds.

Garvey, Catherine. *Play.* Cambridge, MA: Harvard University Press, 1977.

This is a basic book that defines play and then discusses play with objects, play with language, play with rules, and ritualized play. It is a good source of basic information.

Isenberg, Joan P., and Mary Renck Jalongo. *Creative Expression and Play in the Early Childhood Curriculum.* New York: Macmillan, 1993.

The title of this book reflects the reality that creative expression and play are closely related. The authors discuss ways of infusing creative activities and play into the content of the curriculum, assessing children through such activities, and communicating with parents. Many practical ideas are offered for teachers.

McCracken, J. B. *Play Is FUNdamental: How Teachers Can Help Encourage Children's Play.* NAEYC 576.

Washington, DC: National Association for the Education of Young Children.

This brochure defines play, explains the benefits of play, provides suggestions for planning play experiences, and encourages caretakers and parents to increase the involvement of children in play. A question-and-answer section entitled "Questions Facing Parents" answers questions about toys, superhero play, play with guns, watching television, using computers, and rules for play.

Van Hoorn, Judith, Patricia Nourot, Barbara Scales, and Keith Alward. *Play at the Center of the Curriculum.* New York: Macmillan, 1993.

Based on the belief that play is the core of developmentally appropriate practice, the authors offer a theoretical discussion of play that is understandable and then provide suggestions for designing a curriculum that is playful. Included are ideas for play in mathematics, literacy, science, and art as well as chapters on assessment and implementing a play curriculum.

REFERENCES

Almy, Millie. "A Child's Right to Play." *Childhood Education* 60 (May/June 1984): 350.

Barnett, Lynn A. "Research Note: Young Children's Resolution of Distress through Play." *Journal of Child Psychology and Psychiatry and Allied Disciplines* 25 (1984): 477–483.

Barnett, Lynn A., and Joan Fiscella. "A Child by Any Other Name: A Comparison of the Playfulness of Gifted and Nongifted Children." *Gifted Child Quarterly* 29 (1985): 61–66.

Bergen, Doris. "Using a Schema for Play and Learning." In *Play as a Medium for Learning and Development,* edited by D. Bergen, 169–180. Portsmouth, NH: Heinemann, 1988.

Bjorkland, Gail. *Planning for Play: A Developmental Approach.* Columbus, OH: Merrill, 1978.

Brown, Nancy, Nancy Curry, and Ethel Tittnich. "How Groups of Children Deal with Common Stress through Play." In *Play: The Child Strives Toward Self-Realization,* edited by G. Engstrom, 26–38. Washington, DC: National Association for the Education of Young Children, 1971.

Christie, James F., and Francis Wardle. "How Much Time Is Needed for Play?" *Young Children* 47 (March 1992): 28–32.

Christie, James F., E. Peter Johnson, and Roger B. Peckover. "The Effects of Play Period Duration on Children's Play Patterns." *Journal of Research in Childhood Education* 3 (1988): 123–131.

Cole, David A. "Facilitating Play in Children's Peer Relationships: Are We Having Fun Yet?" *American Educational Research Journal* 23 (1986): 201–215.

Collier, Robert G. "Reading, Thinking, and Play: A Child's Search for Meaning." In *Claremont Reading Conference 47th Yearbook,* edited by Malcolm P. Douglas. Claremont, CA: Claremont Reading Conference, 1983.

Combs, M. L., and D. Arezzo-Slaby. "Social Skills Training with Children." In *Advances in Clinical Child Psychology,* edited by B. B. Lahey and A. E. Kazdin, 161–201. New York: Plenum, 1977.

Eheart, B., and R. Leavitt. "Supporting Toddler Play." *Young Children* 40 (March 1985): 18–22.

Ellis, M. "The Complexity of Objects and Peers." In *Play and Learning,* edited by Brian Sutton-Smith. New York: Gardner Press, 1979.

"Environment." In *Current Topics in Early Childhood Education,* vol. 3, edited by L. Katz et al. Norwood, NJ: Ablex, 1980.

Frank, Lawrence K. "Play Is Valid." *Childhood Education* 44 (March 1968): 433–440.

Frost, Joe L., and Sue C. Wortham. "The Evolution of American Playgrounds." *Young Children* 43 (July 1988): 19–28.

Garvey, Catherine. *Play.* Cambridge, MA: Harvard University Press, 1977.

Gunsberg, Andrew. "Empowering Young Abused and Neglected Children through Contingency Play." *Childhood Education* 66 (1989): 8–10.

Henniger, Michael. "Learning Mathematics and Science through Play." *Childhood Education* 63 (1987): 167–171.

Isenberg, Joan P., and Mary Renck Jalongo. *Creative Expression and Play in the Early Childhood Curriculum.* New York: Macmillan, 1993.

Isenberg, Joan, and Nancy Quisenberry. "Play: A Necessity for All Children." *Childhood Education* 64 (February 1988): 138–145.

Kamii, Constance, and Rheta DeVries. *Physical Knowledge in Preschool Education: Implications of Piaget's Theory.* Englewood Cliffs, NJ: Prentice-Hall, 1978.

Kostelnik, Marjorie, Alice P. Whiren, and Laura Stein. "Living with He-Man: Managing Superhero Fantasy Play." *Young Children* 41 (1986): 3–9.

Kostelnik, Marjorie, Laura Stein, Alice P. Whiren, and Karen Soderman. *Guiding Children's Social Development.* 2d ed. New York: Delmar, 1993.

Lunzer, E. "Intellectual Development in the Play of Young Children." *Educational Review* 11 (1959): 205–217.

Myhre, Susan. "Enhancing Your Dramatic-Play Area Through the Use of Prop Boxes." *Young Children* 48 (July 1993): 6–11.

Parten, Mildred B. "Social Participation Among Preschool Children." *Journal of Abnormal and Social Psychology* 27 (July/September 1932): 243–269.

Peck, Charles A., Tony Apolloni, Thomas P. Cooke, and Sharon A. Raver. "Teaching Retarded Preschoolers to Imitate the Free-Play Behavior of Nonretarded Classmates: Trained and Generalized Effects." *Journal of Special Education* 12 (Summer 1978): 195–207.

Pellegrini, Anthony D., and Brenda Boyd. "The Role of Play in Early Childhood Development and Education: Issues in Definitions and Function." In *Handbook of Research on the Education of Young Children,* edited by Bernard Spodek, 105–121. New York: Macmillan, 1993.

Pellegrini, Anthony D. "The Relationship Between Kindergartners' Play and Achievement in Prereading, Language and Writing." *Psychology in the Schools* 17 (October 1980): 530–535.

Phyfe-Perkins, Elizabeth. "Children's Behavior in Preschool Settings: A Review of Research Concerning the Influence of the Physical Environment." In *Current Topics in Early Childhood Education,* vol. 3, edited by L. Katz et al. Norwood, NJ: Ablex, 1980.

Piaget, Jean. *The Origins of Intelligence in Children.* New York: International Universities Press, 1952.

Piaget, Jean. *Play, Dreams and Imitation in Childhood.* New York: W. W. Norton, 1962.

Piaget, Jean, and Barbel Inhelder. *The Psychology of the Child.* New York: Basic Books, 1969.

Roeper, Annemarie. "Play and Gifted Children." In *Play as a Medium for Learning and Development,* edited by D. Bergen, 163–165. Portsmouth, NH: Heinemann, 1987.

Rogers, Fred, and Hedda B. Sharapan. "Helping Parents, Teachers, and Caregivers Deal with Children's Concerns About War." *Young Children* 46 (March 1991): 12–13.

Roswal, Glenn, and Greg H. Frith. "The Children's Developmental Play Program: Physical Activity Designed to Facilitate the Growth and Development of Mildly Handicapped Children." *Education and Training of the Mentally Retarded* 15 (December 1980): 322–324.

Rubin, K., G. Fein, and B. Vanderberg. "Play." In *Carmichael's Manual of Child Psychology: Social Development,* edited by E. Hetherington. New York: Wiley, 1983.

Smilansky, Sara. "Can Adults Facilitate Play in Children? Theoretical and Practical Considerations." In *Play: The Child Strives Toward Self-Realization,* edited by G. Engstrom, 39–50. Washington, DC: National Association for the Education of Young Children, 1971.

Spodek, Bernard, Olivia N. Saracho, and Michael D. Davis. *Foundations of Early Childhood Education: Teaching Three-, Four-, and Five-Year-Olds.* Englewood Cliffs, NJ: Prentice-Hall, 1987.

Sutton-Smith, Brian. "The Spirit of Play." In *The Young Child at Play: Reviews of Research,* vol. 4, edited by Greta Fein and Mary Rivkin, 3–13. Washington, DC: National Association for the Education of Young Children, 1986.

Sutton-Smith, Brian. "The Struggle Between Sacred Play and Festive Play." In *Play as a Medium for Learning and Development,* edited by Doris Bergen. Portsmouth, NH: Heinemann, 1988.

Sylva, Kathy, Jerome S. Bruner, and Paul Genova. "The Role of Play in the Problem-Solving of Children 3–5 Years Old." In *Play: Its Role in Development and Evolution,* edited by Jerome S. Bruner, Alison Jolly, and Kathy Sylva, 244–257. New York: Basic Books, 1976.

Van Hoorn, Judith, Patricia Nourot, Barbara Scales, and Keith Alward. *Play at the Center of the Curriculum.* New York: Macmillan, 1993.

Wasserman, Selma. "Serious Play in the Classroom." *Childhood Education* 68 (Spring 1992): 132–139.

Chapter Six

Language
Celebrating the Magic

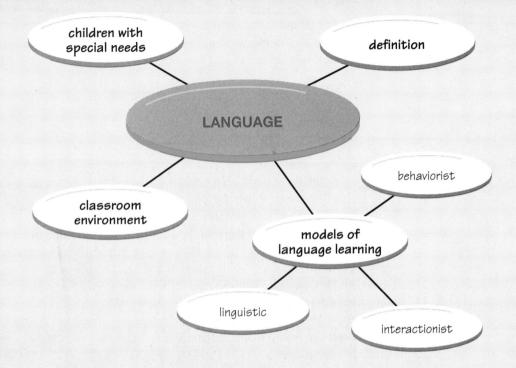

This morning, you visited a nursery school to observe the children's language development. You recorded the speech of three children and found that although they were all four years old, they used language quite differently. One child enunciated words clearly and seemed to have an extensive vocabulary. You noted that his conversation included the words *planetarium* and *Tyrannosaurus rex*. Another child of the same age smiled at the other children, but in the half-hour that you observed, she said nothing. The third child used language to persuade another child to let him have a doll and told a story about his baby sister taking his train the night before.

When you returned to class, you found that your classmates had similar experiences. Those who observed in primary grades also found great variation in children's language use. Some children could tell long, involved stories in which events were sequenced correctly; others seemed not to understand the vocabulary used in instruction in their class-rooms. Some children seemed to be unwilling to initiate conversations with adults but talked freely with peers on the playground.

Given these observations, you now have questions about how teachers assess children's language and how children use language in various situations.

• •

One of the most exciting moments in parenting is when Baby says that first word—when he puts together sounds that communicate meaning. Parents share that moment with all who are close or can be reached by telephone, and the word is dutifully recorded in the baby book.

One of the characteristics that makes us human is our language, which gives us the ability to share with others our ideas, thoughts, dreams, discoveries, and knowledge. That children achieve the ability to communicate so rapidly and seemingly so effortlessly is a marvel to all who observe the process. The ability to communicate with others is learned so rapidly that it almost seems magical. Come celebrate this magic, the wonderful world of children's language.

Two premises underlie this chapter and should be kept in mind as you read. One is the belief, articulated by Goodman et al. (1987), that language is not acquired externally but rather is part of a process of personal development and emerges in the context of social use (p. 38). That is not to say that language is not present in the child's environment but that learning language is a more complex process than simply adopting language that is outside oneself. Therefore, in this chapter, the term that will be used to describe the learning of language is *language development* rather than *language acquisition*. The other premise underlying the chapter is that oral and sign languages are not developed in isolation; they are always related to cognitive development and to the development of other language abilities. One cannot separate spoken or sign language and written language. Each system of language contributes to learning language; one does not precede the other.

DEFINITION OF LANGUAGE

For the purposes of this chapter, *language* is defined as a system of communication used by humans, which is either produced orally or by sign and that can be extended to its written form. Language also has characteristics that define it further. One characteristic is that language is rule governed. For instance, all languages have rules that determine the order in which words occur in sentences. These rules are learned intuitively by speakers of the language; only speakers who make a scientific study of the language are likely to be able to verbalize these rules. An example of one such rule in English is that adjectives usually precede nouns (*white house*); in Spanish, however, adjectives usually follow nouns (*casa blanca*).

Another characteristic of language is that it is arbitrary. There are no logical connections between the sounds that we use to label objects and the objects themselves. Social groups merely agree to use a particular combination of sounds to represent an object. Actually, very few words sound like what they represent, such as *buzz* or *hiss*. Words like *table, chair, bottle,* and so on have no logical connections with their referents.

Language is also changing. New words are constantly entering our lexicon, and others are being discarded. Meanings, too, are changing. With a little thought, you could probably list thirty or forty words that have been added to the English language within the last five years and ten or so that have changed meaning. Even young children use technological words that did not exist a generation ago, such as *CD (compact disc)* and *joystick,* as common vocabulary words.

LANGUAGE SYSTEMS

Every language is a set of systems: phonology, morphology, syntax, semantics, and pragmatics. *Phonology* is the system of sounds that make up the language; it includes the sounds that are used to make words, the rules for combining the sounds, and the stress and intonation patterns that help to communicate meaning. Different languages use different sounds and allow different combinations of sounds in words. In some languages, for instance, words can begin with the "ng" sound, but not in English. The task of the child is to learn to distinguish differences in sounds and intonation patterns that signal different meanings.

A second system of language is *morphology*, which deals with the meanings of sounds. A *morpheme* is the smallest unit of sound that carries meaning. Some words are morphemes; some are combinations of morphemes. *Tiger* is an example of a word that is a morpheme. The plural, *tigers*, is a combination of the free morpheme *tiger* and the bound morpheme *s*. The *s* is bound because it signals meaning but cannot carry meaning alone. Other morphemes signal changes of tense, person, or number rather than meaning. Mastering English morphology includes learning how to form possessives, plurals, and past and progressive verb tenses. For example, in English we say "one apple," but we must say "eight apples." Many other languages signal the number change with the number word only and do not require pluralization of the noun *apple*.

Syntax is a third system of language. In simple terms, the syntax of a language contains the rules for combining words into phrases and sentences and for transforming sentences into other sentences. Syntax provides information about word meanings based on their places in sentences. If you heard *A crad was zagging wickily*, you would know that the action described occurred in the past and that *wickily* described how the *crad* was *zagging*. You would also know that more than one *crad* existed because the article *a* signifies one of something. Children mastering syntax learn how to construct negatives, questions, compound sentences, passives, imperatives, and eventually complex sentences that include embedded clauses.

Semantics is the fourth system of language. Learning semantics means acquiring vocabulary and meanings associated with words. Some words are probably learned by repeated association, such as *bottle*. The word and the object are presented to the child simultaneously, over and over again. Other word usages reflect the child's growing ability to categorize. A very young child may begin by using *doggie* to refer to any four-legged animal but then learns more specific terms, such as *horse* and *cow*. A child's system of meanings is constantly developing and changing as a result of experience and maturation. Cognitive abilities are reflected in a child's speech. For example, a child will begin to use *gone* about the same time that she learns the concept of object permanence. Mastering the semantic system requires that a child learn word meanings and relationships between and among words.

In addition to learning all the other systems of language, the child must learn the rules for using language in social interactions. *Pragmatics* is the use of language to express intention and to get things done. Speakers must learn to adapt their language to achieve their communication goals in different situations and to do so in socially acceptable ways. Pragmatics includes the rules for appropriate language in church, on the playground, and at the dinner table. A speaker of any language would not be considered competent in its use until he had mastered the basic rules for language use in various social contexts. Children reflect their understanding of pragmatics when they learn to say *please* or when they speak more simply to a baby than they normally speak. Hymes (1974) describes the ability to use language and to use it correctly in various interactions as **communicative competence.**

Communicative competence
The ability to use language to achieve one's needs, regardless of the social correctness of the utterances.

As an illustration of communicative competence, Dyson and Genishi (1993) describe a first-grade classroom in which the children have just taken a standardized test. When the children learn that the school board requires that they take such tests, they want to write to the school board. In the course of the discussion, the children talk about what kinds of things one can say to a school board and decide that their teacher should probably read the letters before sending them "cause they [the school board] might not be able to understand them" (p. 123). Communicative competence is learning to use language in different situations and for different purposes.

Sociolinguistics, the study of language in a social context, is closely related to pragmatics. Sociolinguists ask: "What are the key aspects of a communication encounter and how do they influence one another? How do we adapt the language to various social contexts? And how does the language style used affect the social context itself" (Lindfors 1980, p. 6)? A speaker's ability to produce language does not automatically include the ability to communicate effectively in a given social situation. Figure 6.1 illustrates the relationship between linguistic competence and communicative competence.

Sociolinguistics
The study of language as used in a social context.

FIGURE 6.1 Linguistic and Communicative Competence

LC = linguistic competence
CC = communicative competence

Source: Celia Genishi and Anne Haas Dyson, eds., *Language Assessment in the Early Years* (Norwood, NJ: Ablex, 1984). Reprinted with the permission of Ablex Publishing Corporation.

Anyone who has ever studied a foreign language should be familiar with the concept of knowing more language than one can use effectively. Early lessons in Spanish, for instance, will include learning words for foods, places, colors, numbers, and so on. One's ability to communicate, however, will be quite limited until he knows some of the systems of that language (for example, that adjectives follow nouns) and has experience in applying them. Similarly, a child learning a first language will know words that she cannot use effectively; competence will come with experience.

MODELS OF LANGUAGE LEARNING

Three major theories attempt to explain the development of children's language: the *behaviorist* model, the *linguistic* model, and the *cognitive developmentalist*, or *interactionist*, model (Butler 1974; King 1987; Berko-Gleason 1987). Each theory will be examined briefly.

Behaviorist Model

The behaviorist model of learning language describes the process as consistent with the rules of operant conditioning, based upon a stimulus-response model. In the simplest terms, infants are presented with language, they imitate the language, they are rewarded for their imitations, and they continue to repeat what they have heard. Imitation does not have to be exact or immediate in order for children to make use of it in learning language.

Behaviorist explanations fail to account, however, for the fact that much of children's language is constructed in ways that have never been modeled by mature speakers. For example, a child may say "Higher the swing!"—a construction not used by any other speaker in the child's experience. Behaviorists also have difficulty explaining regressions in children's language. Typically, a young child will use the correct form of a past-tense verb, such as *went*. But as the child matures and generalizes the rules for constructing past-tense verbs, he replaces *went* with *goed*. Later, as the child learns that some words are exceptions to the general rules, *goed* is replaced by *went*.

The difficulty of modifying language through adult input is another problem for behaviorists. According to the stimulus-response model, the child should respond to adult correction of her language use. But as anyone who has attempted to correct a young child knows, this does not always happen. Literature on this subject contains many stories of adults' attempts to correct young children's language (McNeill 1966). The fact is, children do not change the forms of their language easily.

On the other hand, the behaviorist point of view does have some validity. Children obviously speak the language of their homes. Any human child can learn any human language. No human language can be said to be more complex or more difficult than other languages. Children learn to produce the sounds needed in their native language and to eliminate the sounds that are not required. Children also learn to repeat words and phrases that they hear around them, even when they do not know what they mean.

Linguistic Model

Another explanation for the development of language is the linguistic, or nativistic, model. Linguist Noam Chomsky (1965) was instrumental in developing this model. The theory holds that language is inherent in the child at birth and needs only be triggered by social contact with speakers in order to emerge.

When the linguistic explanation for language acquisition was developed, the study of language was dominated by behaviorist thinking. Some theorists began to question whether children could learn language as quickly as they obviously did solely through interactions based on stimulus and response. These theorists reasoned that language must be part of children's human inheritance. Chomsky (1965) theorized that humans were equipped with a *language acquisition device*—a structure in the brain that made possible the learning of language.

Evidence in support of this theory is that humans are the only species to acquire language, which they use to communicate ideas and pass on to other generations knowledge they have gained. Linguistic theorists also point out that language development is almost universal among humans. Only humans suffering from severe trauma or mental retardation are unable to use language; the vast majority of humans use language at some level of competence. Linguistic theorists have contributed to the field of language development by forcing researchers to examine their models and more carefully observe what children actually do in learning language.

Cognitive Developmentalist (Interactionist) Model

A third theory for explaining language development is that of the cognitive developmentalists, or interactionists. This group of theorists—represented by Jean Piaget (1959), Jerome Bruner (1983), and Lev Vygotsky (1962)—believes that children learn language quickly because human brains seek patterns and order in language, just as they constantly seek patterns and order in the environment. For evidence, these theorists point to examples of language that is produced when there has been no previous model; to the uniqueness of language (the fact that except for clichés, one may never hear exactly the same sentence used in the same context more than once); and to the obvious reliance of the child on the so-called rules of language, which are never taught but which are abstracted from examples presented to the child.

Learning language is not an effortless process. Children make a conscious effort to learn the names of things, feelings, and actions. The developmentalist model views the learner as vital in the process of learning language. The learner is active in seeking and constructing meaning and in seeking communication with others (Jaggar and Smith-Burke 1985; Shuy 1987; Bruner 1983). Learning to discriminate and correctly label a cat or a dog illustrates the active nature of language learning. If a child sees a dog and says "doggie," the caregiver will likely respond "Yes, it's a dog." If the child labels the animal "kitty," the response will likely be "No, it's a dog." The child is left on his own to determine the features of each animal that are distinctive, because it is difficult to describe the features verbally in a way that has any meaning for a very young child.

Developmentalists also recognize the importance of social interactions in the development of language. Many of the words learned first, such as *bye-bye* and *hi*, only have meaning as parts of interactions with others. For developmentalists, many factors affect language learning. These factors (social, maturational, biological, cognitive) interact and modify one another as a child learns language (Berko-Gleason 1985). Many developmentalist researchers believe that infants control much of their interaction with adults in their environments by smiling, making sounds, and repeating adult sounds to continue the interactions.

Bruner (1983) describes the language acquisition support system that adults create for children who are learning language. The support system is "scaffolding" that provides a framework and supports the child until she has mastered language forms at a given level; the scaffolding is moved to a higher level when the child's language forms become more complex. For example, when a very young child in a high chair drops a cereal bowl to the floor, her parent says "uh-oh." When the child has learned to say that phrase each time she drops something, the parent begins to say "down" or "gone" each time. As the child's language abilities increase, the parent begins to use longer sentences when something is dropped, such as "Please don't drop your cereal bowl on the floor."

Children learning language produce hypotheses and test them with the speakers in their environments. They try different combinations of sounds and words in different situations. Developmentalists believe that this problem-solving behavior is very important in learning language. They also believe that the errors in children's speech reflect new knowledge about language rules.

SEQUENCE OF LANGUAGE DEVELOPMENT

Language development follows a sequence, which is fairly predictable even though there are many individual variations. Most children move from differentiated crying (crying that sounds different in response to different stimuli: being pricked by a pin, feeling cold or wet, and so on) through cooing and babbling to expressive jargon and one-word sentences. Some children learn the names of objects before other words. Nelson (1973) classifies children's language as *referential* or *expressive*. Common nouns are referential; social words are expressive. Many children develop *idiomorphs* (not real words), which they apply to objects that they evidently find related. For example, when shown flowers or pictures of flowers, the child may make a sniffing sound. For a period of time, this sound will represent anything to be smelled. Soon the child will develop longer utterances and learn to produce negatives and questions. Then the child's language consists of some mature forms and some immature forms. By the time children are eight to ten years old, their language is mostly mature. At the same time, the child's comprehension of language is developing rapidly.

Language development is not complete at the end of infancy; it continues throughout one's lifetime. Children continue to make rapid gains in vocabulary during the early childhood years. Three- and four-year-olds learn to construct questions and negatives. "Why he no go?" changes to "Why isn't he going?" and "Me no do it" becomes "I didn't do it." Children also begin to use and understand more complicated sentences, such as "The dog under the table is mine." By the time a child begins kindergarten, she will have mastered most of the basic forms in her native language. Some fives will continue to use such forms as "gots" and "goed." Even children of eight and nine can be confused by such sentences as "The boy was bitten by the dog," since they respond to sentences as if the first noun named is doing the acting.

Older primary children are learning vocabulary and learning to use more complex sentence forms correctly. They are also becoming more aware of their audience. Very young children assume that their listeners share their context; older children can take the point of view of the listener and not assume a shared context. They gain skill in giving directions and relating stories in a sequence. They also gain abilities to use language that is not context bound and to discuss objects, events, and some abstract ideas, such as love.

Language play begins in infancy as children play with sounds and continues as young children create rhyming words or make up preposterous names or other silly words. The play of older children usually depends on changes in form or word meanings. Children may create secret languages, such as Pig Latin, and a host of sayings for all types of situations, such as lying, cheating, name calling, begging, telling the truth, using table manners, and so on.

Older children and adults continue to learn language. People learn the vocabulary related to their professions and their hobbies, and they learn to use more formal speech when it is appropriate. Even the most literate person discovers new vocabulary words or new expressions as he listens and reads; language development does not end as long as a person is mentally active and an environment for learning is available.

CREATING AN ENVIRONMENT FOR LANGUAGE LEARNING

Since almost all children learn language and can use it to satisfy their communication needs, observations of what parents and caregivers do naturally to encourage language development is helpful when planning for successful language learning. Parents or other caregivers teach language informally, focus on the intent or meaning of the child's utterances rather than on the form, expect success, recognize that language learning is wholistic, and celebrate the child's unique, creative uses of language.

Use an Informal Approach

Adults or older children in an infant's environment do not teach language formally. What they do is talk to the child about the environment and happenings in the environment. Long before an infant can produce language, speakers around the child will be talking to her: "Oh, are you thirsty? Here is a bottle of water" or "It's time for your bath now." They also make attempts to talk about what is interesting to the child. If the baby is look-

Language is learned most easily in situations in which communication is the intent of the learner.

ing at something, the adult will attempt to determine what has caught the child's interest and talk about it. As the child grows and becomes mobile, the parent's or caregiver's language is more controlling, but it is still closely related to the context (for example, "Play here with your ball. Roll the ball on the floor."). Parents do not plan language lessons each day. They just talk to their children as they make cookies, repair the sink, wash the car, cook dinner, and go through the daily household routines. Language is learned through meaningful interactions, not by talking about it or analyzing it.

In school settings, teachers can attempt to follow the child's lead in conversations and talk about topics that are meaningful and interesting to the child. Sometimes teachers are so determined to follow the given curriculum or their own agenda that they fail to respond to children's interests or to concentrate on topics that are actually important to the children. It is not as easy to follow the child's lead at school as it is at home, where only one or two children are present, but teachers do need to think about children's needs and interests in communication experiences.

Focus on the Speaker's Intent

Learning language is a self-generated process. It is controlled by the learner and is not dependent on external rewards. Achieving communication with significant others seems to be reward enough to keep the child learning. Parents and other adults seem to know this intuitively, because the majority of their responses to a child's language are focused on the child's intent, rather than on the perfection of the utterance. Even parents who do correct their children's speech are much more likely to correct content than form. If the child runs into the house and shouts "Daddy gots a new car!" the adult is more likely to respond "No, Daddy has borrowed that car" than to instruct the child to say "Daddy *has* a new car." In fact, if Daddy does have a new car, the response is likely to be "Let's go see it!"

In the early childhood classroom, teachers can make a real effort to focus on what children are trying to say rather than the form that they use. Teachers should concentrate on providing new objects and new experiences to help build the young child's vocabulary. Efforts to correct grammatical structures are relatively useless with this age group. A study that compared teachers trained to repeat the child's incorrect utterance in correct form and those trained to extend the conversation based on the child's utterance showed that extension is more useful in helping children achieve more language growth (Cazden 1965). If a child says "See red car," the teacher using extension would say "Yes, I see a red car and blue car going down the street." These responses are much more closely related to what parents do in responding to the meaning rather than to the form of utterances. In primary classrooms, teachers can help children learn the vocabulary of topics that interest them, provide opportunities to express their own ideas, and continue to focus on children's meanings.

Expect Success

If you went to the local hospital and interviewed parents of newborn infants about their expectations of whether their babies would learn to talk, you would probably get emphatically positive answers (along with strange looks for asking such a question!). Parents expect that their children will become mature speakers. When the baby makes errors, they know that it is a normal part of the process in learning language. They do not expect that their child will be able to say "My bowl of cereal has fallen to the floor" when he drops his oatmeal off the high chair. They do know that their child's language will mature over time and that immature forms will be replaced by more mature and more complex forms.

In early childhood classrooms, teachers can also expect success as children are learning language. Teachers who view errors such as the use of irregular plurals (*mouses, feets*), adding *-ed* to form the past tense of verbs (*goed, runned*), and the use of incorrect verb forms as indicators of the child's growing mastery of the rules of English will treat those errors differently than teachers who view them as mistakes to be corrected. Language is learned through active exploration of the systems, not by direct imitation of models. Errors are indications of the active nature of language learning as well as growth and maturation.

Emphasize the Wholistic Nature of Language Learning

Children learn language, language functions, and how to use language in social interactions all at the same time (Halliday 1982). Parents do not set out to teach language to their children by limiting their children's learning to one piece of the complex system of language. They help their children learn language by conversing with them in meaningful contexts and in social situations. They present language as a whole, within a context, and within a social milieu. Few parents would drill their children by asking them to learn a list of nouns, followed by a list of verbs, and then some adjectives. They would not expect their children to practice language outside a real context. The idea of a parent's asking a child to go to his or her room and practice saying "I would like a drink of water" is ludicrous.

Teachers of young children can also preserve the wholistic nature of language learning by not breaking language into bits and pieces for study in school. Words in isolation—or worse, sounds in isolation—have no meaning that can be constructed. Children do not need to practice isolated elements of language; they do not learn the parts and then put them back together and use them. They do need to use language in a variety of situations and with a variety of speakers. They need to talk about topics of interest to them and to learn to adjust their language to meet the requirements of the speaking situation. Real talk provides young children a chance to practice their developing language.

Celebrate Creativity

Goodman et al. (1987) describe a child learning language as always creative or inventive and at the same time pulled back into conformity. Children are always creating new words and phrases, but when they find that their words fail to communicate what they intended, they conform more to the usual social forms. This inventiveness in language is important. We could not create new terms when they were needed if we lost our capacity to be inventive language users. Parents and others tend to celebrate some of the creative language of children. For example, many people have nicknames invented when they were children by younger siblings who could not pronounce their real names. Almost all families use special words that were either errors in pronunciation or words invented by their children.

In the classroom, teachers can celebrate children's unique expressions by recording them to share later or by posting them on a chart or bulletin board. Some of the expressions children use are very poetic. Teachers can also celebrate children's language by not changing it. If a child uses a dialect, these expressions can also be celebrated and recorded. There are appropriate times and strategies for helping young children develop skill in speaking effectively in different contexts, but for very young children, the focus should be on the child's unique ways of expressing that meaning. Children need to have their language accepted and valued.

Recognize Language Achievements

Children have made such amazing progress in mastering their native language before entering preschool that teachers sometimes fail to recognize how much they have accomplished. Children's linguistic competencies include the ability to select meaningful parts of a message, to recognize differences in linguistic contexts, and to use syntactic rules. If you say to a very young child "Your father has gone to the office to work," the child will respond "Daddy gone." Obviously, the child knows what is significant in the message. Children adapt their language to listeners when they are very young. This is particularly noticeable in children from bilingual families, who sort out which language they should speak with which people. Children also use correct syntactical rules from the time they begin to use sentences of more than one word. They say "More milk" as opposed to "Milk more," for example.

In summary, children learn language when they are in environments where language is used and when they interact with others. They learn best when meaning rather than form is stressed. Parents set the stage for successful language learning by using language in real-life situations, by dropping specific intentions to teach language, and by accepting approximations that gradually become closer to adult models. Parents should also take delight in the child's progress and celebrate the child's imaginative and poetic uses of language.

CHILDREN WITH SPECIAL NEEDS

Some children will have special needs when it comes to learning language in school settings, such as those who come to school speaking a dialect, children for whom English is their second language (ESL), and children with language delays. In thinking about the first two of these groups, teachers need to remember that language and culture are closely related. In fact, one of the elements that defines a cultural group is its language. It is a myth that one language is better than others for communicating. Several years ago, children from culturally different groups were labeled "nonverbal" because they often were not responsive in interview settings. Labov (1970) was among the researchers who helped change this practice by observing the language of children in several social contexts. He determined that verbal behavior was highly dependent on social situation and that children from poor families and cultural/ethnic minority groups could use language effectively given comfortable social situations.

Children Who Use Dialects

A **dialect** is a systematic variation of the common language spoken by a particular group. All of us speak dialects of some sort. There are regional dialects, social class dialects, and cultural/ethnic dialects. By definition, a dialect is rule governed and consistent.

Dialect
A systematic variation from the common language that is used regularly and shared by a social group. The variation can be in word order, meaning, or pronunciation.

Children who speak dialects are not merely making errors in their grammatical constructions; they are following the rules of their dialects. The most important thing for teachers to remember is that children who speak dialects are not less capable of learning language than other children, nor is the dialect less effective for communication than more standard English. When judgments are made about the correctness of children's speech, these judgments are usually social, not linguistic (Jaggar 1980).

Dialects may differ in terms of vocabulary, syntax, and morphology. Vocabulary differences include all the various terms used to describe, for example, the parts of a car, the seed in a peach, or an ice cream drink. Vocabulary differences may also include some verb usages, such as the use of *carry* for *take* (as in "He will *carry* you to town"). Syntactical differences often include deleting some words. In some dialects, the correct form of "He is working today" is "He be working," which indicates that the subject is presently working. Morphological differences include dropping some inflectional endings so that possessives are formed differently ("That girl shoes") or tense or number are indicated differently ("He go there yesterday"). The differences in dialects and more standard speech are usually only minor, surface differences.

Teachers of young children who speak dialects that are different from the dialect of the majority should be especially sensitive to each child's use of language and be prepared to honor the child's ability to learn language. The child's dialect is certainly effective for communicating in her home or neighborhood. Exposure to literature and to models of other, more standard dialects may give the child alternative ways of expressing needs and thoughts over a period of time, but the teacher's goal should not be eradication of the dialect.

Ideas for the Classroom

Children who speak dialects need teachers who accept and respect their speech. The ideas below offer ways to help children develop their language skills in standard English while maintaining their dialect when it is appropriate:

1. Involve children in drama. They can dramatize stories and role-play various speaking situations.
2. Invite speakers to the classroom who are skilled in both the children's dialect and standard English.
3. Read the children books that use dialects.
4. Record the speech of several children saying essentially the same thing, and compare the words used.
5. Record what children say in standard spelling, but allow them to read what you have written in dialect.
6. Provide opportunities for children to talk to many different speakers.

English-Second-Language (ESL) Children

English-second-language (ESL)
A term describing speakers whose native language is not English.

In the typical U.S. classroom today, many children do not speak English as their native language. To facilitate communication with these **English-second-language (ESL)** children*, a number of approaches may be used: Some schools offer special bilingual programs for students who do not speak English; other schools provide tutors whose goal is to help children learn English; and some schools expect classroom teachers to provide for ESL children in the regular classroom context. Since most teachers will have ESL children in their classrooms, they should be aware of some of the research on second-language learning and its implications for instruction.

*In some school systems, ESL students are referred to as having *limited English proficiency (LEP)*.

Given the opportunity, many children become competent in more than one language.

To learn a second language successfully requires the same conditions that foster learning one's native tongue (Krashen 1981). Specifically, the ESL learner needs someone with whom to talk and needs support for attempts at communication. Language is learned best within a social context in which success at communication is expected. Since second-language learners use the strategies of simplification and overgeneralization, which are also common in original-language development, they will benefit from encouragement rather than correction during the early stages of learning English. For example, ESL learners may simplify all verbs to one tense and depend on context to help communicate the real message. Finally, second-language learners pick up more details in order to make their communication more effective. They learn to say "I went there yesterday in the afternoon" rather than "I go there." For young children, this process may take only a few months; for older children, it may take longer.

In summary, the best environment for ESL learning includes support, encouragement, meaningful purposes for communication, and an expectation that children will talk with others who speak the language to be learned. "For a learner to be free to learn another language, the learner must be able to trust others to respond to the messages communicated and not be laughed at or singled out. In addition, a learner must be active in seeking people to talk with" (Urzua 1980, p. 38).

Ideas for the Classroom

Teachers who want to help ESL children achieve competence in English will be thoughtful about the classroom environment and activities that make learning English as much like learning a first language as possible. The following suggestions may stimulate teachers' thinking:

1. Plan for activities that require children who speak English and children who are learning English to work together (Hester 1987). This is one of the best strategies for helping children learn English. In the early childhood classroom, it is not difficult to arrange for such cooperative experiences.
2. Encourage ESL children to share their native language through songs, fingerplays, or books.
3. Share (or find someone to share) with the class stories or poetry in a foreign language and then in English.
4. Be careful not to separate non-English-speaking children or to exclude them from activities that you fear they will not understand. ESL children learn language by listening, watching, and following examples.
5. Writing and reading activities can be based on children's growing vocabulary in English. At first, children can make books of the words that they are learning. After only a few weeks, teachers will find that most children are learning too rapidly to use this technique.

Children with Language Delays

Language delay
A delay in the development of an individual child's language ability that results in his skills not matching what is typical of peers.

A **language delay** results in a child's using language that is noticeably deficient for his age (Dumtschin 1988). Sometimes, delays in language can be attributed directly to specific causes, including physical problems (such as loss of hearing or structural problems in the speech-producing organs) or disease (for example, cerebral palsy); mental retardation; or emotional problems (such as autism) (Cole and Cole 1989). Other delays in language have no apparent cause; the child seems normal in other areas, but his language is not typical for his age group.

One of the first steps in providing for the needs of a child with a language delay is to make a referral to diagnose or rule out any underlying cause for the delay. Some schools have speech and language therapists who can be consulted. If the center or school does not employ a therapist, the referral may be to a therapist in private practice. If no professional can be located, the National Association for Hearing and Speech Action can provide assistance. If a cause for the delay can be identified, the therapist will make recommendations for activities or strategies that will be helpful to the teacher and parents. If no cause can be identified, the teacher will want to provide as much support for the child's language growth as possible.

Research has shown that conversation between children and adults can be helpful in assisting children with language delays (Cross 1984; Lasky and Klopp 1982). As noted earlier, most adults respond to the meaning of a child's speech and continue conversations on topics introduced by the child. Children whose language is less mature than that of age peers may need even more conversation with adults that focus on their meanings and intentions. Teachers need to be especially careful not to assume that children cannot understand normal conversation just because they cannot produce language typical of age-mates. Restricting a child's language environment is not appropriate.

Researchers have also found that children with language delays have more interactions with adults who are critical of their language productions than do children who are making normal progress (Bondurant, Romeo, and Kretschmer 1983). Teachers should respond to children by supplying the correct labels for objects or actions without being negative. For example, if a child is looking at a book of zoo animals and mistakenly calls the tiger a lion, the teacher might respond, "This tiger is very large. Tigers and lions are both in the zoo."

Teachers should also be aware of their use of controlling language with children who have language delays. Cross (1984) found that children with language delays experienced more directive language from adults than did children whose language development was normal. Language that is controlling fails to help children develop positive interaction patterns or increase their vocabulary. For example, consider the message delivered by the command "Pick these up now!" with that of the direction "Please help me pick up the large blocks and put them on the top shelf."

Explicitly instructing children in the social uses of language and involving them in direct imitations have been found to be effective with children with language impairments but not with normally developing children (Connell 1987; Zirkelbach and Blakesley 1986). Such instruction must be geared to the observed needs of the individual child.

Jones and Warren (1991) make several suggestions for working with children with language delays. First, the teacher should follow the child's lead, establishing dialogue and planning novel activities that reflect the child's interests. The teacher should also provide support for the child's language by commenting on the child's utterances but not necessarily expecting a response.

Finally, teachers also need to be aware of the amount of talking by adults and the amount of talking by children encouraged in classrooms. If children are constantly involved in teacher-directed activities, in which listening and following directions are the accepted behaviors, then little time will be left for active language production (Hough, Nurss, and Goodson 1984). Children need to talk to adults and to other children if their language is to improve. Most of the children's day should be structured so that language is an integral part of activities. Teachers should make every effort to talk *to* children, not *at* them, and to accept children's language. All children need the same conditions in order to achieve maximum growth in language: an accepting environment, interesting things to talk about, and adults with whom to engage in meaningful conversations.

Ideas for the Classroom

Teachers who want to help all children develop their language abilities will encourage children to use language in classroom settings. This is especially true for those children whose language development is atypical. The following strategies may be useful in planning activities that enhance language development:

1. Encourage children to retell stories that you have read or told. A flannel board may encourage older preschoolers to be more confident in their retellings.
2. Encourage children to use puppets to tell stories or to carry on conversations among puppet characters.
3. Involve children in learning fingerplays, song lyrics, chants, and choral readings.
4. Plan cooperative classroom activities in which children use language freely, such as card games or board games or building projects.
5. Be sure that children with language delays are not "talked down to" by anyone in the classroom and that their participation in activities is not limited.

OBSERVING LANGUAGE LEARNERS

Yetta Goodman (1985) has coined the term *kidwatching* to describe how teachers should pay attention to children—to what they are thinking and saying and how they are responding—which is extremely important in

D EVELOPMENTALLY A PPROPRIATE P RACTICE	*As you think about language development and developmentally appropriate practice, reflect on the following:*

- Many children learn to use language differently than middle-class White children. These differences are not just dialectal but reflect culturally appropriate uses of language in telling stories or entertaining groups. In a developmentally appropriate classroom, what goals and standards should be set for children's language use? For example, should all children be expected to achieve the middle-class model of language use? Why?
- Language is best learned when it is used for a real purpose; thus, contrived activities to practice language skills are rarely effective. How should real language be used in activities for children of different ages—say, preschoolers versus primary-grade children?
- The teacher must accept and respect the language of all children in a developmentally appropriate classroom. How can the teacher demonstrate acceptance and respect for an ESL student?
- The best environment for learning language includes the critical elements of DAP, such as choice, active involvement, age and individually appropriate expectations, and so on. How do these elements enhance learning language?

assessing language development. Teachers have to learn how to observe children's language and how they use it. Teachers must also learn how to provide the environments that foster children's growth in language abilities and what specific activities can be most helpful to a given child at a given time (Goodman 1985).

The following guidelines will be helpful as teachers observe the language of young children:

1. Always observe a child's language in a variety of contexts before drawing any conclusions about the child's abilities. Some children who are almost nonverbal in school settings will be extremely verbal on the playground. Some children will not contribute to conversation even in small groups but can communicate effectively one to one with a child or an adult.

2. Look for competence in using language for a variety of purposes. For example, how does the child share information, get what is needed or wanted, or use imaginative language? Can the child communicate both with adults and with other children?

3. Look for effectiveness in communication rather than for specific abilities, such as "The child speaks in complete sentences." Often, the most effective communication does not require the use of complete sentences. What teachers need to know is whether children can adapt their language to the requirements of different speaking situations.

4. Look for signs of growth in the child's knowledge of language systems. For example, are there changes in the child's use of inflectional endings and clauses?

5. Look for growth in vocabulary. As a child participates in the activities provided in the classroom, are labels for objects and actions becoming a part of his vocabulary?

Careful observation of children's language will provide insights that will help teachers plan activities and structure the environment to foster growth in language. The teacher who observes that a child does not know the language for expressing emotions, for example, will help by providing some of the labels for feelings when the child needs them. Other children may need more opportunities to recount incidents in sequential order. The teacher may guide by asking "What came first?" or "Then what happened?" and so on. Plans and guidance that meet children's individual needs can only be provided on the basis of careful observation. Without knowledge of children's language, effective instruction is almost impossible.

LANGUAGE DEVELOPMENT IN SCHOOL SETTINGS

Commercial Programs

Encouraging the development of language is always one of the primary goals of teachers of young children. Toward this goal, various commercial programs are available, often consisting of a teacher's guide, pictures of objects in various categories, and sometimes plastic models of objects. These materials may also be accompanied by audiotapes or computer programs designed to allow children to practice repeating words or phrases.

Commercial programs designed to teach children language are objectionable for several reasons. One, of course, is that these programs ignore the interactive and active nature of language learning. Another objection is that most programs are designed for small-group instruction, yet it would be rare to find a group in which all the children needed to learn the same words or phrases. A third objection to commercial language programs is that most of the actual production of language is done by the teacher, rather than by the children. Finally, most of these programs are expensive.

Using a commercial program is not the answer for promoting children's language growth. Setting up an environment that encourages language growth and that is responsive to children's language *is* the answer. Language is learned best when children use it for meaningful purposes. In the best classrooms, children have many opportunities to talk with each other and with adults. Children playing with clay, sand, water, blocks, and other classroom materials are encouraged to talk about their experiences. As adults move around the play areas, they listen to the children's language, make observations, and expand on the children's language in meaningful interactions that are developmentally appropriate. If a three-year-old is playing with the sand, the adult might offer the language to describe what is taking place by remarking, for example, "You are filling the cup with sand." An eight-year-old playing with water and boats might be encouraged to use the vocabulary connected with boating: *deck, port, stern, aft, dock,* and so on.

Wells (1986) reached several disturbing conclusions following an extensive longitudinal study of the language of children in Bristol, England. For *none* of the children studied was the language used in the classroom as linguistically rich as that used at home, which was self-motivated, spontaneous, unstructured, and supported by adults. Wells concluded that several factors made language development at school much more difficult than it was at home: a large number of students per teacher, a curriculum dominated by norm-referenced tests, and the fact that many teachers did not believe that talking was important for learning.

Activities That Encourage Language Growth

Almost everything that happens in the early childhood classroom will contribute to children's language development. If children are arguing over a toy, the teacher can help them use language that is appropriate for disagreeing and for solving the problem. If an adult visits the class, the children can have opportunities for interaction with the visitor, who serves as another model of language use. If the children go on a field trip, they will have the opportunity to learn the vocabulary connected with what they are observing. Language development goes on all through the schoolday.

The activities described in the following sections are merely suggestive of the opportunities teachers have for helping children develop more competency as language users.

Literature

Language in children's books is very important. When an entire book contains three hundred words, an author cannot waste words but must choose the best ones to convey the ideas. Martin (1986); Harste, Woodward, and Burke (1984); and Blackburn (1985) point out that everyone stores up all the words, phrases, and story elements they hear and that this language become theirs after a time. Books help children fill up their storehouses of beautiful words. Even simple stories can do this.

In *Whose Mouse Are You?* (Kraus 1970), when the little mouse is asked about his brother, he replies, "I have none." That is probably not the way most children would respond nor is it the language most children would hear at home, but it is elegant. Sometimes we choose books or stories just because the words sound so wonderful. The elephant's child says, "Good-by. I am going to the great, gray-green greasy Limpopo River all set about with fever trees to find out what the Crocodile has for dinner" ("The Elephant's Child," in Kipling 1965, p. 132). We read such language because we love to hear the sound of it. Children, too, love the sound of language, whether they understand the meaning of every word or not. The language in books allows teachers to expand children's language in supportive and creative ways. Books with simplified vocabularies are somewhat useful for beginning readers, but for all other purposes, books should be chosen because they have beautiful language.

Narrative Stories   Children's literature often serves as a focus for learning new vocabulary or new ways of expressing ideas and can provide the foundation for countless activities, including the following:

1. Compare the words used in different versions of familiar folk stories. For example, several words are used to label the woodcutter in versions of "Little Red Riding Hood." Children might discuss what they think is the best choice of words and what pictures the different words bring to mind.
2. Dramatize stories or rhymes. Actually speaking the words and performing the actions that go with them help children make vocabulary real and personal.
3. Have children retell stories in their own words and/or use puppets to recall stories.
4. Ask children to create new versions of stories by selecting words to fit the patterns in repetitive books. For example, in *Someday* (Zolotow 1965), the pattern is "Someday I'll _____." Children can think of what they will do "someday."
5. Encourage children to tell their own original stories and record them either in writing or on audiotape. Having children tell their own stories results in more complex language use and more detailed stories than is the case when children are asked to tell stories about a picture or wordless picture book (Hough, Nurss, and Wood 1987).

Storytelling   Telling stories can also aid in children's language development. Storytelling has the advantage of being a direct communication between the listener and the teller. Children listening to a story are required to be active listeners. If they tune out, the story will go on; there will be no instant replay. Storytelling also invites children to become active by participating in the story, repeating phrases or words or creating voices or gestures for the characters.

Storytelling is also flexible. If the audience gets restless, the storyteller can add more drama to the voices, shorten the story, end the story immediately, or whatever is required to make the session successful. Of course, this requires that the storyteller pay close attention to the audience and respond accordingly.

Stories told to children should contain language that they can understand from context so that the storyteller will not have to stop for explanations. Stories for children should also be about topics and situations that appeal to them; if the children are not interested in what the story is about, they will tune out and become restless.

The storyteller should invite participation in the tale, especially after the first telling. Possible activities include the following:

1. Invite children to dramatize a story as you tell it. For example, "The Turnip," a Russian folk tale, works very well (Morgan 1990).
2. Provide materials so that children can retell stories during activity periods. Make flannelboard pieces, wooden characters, finger puppets, or puppets available, depending on the age and experience of the children.

Children need to use language for many different purposes, including storytelling and drama.

3. Encourage children to tell their own stories. Older children can write and produce their stories in many forms: a skit for TV, a scroll story, a flannelboard story, and so on.
4. Encourage children to join the storytelling by repeating certain phrases or sounds.

Poetry/Chants/Rhymes   Fingerplays and choral readings help children learn new vocabulary words and new sentence patterns that add to their repertoires. Teacher should plan activities such as the following:

1. Create new versions of song lyrics or rhymes by selecting words that fit the rhymes. For example, after learning *Alligator Pie* (Lee 1974), children can write or dictate new versions.
2. Dramatize rhymes or song lyrics. When children participate in drama, their actions indicate comprehension of the words. For example, the words of the various versions of "Bear Hunt" describe different actions; children can do the actions to demonstrate that they understand the words.
3. Dramatize concepts in science or social studies—such as the attraction and repelling of magnets or the arrival of a famous explorer—so that the language has real meaning for children.

Sharing Time

Sharing time can have many positive benefits for language development if managed appropriately. For instance, sharing time should be conducted in small groups so that children do not have to sit for long periods while each person has a turn. Objects should be displayed to the group, rather than passed around. Teachers should also help children learn how to begin and end presentations, and sessions should be structured so that children are not required to stand up or come to the front of the class in order to participate (Oken-Wright 1988).

Teachers should also control sharing time so that it does not turn into a session in which children show off their latest possessions. The following activities may help achieve that control:

1. Sharing can be organized so that children describe the details of the process for making objects they have created in class. For example, a child might share how a textile print or clay object was made. Cooking experiences and building with blocks are other activities that provide interesting topics for sharing.
2. Children can bring objects from home that are related to a theme or topic of study. For example, they might bring something square when the class is learning shape concepts.

3. Children can share personal experiences that are important to them. They might talk about a special trip or an exciting event that occurred at home, such as the birth of kittens.
4. Sharing time can be used as a brainstorming session for solving class problems and planning class activities.

Teachers must also consider children's ages in planning activities for sharing time. For instance, in considering the classroom, younger children might be asked to offer suggestions for classroom or playground safety, and older children might be asked to think about the room arrangement and how it might be altered for better traffic patterns. In planning themes and projects, older children might be asked to persuade others that a topic of study that interests them would be a good choice for the next class theme.

Classroom Centers and Activities

Classroom centers such as the block area, where several children work together, tend to encourage more language use than centers where the activities are more solitary. It follows that teachers who want to encourage children's language development and use will arrange learning areas so that children can talk to each other and will prompt children to work together.

Materials will also need to be interesting and novel enough that children will want to talk about them. Several recent research studies (Isbell and Raines 1991; Dyson and Genishi 1991; Anen 1991) have verified the common-sense knowledge that children who are encouraged to participate in active and interesting activities are more likely to use language and produce more language than children who are asked to complete skills activities. A classroom environment in which teachers and children use language for many purposes will contribute to the communicative competence of the children.

Encouraging Different Language Functions

Children need opportunities to use language for a variety of purposes:

1. *Descriptive language*—Children can describe objects that are hidden from others (in a box or bag) using as many details as possible; the listeners must guess what has been hidden.
2. *Persuasive language*—Children can convince others to share a toy, to take a role in cooperative play, to participate in a game, and so on.
3. *Personal language*—Children can participate in interpreting what concepts mean in personal terms. For example, a child might describe what *family* means.

4. *Imaginative language*—Children can strengthen their language of fantasy and "let's pretend" through dramatic play, drama, poetry, and stories.

5. *Informative language*—Children can use language to communicate information. For example, a child might bring a caterpillar to school and share all the information that she has about caterpillars.

Overview of Activities

It is obvious from these brief lists of suggested activities that almost every activity in an early childhood classroom can provide an opportunity for language growth. Teachers and children together can talk about personal experiences, classroom activities, feelings and emotions, and plans and expectations. A classroom in which children can talk with other children and with adults who respect and value their ideas as well as the way they are expressed will be a place where language flourishes.

CHAPTER SUMMARY

- Language is composed of the systems of phonology, semantics, syntax, morphology, and pragmatics. Each of these systems offers a challenge to the learner.

- Three different theoretical explanations were offered of the process of learning language: behavioristic, linguistic, and cognitive developmentalistic. The cognitive developmentalist, or interactionist, view is based most directly on observations of children learning language and using it to communicate.

- Children all over the world learn language in a similar sequence, although with individual variations. The basic sequence begins with crying and moves through cooing, babbling, and echoing to the use of single words, multiple words, and then complete sentences.

- Observations of children learning language reveal that it is learned informally; that adults should focus on the intent of the learner; that adults should expect success; that language learning is wholistic; and that language is creative.

- The language achievements of young children are quite remarkable. By the time children are five or six, they have mastered most of the basic forms of their native language and have an extensive vocabulary.

- Children who speak dialects other than the dialect of the majority and children for whom English is their second language (ESL) can be helped by knowledgeable teachers who structure supportive learning environments.

- Some children do not achieve language competence at the same rate as their peers. Children with language delays need teachers who are aware of the strategies that research has shown to be most important in helping them achieve growth in language.

- Observing language development is important for planning activities and strategies that will help each child maximize language development. Observers should not merely look for discrete skills from a checklist but should observe children carefully in a variety of language contexts.

- Activities that foster the growth of language take place in the classroom every day. Children need opportunities to talk with other children and with adults. They need something interesting to talk about, and they need teachers who celebrate their use of language.

WHAT WOULD YOU DO?

Reflect on your reading and your own experiences with young children as you think about the following situations:

1. Your principal believes that all quiet classrooms are good classrooms. How would you explain the noise level in your classroom?
2. The second-grade teacher down the hall does an activity each morning called "oral language development." The activity begins when the teacher writes a sentence on the chalkboard that contains two or three errors—spelling, punctuation, or grammatical errors. The children are asked to read the sentence and then called on to find and correct the errors. The activity continues until the sentence has been corrected. Would this activity be appropriate for second-graders?
3. You have children who speak four different languages in your preschool class. How would you address this in planning activities?
4. A parent is concerned that you do not correct the children when they use words such as *goed* or *gots* in speaking. What would you tell her?

THEORY INTO PRACTICE

1. Tape record the language of a two-year-old, a four-year-old, and a six-year-old engaged in a similar activity—playing with clay or playing with another child outdoors, for example. Listen to the tapes several times, and compare the differences in the children's language in terms of vocabulary, length of sentences, use of adjectives, and so on.
2. Interview the caregivers of three two-year-old children about the vocabularies of their children. Make a list of the words that each caregiver reports. Compare these lists. Do they contain similar words? Do they contain similar types of words? For example, do some children use more nouns as opposed to more words of social interaction? Based on your observations, can you conclude that children in different environments learn different words? Explain your findings.
3. Observe an adult reading the same book on two occasions: once to a two-year-old and once to a four-year-old. How does the language of the adult differ in the two situations? Does he ask more questions or different kinds of questions of one child than the other? Does he expect more responses or different kinds of responses from either child? Explain your observations.
4. Observe the home language of a child of five or six and the school language of the same child for the same amount of time. Do the number and kinds of verbal interactions differ in the two situations? Explain your observations.

RECOMMENDED FOR FURTHER READING

Cazden, Courtney, ed. *Language in Early Childhood Education.* Washington, DC: National Association for the Education of Young Children, 1981.

   This collection of articles covers a variety of topics, such as programs for language development, second-language learners, and community and parental responses to the treatment of dialects in school settings. One of the most helpful features is a list of questions that teachers can use to evaluate their own language performance in the early childhood classroom.

Piaget, Jean. *The Language and Thought of the Child.* 3d ed. London: Routledge and Kegan Paul, 1959.

   This study, along with that of Lev Vygotsky, is considered a classic. Both theorists describe the development of children's language and its relationship to their thinking. Piaget was not an educator and was much more interested in the psychological explanations of language than in classroom applications of these explanations.

Piper, Terry. *Language for All Our Children.* New York: Macmillan, 1993.

> *Good chapters are included on the theories of language development and bilingual language development, including many anecdotal incidents. The chapter that describes what constitutes an outstanding school is especially good.*

Vygotsky, L. S. *Thought and Language.* Edited and translated by Eugenai Hanfmann and Gertrude Vakar. Cambridge, MA: MIT Press, 1962.

> *This is a more theoretical exploration of language than those presented in the classroom-oriented books*

mentioned in this list of readings. *Vygotsky was interested in psychological explanations for growth and development in language rather than in direct classroom applications of these explanations.*

Wells, Gordon. *The Meaning Makers: Children Learning Language and Using Language to Learn.* Portsmouth, NH: Heinemann, 1986.

> *This report of an extensive longitudinal study of children's language conducted in Bristol, England, is easy to read, and its findings are reported in nontechnical terms. The author makes clear the need for teachers who can understand children's language development and the importance of children's using language in school.*

REFERENCES

General Sources

Anen, Judith. *Enhancing the Curriculum Through the Addition of Rich and Diverse Language Development Activities.* ERIC Document Reproduction Service 329944, 1991.

Berko-Gleason, Jean, ed. *The Development of Language.* Columbus, OH: Merrill, 1985.

Blackburn, Ellen. "Stories Never End." In *Breaking Ground: Teachers Relate Reading and Writing in the Elementary School,* edited by J. Hansen, T. Newkirk, and D. Graves. Portsmouth, NH: Heinemann.

Bondurant, J. L., D. J. Romeo, and R. Kretschmer. "Language Behaviors of Mothers of Children with Normal and Delayed Language." *Language, Speech and Hearing Services in Schools* 14 (1983): 233–242.

Bruner, Jerome. *Child's Talk: Learning to Use Language.* New York: W. W. Norton, 1983.

Butler, Lester G. "Language Acquisition of Young Children: Major Theories and Sequences." *Elementary English* 51 (1974): 1120–1123.

Cazden, Courtney. "Environmental Assistance to the Child's Acquisition of Grammar." Doctoral dissertation, Harvard University, 1965.

Chomsky, Noam. *Aspects of a Theory of Syntax.* Cambridge, MA: MIT Press, 1965.

Cole, Martha L., and Jack T. Cole. *Effective Intervention with the Language Impaired Child.* 2d ed. Rockville, MD: Aspen, 1989.

Connell, Phil J. "An Effect of Modeling and Imitation Teaching Procedures on Children With and Without Specific Language Impairment." *Journal of Speech and Hearing Research* 30 (1987): 105–113.

Cross, T. G. "Habilitating the Language-Impaired Child: Ideas from Studies of Parent-Child Interaction." *Topics in Language Disorders* 4 (1984): 1–14.

Dumtschin, Joyce Ury. "Recognize Language Development and Delay in Early Childhood." *Young Children* 43 (1988): 16–24.

Dyson, Anne Haas, and Celia Genishi. "Visions of Children as Language Users: Language and Language Education in Early Childhood." In *Handbook of Research on the Education of Young Children,* edited by B. Spodek. New York: Macmillan, 1993.

Dyson, Anne Haas, and Celia Genishi. *Visions of Children as Language Users: Research on Language and Language Education in Early Childhood.* Technical Report No. 49. ERIC Document Reproduction Service 335678, 1991.

Genishi, Celia, and Anne Haas Dyson, eds. *Language Assessment in the Early Years.* Norwood, NJ: Ablex, 1984.

Goodman, Kenneth, E. Brooks Smith, Robert Meredith, and Yetta Goodman. *Language and Thinking in School.* 3d ed. New York: Richard C. Owen, 1987.

Goodman, Yetta. "Kidwatching: Observing Children in the Classroom." In *Observing the Language Learner,* edited by Angela Jaggar and M. Trika Smith-Burke. Newark, DE: International Reading Association/National Council of Teachers of English, 1985.

Halliday, M. A. K. "Three Aspects of Children's Language Development: Learning Language, Learning Through Language, Learning About Language." In *Oral and Written Language Development Research: Impact on the Schools,* edited by Y. Goodman, M. Haussler, and D. Strickland. Urbana, IL: National Council of Teachers of English, 1982.

Harste, J., V. Woodward, and C. Burke. *Language Stories and Literacy Lessons.* Portsmouth, NH: Heinemann, 1984.

Hester, Hilary. "Peer Interaction in Learning English as a Second Language." *Theory into Practice* 26 (1987): 208–217.

Hough, R. A., J. R. Nurss, and M. S. Goodson. "Children in Day Care: An Observational Study." *Child Study Journal* 14 (1984): 31–46.

Hough, Ruth A., Joanne R. Nurss, and Dolores Wood. "Tell Me a Story: Making Opportunities for Elaborated Language in Early Childhood Classrooms." *Young Children* 43 (1987): 6–12.

Hymes, Dell. *Foundations of Sociolinguistics: An Ethnographic Approach.* Philadelphia: University of Pennsylvania Press, 1974.

Isbell, Rebecca, and Shirley Raines. "Young Children's Oral Language Production in Three Types of Play Centers." *Journal of Research in Childhood Education* 5 (Spring/ Summer 1991): 140–146.

Jaggar, Angela. "Allowing for Language Differences." In *Discovering Language with Children,* edited by Gay Su Pinnell. Urbana, IL: National Council of Teachers of English, 1980.

Jaggar, Angela, and M. Trika Smith-Burke, eds. *Observing the Language Learner.* Newark, DE: International Reading Association/National Council of Teachers of English, 1985.

Jones, Hazel A., and Steven F. Warren. "Enhancing Engagement in Early Language Teaching." *Teaching Exceptional Children* 23 (Summer 1991): 48–50.

King, Martha L. "Language: Insights from Acquisition." *Theory Into Practice* 26 (1987): 358–363.

Krashen, Stephen D. *Second Language Acquisition and Second Language Learning.* New York: Pergamon Press, 1981.

Labov, W. "The Logic of Non-Standard English." In *Language and Poverty,* edited by F. Williams. Chicago: Markham, 1970.

Lasky, E. Z., and K. Klopp. "Parent-Child Interactions in Normal and Language-Disordered Children." *Journal of Speech and Hearing Disorders* 47 (1982): 7–18.

Lindfors, Judith Wells. *Children's Language and Learning.* Englewood Cliffs, NJ: Prentice-Hall, 1980.

Martin, Bill, Jr. "Celebrating Language." Seminar sponsored by the School of Education, Oregon State University, Corvallis, Oregon, Summer 1986.

McNeill, David. "Developmental Psycholinguistics." In *The Genesis of Language,* edited by Frank Smith and George Miller. Cambridge, MA: MIT Press, 1966.

Nelson, Katherine. "Structure and Strategy in Learning to Talk." *Monographs of the Society for Research in Child Development* 38 (1973): 149.

Oken-Wright, Pamela. "Show and Tell Grows Up." *Young Children* 43 (1988): 52–58.

Piaget, Jean. *The Language and Thought of the Child.* 3d ed. London: Routledge and Kegan Paul, 1959.

Shuy, Roger. "Language as a Foundation for Education: The School Context." *Theory into Practice* 26 (1987): 166–174.

Urzua, Carole. "Doing What Comes Naturally: Recent Research in Second Language Acquisition." In *Discovering Language with Children,* edited by Gay Su Pinnell. Urbana, IL: National Council of Teachers of English, 1980.

Vygotsky, Lev S. *Thought and Language.* Cambridge, MA: MIT Press, 1962.

Wells, Gordon. *The Meaning Makers: Children Learning Language and Using Language to Learn.* Portsmouth, NH: Heinemann, 1986.

Zirkelbach, Thelma, and Kathryn Blakesley. "The Language Deficient Child in the Classroom." *Education Digest* 51 (January 1986): 52–55.

Children's Books

Kipling, Rudyard. *Just So Stories.* New York: Grosset and Dunlap, 1965.

Kraus, Robert. *Whose Mouse Are You?* New York: Macmillan, 1970.

Lee, Dennis. *Alligator Pie.* Toronto: Macmillan of Canada, 1974.

Morgan, Pierr. *The Turnip.* New York: Macmillan, 1990.

Zolotow, Charlotte. *Someday.* New York: Harper and Row, 1965.

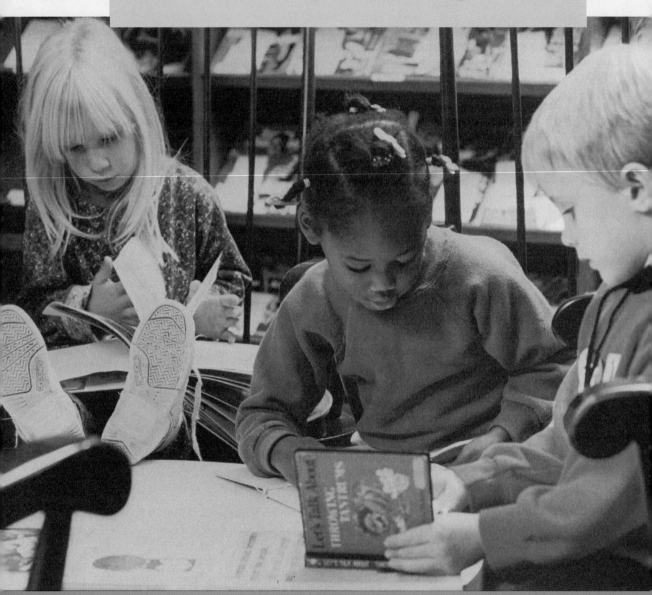

Chapter Seven

The Development of Literacy
Reading and Writing

learning to read

children with special needs

instructional goals

READING AND WRITING

handwriting instruction

classroom environment

learning to write

activities

This week, your observations focused on children's reading and writing activities. You observed in a preschool, where threes and fours were in the same class. You noticed that as they played, some children wrote several signs. You could not read the signs, but the children seemed to think they were important. Other children spent part of their play time looking at books, and several children could retell the stories in their favorite books. You know that parents are concerned that their children do well in reading, and you wonder if these children will be readers by the time they are in first grade.

Others in your class reported on their visits to primary-grade classrooms, where they observed many different approaches to reading and writing. In some classrooms, the teachers used a series of books designed for teaching reading (basal readers) almost exclusively. In other classrooms,

children were engaged in reading and writing activities about topics of interest to them. You think that reading about topics of personal interest sounds
very appealing. After all, when you read on your own for pleasure, you
choose what you want to read. But if the children choose their own topics,
how does the teacher manage to teach every child? It all seems very complicated at the moment. How do you know what is best for children?

· ·

Nothing in the early childhood curriculum is as likely to cause concern among parents and administrators as the teaching of reading
and writing. Few parents have much to say about how art or science is taught, but most parents today have a set of expectations about
reading instruction. Only a few years ago, preschool and kindergarten
teachers were not expected to teach reading. Many present-day kindergarten and preschool teachers have had the experience of having carefully
explained to parents the goals and activities to be included in a developmental program, only to hear them say, "Good! But I want my child reading by Thanksgiving." Some schools choose basal reading series that
include workbooks for the children to use before first grade. Some districts
have mandated that all kindergartners master a given list of sight words.

The majority of public schools today require teachers to give reading
instruction or to provide reading-readiness activities in kindergarten
(Karweit 1988). Even preschool teachers have felt pressured to provide
reading instruction for three- and four-year-olds. Many authorities in early
childhood education and child development, however, question the wisdom of formalized reading instruction in preschool and kindergarten. This
does not mean that literacy should not be addressed in the curriculum;
instead, it means that instruction in literacy should be informal. It is imperative that teachers of young children understand the developmental
nature of learning to read and write and be able to communicate that
understanding to parents, program directors, principals, and others. Early
childhood teachers must also know how to use their knowledge to best
foster and encourage growth in literacy with each child.

In the last few years, the generally accepted view of reading and writing instruction has changed rather radically (Sulzby and Teale 1985). Once
educators talked in terms of *reading readiness* as the period when a child
would benefit from reading instruction. The concept of reading readiness
implied that at a certain time, children could be taught skills that were pre-
cursors to real reading (Durkin 1982). Readiness activities consisted of
exercises such as finding a shape that was different in a row of shapes or

finding the pig whose tail was different from the tails of the other pigs in the row. Although visual discrimination ability is necessary for success in reading, attempting to teach it with shapes and pigs is not a very useful reading activity. Similarly, educators once believed that writing instruction should begin with teaching children to form letters, usually in first grade.

Today, literacy—a more broadly defined ability that includes reading and writing—is conceptualized as a continuum beginning with the child's development of language in infancy and (ideally) continuing throughout a person's life span (Harp and Brewer 1991). Just as there is great variability in children's use of oral language, there is great variability among individual children's understanding of the printed language system. Not all children of a given age will be at the same level of development. The task faced by teachers of young children is to discover what each child knows about printed language and then to plan for activities and experiences that will promote continued literacy development.

It is virtually impossible to talk about reading and writing instruction as separate subject-matter areas. Given the integrated nature of literacy— indeed, of all children's learning—teaching young children reading and writing as separate subjects is not recommended. Additionally, both reading and writing are learned best through meaningful activities, not through instruction in isolated skills. Keep in mind this wholeness of language and the need for real experiences with print as you read this chapter, which will discuss research on reading and writing and describe some examples of appropriate classroom experiences for young children.

LEARNING TO READ

Recent research on the emergence of literacy in young children (Ferreiro and Teberosky 1982; Kontos 1986) makes it clear that reading, as well as oral language and writing, develops over a period of time; the beginnings of these skills, however, are not always obvious to the untrained observer. The development of reading is closely tied to the development of both oral language and writing; all are aspects of literacy. The isolation of so-called reading skills from activities designed to promote oral and written language development ignores this vital link and unnecessarily handicaps a young beginning reader.

The young child is constantly learning about language in its oral and written forms. For example, around two years old, the child may be learning to string together words to create sentences several words long. At the same time, the child likely will be learning to use crayons or pencils to make scribbles. Later, the child will be able to determine which of the forms produced in scribbling can be discriminated as letters.

Young children learning oral and written language respond to the *functions* of language before they attend to its *form*. In learning oral language, children do not learn the proper set of phonemes to produce the word for "cracker"; they learn that producing such a word (or an approximation of the word) will help them get a snack. In the same way, children learn about the functions of print before or concurrent with learning about its form. Children in a print-rich society (such as that in the United States) are exposed to print in a variety of situations, simply as part of their daily activities. They observe stop signs, labels on cereal boxes, and slogans on their clothing; they observe adults around them reading newspapers, magazines, and books. Children observe others writing letters, clipping coupons, looking up recipes in cookbooks, sending greeting cards, and making grocery lists. Ideally, children observe print as they sit on someone's lap and listen to their favorite story being read. Again, children attend first to the functions of print (entertainment, information, communication) and then to the details of its form (word formation, sentence structure, punctuation).

Environmental print
Print that occurs in the everyday environment, such as stop signs and candy labels.

The young child is constantly responding to **environmental print** without being introduced to formal reading instruction. The work of Goodman and Altwerger (1981) with three- and four-year-olds clearly indicates that children respond naturally to environmental print in ways that are meaningful. A child will respond to a trademark for toothpaste, for instance, by pronouncing the word *toothpaste* even if he cannot read the label on the tube. Children categorize print as food labels, signs, and so on, depending on their own experiences.

Given the opportunity, most children are able to apply problem-solving techniques to the task of learning about print. Children learning to use oral language, for instance, make hypotheses about what language is needed to achieve their goals, try out these hypotheses, and use any feedback they get to confirm or adapt their original hypotheses. Children learning about printed language employ similar problem-solving behaviors. A child may point to the printed sign on a storefront and say "That says Safeway." The adult will normally respond by verifying that the sign does indeed say "Safeway" or by correcting the child: "No, that says Smith's." The child will use that feedback in making her next informed guess about print.

Learning to break the code of written language is not exactly the same as learning oral language, although the two processes have many elements in common. Children normally learn to talk without any instruction, but learning to read requires direct instruction. This is not to suggest a return to traditional reading groups, where children were organized by ability and given daily lessons. Rather, teachers and parents should provide informal instruction when they answer children's questions about letters, sounds, and words. For example, if a child is playing with a set of magnetic letters and places an "H" on the refrigerator door, he may ask "What is this?" The parent should respond "That is an 'H.' It's the first letter of your friend Harry's name."

Schickedanz (1993) relates the story of a child who was returning two books from the classroom library. He asked the teacher, "How does this work?" She replied, "You put the cards in the pocket at the back of the book." Having checked out books before, he probably knew that part; what he was likely asking was how to tell exactly which card went in which book. This would have been an excellent opportunity for the teacher to teach the child to match the words of the book titles to the words on the checkout cards. Durkin (1966), in her classic study, found that children who taught themselves to read at an early age actually received considerable help from their parents and siblings, but the assistance was so informal that it went unnoticed by adults in the environment. Nonetheless, others spent considerable time giving the children feedback and answering their questions about print.

Vygotsky and Reading Instruction

Vygotsky's model of learning has been applied to reading instruction and is described by Mason and Sinha (1993). They list the following steps in the model:

1. Natural involvement
2. Mediated learning
3. External activity (child-directed learning and practice with the aid of props and occasional coaching by an adult)
4. Internal or independent activity

When applied to reading instruction for young children, Vygotsky's model provides that first, children are naturally involved in literacy activities: hearing stories read, observing others read, observing others write, attempting to write on their own, and so on. Next, children are engaged in mediated learning, such as having adults point out letters and words as stories are being read or as children are involved in writing activities. In the third stage, children begin to participate in such activities as rereading familiar stories (with books as props) and ask for adult assistance when faced with difficulties. Finally, children internalize the knowledge of print and how the "code" works so that their reading is independent.

To implement Vygotsky's model, teachers must plan appropriate classroom activities for the children. Appropriate activities are those that are useful, meaningful, flexible, shared, and wholistic.

This model seems to fit the early childhood classroom because the child is central at all stages and chooses the activities she wishes to complete. The teacher acts as a coach and helper to the child but does not dictate what the child will learn next or the strategies that the child will use in certain situations.

GOALS OF READING INSTRUCTION FOR YOUNG CHILDREN

The basic goals of reading instruction for young children include (1) continuing their language development, (2) giving them personal knowledge of the functions of print, and (3) helping them learn about books and the importance of reading. This third goal can be divided further into several secondary purposes: to develop phonemic awareness, to learn about story structure, and to learn about what readers do. Children in the primary grades will continue language development, learn to apply reading strategies, and become independent readers.

None of these goals can be met by engaging a child in isolated practice activities that are designed to teach a specific skill. These goals are best met through an integrated curriculum in an environment that includes interesting play opportunities. Examples of activities that help children achieve these goals are described briefly in the sections that follow.

Developing Oral Language Skills

Oral language development is important for growth in literacy; both reading and writing are language skills (Glazer 1989). The more competent a child is in using oral language, the more she will know about how language works and the more able she will be to transfer this knowledge to the written language system. Oral language development will take place if children are provided with interesting activities in which to participate and are allowed to talk with each other and with adults. Dramatic play, for instance, allows children to "try on" the vocabulary and speaking mannerisms of various adults as they play "grocer," "shopper," "mechanic," "bus driver," "teacher," "cook," "parent," or "Superman."

Some children may need to learn the meanings of words they will meet in print later in school. Teachers can create opportunities for developing concepts by providing children with objects, activities, or experiences. When children play with lariats, classify leaves, or go on field trips to experience elevators, circuses, or restaurants, they are developing meanings. When they are expected to read words such as *lariat, maple leaf, elevator, circus,* and *restaurant,* they will have the knowledge to make the print meaningful for them. Language development activities can be extended to print as children observe the teacher recording their words as they dictate a story or see a chant or song they have learned printed on a chart. Young children need many opportunities to initiate and participate in verbal interactions with each other. They also need to engage in real conversation with adults rather than being limited to responding to questions posed by a teacher.

Learning about the Functions of Print

Children are not likely to be motivated to learn to read and write without some knowledge of the **functions of print.** Knowing that print can be decoded to reveal wonderful stories and secrets is strong motivation for learning to read. Children learn the functions of print by observing the teacher using a book to find information about the insects a child brings to school or by watching an adult follow directions for putting together a class incubator. Children learn about the pleasure print can bring by hearing the teacher read poetry and stories to them. They learn the usefulness of print for sending messages when they write thank-you notes to the clown who visited their class or when they see that an invitation to their parents to share a special event results in their parents' coming to school. Children learn that a shopping list can help them remember needed items. Using print all through the day and experiencing the pleasures of being read to are necessary activities for learning about the functions of print.

Functions of print
The purposes of print: to provide directions, pleasure, information, and so on.

Learning about Books

Learning about books is a goal that can provide joy for both students and teachers. When children know about books and what is in them, they are much more likely to be interested in learning to read and to know what to expect when they begin reading. Both teachers and children cherish time spent sharing favorite story books and poems. When children listen to teachers or parents read to them, they learn to appreciate the sounds and rhythms of language and the pleasures to be found in books.

Of course, books also provide information and directions. Teachers can supply books that will enhance ideas developed in play. For example, children playing "going to the moon" would be interested in books about planets and space travel. Other children might be interested in books that give directions for making an insect cage, that tell how to care for the classroom animals, or that provide information about snakes, dinosaurs, or monsters. An observant teacher will find many opportunities to share both informational books and stories. Children will unlikely exert all the effort it takes to learn to read if they do not know there are treasures to be found in print for those who can read.

Phonemic Awareness

Phonemic awareness
The ability to examine language separate from meaning and manipulate its component sounds.

Phonemic awareness has been defined by Cunningham (1988) as "the ability to examine language independently of meaning and to manipulate its component sounds" (p. 516). Phonemic awareness is a cluster of skills of different ability levels, not a single skill that one does or does not have. For example, recognizing rhyming words is one level of phonemic awareness, distinguishing the beginning sound of a word from the remainder of the word is another level of awareness, and completely segmenting the phonemes in a given word is yet an even higher level.

Phonemic awareness should not be confused with *phonics;* the two are not synonymous. Phonics involves teaching children sound-letter relationships through direct instruction (Griffith and Olson 1992). Phonemic awareness involves a broader range of skills and is achieved through less formal means.

Phonemic awareness is best achieved through children's daily interactions with print. For example, a child who wants to write a note might ask how to spell a certain word. The teacher might say the word slowly and ask what sound the child hears. When the child has identified that sound and recorded it, the teacher would repeat the whole word and ask what sound the child hears next. This pattern would be repeated until the child has spelled the word in full (or at least all the letters that have been sounded).

Children who write words using so-called invented spelling are well aware of the phonemic nature of language and do not need instruction in phonemic awareness. Teachers can also point out the phonemes of words in stories the children are reading. If the teacher were reading a big book about a greedy cat, he might remind the children that they can read the word *greedy* every time they see it because the *gr,* the *ee,* and the *dy* stand for the same sounds whenever they are printed together.

Several studies have found that phonemic awareness is a good predictor of reading success. For most children, the skills that constitute phonemic awareness will develop with repeated experiences in reading and writing. For those children who have difficulty developing these skills on their own, the teacher should offer guidance, for instance, regularly pointing out the phonemic nature of words. Eventually, the children's own phonemic skills will mature, and such specific help will no longer be needed.

Learning about Story Structure

Every time a reader chooses material to read—a magazine, a newspaper, a mystery novel, or a cookbook—he brings to that reading experience expectations of how the material will be written and what its structure will be. Knowledge of **story structure** is important because the more a reader knows about what to expect from printed material, the more likely he is to be successful in reading it. A skilled reader knows that a newspaper will be written in a distinctive style; that most of the information will be found in the beginning of the article, with details following; that certain types of articles will be in certain sections of the paper, maybe even on certain days; and so forth.

Story structure
The organizational pattern of printed material that is typical of its genre.

　　Children who are learning about reading are also developing knowledge of story structure and what to expect from various reading materials (Jensen 1985). Knowledge of story structure cannot be taught using skills worksheets. Such knowledge is developed through experience—reading many kinds of materials over a long period of time. For example, teachers can help children compare the structures of *Too Much Noise* (McGovern 1967) and *It Could Always Be Worse* (Zemach 1976), two stories that have the same plot structure. Even young children can begin to recognize cumulative structure in such stories as *The Turnip* (Tolstoi no date) and in *circle stories* (in which the main character begins at a point, usually home, has adventures, and returns to the beginning point) such as *The Runaway Bunny* (Brown 1942), *The Story of Ping* (Flack and Wiese 1933), and *Sylvester and the Magic Pebble* (Steig 1969).

Learning What Readers Do

Children learn what readers do as they observe people reading. Young children need to know that readers attend to the print of the text and that they think as they read. Even three- and four-year-olds begin to understand that it is the print that is being read, rather than the pictures, and that reading is constrained by *directionality* (Goodman and Altwerger 1981). Children who look at "big books" or class charts while the teacher reads them have the opportunity to develop this knowledge of directionality, as a hand or pointer moves from left to right under the print. Listening to "big books" being read aloud also gives children an opportunity to observe the changes in inflection indicated by punctuation.

Children also begin to learn that print is constant, that the same configuration of letters stands for the same word every time (except with homonyms, of course). One good way to encourage this observation is to use pocket charts with word cards. Poems and chants can be printed on cards that can be changed. If the children have learned "One, Two, Buckle My Shoe," the teacher might use the cards to prompt children to substitute new words for *shoe, door,* and so on; this allows children to recognize that some words remain the same, no matter what context they are in. The teacher can also demonstrate that readers make predictions about what they read. For instance, she might introduce a book by showing the children its cover and asking for predictions of what the story might be about.

Young children also learn what readers do when they engage in writing. As they record their own ideas, they become more aware that reading is the unlocking of an author's ideas, not just the pronouncing of words.

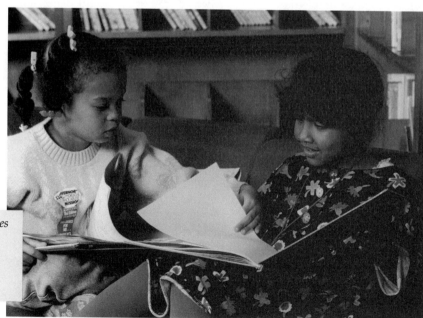

Readers use a variety of cues in order to get information from the printed page.

Six-year-old Jason is a good example of a child learning to read by writing. He has "published" several books of his own and feels quite confident in his ability to read them and to write others. Jason reads the ideas from the books but certainly does not produce a word-perfect reading of the text. In fact, he pays little attention to the exact text. What is important is that he believes that he can read, that he is capable as a reader and writer, and that others value his ability. He is gaining in ability to recognize individual words and is becoming more aware of the importance of the text. Nothing in his reading experience is teaching him that he is not able to read.

This is the goal of an early childhood reading program for beginning readers. Not all children experience such success and support for their developing reading abilities. In a skills-based classroom, Jason might be placed in the low reading group because he cannot read the exact text yet. That placement would deliver a clear message to Jason each day: that he cannot achieve what his teacher and parents expect of him. He would learn that reading is a painful experience and one to be avoided, if at all possible.

Applying Reading Strategies

As children become more independent as readers, teachers can help them apply the strategies used by effective readers: sampling print, predicting what is coming, confirming predictions, and integrating new information with what is known (Weaver 1988). Children need opportunities to use what they know about language and how it works and to apply their own experiences to reading tasks. For example, children who know oral language can use their knowledge of semantics and syntax to predict the meanings of words, if the reading materials make sense to them. Materials for reading must be selected with the children's experiences in mind; children must be able to apply what they know about how the world works to their reading. A story about a caterpillar will not make sense if the reader has no concept of what a caterpillar is.

Readers use a variety of cues from the printed page in order to get meaning, including the following:

- *The graphophonic system*—In English, the alphabet letters and their related sounds
- *The schematic system*—What one knows about the topic before beginning reading and what one knows about the genre one is reading
- *The semantic system*—What words mean
- *The syntactic system*—How words fit into different slots in sentences

Which cues are used most depends on the skill of the reader and the nature of the material being read. For instance, as you read this textbook, you probably rely most heavily on the schematic system and pay least attention to the graphophonic system. You will realize that you do not look at every letter when you read if you think about how difficult it is to proof-read your own work—it's nearly impossible. You know what you said, so to actually look at each letter is very difficult. Consider another demonstration of how little most readers use the graphophonic system: When you read an article that has been photocopied and the words on the edge of the page are blurred, you read over and fill in those words, usually without even thinking about them. A beginning reader, on the other hand, may focus so much on the print that she will fail to use the other systems. Reading will be more difficult for you when you are not familiar with the topic because you will not have adequate background knowledge. If you doubt the importance of background knowledge, pick up a biology journal next time you are in the library, and read an article or two.

A good reader coordinates the cues from all these systems through the use of learned strategies and does it so rapidly that she is unaware of even using the separate systems.

Becoming an Independent Reader

Teachers can help children gain independence as readers by providing reasons for them to read. In other words, reading should meet children's needs for gaining information or solving problems. If children are learning about spiders, the teacher should provide a wide variety of books about spiders. Children will need to read in order to obtain information and to write in order to share that information. Print can be used in the classroom to help children organize their activities, keep records, and make plans. The more reasons children have for using print for their own needs, the more easily they will become able to read independently.

Meeting School or District Requirements

If a school or district has established specific reading requirements for kindergartners or children in primary grades, teachers can use a variety of means in order to achieve those goals while keeping the children's contact with print appropriate and meaningful. For example, if the district requires mastery of a list of sight words, the methods for teaching those words will be determined by individual teachers. Teachers can point out those words in poems, stories, or chants and emphasize them on charts or "big books." Teachers can also focus children's attention on words from the list while taking dictation from them or when using language experience stories. Very few stories dictated by five-year-olds fail to contain *I, me, you, see, run,* or other common sight words. Teachers can then help children read those words. Multiple repetitions of such activities will usually result in children's learning to recognize the required list of sight words, even when the words are presented in isolation. Teaching a sight-word vocabulary does not require drill and practice that is isolated from the children's experience or other practice that can cause some children to feel inadequate.

When reading is viewed as part of a developmental process, rather than as a set of discrete skills, both teachers and parents can place learning specific reading skills in better perspective and can celebrate a child's growth without pressuring him to perform a given skill at a particular time. Only then will our expectations be reasonable: growth for every child on a timetable set by the child himself.

SOUND-LETTER RELATIONSHIPS

In some programs for young children, the reading curriculum centers around teaching sound-letter relationships. Teachers in such programs may feature a "letter of the week" and give children exercises in tracing or copying the selected letter. Teachers might require that objects brought for sharing time be objects whose names begin with the sound represented by the letter and that snacks be food whose names begin with the given letter.

There are several significant flaws in the "letter-of-the-week" curriculum. One is that a letter alone has no context and thus has no meaning. By themselves, letters have little value. Only when they are combined with other letters to form sounds and words do letters have context and meaning. Focusing on an individual letter therefore means focusing on the most insignificant piece of information that is useful for real reading. Another flaw in the "letter-of-the-week" curriculum is that concentrating on sound-letter relationships leads children to believe that other strategies for reading are less important. But in fact, mature readers use sound-letter relationships much less frequently than other strategies. A third problem is that stressing sound-letter relationships tends to encourage parents to believe that mastery of this one aspect of reading is tantamount to mastery of reading, which is certainly not true. In addition, a focus on sound-letter relationships ignores what children already know about such relationships and may involve boring repetition of information for some children. In this sense, teaching a "letter of the week" violates the principle of good skills instruction that says such instruction should always be presented when it is needed by the learner.

These criticisms of the "letter-of-the-week" curriculum should not be interpreted to mean that learning about sound-letter relationships is unimportant. Understanding sound-letter relationships is another important skill in learning to read. To help children gain this skill, teachers should plan activities that are developmentally appropriate and designed for individual children. For children who are having difficulty with sound-letter relationships, alternatives to a "letter of the week" include focusing on a given letter in stories, charts, chants, poems, song lyrics, or other print. Reutzel (1992) recommends a number of activities: creating alphabet books from environmental print; creating an alphabet center in the classroom with wooden, magnetic, and sandpaper letters as well as stencils, chalkboards, and other writing materials; and using alphabet cookies and cereals, especially in pairs or small groups so that children can sort and eat the letters while talking to one another about which letters they have. Reutzel goes on to suggest that art experiences are also enjoyable and meaningful, such as compiling a collage of objects that begin with a given letter. Finally, he suggests the frequent use of alphabet books in the classroom. After repeated readings, children can create their own alphabet books.

Allowing children to write is the most sensible approach to teaching sound-letter relationships. When children write, they demonstrate their knowledge of such relationships. As they hear others read aloud; watch adults record their words; see the words to songs, poems, chants, and fingerplays on charts; and read books and messages, their knowledge of sound-letter relationships grows and is reflected in their writing.

The Beginning Reader

In the early stages of learning to read, children continue to need teachers who recognize what reading strategies children know and how they use them. Certainly, instruction in various strategies is needed, but it must be tailored to fit individual children. Girard (1993) describes a first-grade classroom in which the children learned to use multiple strategies for solving their reading problems. They learned the vocabulary of such strategies as *predicting* and *confirming* and learned that they have many alternatives in approaching an unfamiliar word in text.

For beginning readers, teachers should select books carefully. The best choices are books that are interesting yet have repetitive vocabularies; picture books containing beautiful illustrations and books using complex language are not good choices. In introducing a new book that is unfamiliar to readers, Clay (1991) recommends these guidelines:

- Invite the children to respond to the new book by focusing on its illustrations and linking it to other stories the children know.
- Ask the children about any of their own experiences that may relate to the new book, not only to make the book relevant but to straighten out anything that may be confusing about it.
- Create an overview of the story structure to provide a framework for anticipating what will happen throughout. Perhaps sketch the plot or structure the sequence of the story up to the climax, leaving the resolution a surprise.
- Encourage children to draw on personal experiences or to remember other stories shared previously, which will develop understanding of the theme or topic. Conceptual problems may also be addressed; for instance, some of the children may not understand cultural issues or underlying assumptions (such as why the fox is stalking the hen). Discussion will explore this facet of the plot.
- Use novel language features in talking about the story, and enunciate these words or terms very deliberately. This means anticipating anything that will not clearly link to the children's own language, such as literary devices, unusual names, and odd syntactical sequences.
- Intentionally use one particular sentence pattern two or three times, and have children repeat a phrase or sentence, trying the difficult language or pronunciation themselves. This allows children to hear and remember a model of the language, which will support their reading of the text. This does not mean memorizing the lines of the book but rather "readying the mind and ear to grapple with novelty" (pp. 266–267).

As children learn to read independently, they need teachers who support their efforts and set the stage for successful reading experiences.

STAGES OF READING DEVELOPMENT

Because teachers need to provide children with experiences that encourage growth in literacy, knowledge of the stages of reading development is useful. These stages cannot be defined in terms of ages because individual children move through the stages at their own pace. Similarly, these stages are not to be used to determine if individual children are making appropriate progress for their age. Rather, knowledge of the stages of reading development should help a teacher conceptualize the developmental nature of the reading process and feel comfortable about the progress individual children are making, knowing that growth takes place over time.

Cochrane et al. (1984) describe reading behaviors in five stages: the magical stage, the self-concept stage, the bridging reader stage, the take-off reader stage, and the independent reader stage. These stages are described in more detail in Table 7.1.

Table 7.1 Stages in Reading Development	
STAGE	**PARENT/TEACHER ROLE**
Magical Stage The child is learning the purpose of books; begins to think that books are important; looks at books, holds books, often takes a favorite book with him or her.	Model the importance of reading; read to the child; talk about books.
Self-Concept Stage The child views himself as a reader; begins to engage in readinglike activities; may pretend to read books; imposes meaning from pictures or previous experience with books; uses booklike language, even though it does not match the text.	Read to the child; provide access to books the child knows; participate with the child in reading books.
Bridging Reader Stage The child becomes aware of actual print. He may be able to pick out familiar words; notices personally significant words; is able to read back stories that he has written; can read familiar print from poems, songs, or nursery rhymes. The child may believe that each syllable is a word and can be frustrated with attempts to match print and sounds; usually begins to recognize alphabet.	Read to the child; present words of familiar songs or poems on charts or in booklets; provide opportunities to write frequently.
Take-Off Reader Stage The child begins to use the three cueing systems (graphophonic, semantic, and syntactic) together. He is excited about reading; begins to recognize print out of context; attends to environmental print and reads everything (cereal boxes, signs, and so on). A danger in this stage is giving too much attention to each letter.	Read to the child; encourage reading in a variety of situations; do not force letter-perfect reading.
Independent Reader Stage The child is able to read unfamiliar books independently; constructs meaning from print and from previous experience and authors' cues; is able to make predictions about reading material. Material related directly to experience is easiest to read, but the child can understand familiar structures and genres and common expository material.	Read to the child; encourage age predictions about reading; select material that is relevant; provide instruction in story structure.

Source: Adapted from Orin Cochrane, Donna Cochrane, Sharon Scalena, and Ethel Buchanan, *Reading, Writing and Caring* (Winnipeg, Manitoba, Canada: Whole Language Consultants, 1984). Used with permission of the authors.

Again, the descriptions of these stages are not meant to indicate to either teachers or parents that any child should be at any stage at any given time. The stages are useful in helping teachers observe and communicate growth in literacy. They also remind teachers and parents that what the child is accomplishing at any given time is not the end product of the process of developing reading ability; that process will take many years. How young children feel about reading during their early years and how they feel about themselves as beginning readers will have a profound effect on that lifelong process.

LEARNING TO WRITE

In the past, teachers and parents assumed that children would learn to write after they learned to read and that these experiences would take place primarily in a school setting. That view of writing dominated the instructional literature for years. Then in 1971, Carol Chomsky made a radical departure from the traditional view when she advocated that nonreaders should be writing and that reading instruction should begin with writing. Since that time, there has been a flurry of research activity focusing on young children and their writing. The resulting information has greatly expanded the view of writing—what it is, how it develops, and how best to teach it.

The more traditional view defined writing in terms that were mostly limited to handwriting. Children were expected to copy letters until they could reproduce close approximations of the teacher's model. Then they were expected to copy sentences. Teachers often gave children exercises in a handwriting text to copy or began the schoolday by writing a poem or a quotation on the board for the children to copy. Children's attempts at writing on their own were basically ignored or perhaps even punished—certainly not encouraged (Atkins 1984). In light of the research conducted since the 1970s, however, writing is generally defined more broadly today to include children's efforts at making marks on paper—beginning with scribbles.

Parents and teachers of young children have always known about young children's interest in writing. (They have been cleaning the results of that interest off walls and tables for years.) Children seem to be intuitively aware of the importance of their efforts. Goodman and Altwerger (1981) found that when they asked three-year-old children if they could write, the children would answer "Of course" and make marks on paper that they expected could be interpreted. (Interestingly, these same three-year-olds claimed not to be able to read because they had not been taught to do so.)

We now recognize that children construct their understanding of written language in a developmental sequence that is observable and very similar in all children. The stages of writing development have been described by Temple, Nathan, Temple, and Burris (1993); Clay (1975); and Ferreiro and Teberosky (1982). These stages are outlined in the following sections.

Development of Writing

Scribble Stage

As soon as children begin to make marks with writing instruments, they are beginning to learn about written language and how it works. The first stage in the development of writing is scribbling. Just as children babble before they use words, they scribble before they learn which forms are letters and which are not. Figure 7.1 is an example of scribbling.

Parents and teachers of scribblers should provide them with a variety of materials, such as paint, books, paper, and crayons. Parents and teach-

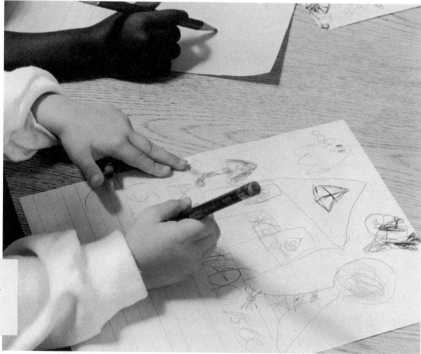

The development of writing occurs in predictable stages.

FIGURE 7.1   Scribbling

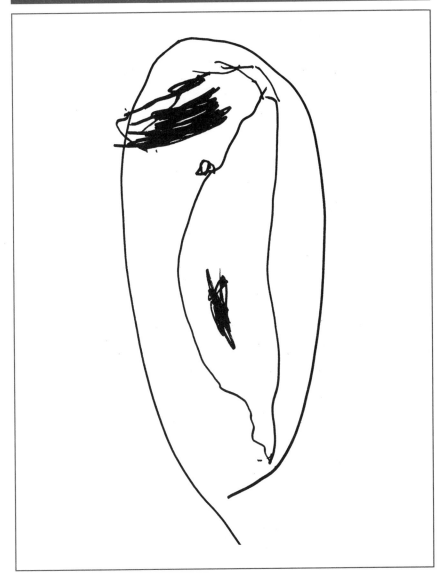

ers should label the children's scribbling as "writing" and model writing just as they model reading for their children. Parents can model writing in everyday situations, for instance, saying "We are almost out of milk. We should write it on our grocery list," or "I am writing a letter to Aunt Sue. Would you like to write something to her?" or "I am going to leave a note

FIGURE 7.2   Linear Repetitive Writing

for Daddy so he will know where we are," and so on. Parents should also read aloud and encourage children to talk to each other and to adults.

Linear Repetitive Stage

The next stage in writing development is the linear repetitive stage. In this stage, children discover that writing is usually horizontal and that letters appear in a string across a page. Children in this stage think that a word referring to something large has a longer string of forms than a word referring to something small (Ferreiro and Teberosky 1982; Schickedanz 1988). In other words, children look for concrete connections between words and their referents. Figure 7.2 is a sample of linear repetitive writing. The child who did this sample mixed some letter forms with the linear scribbles.

Children in the linear repetitive stage need the same support that scribblers need from parents and teachers. Adults might also begin watching for the emergence of letter forms.

Random-Letter Stage

The next stage is a random-letter stage, in which children learn which forms are acceptable as letters and use them in some random order to record words or sentences. Children produce strings of letters that have no relation to the sounds of the words they are attempting to record. They

FIGURE 7.3   Random-Letter Writing

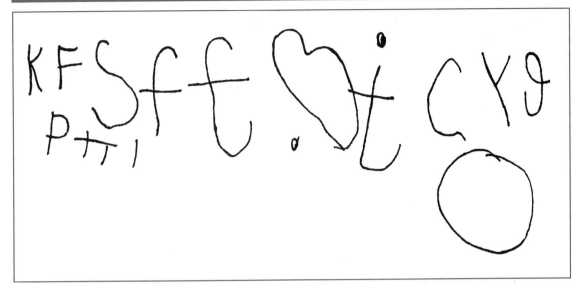

"The 3 bears are so nice and cute."

may also include some forms that are not recognizable as letters because their repertoire of letters is so limited. Figure 7.3 shows an example of random-letter writing in which the message is "The 3 bears are so nice and cute." This sample illustrates clearly the inclusion of some forms that are not letters.

Teachers and parents should encourage children's attempts to write. Children need the adults around them to respond to the intent of their writing, not to correct their form. If the people around them honor their attempts to write and treat their writing as important, children's writing skills will grow. Just as we know that a child who is saying "goed" is actually making progress in learning language, we know that a child who has discovered letters and understands that they stand for thoughts has made progress in learning about written language.

Letter-Name Writing, or Phonetic Writing

The next stage of development is that of early phonetic writing. In this stage, children begin to make the connection between letters and sounds. The beginning of this stage is often described as *letter-name writing* because children write the letters whose names and sounds are the same. For example, they write the word *you* with the letter *u*. They begin to represent words with graphemes that reflect exactly what they hear. Figure 7.4 is an exam-

FIGURE 7.4 Phonetic Writing

"Me and my family are going to Utah for 5 days."

ple of phonetic writing in which the message is "Me and my family are going to Utah for 5 days." In this sample, it is easy to see that the child represented *my* with an *m, family* with *fa, going* with a *g,* and *Utah* with *UTO.*

Transitional Spelling

As children learn more about the written language system, they begin to learn the conventions of written language. They being to spell some words in conventional ways, even though their spelling up to this point has been phonetic. A good example is the word love. Because children are exposed to this word so often, they begin to spell it in its conventional form very early. *The* is another common example.

This stage of spelling is called *transitional* to indicate that children are moving from phonetic spelling to more standard or conventional spelling. Figure 7.5 is an example of such spelling. Beginning on the bottom left, this

FIGURE 7.5   Transitional Spelling

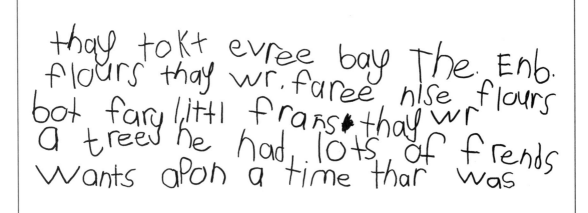

sample reads: "Once upon a time there was a tree. He had lots of friends, but very little friends. They were flowers. They were very nice flowers. They talked every day. The end." This child began her story on the left side of the page, but when she needed more space, she wrote the next line above the first line. She knew about the direction of written English but did not yet know how to place words on a page. (Consider all she *did* know about written English that allowed her to compose and record this story.)

Teachers and parents can foster independence in writing at this stage by asking children how they think words are spelled, by supplying needed information, and by encouraging children to help each other in the writing process. Instruction in spelling as an isolated subject is not necessary at this point. Children will learn to spell conventionally the words they need for writing. In Figure 7.5, much of the writing is correct. Teachers should focus on how much children know at this stage, rather than correcting spellings they do not yet know.

Conventional Spelling

Finally, children achieve mostly conventional spelling. Just as children move slowly from babbling to adult speech, they need time to learn the conventions of written language. Adult speech is not mastered without considerable time and effort from the learner and support from sensitive adults. Children deserve the same support as they move from scribbling to mature writing.

Principles of Written Language

Marie Clay (1975) has been very influential in helping teachers of young children understand children's development in reading and writing. Her work, along with that of Don Holdaway (1980), has served as the basis for reading and writing instruction in all of New Zealand. Many U.S. schools and preschools have adopted the methods of instruction that these two researchers advocate.

Clay (1975) has observed the following principles that govern the development of written language:

1. *The principle of signs*—Children learn that objects or events can be represented with signs; they then move to learning letters as symbols that are arbitrary, that is, not related to their referents.

2. *The copying principle*—Children often copy models found in their environment, such as logos, or they copy their names, since their names are likely to be the print that they see most often.

3. *The flexibility principle*—Children discover that a letter can vary greatly in form and still be recognized as a letter. Children trying out this principle will create variations of letter forms and ask for feedback on the success or failure of their variations. In this problem-solving approach, children learn to construct and to recognize various forms of the same letter.

4. *The inventory principle*—Children often take inventory of their own learning in a very systematic way. They may make lists of all the letter forms they know or all the words they can write. Although teachers might have a reason for asking children to write all the letters or words that they know, children also complete such inventories spontaneously.

5. *The principle of recurrence*—Clay describes *recurrence* as "the tendency to repeat an action," which contributes to the child's ability to form letters quickly and habitually. The child also begins to realize that the same letters or words can recur in different patterns. English-speaking children discover that letters can only be repeated twice in words and that words can only be repeated twice in sentences. For example, in words such as *Mississippi*, the same letter is repeated, and in sentences such as *He had had all he could eat*, the same word is repeated.

6. *The generating principle*—The generating principle causes children to use some of the elements of writing and some of the rules for combining them to produce new statements. Such behavior is basic to the development of oral language because children can never hear every sentence that they want to produce—they can only learn the elements and the rules for

combining them. It is logical that children would use this same technique when attempting to master written language systems.

Conventions of Written Language

Children must learn other elements of written language that are not related to representing sounds with specific letters or combinations of let-ters. One of these elements is *directionality:* the **convention** that in English, writing begins on the left and moves to the right. Other conventions include the use of space around words and the use of abbreviations. Children must also learn to arrange words on a page and in a book. Children may temporarily ignore what they know about directionality if they cannot fit a word on a page or line. Through experience, they learn to carry words over to the next page or to put extra words on the backs of pages. Graves and Stuart (1985) observed that the space around words was negative space and that learning what to do with it was a difficult concept for young children. Some children attempted to fill up negative space by placing periods between each word. They recognized spaces but tried to make them positive rather than negative.

Convention
A rule of written language that is determined by social agreement, such as the use of capital letters.

Only children with well-developed concepts of words will understand abbreviations. The use of abbreviations signals that children understand that the letters of abbreviations stand for words and could be expanded into the words for which they stand. Clay (1975) cites an example of a child who used abbreviations in squares to be colored a given color. The child marked each square with a *b* for *black, w* for *white,* and so on.

In order to make all these discoveries about written language, children need experience exploring writing, opportunities to make hypotheses about how print works, and feedback that verifies their guesses. Teachers and parents who recognize that children are exploring the flexibility of written language and constructing an understanding of what is possible will be able to foster growth in children's writing. They will offer many opportunities for writing, will recognize most mistakes as explorations of the written language system, and will be able to celebrate the growth that they can observe in the children's understanding.

The Writing Process with Young Children

Much has been written in recent years about the writing process and means of implementing it across the curriculum so that elementary chil-

FIGURE 7.6   Writing by a Child in Kindergarten

"I watched T.V."

FIGURE 7.7   Writing by a Child in Kindergarten

OCVLWNPGmBA

"We went to the woods and we was gonna shoot the rabbit."

FIGURE 7.8   Writing by a Child in Kindergarten

HCAURtLES FBDWNav PD J2AM

"My dad is going to buy me a rifle. It's a deer rifle."

dren can achieve competence in writing. The work of Graves (1983) and Calkins (1986) has been helpful to teachers of older elementary children who want to create an environment that promotes writing skills and to take the time necessary to implement the process. The whole point of emphasizing the process of writing is to help teachers move away from giving children isolated bits and pieces of instruction in the conventions of printed language and toward helping children learn those conventions while engaging in relevant and meaningful writing activities.

Helping younger children write meaningfully requires providing the necessary tools (paper, writing instruments) and helping children appreciate the usefulness of writing. Even very young children should be encouraged to keep journals in which they can record their experiences and feelings. Young children may begin by drawing pictures and talking about them. As they participate in classroom activities, they may begin to use letters or words and phrases to aid in expressing their ideas. Gradually, the amount of writing will increase. Teachers of young children should be aware that not all children will choose to write in journals. Children are to be encouraged but not forced to write in their journals regularly. Figures 7.6, 7.7, and 7.8 are examples of journal entries from a kindergartner that were recorded over a period of a week.

Children should be encouraged to make use of print in play situations and in other activities. For example, a child was observed carefully writing a list, which he took home. The next day, his mother came to the classroom to ask for a copy of the recipe that had been used in a cooking experience. Her son had brought home a list of ingredients, but she didn't know what to do with them. From this experience, the child learned more about writing than would have been possible if he had completed a whole ream of worksheets. He learned that print is important in communication, that some lists require much detail, and that writing gets a response. Children might write dialogue for puppets or make signs to label the parts of the airport they have constructed with blocks. The teacher's tasks are to make sure that materials are available and accessible and to value and encourage what children do.

For younger children, the writing process will not include the usual steps that older children can complete, such as editing and writing revisions. Just writing for themselves, watching an adult write down what they dictate, and listening to well-written material being read is enough writing instruction for most young children. Primary children can be helped to edit their own writing and as they grow more skillful, the writing of their peers. By second grade, many children can look for capital letters at the beginnings of sentences, punctuation marks at the ends of sentences, and conventional spellings of familiar words. Children can also help each other by responding to each other's writing.

HANDWRITING INSTRUCTION

Instruction in the correct formation of letters should be part of the curriculum for young children only as it meets individual needs. The focus of all writing with young children should be the content of the message, rather than the formation of the letters. Children will explore the variability that is possible in producing letter forms and make judgments about the appropriateness of given forms based on the feedback they get when they use those forms for communication. Children do not need to practice forming letters for no reason. Some children may choose to copy models of print found in the classroom environment. Teachers can certainly allow children to copy such print, but they should not assign children the task of writing letters over and over. When children have real reasons for writing legibly, they will want to learn to write letters that others can read. The desire to create letters, signs, displays, notes, invitations, and a multitude of other written forms is reason enough for children to practice legible handwriting.

In the beginning stages of writing, young children often produce letters that are backward. In a child's world, the orientation of most objects is not important—a chair is a chair, no matter which way it is facing. Children may not always attend to letter orientation, and backward letters are not indications of some sort of disability. Children may not only make letters backward; they may also begin writing on the right of the paper and produce whole words backward. Given many opportunities to engage in writing designed to communicate, children will correct these errors. A teacher should model correct grammar for children but without correcting their use of language. For example, if a child said "I goed to the store yesterday," the teacher would probably respond "Oh, what did you buy when you went to the store?"

The same sort of response is most useful in helping children correct backward letters. Often, the teacher can write a response that models the correct letter formation or provide reading materials in which the letter is prominent. If a child had trouble producing given phonemes after age seven or so, the teacher would ask for some professional help. The same rule of thumb applies to children who produce backward letters. For most preschoolers and primary-grade children, however, providing more opportunities to write and read is the best prescription.

<table>
<tr><td>

DEVELOPMENTALLY
APPROPRIATE
PRACTICE
....

</td><td>

As you reflect on your own experience in learning to read and what you know about developmentally appropriate practice, think about these statements:

</td></tr>
</table>

- According to the tenets of DAP, reading instruction should not begin until the child is about six years old.
- Literacy is a continuum of learning that begins at birth. The teacher's task is to find where each child is on that continuum and what she wants and needs to know next.
- A teacher who wants to be as developmentally appropriate as possible will not engage in any direct literacy instruction unless the child

specifically asks for guidance (such as "What is this letter?").
- Adding play materials that will encourage literacy activities does not necessarily make the classroom less playful.
- Isolated skill instruction (such as teaching the names of letters and how to recognize sight words) is rarely developmentally appropriate.
- Literacy is not the whole focus of instruction in a developmentally appropriate classroom.

CLASSROOM ENVIRONMENTS THAT FOSTER THE DEVELOPMENT OF LITERACY
....

Classrooms that foster the development of literacy have several distinguishing characteristics: They are interesting and full of activity, they allow for participation in many different experiences, and they connect reading and writing to children's experiences. Classrooms where literacy emerges are also print rich: They contain a wide variety of reading, writing, and listening materials that are accessible to children.

In a stimulating, active environment, children will be encouraged to participate in a wide variety of experiences. Such a classroom will not be a quiet place! Children developing new concepts should want to talk about them, read about them, and write about them. For example, as a science activity, children might observe hatching silkworms. This activity would require research about when silkworms hatch, when the mulberry leaves that they eat are available, what will happen to the silk if the larvae are allowed to mature, and how to preserve some eggs so that another generation of silkworms can be grown. This activity might also involve gathering food for the larvae and observing the metamorphosis of the larvae into silkworms. Children involved in such experiences will be constantly talking about their observations, reading from a variety of sources, listening to others read, and writing about their experiences and feelings. Activities that encourage thinking, talking, reading, and writing should be part of every schoolday.

Several studies have found that adding selected materials to the play environment and guiding their use can encourage children to participate in more literacy activities in their play (Neuman and Roskos 1993; Christie 1990; Morrow and Rand 1991). Christie (1990) notes that giving children time to play is simply not enough. Teachers must also intervene to promote literacy activities, perhaps thinking about what literacy materials could be added to play areas, encouraging children to play in theme centers where literacy is a natural response to a theme, or modeling literacy behaviors in play areas. For example, a teacher might set up an office or a grocery store or invite children to write labels for their block constructions. Theme areas that involve literacy experiences include a doctor's office, a shoe store, a restaurant, a home (making lists, checking the TV guide, reading the newspaper, reading to babies, and so on), and a post office.

Neuman and Roskos (1993) recommend using real literacy objects rather than pretend objects. An office might be equipped with real file folders and forms. The materials selected should be familiar to the children from their real-world experiences. Morrow and Rand (1991) suggest that literacy materials be kept in clearly marked places, that they be changed frequently to keep children's interest in them high, that teachers model the

Growth in literacy is enhanced by many experiences with print.

uses of materials as needed or suggest possible uses when appropriate, and that all levels of development be accepted for the most positive results.

Language, including printed language, is a tool for communicating effectively. Teachers use all kinds of language to help children express their understanding and to help them gain new knowledge. The activities described in the following list will help children connect concepts and oral and printed language:

Reading and Writing Activities
for the Early Childhood Classroom

- The children construct an ambulance after they observe an ambulance go by while they are playing outside. The play grows into a need for a hospital and patients and doctors. The teacher can contribute by offering books about ambulances or hospitals for browsing and by recording and reading back some of the children's statements about their play. The children might describe the ambulance and its sounds, and these descriptions could be recorded on a large piece of paper, to be reread several times as the play continues. Children might also choose to draw and write about their own hospital experiences.
- The children have learned to sing a song by rote. The teacher prepares a chart with the lyrics to the song printed on it. It is hung in the classroom, and children can follow the words as they sing. The words might also be printed on cards to be placed in a pocket chart; the children could then read the cards whenever they like. Children might be given copies of the lyrics in their own booklets. Primary children can write new lyrics to known melodies. As children engage in writing stories or song lyrics, they can get instruction in punctuation as it is needed, learn about editing, and decide about publishing their work. Barclay and Walwer (1992) suggest using song picture books to link the lyrics of songs to children's growing literacy abilities.
- The children have made some puppets. The teacher records the story that they tell with the puppets on a chart and places the chart near the puppet stage. Some children will be able to read it to others who want to play with the puppets. Some children might want to make their own books of the story. Other children might want to create new stories or sequels to the first. Older children can learn simple bookbinding techniques and about the punctuation needed in the script for a puppet play.
- The children learn the text for a pattern book such as *Brown Bear, Brown Bear* (Martin 1970) and then write their own books using the same pattern. They might write "Jennifer, Jennifer, what do you see? I see Steven looking at me." *Brown Bear, Brown Bear* and *Whose Mouse Are You?*

(Kraus 1970) are excellent models for helping children learn to use punctuation marks.

- The children visit the local fire station. The teacher arranges for photographs to be taken of the entire trip. The children might write about the trip and use the photographs as illustrations. The photographs and the children's writing could be bound into a book.

- The teacher reads a "big book" aloud to the children and explains what a reader does while reading (thinking, following along the lines of print, predicting, and so on). When the teacher rereads the book, the children join in when they recognize words. The teacher can plan any number of activities, depending on the needs of the group. Some children might write new stories based on the model in the "big book." For some children, the teacher might cover some of the words in the book with Post-it notes, print other words on them, and ask the children to read the new version of the story that is created. Other children might find all the words that begin with a given sound. Others will be able to read the student versions of the "big book" independently.

- The children dictate a report about their experience catching tadpoles in the pond, and the teacher records their report on a large chart. This report might be reread and used as described in the "big book" example above. If older children have written their own reports about tadpoles, the teacher might help them compare their reports to those written by other authors. They might discuss what an author had to know to write the piece, what information might have been excluded, the expected audience of the piece, the point of view taken by the author, and the author's style.

- The children have listened to the teacher read *The Lion, The Witch, and the Wardrobe* (Lewis 1951). Several children might be interested in reading the other books in the series, *The Chronicles of Narnia*. Other children might write responses to the reading in their journals; some children might create wardrobes through which to enter the kingdom of Narnia; some children might adapt their favorite scenes for readers' theater; and some might create a board game based on the Lewis stories.

- A group of first-graders liked *Whistle for Willie* (Keats 1964) so much that the teacher decided to do an author study on Ezra Jack Keats. The class might read several more of his books, discuss the language used, read reviews of his books, study the art in his illustrations, create skits for the characters in some of his books, read about how to put on a puppet play, or produce a play of their own.

- In response to her class's interest in the squirrels on the schoolgrounds, a teacher reads aloud *Nuts to You* (Ehlert 1993). Those children who are

INTEGRATING THE CURRICULUM

As promised in the Preface, the theme of patterns will be illustrated in each of the content-area chapters of this book (Chapters Seven through Twelve). The point of these examples is to help you understand more clearly how any well-chosen theme could include any of the traditional subject-matter areas. Consider the following activities in promoting literacy:

- Find the verse and chorus patterns in song books such as *Old MacDonald Had a Farm* (Pearson 1984) or the cumulative patterns of such songs as *This Old Man* (Jones 1990).
- Find the patterns in chants and rhymes; for example, *The House That Jack Built* (Stevens 1985) has a very strong pattern that can be clapped or tapped.
- Find the repeating patterns in books such as *Over in the Meadow* (Galdone 1986); *Black Crow, Black Crow* (Guy 1991); and *Brown Bear, Brown Bear* (Martin 1970).
- Discover the patterns in *A Seed A Flower A Minute, An Hour* (Blos 1992) and *Summer Is . . .* (Zolotow 1967).
- Call attention to the organizational patterns of alphabet and counting books.
- Explore the plot patterns of cumulative stories, circle stories, and parallel stories such as *Blueberries for Sal* (McCloskey 1963). Construct plot lines or draw pictures to illustrate these patterns.
- Compare the patterns of several different pieces of poetry. Focus the children's attention on how words are placed on pages for particular emphasis. Examples of acrostic, alphabet, or concrete poetry would be especially useful for examining the patterns.
- Write stories that follow given patterns; for example, choose a cumulative pattern and create a story.
- Encourage children to think about the pattern of rhythm in language as they compose sentences. Read examples of short, staccato patterns as well as more languid patterns that are used to create certain moods or tones.

still interested in squirrels might go through the card catalog in the library looking for other books on squirrels, use the CD–ROM to find entries about squirrels in the encyclopedia, or write their own stories and reports about squirrels.

These few examples illustrate how a teacher can use everyday class experiences to encourage children's developing abilities in reading and writing. It is important to remember that not every child will be interested in participating in all these experiences. Some children will be just becoming aware of the print around them; others will be interested in making their own books. The teacher must not expect total participation by everyone. If a child is not interested in print, the teacher must discover things that do interest the child and then help the child find ways to enhance that interest with print in a very personal way.

It is also important that the teacher not treat reading and writing as the only important activities in which children are involved. Children need to be involved in play, art, music, and so forth, and the teacher must value these experiences for themselves, without always tacking on a reading or writing component to supposedly legitimize the experience. To do otherwise would send children the subtle message that only reading and writing are important.

The communication triad—speaking, reading, and writing—should permeate all instruction in every subject. But each child's efforts in these areas should be natural—resulting from her own inclination and growing ability in each area. The artificial separation of learning into distinct instructional subjects must be avoided. When instruction is separated from experience, children develop the misconception that learning takes place only in school. Ideally, education is entering an era in which teachers will refocus on children's learning, rather than on defining education in terms of instruction.

CHILDREN WITH SPECIAL NEEDS

Teachers need to give special consideration to planning reading and writing activities for children with special needs, including those who have physical disabilities or language delays, who speak dialects, or for whom English is a second language (ESL). Chapter Six included suggestions of oral language experiences for children who speak dialects, whose first language is not English, or who have language delays. Teachers should consult with the parents of children who need special adaptations and with district or school specialists who can provide help in planning. Parents can provide information about the child's home experiences in literacy development and can help teachers by providing a supportive environment at home.

The following examples illustrate only a few of the possible adaptations that teachers may make to provide reading and writing experiences for children with special needs:

- Children with physical disabilities, such as sight or hearing losses, may need special materials to make their encounters with print successful. Teachers may need to provide materials printed in braille or very large print for children with vision limitations. Teachers may need to learn to sign or to have an interpreter present to take dictation from children who use sign rather than spoken language. Children who cannot hold ordinary writing instruments may need an adult or older child to act as a scribe for them; some children who have difficulty with controlling pens or pencils learn to use typewriters or computers to communicate.

- Children who have not achieved the oral language skills typical of their age group may need more opportunities to learn and practice oral language forms. When words are introduced in print, some children may need more background experiences in order to develop meanings for these words. Teachers should arrange for children who have language delays to interact with other children as much as possible and to talk with adults, as well.

- Teachers of children who speak dialects need to value the children's language and encourage them to develop their dialectal abilities while providing models of standard English when appropriate. For example, a child may communicate more effectively in his dialect on the playground but need a model of standard English when he has the opportunity to interview a guest speaker. Teachers who value children's language will not correct the use of dialects but will acknowledge that use as an acceptable form of communication. When taking dictation from a child who speaks a dialect, the teacher should record the words in conventional spelling but not change the syntactical structure of the child's utterances. As a child reads from charts or books, the teacher should not correct the child who reads the text "My mother is going to work" as "My mama be going to work." Such a child has demonstrated an understanding of the printed text, and that is much more important than an absolutely perfect rendering of the text at this point.

- ESL children need many opportunities to interact with English-speaking children and adults. The worst possible approach would be to isolate such children from the other children in order to give them special help in learning English. Children who play and talk with other children who speak English will learn the language quickly. Teachers should allow children to use their native languages when necessary for communication. In past years, schools often limited children's use of native languages in order to force them to speak English more quickly. That approach does not facilitate more rapid learning of English; rather, it does much harm to children's self-concepts and feelings of acceptance and actually hinders language development. The goal is not to eliminate children's first language but to help them achieve competence as speakers of a second language.

The concerned teacher will also learn enough about a child's native language to recognize where the child might have particular difficulties with English. For example, some sounds used in English, such as the *ch* at the beginning of *chair,* are rare in Spanish; there are differences in syntactical patterns between the two languages, as well. Chapter Six mentioned the differences in placement of adjectives in Spanish sentences; Spanish also allows redundancy. A Spanish-speaking child might say "My mother, she," which is acceptable in Spanish. Some languages, such as Chinese, are not alphabetical; for Chinese children, teachers can provide experiences with sound-letter relationships in meaningful contexts. As a child begins to learn words in English, the teacher will record those words in print for the child and will make sure that the child has many opportunities to write and explore English (Brewer 1990).

READING, WRITING, AND LANGUAGE EQUAL LITERACY

Table 7.2 suggests a way of relating the development of oral language, writing, and reading: literacy. The chart is not meant to indicate that the stages coincide exactly but simply that children develop knowledge in each system simultaneously. The point is that achieving literacy is a developmental process, similar in nature to the development of oral language. Teachers and parents who view literacy in this way are much more likely to support children, wherever they are in the process, and to understand that it takes time to be a skillful user of language systems.

Table 7.2   Stages in Different Aspects of Literacy

STAGES IN ORAL LANGUAGE DEVELOPMENT	STAGES IN WRITING	STAGES IN READING
Babbling	Scribbling stage	Magical stage
Expressive jargon	Linear repetitive state (with some scribbling)	Self-concept as a reader
One-word expressions, questions, negatives	Random-letter spelling	Bridging stage
Mature patterns mixed with immature forms	Letter-name writing, or phonetic writing	Take-off stage
Mature speech	Transitional spelling	Independent reading
	Conventional spelling	Skilled stage
		Advanced skilled stage

CHAPTER SUMMARY

- Literacy is developed over a long period of time. It is a complex process that cannot be promoted by readiness activities alone. Children who are learning reading and writing need to be actively involved in the process. Isolated skill lessons are not appropriate.
- Literacy development takes place in observable stages, but the length of time a child spends in each stage is highly individual. Children exhibit some predictable behaviors as they move along the continuum of literacy, but each child does so at her own pace.
- The beginning stage of learning to read is marked by the child's interest in books, followed by the child's developing a concept of himself as a reader. In the bridging stage, the child learns to attend to the print in the text, and in the take-off reader stage, he learns to use all the cueing systems simultaneously. The child then becomes an independent reader. Ideally, the ability to read continues to develop throughout one's life.
- Long before formal instruction begins, children are doing important work in literacy development as they explore the world of print. Children need opportunities to write and to construct their

knowledge of letters and the written language system.
- The child's control of the form of written language progresses through a number of stages: scribbling, linear repetitive scribbling, random-letter spelling, letter-name spelling (or phonetic spelling), transitional spelling, to conventional spelling. The child's use of written language provides the teacher with an understanding of what the child knows about written forms that is invaluable in planning literacy experiences for her.
- The development of literacy is best achieved in an interesting, active classroom where a wide variety of activities are available to the children. Children who are involved in interesting activities can be encouraged to use print in connection with these activities in meaningful ways.
- Exercises in isolated skills are not appropriate for young children. Children cannot practice skills out of context and then apply what has been learned to actual literacy experiences.
- Instruction in handwriting should be part of the curriculum for young children only as it meets individual needs to communicate more effectively.

WHAT WOULD YOU DO?

Reflect on your reading and your own experiences with young children as you think about the following situations:

1. You are asked by a group of kindergarten parents to assure them that their children will be reading by the end of the term. What would you tell them?
2. Some of the parents of the three-year-old children in your class are sure that their children would benefit from reading instruction using words on flashcards. What would you tell them about emergent literacy?
3. You have listened to and read of many opinions about instruction in reading. It seems that everyone who can read feels he is an expert on such instruction. How would you know to whom to listen?
4. You want to have a developmentally appropriate reading program, in which literacy is integrated into real and authentic experiences, but your school district requires an isolated phonics program. How would you explain your belief in the value of DAP in teaching reading?
5. A parent has asked you what he can do at home to help his child learn to read and write. What advice would you give?
6. You are asked to speak to the parent-teacher association on the concept of emergent literacy. What information would you present?

THEORY INTO PRACTICE

1. Observe several young children as they write. How do they react to the opportunity to write? Do you find writing behaviors that you can now identify as part of the developmental process of learning to write? Explain your answer on the basis of your observations.

2. Observe a class of four-year-olds and a class of second-graders. What are some of the develop-mental differences that you can observe in their reading behaviors?

3. Plan two or three classroom activities that would promote the development of literacy in developmentally appropriate ways.

4. Role-play a conference in which you explain to a parent how you will teach phonics.

RECOMMENDED FOR FURTHER READING

Clay, Marie M. *Becoming Literate: The Construction of Inner Control.* Portsmouth, NH: Heinemann, 1991.

For those who want a detailed study of children learning to read, this book provides excellent information. Clay discusses preschool children, the writing process, learning to spell, choosing books for reading instruction, and other topics in very readable and informative chapters. Some of what she says applies to New Zealand schools, but U.S. teachers can certainly use the basic information.

Fields, Marjorie V., Katherine L. Spangler, and Dorris Lee. *Let's Begin Reading Right: A Developmental Approach to Beginning Literacy.* 2d ed. New York: Macmillan, 1991.

This book includes excellent discussions of the relationship of literacy development to other areas of a child's development. Reading and writing are approached through interesting activities, not as separate skill areas.

Gentry, J. Richard, and Jean Wallace Gillet. *Teaching Kids to Spell.* Portsmouth, NH: Heinemann, 1993.

The authors present a thorough treatment of how spelling is learned and then suggest a practical program for use in the classroom. This book is a good resource even if you choose not to include formal spelling in your classroom.

Goodman, Ken. *Phonics Phacts.* Portsmouth, NH: Heinemann, 1993.

Although this book is short, it is powerful. The explanation of phonics is clearly written and under-standable. Goodman also presents thorough explanations of the place of phonics in writing and reading instruction and an interesting chapter on the politics of phonics.

International Reading Association. *Literacy Development and Pre-First Grade: A Joint Statement of Concerns About Present Practices in Pre-First Grade Reading Instruction and Recommendations for Improvement.* Newark, DE: IRA, 1985.

This statement was prepared by a committee representing the Association for Childhood Education International, the Association for Supervision and Curriculum Development, the International Reading Association, the National Association for the Education of Young Children, the National Association of Elementary School Principals, and the National Council of Teachers of English. It was printed in the journals of these organizations and is available as a pamphlet from the International Reading Association, 800 Barksdale Road, P.O. Box 8139, Newark, DE, 19714-8139. The statement is a helpful resource in responding to parents and others who have questions about reading programs for young children.

Kamii, Constance, ed. *Early Literacy: A Constructivist Foundation for Whole Language.* NEA Early Childhood Series. Washington, DC: National Education Association, 1991.

This book provides a foundation for understanding constructivist thinking. This explanation for how children learn is especially important to the whole-language movement in reading instruction, as it provides a strong philosophical base for whole-language programs. Some useful and practical chapters are offered on how children learn to spell, the writing process, and teaching reading with storybooks.

Ministry of Education. *Dancing with the Pen.* Wellington, New Zealand: Ministry of Education, 1992.

This book was written to support the work of teachers in New Zealand who are engaged in process writing. It offers clear explanations of why it is so important for children to choose their own topics, think about the audiences for their pieces, and seek the help of others in completing their writing. The stages of the writing process are explained clearly, and the many examples of children's writing add to the practical applications in this book.

Morrow, Lesley Mandel. *Literacy Development in the Early Years.* 2d ed. Boston: Allyn and Bacon, 1993.

This book begins with language development and the development of literacy in the home and moves on to managing reading instruction in the classroom, developing thematic units, and creating portfolios for assessments. The book is very useful for teachers of young children. Primary teachers will especially appreciate the suggestions for the physical environment and the checklists for evaluating the reading and writing development of children.

Schickedanz, Judith A. *More Than the ABC's: The Early Stages of Reading and Writing.* Washington, DC: National Association for the Education of Young Children, 1986.

This book includes much information about selecting books for young children and good chapters on the development of reading and writing. The strategies for combining print with play activities are especially useful.

Strickland, Dorothy S., and Lesley M. Morrow, eds. *Emerging Literacy: Young Children Learn to Read and Write.* Newark, DE: International Reading Association, 1989.

This collection of articles contains many practical ideas for the classroom teacher. There are chapters on reading to children, choosing children's literature, and assessing young children's reading and writing.

REFERENCES

General Sources

Atkins, Cammie. "Writing: Doing Something Constructive." *Young Children* 40 (November 1984): 3–7.

Barclay, Kathy Dulaney, and Lynn Walwer. "Linking Lyrics and Literacy Through Song Picture Books." *Young Children* 47 (May 1992): 76–85.

Brewer, Jo Ann. "Literacy Development When Children's First Language Is Not English." In *Literacy in the 90's: Readings in the Language Arts,* edited by Nancy Cecil, 221–230. Dubuque, IA: Kendall Hunt, 1990.

Calkins, Lucy. *The Art of Teaching Writing.* Portsmouth, NH: Heinemann, 1986.

Chomsky, Carol. "Write First, Read Later." *Childhood Education* 47 (March 1971): 296–299.

Christie, James F. "Dramatic Play: A Context for Meaningful Engagements." *Reading Teacher* 43 (April 1990): 542–545.

Clay, Marie M. "Introducing a New Storybook to Young Readers." *Reading Teacher* 45 (December 1991): 264–273.

Clay, Marie M. *What Did I Write? Beginning Writing Behavior.* Portsmouth, NH: Heinemann, 1975.

Cochrane, Orin, Donna Cochrane, Sharon Scalena, and Ethel Buchanan. *Reading, Writing and Caring.* Winnipeg, Manitoba, Canada: Whole Language Consultants, 1984.

Cunningham, A. E. "A Developmental Study of Instruction in Phonemic Awareness." Paper presented at American Educational Research Association, New Orleans, LA, 1988 (as cited in Griffith and Olson 1992).

Durkin, Dolores. *Children Who Read Early.* New York: Teacher's College Press, 1966.

Durkin, Dolores. *Getting Reading Started.* Boston: Allyn and Bacon, 1982.

Ferreiro, Emilia, and Ana Teberosky. *Literacy Before Schooling*. Portsmouth, NH: Heinemann, 1982.

Girard, M. "Bringing Children to Literacy Through Guided Reading." In *Bringing Children to Literacy: Classrooms at Work,* edited by B. Harp. Norwood, MA: Christopher-Gordon, 1993.

Glazer, Susan Mandel. "Oral Language and Literacy Development." In *Emerging Literacy: Young Children Learn to Read and Write,* edited by Dorothy S. Strickland and Lesley Mandel Morrow, 16–26. Newark, DE: International Reading Association, 1989.

Goodman, Yetta, and Bess Altwerger. "Print Awareness and Pre-School Children: A Working Paper." Tucson, AZ: Arizona Center for Research and Development, College of Education, University of Arizona, 1981.

Graves, Donald. *Writing: Teachers and Children at Work.* Portsmouth, NH: Heinemann, 1983.

Graves, Donald, and Virginia Stuart. *Write From the Start.* New York: New American Library, 1985.

Griffith, Priscilla L., and Mary W. Olson. "Phonemic Awareness Helps Beginning Readers Break the Code." *Reading Teacher* 45 (March 1992): 516–523.

Harp, Bill, and Jo Ann Brewer. *Reading and Writing: Teaching for the Connections.* San Diego, CA: Harcourt Brace Jovanovich, 1991.

Holdaway, Don. *The Foundations of Literacy.* Portsmouth, NH: Heinemann, 1980.

Jensen, Mary A. "Story Awareness: A Critical Skill for Early Reading." *Young Children* 41 (November 1985): 20–24.

Karweit, Nancy. "Effective Preprimary Programs and Practices." *Principal* (May 1988): 18–21.

Kontos, Susan. "What Preschool Children Know About Reading and How They Learn It." *Young Children* 42 (November 1986): 58–66.

Martin, Bill, Jr. "Celebrating Language." Seminar sponsored by the School of Education, Oregon State University, Corvallis, Oregon, Summer 1986.

Mason, Jana M., and Shobha Sinha. "Emerging Literacy in the Early Childhood Years: Applying a Vygotskian Model of Learning and Development." In *Handbook of Research on the Education of Young Children,* edited by B. Spodek, 137–150. New York: Macmillan, 1993.

Morrow, Lesley M., and Muriel K. Rand. "Promoting Literacy During Play by Designing Early Child-hood Classroom Environments." *Reading Teacher* 44 (February 1991): 396–402.

Neuman, Susan B., and Kathleen A. Roskos. *Language and Literacy Learning in the Early Years.* Fort Worth, TX: Harcourt Brace Jovanovich, 1993.

Reutzel, D. Ray. "Breaking the Letter-a-Week Tradition." *Childhood Education* 69 (Fall 1992): 20–23.

Schickedanz, Judith. "Teacher Interaction: The Key to Instruction in the Early Childhood Classroom." Paper presented at the New England Reading Conference, Hyannis, MA, October 1993.

Schickedanz, Judith. "Views of Literacy Development: Then and Now." Paper presented at the annual conference of the National Association for the Education of Young Children, Anaheim, CA, 1988.

Sulzby, Elizabeth, and William H. Teale. "Writing Development in Early Childhood." *Educational Horizons* (Fall 1985): 8–12.

Temple, Charles A., Ruth G. Nathan, Frances Temple, and Nancy A. Burris. *The Beginnings of Writing.* 3d ed. Boston: Allyn and Bacon, 1993.

Weaver, Constance. *Reading Process and Practice.* Portsmouth, NH: Heinemann, 1988.

Children's Books

Blos, Joan W. *A Seed A Flower A Minute, An Hour.* New York: Simon & Schuster, 1992.

Brown, Margaret Wise. *The Runaway Bunny.* New York: Harper and Row, 1942.

Ehlert, Lois. *Nuts to You!* San Diego: Harcourt Brace Jovanovich, 1993.

Flack, Marjorie, and Kurt Wiese. *The Story of Ping.* New York: Viking, 1933.

Galdone, Paul. *Over in the Meadow.* New York: Simon & Schuster, 1986.

Guy, Ginger Fogleson. *Black Crow, Black Crow.* New York: Greenwillow, 1991.

Jones, Carol. *This Old Man.* Boston: Houghton Mifflin, 1990.

Keats, Ezra Jack. *Whistle for Willie.* New York: Viking, 1964.

Kraus, Robert. *Whose Mouse Are You?* New York: Macmillan, 1970.

Lewis, C. S. *The Lion, The Witch, and The Wardrobe.* New York: Macmillan, 1951.

Martin, Bill, Jr. *Brown Bear, Brown Bear.* New York: Holt, Rinehart and Winston, 1970.

McCloskey, Robert. *Blueberries for Sal.* New York: Viking, 1963.

McGovern, Ann. *Too Much Noise.* New York: Scholastic, 1967.

Pearson, Tracey Campbell. *Old MacDonald Had a Farm.* New York: Dial Books, 1984.

Steig, W. *Sylvester and the Magic Pebble.* New York: Scholastic, 1969.

Stevens, Janet. *The House That Jack Built.* New York: Holiday House, 1985.

Tolstoi, A. *The Turnip.* Moscow: Malysh, no date.

Zemach, M. *It Could Always Be Worse.* New York: Scholastic, 1976.

Zolotow, Charlotte. *Summer Is . . .* New York: Crowell, 1967.

Chapter Eight

Manipulation and Discovery

Mathematics

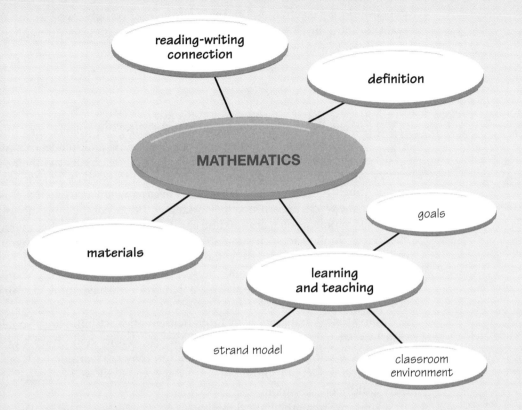

When you went to the primary school today, you found first- and second-graders using math in many more ways than you remember from your own school experience. Some children were building structures with geoblocks and seemed to be familiar with these three-dimensional shapes and their names. Other children were busily recording the scores of a game. Some were measuring objects in the classroom with a block from the block area; they were comparing their measurements with the results others had obtained.

You were very surprised to see all this activity during math time. You remember math as the period right before lunch, when the teacher taught how to solve a problem by demonstrating the steps on the chalkboard. After watching this demonstration, you worked pages and pages of similar problems on your own. In your experience, math always involved paper-and-pencil activities. But that wasn't what you observed today. You want to know how that teacher gets her children interested in math and helps them learn concepts and algorithms.

• •

This chapter and the next, on mathematics and science, are titled "Manipulation and Discovery" because young children learn mathematics and science from their manipulation of objects and their discovery of relationships and patterns in their environments. *Mathematics* means much more than just *arithmetic*. Perhaps when you were a child, math meant practicing arithmetic: working addition, subtraction, and multiplication problems on reams of ditto sheets. If you think of math for young children as limited to such simple equations as $1 + 1 = 2$, observe young children for a few minutes while they play. You will become aware of both their interest in mathematics and the scope of mathematics itself: "You got a bigger cookie than me!" "I am taller than you." "I have more clay than you." "I gots five pennies."

Many topics that seem relevant to mathematics activities are also relevant to science activities. As children learn to classify and group and as they think about functions and relationships, they are learning both math and science. In fact, it is often difficult to separate math and science in the early childhood classroom.

Children are mathematical thinkers outside of school. The challenge is to keep that interest, enthusiasm, and curiosity alive in the school setting. Teachers must make real efforts to make math easy for children to learn (Price 1989).

DEFINITION OF MATHEMATICS
• •

The dictionary defines *mathematics* as "the science of numbers and their operations, interrelations, combinations, generalizations, and abstractions, and of space configurations and their structure, measurement, transformations, and generalizations." But for young children, mathematics is a way of viewing the world and their experiences in it. It is a way of solving real problems. It is an understanding of number, operations on number, functions and relations, probability, and measurement. It is much more than the pages of simple equations that you may remember working as a child.

As children grow and develop, their mathematical activities change. The youngest children explore, begin to group and sort objects, and make comparisons. As children enter school, they may be ready for labels for

Mathematics includes much more than simply arithmetic.

their mathematical thinking and for recording their discoveries using mathematical symbols. Through the early childhood years, mathematics should continue to be a manipulative activity (McCracken 1987).

The National Council of Teachers of Mathematics (NCTM 1989) calls for curricula that provide students with opportunities to **construct** their concept of mathematics across all grade levels. "Mathematics should be viewed as a *helping discipline,* not as a subject area that sorts and rejects students on their inabilities to perform" (p. 22).

Construct
To build personal mental structures that organize information and knowledge.

HOW MATHEMATICS IS LEARNED

Piaget (1970) describes three ways that human beings can learn. He believes that they can learn from:

1. *The physical world*—Concepts such as "hot," "cold," "rough," "smooth," and so on
2. *The social world*—Concepts such as "language," "religion," "superstition," and so on
3. *The construction of mental relationships*—Concepts such as "counting," "seriation," "numeration," "conservation," and so on

Piaget calls the construction of mental relationships *logico-mathematical learning*. This type of learning will be our focus in this chapter (Piaget 1970; Kamii and DeClark 1985; Kamii and Joseph 1989; DeVries and Kohlberg 1987).

Logico-mathematical thinking requires that the learner create categories and hierarchies of objects without regard to their physical properties. For example, if you hold three yellow, wooden pencils in your hand, you will observe that they are made of wood and that they are inflexible. Those are physical facts. You cannot decide those characteristics. However, that there is a set of three pencils is a mental construct. They are physically separate objects, but their forming a set of three is a mental relationship. Think about the concept of "threeness." It is not dependent on the physical properties of the objects to which you are applying it. You could have three houses, three whales, three mustard seeds, three amoebas, and so on. In sum, the physical characteristics of the objects (including size, shape, color, texture, or temperature) do not determine that there are three; your placing them in a relationship is what makes that determination.

Simple abstraction
Abstracting a concept from repeated experiences with objects.

As learners, children abstract certain information from their experiences. For example, children learning color names learn to ignore other properties of objects and to focus on the property of color. Piaget (1970) calls this **simple abstraction** (also known as *empirical abstraction*). Although theorists do not agree on exactly how simple abstraction is accomplished, most believe that children abstract the rules that make language work from their experience with examples of language.

However, logico-mathematical concepts cannot be abstracted from experience. If, for example, a child plays with three dolls, he must reflect on the relationship he has created among the dolls; he cannot merely abstract the concept "three" because there are three dolls. We know that this is true because we can think about millions, billions, and trillions even though we have probably never had any experience with sets of this magnitude. We are able to think in these terms because we understand the hierarchical nature of the number system; that is, we understand that millions, billions, and trillions are comprised of thousands, hundreds, tens, and ones.

Reflective abstraction
Thinking about the results on one's manipulations on objects.

Piaget (1970) explains that we construct ideas via logico-mathematical learning by a process called **reflective abstraction.** This process works as follows: The learner manipulates objects and then reflects on the results. This reflection leads to reorganizing her mental constructs. Once this reorganization has taken place, it is impossible for the learner to think in exactly the same way again.

To illustrate the process of reflective abstraction, consider an example from mathematics. Most young children lack number conservation skills. Suppose a young child is presented with two identical sets of objects, such as plastic chips. In one of the sets, the chips are arranged in a row so closely that they almost touch each other; in the other set, the chips are arranged so that there are large spaces between the chips. Observing these two sets of chips, the young child will believe that the set that occupies the most space contains the most chips. After experience with manipulating sets and reflecting on the number of items in sets arranged in various physical configurations, the child will learn that the physical arrangement has no bearing on the number of objects in the set. This observation will produce a mental reorganization of sorts, such that the child will never again think that physical configuration influences number.

Even very young children can recognize the difference between numbers of items in small sets—for instance, 2 cookies compared to 5 cookies. Piaget (1970) calls these *perceptual numbers*. But with numbers larger than 8 or so, perceptions are no longer reliable, and a system of numbers must be constructed. This system must be based on the relationship among numbers: that 1 is included in 2, 2 in 3, and so on. When a child has created this system, he can begin to understand operations on numbers, such as addition, subtraction, multiplication, and division. Children can be taught that $2 + 3 = 5$, but *"they cannot be taught directly the relationships underlying this addition"* (Kamii and DeClark 1985, p. 14; italics in original). These relationships must be constructed by the learner, based on his observations.

When we count objects, we have to order them, so that each is counted only once. Creating that order is a mental operation. When we order objects from largest to smallest, for instance, we create a relationship among the objects. Concepts of size, time, and geometry must also be constructed by the learner.

Applied to mathematics, Vygotsky's (1978) view would prompt teachers to think about what children might be on the verge of discovering and to provide the materials and assistance that would enhance making those discoveries. Vygotsky's view would not support a step-by-step curriculum that fails to take into account the individual achievement of each child.

Think once again about your own experiences with math and math teachers. Most students have been in the situation of having a math teacher who truly understood geometry or calculus but could not teach students what he knew. If math could be taught directly from one person to another, then students could learn what was in the teacher's head. Obviously, that is not the case.

If one accepts the thesis that mathematical concepts must be constructed by each learner, based on observations with real-life materials and situations, then what are the responsibilities of the teacher? One responsibility is to supply the language for the concepts that the child is constructing. A child can discover the concept "five" but must have the label *five* supplied. Another of the teacher's responsibilities is to arrange the environment so that the materials that best represent a concept are available for manipulation and to provide time for manipulation. When children are involved physically, the teacher must also involve them mentally by engaging them in reflective thinking; this can be accomplished simply through asking questions about what the children observe.

One can conclude, then, that mathematics instruction must be based on the hands-on manipulation of objects by learners and that symbols should be introduced after concepts are well in place.

HOW MATHEMATICS IS TAUGHT

Goals of Mathematics Instruction

The goals of mathematics instruction include:

1. Giving children opportunities to participate in many activities that encourage the development of mathematical concepts
2. Encouraging children to use mathematical knowledge to solve problems and understand relationships
3. Helping children develop a concept of mathematics as relevant to their own problems and environment, as opposed to viewing mathematics as something one memorizes and repeats
4. Helping children view themselves as learners who are capable of succeeding in mathematics

These are very broad goals, and more specific objectives must be developed for introducing children to counting, measuring, grouping, adding and subtracting, and geometry. If the broad goals are achieved, no child will believe that she is not good in mathematics or that only adults know the answers and the only way a learner can know the answers is to be told them.

Mathematics in the Classroom

The curriculum standards established by the NCTM for kindergarten through fourth grade (K–4) are based on the following assumptions:

1. *The K–4 curriculum should be conceptually oriented. . . .*
2. *The K–4 curriculum should actively involve children in doing mathematics. . . .*

3. *The K–4 curriculum should emphasize the development of children's mathematical thinking and reasoning abilities. . . .*
4. *The K–4 curriculum should emphasize the application of mathematics. . . .*
5. *The K–4 curriculum should include a broad range of content. . . .*
6. *The K–4 curriculum should make appropriate and ongoing use of calculators and computers. (NCTM 1989, pp. 17–19)*

In the early childhood classroom, there are many opportunities for teaching mathematics that fit the NCTM standards. For example, most math in early childhood classrooms focuses on developing concepts rather than learning algorithms. A day in an early childhood classroom presents many problems that help children explore concepts: How many pieces of paper do we need for art? How many boys are here today? How many girls are here today? How many children are present? This is the ninth day of the month; what day will be next? How many days have we been in school this year? How many want to read Book A next? How much space will we need to store this game?

By asking questions such as these, the teacher can demonstrate to children the application of mathematics in the real world and cover a broad range of content. When learning mathematics is approached in this way, children will develop concepts as well as thinking and reasoning abilities. If children employed calculators or computers in finding answers to these questions, then all the standards would be met through answering the everyday math problems that arise in any classroom.

Greenberg (1993) explains the teacher's role as having four dimensions:

Procurement and management of appropriate materials; management of content offerings, inviting opportunities and choices.
Knowledge of the basic skills and concepts to be developed, of the process of spotting possible teaching moments, of how to converse with children, and of how to pose challenging questions.
Relationships with and knowledge of the individual child.
Knowledge of the nature of children in this age range—their emotional, social, physical, and intellectual needs, and their interests. (p. 78)

Children need to employ a variety of strategies to answer questions and solve problems. If the teacher supplies the strategy, it may not make sense to the child. For example, suppose that just before beginning an art activity, the teacher poses the question: How many pieces of paper are needed in order for every student to have one? Some younger children will need to get a piece of paper, bring it to a classmate, and repeat this procedure until everyone has a paper. Others may be able to count the number of children in the class and get the corresponding number of papers. Some first- and second-graders will pass out the papers without counting the number needed in advance. Some children will be able to use the attendance figures to calculate how many classmates are absent from the class; others will need to count and may not know how to find the number who are missing.

Kamii and DeClark (1985) cite an example of first-graders who were voting. The class included twenty-four students, and when the vote for the first choice was thirteen, one child said they did not need to vote for the other choices. Even after hearing the child's explanation of having a majority vote, the other children did not understand why this could be so and needed to continue the vote. Some children will be able to measure the size of a game and find an appropriate storage space; others will have to use trial and error. Children will be in many stages of understanding; they must use their own thinking to make sense of problems.

Mathematics in an early childhood program should not be scheduled for a specific period of instruction but should be an integral part of the schoolday. In the primary grades, math should be integrated into themes as much as possible, but if a theme is not appropriate for meaningful mathematics, then a math period should be scheduled.

Math instruction should also be part of the children's play time. Children can play games with cards, dominoes, or dice that help them think about math. (In some communities, such gaming materials might be unacceptable, and teachers will need to be creative in selecting other materials that encourage the same kinds of thinking.) Children in play also group, sort, classify, and seriate objects. They construct sets of blocks, beads, crayons, and other materials. Calendars, attendance records, and weather charts provide many opportunities for thinking mathematically. As children play "grocery store" or participate in cooking activities, they can weigh, measure, and count in meaningful situations. Almost any topic of study lends itself to helping children develop mathematical concepts in addition to other knowledge. For example, if the class is studying shells or leaves, then classification, seriation, graphing, counting, and measuring will be integral parts of the study.

Instruction in mathematics should focus on providing experiences and activities for young children and asking questions to guide children's reflections. Children should be encouraged to think of mathematics as real problems to solve, not simply as calculations to complete. Burns and Richardson (1981) have identified the problem of teaching arithmetic first: "We teach the abstract processes of arithmetic first and then hope that children will learn to use these processes to solve problems. . . . The emphasis on problems must come first; it's the starting place for developing arithmetic understanding and for establishing the need for computation" (p. 39).

The Strand Model

The NCTM and several states have conceptualized the curriculum for mathematics in a *strand model* (see Figure 8.1). (The word *strand* is meant to

---

FIGURE 8.1   The Strand Model of Mathematics

MATHEMATICS

Source: © Karen Clark Smith, 1988.

imply that the components of mathematics are all necessary and interrelated.) The strand model was developed to help teachers view mathematics as much more than arithmetic and to be an organizer for presenting information about mathematics. It is not a teaching model; rather, it illustrates that the real world of problem solving (through inquiry, exploration, investigation, questioning, discovery, and reflection) is the environment within which the different strands of math are used. The model is an artificial representation of mathematics because actually each strand is interrelated. Logical thinking is required to understand patterns and functions, measurement is involved in geometry, relationships are important in statistics, and so forth. The sections that follow will discuss each strand and offer some teaching suggestions for helping children develop concepts related to that strand.

As Figure 8.1 shows, each strand of mathematics is embedded in problem solving; problem solving is the background for thinking in any area of instruction in math. Problem solving does not mean working word problems; it is an attitude of looking for real problems, finding ways of expressing those problems, and finding solutions to them through mathematics. Problem solving is not a set of standard procedures that children memorize and apply in given situations. Most real-world problems are not clearly defined; they do not lend themselves to solution by memorized strategies. Arithmetic is at the center of the model because it can be used to find and record solutions to real problems in all the strands of mathematics.

Logical Thinking and Mathematical Reasoning

One of the strands in the model is logical thinking and mathematical reasoning. *Logical thinking* is sorting and classifying information. Any time children are faced with problems that require sorting and classifying, they must use logical thinking. Since number is one category of classification, sorting and classifying are important in creating mathematical categories. (Recall the three pencils mentioned at the beginning of the chapter; they can be classified as writing tools, wooden objects, painted objects, and so on as well as by number.) Some appropriate activities to help threes and fours learn to think logically include:

- Putting all the sand toys in one container
- Sorting the dishes in the housekeeping area into storage areas for plates, silverware, cooking utensils, and so on
- Classifying the unit blocks into different sizes for storage
- Sorting all the crayons, markers, and pencils into containers
- Comparing sets and using categories such as "more" and "less"

As you can imagine, this list could go on for pages and pages, as almost all the play materials in the classroom must be sorted and classified for storage each day. As children do these tasks or help teachers do them, teachers can talk to them about what they are doing and the criteria being used for sorting and classifying. As children mature in their understanding, teachers should refine the criteria for classification so that items are sorted on the basis of increasingly complex criteria.

Fives and sixes engage in logical thinking when they sort materials, define the criteria for classifications, and seriate objects. Examples of problems for fives and sixes include:

- Sorting buttons, keys, or other objects into groups and then explaining the criteria by which the classifications were made—The teacher might then encourage children to think of other criteria by which the same objects could be grouped. If the children had already grouped buttons by color, then they might group them by size, by number of holes, by whether they are shanked or unshanked, or by what they are made of.
- Creating Venn diagrams with yarn circles—If one circle contains objects that are blue and the other contains objects that are square, the intersection of the circles will contain square, blue objects—yet another category.
- Sorting models of zoo animals and farm animals for storage—As each is placed in the container, the child makes a tally mark and then compares the sizes of the sets of animals. This is a meaningful and logical extension of classification into arithmetic.
- Going on a "circle hunt" to find as many circles as possible while on a walk—Groups record and then compare the numbers of circles they find. These numbers can be saved and compared to the numbers of squares or triangles found on other hunts.
- Playing card games (Old Maid, Rummy, Go Fish, and so on)

Sevens and eights can continue to classify objects and compare sets that are created. Tasks for sorting and classifying can be extended to sets of numbers; for most tasks, children can use arithmetic to record the operations. Teachers can stimulate sorting and classifying skills in the following ways:

- Asking questions—"If all these numbers are even numbers, can seven be included in this set?"
- Getting children to think about what pieces of information are needed to solve problems—"We know that our classroom is forty tiles long and thirty tiles wide and that it has eight windows. How many tiles cover the floor?"

- Posing "if-then" statements—"If you double your score and then find half of it, what will you have?"
- Asking children how many ways they can think of to get an answer to a problem
- Having children solve problems and defend their solutions

Seriation Seriation tasks are inherent in the play experiences of even very young children. Seriation requires keeping in mind the characteristics of one element while comparing it to another element. Most very young children can compare two objects and determine which is larger and which is smaller. When asked to create a series based on size from a set of items, most four-year-olds will pick up two items at a time, compare them, determine the larger of those two, and then pick up two more items without considering the previous items. In their play, threes and fours will begin to place objects such as cans on the grocery store shelves in some kind of order, but seriating a large number of items is not an appropriate task. Appropriate seriating tasks for threes and fours include arranging dolls in the doll bed; arranging pairs of objects from the classroom (crayons, spools, spoons, plates, and so on) into sets of larger objects and smaller objects; arranging trucks in the block center by size; and arranging sets of three or four blocks into series.

Most fives can complete a simple seriation of more than three items. As children become more skilled, the numbers of objects to be seriated can be increased. Some classroom problems involving seriation for this age group include arranging stacks of paper by ascending size on the art shelves; arranging blocks in the unit block area by ascending or descending size; arranging strips of paper that represent the heights of each class member; and arranging stacks of blocks in ascending order (one block, three blocks, five blocks, and so on).

Sevens and eights can accomplish the following kinds of seriation tasks: arranging sets of numbers in order or in patterns (a seriation task similar to arranging stacks of blocks); finding missing items in a series; and creating double series (a set of balls to match a set of bats).

Statistics and Probability

Another strand in the model is statistics and probability. Statistics is an appropriate topic in the early childhood classroom when it is defined as comparing and analyzing information. Many activities in the classroom involve relationships that can be compared and analyzed. Some appropriate tasks for threes and fours include:

- Observing differences when snack choices are arranged on trays—If the children had a choice of orange juice or milk, the teacher could arrange the juice cups in a set and the milk cups in another set and then create a chart or graph with pictures of the snack choices to represent the information. If eleven children chose orange juice and nine chose milk, there would be eleven squares with pictures of orange juice and nine with pictures of milk.
- Observing and comparing the number of sunny days, cloudy days, snowy days, or rainy days marked on the calendar

Fives and sixes can carry out the following kinds of tasks:

- Creating graphs of information, such as their choices at snack time
- Graphing how many children walk, ride the bus, or come by private car to school
- Graphing how many children have on certain types of shoes
- Voting for their favorite books and recording the results with tally marks

Sevens and eights can work with information that is important to them by:

- Graphing how many children eat the school lunch and how many bring their lunch each day for a month—Children can then try to determine why the choices were made. (Were there more children eating the school lunch when hamburgers were served as opposed to meat loaf?)
- Surveying the school to determine the students' favorite play equipment
- Tallying the number of books checked out of the class library, comparing the information for several weeks, and trying to determine the reasons for any variations

In the process of solving these problems, children use computation and logical thinking as well as statistics.

Children do not develop a firm concept of probability until they are in the concrete operational stage of thinking. However, sevens and eights can begin some interesting activities with probability involving small numbers. For example, they might flip a coin for a given number of times and record the number of heads and tails. Or they might draw colored cubes from a bag containing ten cubes: seven red and three blue. As each draw is completed, the child tallies the color of the cube and then returns the cube to the bag. After ten draws, the child predicts how many cubes of each color are actually in the bag. Drawing, tallying, and predicting can be repeated several times.

Measurement

Measurement is a third strand in the model. Measurement experiences for young children must be based on their ability to conserve length and area. Many children are interested in measuring, and some measurements are meaningful to them. For instance, children are usually quite interested in their own heights, weights, ages, and so on.

Threes and fours can take part in activities such as the following:

- Exploring measurement through materials such as balance scales
- Finding a block of the proper length to fill a given space
- Measuring each other for new shoes or new clothes
- Using different-sized containers in the sand and water areas—Children can use one container to fill another and thereby develop concepts of "larger" and "more."
- Using blocks to build walls or towers with lengths and heights equal to those of other objects

Fives and sixes still do not have stable understandings of linear measures, but they can begin to use nonstandard and some standard measures to measure objects of interest to them. Children of this age are still usually most interested in measuring themselves. The following kinds of measurement are appropriate:

- Measuring their height with strips of paper or yarn and hanging the strips on the wall for comparison
- Measuring their tables with their hands or some other personal item like their shoes
- Measuring the classroom by counting how many steps it takes to cross it
- Determining the number of pieces of paper that are required to cover their tables—If each group is given a different size of paper to use, the children can begin to recognize the need for standard measures.
- Measuring the cloth needed to cover the doll bed
- Using containers in the sand and water that are standard measuring cups or metric measures—The children can count how many cups are required to fill a quart or half-gallon milk carton.
- Measuring ingredients required in cooking experiences—Remember that a container that holds one-quarter cup is still one cup to the preoperational child; therefore, a real understanding of fractions usually will not be gained from cooking experiences.

- Estimating the sizes of objects using strings—The children can cut strings that they think will fit around their heads or their waists and then try them out to check their predictions. They can use this same technique for estimating the girth of their Halloween pumpkins, a watermelon, or their teacher.
- Measuring the heights of their block constructions or determining how many tiles their constructions cover on the floor

Sevens and eights can continue to use nonstandard linear measurements. Some children may be able to make the transition to standard measures, especially when a task does not require repeated measures. Some appropriate measurement tasks for this age group include:

- Choosing the appropriate measuring device for measuring a piece of paper for a book cover or a piece of wood for something they are building in the woodworking area
- Accurately measuring given quantities of liquid, such as cups, pints, quarts, liters, and so on
- Using units (squares of paper or wooden blocks) to measure surface areas and making comparisons with arithmetical computations

As always, the emphasis should be on meaningful measurement tasks; a transition to standard measurements should be based on individual development.

Time   Time is a component of measurement that is often emphasized in programs for young children. However, children do not have the ability to quantify and integrate durations of time until about age ten (Levin, Wilkening, and Dembo 1984). Preschoolers are certainly aware of time, as they hear adults talk about time for snack, time for outdoor play, time to get ready to go home, and so on, but they believe that they can influence the passage of time.

One approach to assessing a child's concept of time involves first determining if she is familiar with an egg timer and then asking her to observe the flow of sand in the timer as she completes a task such as walking around a table. Most preoperational children will think that the flow is slow if they go slowly and fast if they move more quickly. Preschoolers can predict whether it will take more or less time for sand to flow out of containers of different sizes, but they do not have a stable understanding of the concept of time.

Teaching young children to tell time is not an appropriate goal. Preschoolers can be shown the clock face when it is time for certain events in their day, but they should not be expected to use that information. No one should expect to hear a preschooler say "It is ten minutes until time for snack." For a preschooler, a digital clock is easier to read than a clock with a dial because he only needs to recognize the numerals. A dial requires that the child translate the numbers 1, 2, 3, and so on to 5, 10, and 15 to indicate minutes, while also remembering that the numbers stand for the hour. Reading the time from a digital clock does not mean that the child understands time; it just means he can recognize the numerals and read them in two parts.

Fives and sixes may attach more meaning to the passage of time, but learning to read time is still only appropriate for individual children who are ready for the information. Some sevens and eights will begin to make the transition to a stable view of time and will need to learn to tell time. For other children, time still will not be a stable concept, and they will need to know only the times that are important in their daily schedules.

Money The money system is another component of measurement that is often included in curriculum plans. Remember that for young children, bigger means "more." Shel Silverstein (1974) describes the young child's idea of money very accurately in his poem "Smart":

Smart

My dad gave me one dollar bill
'Cause I'm his smartest son,
And I swapped it for two shiny quarters
'Cause two is more than one!

And then I took the quarters
And traded them to Lou
For three dimes—I guess he don't know
That three is more than two!

Just then, along came old blind Bates
And just 'cause he can't see
He gave me four nickels for my three dimes,
And four is more than three!

And I took the nickels to Hiram Coombs
Down at the seed-feed store,
And the fool gave me five pennies for them,
And five is more than four!

And then I went and showed my dad,
And he got red in the cheeks
And closed his eyes and shook his head—
Too proud of me to speak!*

It is very difficult for a young child to understand that a dime is worth more than a nickel when a nickel is physically larger than a dime. Money should be a topic in the curriculum only if children have a real use for the knowledge. Preschool children certainly do not have a concept of how much money is needed to buy objects. Some preschoolers think that if one needs more money, one need only write a check. Preschoolers can begin to explore the ideas of money as they play "grocery store," "shoe store," or "riding on the bus." Teachers may make play money available for the children. Some fives and sixes may need more knowledge of money if they receive a small allowance and save money for special purchases. Sevens and eights can begin to use computations that involve money and change if the problems are real. For example, they might learn about change if some of them buy lunch at school: What amount of money did each student bring to buy lunch? Is it enough? Will there be change? If there is change, how much will it be? Can anyone buy an extra carton of milk today? How much more must the teacher pay for lunch?

Geometry

A fourth strand of mathematics is geometry. Geometry is more than Euclidean shapes. It includes topology (the connectedness of objects) and concepts of how shapes and forms are related to each other. The sequence of development of geometric concepts includes recognition of familiar shapes such as spoons, recognition of figures as open or closed, and recognition of Euclidean shapes such as squares and triangles (Copeland 1984). Very young children have difficulty recognizing the differences between shapes such as squares and rectangles. The emphasis for young children should be on experiences that help them develop concepts of space and the relationships of objects in space. Some examples of activities to encourage geometric understanding follow.

Threes and fours can use two- and three-dimensional objects of various shapes in their play and discover the properties of these shapes. At this age, children do not necessarily need to learn the names of shapes. They can build with blocks and begin to discover how space can be enclosed with lines and that objects can be inside or outside these lines.

*"Smart" text from *Where the Sidewalk Ends* by Shel Silverstein. Copyright © 1974 by Evil Eye Music, Inc.

Fives and sixes can do activities such as playing with blocks; playing with pattern blocks and exploring these shapes and their relationships; constructing a square from four smaller squares; and discovering that a regular hexagon can be divided into two regular trapezoids.

At any age, the emphasis should be on manipulation and on reflecting on what has been constructed, rather than on learning labels. Some children will be interested in labels and will want to know them, but drill and practice are not appropriate for children of this age.

Teachers can encourage sevens and eights in the following kinds of tasks:

- Continuing to explore both two-dimensional and three-dimensional shapes
- Exploring area and volume of different shapes—Children can fill hollow three-dimensional shapes such as cylinders, cubes, rectangular prisms, and spheres with sand or water and determine how they could compute the volume of each.
- Exploring spaces on a geoboard and constructing various shapes and repeating or rearranging them
- Using geometry and measurement in planning room arrangements that will fit everything, use space to the best advantage, and allow for the best movement patterns
- Applying their growing knowledge of geometry to problems in arranging the furniture in their rooms at home

Patterns and Functions

The fifth strand of mathematics is patterns and functions. Patterns are visual, auditory, spatial, numerical, or combinations of these. The base 10 system is organized in patterns of ones, tens, hundreds, and so on, and patterns are evident in all the strands of mathematics. Promoting recognition of patterns is extremely important in helping young children develop mathematical concepts (Ditchburn 1982; Burton 1982). Recognizing and creating patterns helps children learn to order, predict, and estimate. Children can make patterns with beads, blocks, tiles, pattern blocks, pieces of paper, shoes, their bodies, leaves, flowers, seeds, and numerous other materials. Children can be helped to recognize patterns on the calendar, in blocks, in games, and in art materials.

Functions are the patterns created when certain actions are performed on objects or numbers. When a piece of paper is folded once, the result is two sections of paper. When it is folded twice, the result is four sections, and so on. When preschoolers can begin to observe how many sections are created when they fold pieces of paper or that there are two shoes for every

INTEGRATING THE CURRICULUM

The theme of patterns is integral to a math program for young children. The following are only a few of the possible activities for children of different ages:

Activities for Threes and Fours

➤ Working with simple patterns in their bead and block constructions
➤ Building patterns with two colors of Unifix cubes or with two shapes of pattern blocks
➤ Recording the days of the week on the calendar in an alternating pattern of leaf, flower, leaf, flower, and so on
➤ Constructing a pattern with two colors of napkins at snack time
➤ Creating patterns with large and small unit blocks
➤ Clapping the rhythms in their names
➤ Creating two-part rhythmical patterns to music

Activities for Fives and Sixes

➤ Continuing to construct patterns with various play materials
➤ Adding more elements to letter patterns or three-dimensional patterns to make them more complex
➤ Creating patterns from their names and working with numerical patterns
➤ Coloring every second or fifth or tenth day on a calendar of days in school
➤ Finding number patterns on the calendar, on graphs they have constructed, and in other numbers used in the class
➤ Exploring patterns in wallpaper and noticing the changes in patterns as a result of rotations, slides, and flips

Activities for Sevens and Eights

➤ Constructing more three-dimensional patterns
➤ Recognizing numerical patterns by finding different patterns on hundreds charts, in the products of multiplying by twos, threes, or fours, and so on

one person, that is functional thinking. Some ideas for encouraging functional thinking in threes and fours include having children observe the number of shoes per person when they take off their shoes for a movement experience; observe the number of crayons or pencils per person; and fold paper and observe the number of sections created.

Fives and sixes can record their findings about activities in function tables. For example, if every person has two shoes, a function table of this information would look like this:

People	Shoes
1	2
2	4
3	6
4	8

The children should be encouraged to find patterns among numbers in the table. Function tables could be created for a variety of activities.

Sevens and eights can work on creating more involved function tables. A child might create a table of a mathematical operation, such as multiplying by 4, and let a partner determine the function illustrated. Tables could be created for addition, subtraction, multiplication, or division problems from the children's experiences. (Note that this is *not* a suggestion to teach children mathematical operations formally.)

Guess the Function

2	8
3	12
4	16

Arithmetic

As noted earlier, arithmetic is at the center of the model, and like problem solving, it is a part of every strand of mathematical thinking. Young children can use basic arithmetic concepts in solving problems. Arithmetic includes the concepts of one-to-one correspondence, counting, number, place value, operations on whole numbers, and fractions.

One-to-One Correspondence   One-to-one correspondence is the concept that one object can be related to another object. Thousands of pages of workbook exercises have been filled with pictures of rows of dogs and rows of bones, with directions to the child to draw a line from one dog to one bone. Worksheets like these are supposed to help children recognize that if there is a bone for each dog, then the sets are equivalent.

In fact, these practice sheets are not very effective in helping children understand one-to-one correspondence because children need to create their own sets and construct their own understanding of equivalency. Providing them with sets that someone else has constructed does not allow them to develop the concept. For those of us who are no longer preoperational thinkers, it seems obvious that equivalency of sets can be established by counting. But for preoperational children who do not conserve number, counting is not a reliable strategy.

In one study (Kamii 1982), the researcher presented children with two sets of cubes, one set larger than the other. The experimenter told the children, "I will add cubes to the smaller set. Tell me when it has the same number of cubes as the large set." The researcher found that preoperational children continued to watch as blocks were added and spoke up when they believed that the set to which blocks were being added had more. The children failed to notice when the sets were equal.

Some teachers have tried to teach children one-to-one correspondence by having them physically attach one element of each set to an element in another set. Even these physical connections are not as effective in helping children develop the concept as are repeated experiences in creating sets of their own. What children must do is create sets and then think about the relationships that exist between the sets. Children create sets that help them understand one-to-one correspondence when they place one chair at the table for each person, put one brush in each jar of paint, pass out one sheet of paper for each person, or give each person a carton of milk. Teachers can help guide children's reflections by asking them if they had too few, enough, or too many chairs, papers, or cartons of milk. One-to-one correspondence also figures in seriation tasks, as children relate items in one series to items in another.

Counting   If you asked the next three or four people that you met on the street what young children should learn first about mathematics, it's likely they would all say counting. Some program goals include counting to 10 as appropriate objectives for fours and counting to 100 as appropriate objectives for fives or sixes.

Counting can be either rote counting or rational counting. *Rote counting* is naming the numbers in order without making any connection between numbers and sets or real-life objects. *Rational counting* is the ability to order and enumerate objects in sets. Rote counting is often encouraged by parents and teachers, but when children learn to count by rote it is *social knowledge* (that is, things children learn merely because they are told to do so by an adult) and not really related to mathematical understanding.

Learning to count proceeds in stages: The child knows that each object must have a distinct tag (counting word); the child knows that the list of tags must have a particular order; and the child makes the connection between counting and number. Teachers of young children can appreciate these stages, just as they appreciate stages in learning to walk or to write (Price 1989). Two-year-olds have a concept of counting and often attach number words to objects, even though it is almost impossible for them to count correctly. Researchers (Gelman and Tucker 1975; Bullock and Gelman 1977) have found that very young children can attach number tags to objects in ascending order (1, 5, 7) long before they can count accurately.

Leeb-Lundberg (1985) relates a story about counting that many teachers of young children have experienced:

Five-year-old Mary was walking through the park with her parents and some of their friends. It was spring and on the pond a mother duck was swimming with some ducklings behind her. The proud parents, knowing that Mary could count beyond twenty and "knew her numbers," wished to show her ability to their friends. Her father asked her, "How many duck-lings are there swimming behind the mother duck?" Mary, fearful and reluctant, was not able to tell her father how many ducklings there were. Her father, seeing her upset, wished to help her and said, "But Mary, you know that the mother duck has five ducklings." Mary burst into tears and said, "There is no one in the middle." Mary's mother and father were con-fused. They could not understand why Mary could not count the ducklings and decided to speak with Mary's teacher. Monday morning, as they entered the kindergarten classroom, there on the wall was the answer to the puzzle. They saw big cards with domino pictures of numbers from one to ten. This pattern represented the number five. This domino pattern of five was the only thing Mary knew about the number five. It became clear to her parents that Mary did not understand the concept of five—the fiveness of five in dif-ferent pattern situations. When the pattern changed, she could no longer recognize five.

It was impossible for Mary to understand that the swimming ducks could also be five because her concept of fiveness was not based on her own experiences, but rather on an abstract representation. (p. 9)*

Counting is, of course, a very useful problem-solving strategy. It is best if the child discovers the strategy rather than having it imposed by the teacher or parent. For example, rather than saying "Count the plates and get a nap-kin from the cupboard for each one," a parent or teacher might say "Make sure that we have enough napkins for each plate." Discovery of counting as a problem-solving strategy takes some time, but it is worth it to the child.

Kamii (1982) relates the following story:

A mother asked her five-year-old to put a napkin on everybody's plate for the main meal every day. There were regularly four people at the table. Jean-Pierre knew how to count to thirty or more. However, he went to the cup-board to take out the first napkin, which he put on a plate, returned to the cupboard to take out the second napkin, which he put on the second plate, and so on, making a total of four trips. At five years, three months, and six-teen days, he spontaneously thought about counting the plates, counted four napkins to take out of the cupboard, and distributed them at the table. He proceeded this way for six days.

On the seventh day there was a guest and one more plate than usual. Jean-Pierre took his four napkins as usual, distributed them, and noticed that one plate remained empty. Instead of getting an additional napkin, he collected the four already on the plates, and put them back in the cupboard. He then began all over again and made five trips to accomplish the task.

The next day, the guest was not there, but Jean-Pierre continued to make four trips, and continued the same thing for five more days, until he thought again about counting. After using this method for ten days, Jean-Pierre was told that there was a guest again. He distributed his four napkins as usual, but this time simply went to get the missing napkin when he saw the empty plate. The next day, when there were only four people again, he counted the number of plates before fetching the same number of napkins. The arrival of a new guest never bothered him after that. (pp. 31–32)*

Teachers will find many opportunities for helping children develop the concept of counting. Threes and fours are likely to be able to count only a limited number of objects correctly; therefore, counting activities should be individualized to match each child's abilities. Threes and fours can count:

- Pieces of paper needed for art
- Number of place settings needed in the housekeeping center
- Blocks used to build a structure
- Chairs or mats needed for the group
- Dolls in the doll center
- Trucks and cars

Most counting experiences for fives and sixes will involve larger numbers, such as the number of papers needed for the whole class, and will involve recording and comparing different numbers. Children this age can become involved in:

- Counting the pieces of equipment taken outdoors and recording the number of items so that everything can be put away later
- Keeping score in games
- Counting the number of children absent each day and comparing the records over a month
- Counting the number of pieces of paper needed for a class project and multiplying to find how many would be needed for two projects
- Counting by twos, fives, and tens

*From Constance Kamii, *Number in Preschool and Kindergarten* (Washington, DC: National Association for the Education of Young Children, 1982), pp. 31–32. Reprinted by permission of the author.

Sevens and eights can continue to count, record, and compare numbers that have meaning for them in their daily lives and also learn to count by threes and fours.

Number Children's concepts of number develop fairly rapidly between the ages of about three and six. In their investigation of children's concepts of the magnitude of the first nine numbers in the counting string, Murray and Mayer (1988) found that most three-year-olds recognized 1 as a small number and other numbers as large but did not make other discriminations. Four-year-olds were able to discriminate between small and medium-sized numbers and small and large numbers, but they had trouble comparing medium-sized and large numbers. Five-year-olds could categorize all the numbers correctly.

Number can be explored without computation in many ways. Threes and fours can make books of numbers that relate to them: their measurements, ages, shoe sizes, clothing sizes, birthdates, number of teeth, and so on. Fives and sixes can explore how numbers are used in or on buildings. The teacher might ask the children to talk about what they learn from how the rooms are numbered, how seats in an auditorium are numbered, or how the houses on a street are numbered. The teacher might also have children look for as many other uses of numbers as they can find (Turkel and Newman 1988). Sevens and eights can continue to look for numbers in the environment and explore larger numbers.

Developing a sense of numbers and their relationships to each other (numbers can be less than, more than, or part of other numbers) is basic to being able to carry out operations on whole numbers (Van de Walle 1988). Primary children should have many opportunities to explore numbers and their relationships to each other before they are introduced to formal addition and subtraction exercises.

Place Value Children obviously need to know that 12 and 21 do not represent the same number. Traditionally, place value has been included in the first-grade curriculum and again in the second-grade curriculum before children begin working on two-digit addition problems that require regrouping. Kamii and DeClark (1985) and Kamii and Joseph (1989) recommend that place value not be taught at all in first grade but that it be included in second grade when children use it to solve two-digit addition problems. They cite extensive research and classroom observations in which less than half the children below fourth grade understood that the 1 in 16 represents 10. In traditional mathematics texts, children are taught to write the answers to two-digit problems beginning with the ones column. Kamii believes that this is also social knowledge (as defined earlier). Real understanding of place value is not achieved until children are solid con-servers and can understand the part-whole relationships involved in place value. Building an understanding of tens requires extensive experience in doing arithmetic; teachers cannot foster that understanding simply by sup-plying materials bundled into tens to help the child see the tens and ones in a problem.

Kamii and Joseph (1988) advocate major changes in instruction in two-digit addition. These researchers interviewed hundreds of children in grades one through three and found that almost all the children thought that the 1 in 16 was 1, even after hours and hours of place-value instruc-tion. They encouraged children to work out solutions to two-digit prob-lems and then discuss how they achieved their solutions and provided the children with single cubes that they could use in solving the problems. Most of the children started with the tens column and worked through several solutions. They argued and debated with each other about their answers to the problems.

This problem-solving approach resulted in a much higher percentage of children knowing that the 1 in 16 represents 10 at the end of second grade. These authors are not suggesting that children should work math problems without manipulatives. What they are advocating is the use of materials, such as cubes or chips, that are not prearranged into sets of ten for the children. If the children discover that putting materials into sets of ten makes working the problems easier, then they can arrange the materi-als themselves.

The approach advocated by Kamii and her colleagues requires teach-ers to think carefully about what children can learn (as opposed to what they can do on paper) and to conduct research in their own classrooms to uncover the understandings of their children. A curriculum based on games and the children's arguing and debating their solutions to problems will involve teachers in planning, observing, and evaluating much more than a traditional program in which the teacher's job is to cover the mate-rial in the textbook.

Operations on Whole Numbers   Threes and fours can begin to develop the concepts necessary for addition, subtraction, multiplication, and divi-sion, even though these problems are not presented to them symbolically or formally. Children can observe many meaningful examples of opera-tions on whole numbers at home or in school settings:

- They see that when objects from two separate sets are combined, one larger set is created. While playing in the block center, children may put the blocks from two piles together and create one larger pile. They may pick up the crayons from each place at the table and put them together.

- They observe subtraction when they see a set reduced as elements are taken away. If a plate of crackers for snack is passed around, children see the number reduced as each child takes a portion. After they spend some pennies, they know that they have fewer.
- They observe multiplication when the teacher counts materials by sets or when they count groups such as place settings rather than individual pieces.
- They observe division when materials must be shared in equal portions. Often, it is a child's responsibility to determine how to divide food or play materials so that everyone has an equal share.

Instruction in addition and subtraction should not be attempted formally for fives and sixes until the children have achieved reversibility in thinking and understand subtraction as the inverse of addition. Instruction in multiplication and division should continue informally as they are needed to solve real problems; these operations can be presented as repeated addition or repeated subtraction. Fives and sixes can improve their arithmetic understanding by observing adults recording equations for arithmetic operations; recording the equations themselves; counting the sets of shoes worn by the children in the class; or passing out cards for a game by sets of two.

Sevens and eights will continue the use of addition and subtraction to solve problems. Teachers can begin more formal instruction in multiplication and division with children of these ages.

Each child should have numerous experiences working both multiplication and division problems with manipulative materials before she is asked to use the symbols. Children should not be asked to work problems without access to manipulative materials with which the problems can be solved. As addition, subtraction, and multiplication facts become familiar to children, they may not use the manipulatives on every problem, but they should always be available. Every child should view problems involving operations as something to be worked out, not as something that will be unsolvable if she forgets a fact.

Arithmetic is basic, but it should always be a tool for solving problems, not simply an end in itself. Achieving expertise in computation should be secondary to achieving the thinking and reasoning skills that are possible through all the strands of mathematics.

Fractions   As in other area of mathematics, the symbols for fractions should not be introduced until the concept is fully understood. Teachers of young children can use fractional terms (*one-half, one-fourth*) when they are relevant to children's experiences: one-half of a graham cracker, one-half cup of water, one-fourth of the paper, and so on. But the symbol $\frac{1}{2}$ should not be introduced until second or third grade. Fractions can indicate either how many of a set of equal-sized parts are being considered or a number. For children who are just developing a stable concept of whole numbers, formal fractions will be difficult.

Manipulatives for helping children learn about fractions include pattern blocks, fraction tiles, and teacher-made materials such as cardboard circles, squares, and rectangles cut into various fractional parts. Even for second- and third-graders, work with fractions should involve oral problem solving with manipulatives. Goals of instruction in fractions should include helping children know what halves, thirds, and fourths mean; know the difference between unit fractions (elements of a set) and nonunit fractions (parts of one whole); and recognize equivalent fractions.

MATERIALS FOR INSTRUCTION

Many excellent materials for helping children make discoveries about mathematical concepts are available today. Both commercial and teacher-made materials can be useful in good math programs. Commercial materials such as Unifix cubes, pattern blocks, geoblocks, and base 10 blocks are basic for a sound manipulatives-based program. Teacher-made manipulatives might include bean sticks, boxes of junk to be sorted and classified, glass beads on strings in sets from one to ten, geoboards, and so on. Most of these materials can be purchased as well as made by the teachers. When creating manipulative materials, teachers should ensure that mathematical concepts are presented accurately and that the materials do not distract from the concept to be learned. One does not bring in an elephant to teach the concept "gray."

Some materials—such as Cuisenaire rods, Dienes blocks, and Montessori rods—are not good choices for helping young children develop concepts of number. Remember that most of these children do not yet conserve number or length. When given a Cuisenaire rod that is supposed to represent 5 because it is five times as long as the 1 rod, most preconservers will say that this rod is one (and it is one rod). Piaget (1952) stated that "Cuisenaire rods . . . are open to the most totally opposed methods of using them, some of them genuinely operative if the child is allowed to discover for himself the various operations made possible by spontaneous manipulations of the rods, but the others essentially intuitive or figurative when they are limited to

Materials should be provided that are the best possible models for the given concept to be learned.

external demonstrations and to explanations of the configurations laid out by the teacher" (p. 73).

Better representations of number are individual objects such as Unifix cubes, chips, or beans. Once when observing a group of gifted kindergartners, the author saw a child build a square pyramid with Cuisenaire rods. To determine how many units had been used to construct the structure, she still counted each of the different-sized rods as one unit, even after several explanations by the teacher about how to count each rod.

Other materials may also prove less effective in helping children develop concepts. For children who do not yet conserve length, a counting line is not the best strategy for promoting understanding of addition and subtraction. It is also important to be careful when choosing materials for representing fractional parts of a whole. Objects that cannot be divided accurately are not appropriate for developing fractional concepts. Pattern blocks and fraction tiles are better representations of fractions than apples and pies, which cannot be cut accurately into fractional pieces.

Some teachers continue to use worksheets and workbooks rather than manipulatives. They may believe that manipulatives are too expensive, that manipulatives take up too much time, or that parents expect to see paper-and-pencil evidence of children's work (Stone 1987). Some manipulatives are expensive, but materials of good quality will last indefinitely, and many manipulatives can be constructed by the teacher for very little cost. Using manipulatives does take time, but covering the topics without achieving understanding is not efficient teaching. Taking the time initially to make sure that children understand will save time eventually because the same topics will not have to be taught over and over.

Parents can be kept informed about their children's progress in parent conferences or "math nights," when the use of manipulatives is explained and demonstrated, and through good records of the children's work. Teachers can also help parents participate in family math activities so that they are aware of their children's mathematical knowledge. If the parents encourage children to solve problems at home (such as using one-to-one correspondence to set a table with plates and glasses, classifying and grouping groceries for storage, working with money during shopping trips, and so on), they will help their children find real-world reasons for using mathematics and be aware of their children's thinking processes.

Calculators, Computers, and Young Children

Most young children have had some experience with calculators (Pagni 1987). Almost every middle-class household has one or more calculators that children have observed being used, and many young children have their own calculators.

It is reasonable for children to use calculators to solve arithmetic problems and to check their own and their peers' solutions to problems. But a calculator cannot substitute for real experience as a way of developing a concept of number or appropriate counting strategies. Thinking about the problem and how it can be solved should be the focus of instruction. Teachers should not be so concerned about developing children's basic skills that they do not use calculators. Calculators can be useful in computation.

Young children should be allowed to explore calculators. They may enjoy pushing the buttons and watching the numbers change. Older children can begin using calculators to solve equations and learn the importance of entering the numbers correctly. By the time children are seven or eight, they can use calculators in computation and for exploring functions and relationships among numbers.

Some computer programs can enhance a good manipulatives-based math program. Children who have had real experience with geoblocks and geoboards can extend their experiences with a software program called

DEVELOPMENTALLY APPROPRIATE PRACTICE,

Think about your own experience with math: Did you feel that you could be a successful learner of mathematics? Did you believe that the purpose of mathematics was to help you solve problems? As you reflect on your own experience and the contents of your reading, think about what would make learning mathematics developmentally appropriate:

- What would you expect to see in a classroom where mathematics was taught in a developmentally appropriate manner? Why?
- Will children have a chance to play with and explore a wide range of manipulative materials? Explain the importance of manipulatives in a DAP classroom.
- How will teachers help children recognize the

problems in their own classrooms and homes that are mathematical in nature?
- Will a child be excluded from some math experiences on the basis of having failed to master a given set of math facts? Why?
- Are timed tests on math facts developmentally appropriate? Why?

Logo, especially if they are able to manipulate the turtle. Other software programs are being developed almost daily. Many are simply drill-and-practice on arithmetic problems, but more and more programs ask children to interact with different situations and think logically about outcomes. Teachers should evaluate software carefully and choose programs that allow children to think, rather than simply practice algorithms.

THE READING-WRITING CONNECTION

Teachers can help children use reading and writing to record their questions, their discoveries, and their solutions to problems. Many teachers (especially those in the primary grades) provide each child with a notebook in which to write his questions and solutions. The teacher responds to the child's work in the notebook, writes questions, and presents new problems to be solved. Children are also encouraged to read each other's notebooks and to discuss their solutions and discoveries.

In describing the reading and writing experiences of her class, Richards (1990) noted that children made books of ways they had solved problems and that their writing about mathematics was quite varied. They wrote summaries, descriptions, definitions, reports, instructions, notes, evaluations, explanations, and personal responses to math. Figure 8.2 is an example of writing about math.

FIGURE 8.1   Writing about Math

Once opon a time ther was
ten cavemen four of them
went into a cave and got lost
the rest got very scared
and ran a way they only
came back to see if they
would come out but they never
did! So if you see a cave or six
cave men running dont ask them why
they are doing it!
by Melanie Kebler

Scott, Williams, and Hyssop (1992) suggest that mathematics is best conceptualized as communication and reasoning, not as a series of mysterious rules and symbols. They found that second-graders responded well to journal writing experiences in the math curriculum, including stories, pictures, and diagrams to explain their understandings.

Literature can also contribute to the instructional program in mathematics. The most obvious types of literature to use are counting books and rhymes. Many excellent counting books are available. In addition, problems in classification, ordering, and the basic operations can be introduced through literature.

Books that introduce addition and subtraction include *The Doorbell Rang* (Hutchins 1986), *Blueberries for Sal* (McCloskey 1948), and *Anno's Counting House* (Anno 1982). Having read these books, children can dramatize the stories and then write the equations from the stories or watch the teacher write them as they discover them.

Pat Hutchins's book *Clocks and More Clocks* (1970) is interesting for children exploring telling time. They can discuss what was wrong with the clocks in the story and try placing clocks in different parts of the building. *Leo, the Late Bloomer* (Kraus 1971) helps children think about the passage of time and the changes such passage brings.

One example of a book that introduces ordinal numbers (first, second, third) is *The Very Hungry Caterpillar* (Carle 1981). Children can review what happened to the caterpillar in sequence and then create their own stories of events that happened to them in sequence. *Freight Train* (Crews 1978) is another example of a book that encourages thinking about ordinal numbers. It can also be useful for classification; children can classify the types of cars illustrated (Harsh 1987).

Classification is also important in the story "The Lost Button" from *Frog and Toad are Friends* (Lobel 1970). In that story, Frog and Toad go for a walk. When they return, Toad discovers that he has lost a button. As they retrace their path, they find several buttons, but none matches the description Toad gives until his button is found. In dramatizing the story, children can be encouraged to think about classifications from their own button collections. Tischler (1988) suggests a game in which one child plays Toad and rejects buttons by naming the criteria they do not meet. The child who has the correct button becomes the next toad. Many different activities based on the buttons are possible.

Children learning mathematics concepts need to know the language to express the concepts, but knowing the language is not equivalent to understanding the concepts. Children may actually understand concepts before they are able to verbalize their understanding. Therefore, teachers must be sure to allow children to demonstrate their understanding with manipulatives rather than just writing their answers or telling what they understand.

ASSESSMENT

When assessing their knowledge of mathematics, it is not enough to find out what children can do—it is important to know what children understand. Historically, educators assumed that if children could do things such as counting and adding, they understood what they were doing. Research has proven otherwise.

Richardson (1988) found that children who could count often had no concept of number and some who could do place-value problems in their workbooks could not use place-value information to solve real problems. Labinowicz (1980) reported similar findings: Only about one-half the children who could work out equations such as $5 + 4$ could work out the same problem logically when presented with real objects to add. In a later work, Labinowicz (1985) reported that children who had completed drills of number combinations could not automatically recall the correct answers. In interviews about how they solved problems, many children reported that they had taught themselves other ways of thinking about the number combinations in order to make sense of the problems. Children who can do tasks assigned by teachers but who do not understand them may not have enough time to engage in the experiences needed for them to develop the concepts. They may simply continue to do more tasks for which they memorize procedures.

The most effective type of assessment presents the child with a problem and has the teacher observe carefully the strategies the child uses in solving that problem. For example, to assess counting abilities, the child should be presented with real objects to count; the number of objects should be larger than the teacher estimates the child can count. To check a child's understanding of place value, the teacher should try to determine how she organizes objects in a large set for counting and question her about her strategies to try to reveal her thinking processes. Problems in creating patterns, in classification, and in basic operations should be presented with manipulative materials that the child can use to find solutions. Paper-and-pencil tests may help determine what a child can do, but only by giving a child real problems to work can a teacher uncover what he understands.

Teachers will need to assess children's abilities to conserve number and length in order to plan experiences. If children cannot conserve, it does not mean that the teacher must wait until they can before offering them mathematics instruction. Problems and tasks must be evaluated in terms of the kinds of thinking required to solve them; appropriate experiences can be selected based on children's levels of thinking. Children learn a great deal about mathematics before they can conserve number and length (McClintic 1988).

Teachers should not limit themselves to assessing children's computation abilities or problem-solving skills. Teachers should also assess how children feel as learners of mathematics, how children view mathematics, and what abilities children have to apply mathematical thinking to everyday problems.

CHAPTER SUMMARY

- Mathematics is more than just arithmetic. Mathematics includes classification, seriating, grouping, relationships, statistics, probability, fractions, geometry, and arithmetic.
- Mathematics is not a subject at which one is innately good or poor. Neither is knowledge of mathematics transmitted from a person who knows to one who does not. Each individual learns mathematics by constructing understanding. Mathematical relationships are mental constructs.
- Mathematics in the classroom setting should be based on real problems that children are interested in solving. Some problems will involve the use of arithmetic; others will not.

- Instruction in mathematics should focus on helping children understand mathematical concepts before mathematical symbols are introduced.
- Writing down their questions, discoveries, and solutions can be very helpful to children learning mathematical concepts.
- Some mathematical concepts can be introduced through children's literature. Counting books and rhymes may interest children, and other books may introduce the basic operations, classification, or ordering.
- Assessment in mathematics should focus on the child's understanding, thought processes, and attitudes about mathematics.

WHAT WOULD YOU DO?

Reflect on your reading and your own experiences with young children as you think about the following situations:

1. The curriculum guide suggests some topics, such as a unit on telling time, that you feel are inappropriate for most of the children in your group. How would you present your concerns to your principal?
2. A parent asks how you know her child is learning mathematics. What would you tell her?
3. Two children in your kindergarten class are unable to count to ten. What would you do to enhance their learning?
4. One child in your first-grade group understands and can solve problems that are generally found in the fourth-grade math program. What would you do to enhance her learning?

THEORY INTO PRACTICE

1. Observe two or three primary teachers as they conduct mathematics activities. What did you observe about the children's interest? their attitudes?

2. Plan an experience that will help threes and fours develop a concept of number. What adaptations would you make in the experience if the children were older but still had no stable concept of number?

3. Conduct the Piagetian tasks for number and length conservation with two three-year-olds, two five-year-olds, and two seven-year-olds. (These tasks are described in Harp and Brewer 1991.) What differences in thinking do you observe? What are your conclusions about teaching mathematics to children of these ages?

4. Find a children's book that includes some mathematical ideas. Remembering that children need real experience with manipulatives, plan an activity following a reading of the book that involves using purchased or teacher-constructed manipulatives.

5. Write a paragraph explaining your beliefs about how computation should be taught to young children. Discuss your views with members of your group. Try to reach some consensus.

RECOMMENDED FOR FURTHER READING

Copeland, Richard W. *How Children Learn Mathematics: Teaching Implications of Piaget's Research*. 4th ed. New York: Macmillan, 1984.

   This book is often used as a text in math methods courses in teacher-preparation programs. It contains good explanations of how children learn mathematics, useful teaching ideas, and helpful suggestions for setting up and using a mathematics laboratory approach to math instruction.

Kamii, Constance. *Number in Preschool and Kindergarten*. Washington, DC: National Association for the Education of Young Children, 1982.

   Kamii provides an excellent explanation of the Piagetian model of how children learn mathematics. The suggestions for games will help teachers get started using games in their classrooms and thinking about what children learn from games and other experiences.

Kamii, Constance, and Georgia DeClark. *Young Children Reinvent Arithmetic: Implications of Piaget's Theory*. New York: Teachers College Press, 1985.

   This account of a year's work in a first-grade classroom is fascinating. Kamii and the classroom teacher, DeClark, used group games and discussions to help children invent arithmetic for themselves. The descrip-tions are detailed enough that the games and procedures advocated by the authors could be implemented by others. If you teach first grade, this book is a must.

Kamii, Constance, and Linda Leslie Joseph. *Young Children Continue to Reinvent Arithmetic—2nd Grade: Implications of Piaget's Theory*. New York: Teachers College Press, 1989.

   In this book, Kamii describes her continuing explorations of children's mathematical understanding with children in the second grade. Although the book is primarily a report of work in the classroom, Kamii's descriptions are backed up by very readable research. There is enough information on the games and assessment procedures used that teachers could implement the ideas easily in their own classrooms.

Leeb-Lundberg, Kristina. *Mathematics Is More Than Counting*. Wheaton, MD: Association for Childhood Education International, 1985.

   This booklet discusses concepts of number, conservation, one-to-one correspondence, counting and sequencing, sorting and classifying, and equivalence and nonequivalence in short, easy-to-read sections. The author has provided enough examples to help the reader understand the concepts.

McCracken, Janet Brown. *More Than 1, 2, 3—The Real Basics of Mathematics*. Washington, DC: National Association for the Education of Young Children, 1987.

This brochure will help explain to parents and others how children learn mathematics. It contains many suggestions for using mathematics in everyday activities that both parents and teachers will find helpful. It also contains a short list of books that include number ideas. (When ordering from NAEYC, specify brochure 575.)

REFERENCES

General Sources

Bullock, Merry, and Rochel Gelman. "Numerical Reasoning in Young Children: The Ordering Principle." *Child Development* 48 (June 1977): 427–434.

Burns, Marilyn, and Kathy Richardson. "Making Sense Out of Word Problems." *Learning* 10 (January 1981): 39–44.

Burton, Grace M. "Patterning: Powerful Play." *School Science and Mathematics* 82 (June 1982): 39–44.

Copeland, Richard W. *How Children Learn Mathematics: Teaching Implications of Piaget's Research*. 4th ed. New York: Macmillan, 1984.

DeVries, Rheta, and Lawrence Kohlberg. *Constructivist Early Education: Overview and Comparison with Other Programs*. Washington, DC: National Association for the Education of Young Children, 1987.

Ditchburn, Susan J. *Patterning Mathematical Understanding in Early Childhood*. ERIC Document Reproduction Service 218008. 1982.

Gelman, Rochel, and Marsha F. Tucker. "Further Investigations of the Young Child's Conception of Number." *Child Development* 46 (March 1975): 167–175.

Greenberg, Polly. "How and Why to Teach All Aspects of Preschool and Kindergarten Math Naturally, Democratically, and Effectively (For Teachers Who Don't Believe in Academic Programs, Who Do Believe in Educational Excellence, and Who Find Math Boring to the Max)—Part 1." *Young Children* 48 (May 1993): 75–84.

Harp, Bill, and Jo Ann Brewer. *Reading and Writing: Teaching for the Connections*. New York: Harcourt Brace Jovanovich, 1991.

Harsh, Ann. "Teach Mathematics with Children's Literature." *Young Children* 42 (September 1987): 42–49.

Kamii, Constance. *Number in Preschool and Kindergarten*. Washington, DC: National Association for the Education of Young Children, 1982.

Kamii, Constance, and Georgia DeClark. *Young Children Reinvent Arithmetic: Implications of Piaget's Theory*. New York: Teachers College Press, 1985.

Kamii, Constance, and Rheta DeVries. *Group Games in Early Education: Implications of Piaget's Theory*. Washington, DC: National Association for the Education of Young Children, 1980.

Kamii, Constance, and Linda Joseph. "Teaching Place Value and Double-Column Addition." *Arithmetic Teacher* 35 (February 1988): 48–52.

Kamii, Constance, and Linda Leslie Joseph. *Young Children Continue to Reinvent Arithmetic—2nd Grade: Implications of Piaget's Theory*. New York: Teachers College Press, 1989.

Labinowicz, Ed. *Learning from Children: New Beginnings for Teaching Numerical Thinking*. Menlo Park, CA: Addison-Wesley, 1985.

Labinowicz, Ed. *The Piaget Primer: Thinking, Learning, Teaching*. Menlo Park, CA: Addison-Wesley, 1980.

Leeb-Lundberg, Kristina. *Mathematics Is More Than Counting*. Wheaton, MD: Association for Childhood Education International, 1985.

Levin, I., F. Wilkening, and Y. Dembo. "Development of Time Quantification: Integration of Beginnings and Endings in Comparing Durations." *Child Development* 55 (1984): 2160–2172.

Logo Writer. Logo Computer Systems, Inc. Vandrell, Quebec, Canada.

McClintic, Susan V. "Conservation—A Meaningful Gauge for Assessment." *Arithmetic Teacher* 35 (February 1988): 12–14.

McCracken, Janet Brown. *More Than 1, 2, 3—The Real Basics of Mathematics*. Washington, DC: National

Association for the Education of Young Children, 1987.

Murray, Paula L., and Richard E. Mayer. "Preschool Children's Judgments of Number Magnitude." *Journal of Educational Psychology* 80 (June 1988): 206–209.

National Council of Teachers of Mathematics. *Curriculum and Evaluation Standards for School Mathematics.* Washington, DC: NCTM, 1989.

Pagni, David. "You're Never Too Old (or Too Young) to Use a Calculator." *Elementary Mathematician* 1 (December 1987): 10–11.

Piaget, Jean. *The Child's Conception of Number.* London: Routledge and Kegan Paul, 1952.

Piaget, Jean. *Science of Education and the Psychology of the Child.* New York: Orion Press, 1970.

Price, Gary Glen. "Research in Review: Mathematics in Early Childhood." *Young Children* 44 (May 1989): 53–58.

Richards, Leah. "'Measuring Things in Words:' Language for Learning Mathematics." *Language Arts* 67 (January 1990): 14–25.

Richardson, Kathy. "Assessing Understanding." *Arithmetic Teacher* 35 (February 1988): 39–41.

Scott, Deborah, Brenda Williams, and Kathy Hyslip. "Mathematics as Communication." *Childhood Education* 69 (Fall 1992): 15–18.

Smith, Karen Clark. "Strand Model." Oregon State University, Corvallis, OR, 1988.

Stone, Janet I. "Early Childhood Math: Make It Manipulative." *Young Children* 42 (September 1987): 16–23.

Tischler, Rosamund W. "Mathematics from Children's Literature." *Arithmetic Teacher* 35 (February 1988): 42–47.

Turkel, Susan, and Claire M. Newman. "What's Your Number? Developing Number Sense." *Arithmetic Teacher* 35 (February 1988): 53–55.

Van de Walle, John A. "The Early Development of Number Relations." *Arithmetic Teacher* 35 (February 1988): 15–21.

Vygotsky, Lev. *Mind in Society: The Development of Higher Psychological Processes.* Cambridge, MA: Harvard University Press, 1978.

Children's Books

Anno, Mitsumasa. *Anno's Counting House.* New York: Philomel Books, 1982.

Carle, Eric. *The Very Hungry Caterpillar.* New York: Putnam, 1981.

Crews, Donald. *Freight Train.* New York: Greenwillow, 1978.

Hutchins, Pat. *Clocks and More Clocks.* New York: Macmillan, 1970.

Hutchins, Pat. *The Doorbell Rang.* New York: Greenwillow, 1986.

Kraus, Robert. *Leo, the Late Bloomer.* New York: Crowell, 1971.

Lobel, Arnold. *Frog and Toad Are Friends.* New York: Harper and Row, 1970.

McCloskey, Robert. *Blueberries for Sal.* New York: Viking, 1948.

Silverstein, Shel. *Where the Sidewalk Ends.* New York: Harper and Row, 1974.

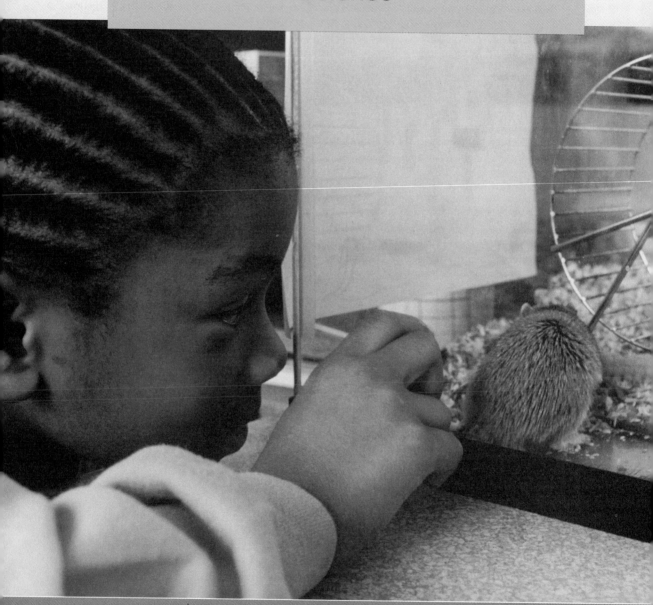

Chapter Nine

Manipulation and Discovery
Science

Your observation task this morning in the preschool was to look for children engaged in scientific learning. You chose to observe a group of three- and four-year-olds for the first hour and a group of seven-year-olds for the second hour. In observing the younger children, you expected to see play and language learning, but you did not expect to see much "science." After all, threes and fours cannot really be expected to do experiments, can they? Once you reviewed your notes, however, you found that children were engaged in many activities that could be labeled "science." Some children compared the textures of sand in different containers; other children tried to sink little wooden barges in water. You also found that many of the children's expressed interests were related to science. You overheard two children asking the teacher what had happened to the orange they had brought for snack several days ago—it was covered with mold. You noticed that the teacher did not throw the orange away but left it out for the children to see and smell.

In the second hour, you watched as seven-year-old children were instructed to take out their science books. They were provided with the materials to complete an experiment described in their textbooks: They were to observe the results of mixing unknown powders with water. At the end of the experiment, the teacher guided the children's discussion of their observations. Then they read the discussion in the text about dissolving.

After observing these two classrooms, you are left with the question: What is science? Is science the informal learning that was taking place in the class of younger children, or is it the more formal guided learning in which the older children were participating?

LEARNING SCIENCE

Just as children learn mathematics through manipulation and discovery, they learn science by manipulation, observation of the results of their manipulations, and discovery of relationships and effects. The role of experience in science is primary—science cannot be done without touching, tasting, feeling, smelling, pushing, pulling, rotating, mixing, comparing, and so on (McIntyre 1984).

In the Piagetian view of how children learn (Piaget and Inhelder 1969), science is basically *physical knowledge*—the knowledge of inherent characteristics and properties of objects—and *logico-mathematical knowledge*—constructed knowledge of the relationships between and among objects. Very few science concepts can be categorized as *social knowledge*—knowledge transmitted from one learner to another. In short, young children must construct their own understandings of science from their experiences. The problem associated with science instruction over the years parallels that in math instruction: Teachers have tried to *tell* students about science. From the work of Piaget and others (Piaget and Inhelder 1969; Kamii and DeVries 1978; Forman and Kuschner 1983), it has become clear that science and math must be learned actively and that learners must construct their own understandings of concepts.

As you read this chapter, you will notice how much math and science are connected in terms of what they teach and how they are learned. Much scientific learning depends on skills such as measuring, classifying, comparing, and finding relationships. These are the same skills fostered in children learning mathematics.

DEFINITION OF SCIENCE

Science is the process of observing, thinking, and reflecting on actions and events. Children engaged in scientific thinking are constructing a framework of relationships within which factual information can be organized into meaningful and useful concepts. Science is an attitude exemplified by curiosity and interest in the world. Science is problem solving. Science is *not* learning facts and memorizing formulas.

Science in early childhood education is encouraging children to explore their environments and reflect on their observations and discoveries. Ideally, science is not a time set aside from other experiences; it is part

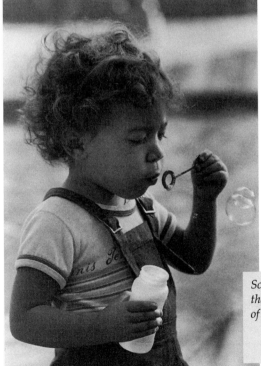

Science is a way of thinking about the world, rather than a collection of facts.

of an ongoing integrated approach in which children think and construct basic understandings about the world. Broadly speaking, a child at the easel follows the basic scientific process when he hypothesizes (predicts that the paint is ready to apply to paper), collects data (paints), revises the prediction (determines that the paint is too runny or too thick), and draws conclusions about how paint reacts under given conditions. He may also discover the interactions of primary colors and explore those interactions very scientifically.

A child experimenting with disappearing ink might hypothesize about the ingredients of the ink and the conditions that make it visible again. She might collect data by trying several recipes for disappearing ink and trying to make it appear under several conditions. After observing what did and did not work, she would draw conclusions about the best formula for disappearing ink and what conditions are necessary to make it appear again. Because young children are so interested in the world around them, science is tightly interwoven in most of their activities and experiences.

Raper and Stringer (1987) have pointed out what science is not:

> *Science is not book learning. We can learn a good deal from books, of course, and there is no other way that we can learn about the lives and discoveries of the great men and women of science except by reference to recorded information. But, fundamentally, the processes of science can only be understood by actively using them. Teachers need to be discouraged from seeing book learning as a substitute for practical activity. (p. 47)*

As Holt (1989) explains:

> *Science is a way of doing things and solving problems. It is a style that leads a person to wonder, to seek, to discover, to know, and then to wonder anew. It is a style in which good feelings of joy, excitement, and beauty accompany these active mental and physical interactions with one's world. Not only children but adults can experience science. It is a way of life. (p. 181)*

Perry and Rivkin (1992) suggest that teaching science requires some essential elements:

> *Time (playing and asking questions takes time), knowing something (some understanding of what can be learned from materials is vital), being open to*

one's own ignorance (teachers can look up information, consult with others, learn along with the children, but it is dangerous not to recognize what is not known), valuing one's own interests and interpretations (science is not right answers, but the asking of questions and thinking about what happens), valuing the symbolizing of experience and knowledge (recording, reworking and rethinking our ideas are as important in science as in any other area), and recognizing the need and being willing to collect and make available ample supplies for sciencing. (p. 16)

Many teachers report that they feel less prepared to teach science than any other subject-matter area (Towsley and Voss 1988). Perhaps such feelings are a result of teachers' misconceptions that science requires complicated materials and is a hard subject to master. This view is changing as more and more teachers at all grade levels are encouraged to think in terms of so-called backyard science or kitchen science—the approach early childhood educators have always taken. *Sciencing*, a term popular with early childhood teachers, implies not only the active nature of science experiences but the idea that both children and teachers are involved in the process of learning science—as opposed to having the teacher teach the children. *Sciencing* also implies that the whole classroom is used for learning rather than setting aside one area as a science area (McNairy 1985).

One of the most positive aspects of science as a field of study for young children is that it has not been affected by the trend to create readiness curricula. In some cases, this has meant that science has been ignored in curricula that focus on academic readiness; in other cases, children have been allowed to explore and investigate unhindered by a preconceived set of objectives that supposedly will make them ready to do science when they are older.

At least teachers do not have to contort their planning so that it reflects ingrained ideas about what children need to do to be ready to study science. Children are natural scientists: They poke the worm they see crawling along the sidewalk, they shake the soft drink can to see the contents spurt out, they take apart their toys to find out how they work, and they watch (and try to copy) the cat lapping up milk with its tongue. Ziemer (1987) describes the world as "a huge hands-on museum, a well-stocked laboratory, a fascinating never-ending field trip" (p. 44).

Teachers just need to take advantage of all that the world offers young children. Science is easy to teach: Just supply children with an interesting environment, make the environment safe for exploration, and provide guidance as children do what comes naturally.

THE SCIENTIFIC PROCESS

Scientific process
A strategy for solving problems that includes making hypotheses, collecting data, testing hypotheses, and drawing conclusions.

The **scientific process** is a cycle of forming hypotheses, collecting data, confirming or rejecting the hypotheses, making generalizations, and then repeating the cycle. The basic skills used in the scientific process include observing, classifying and comparing, measuring, communicating, experimenting, relating, inferring, and applying. Because inferring and applying require more abstract thinking, young children should not be expected to be competent in these skills in a formal sense. Each of these skills, as it applies to an early childhood science program, is discussed in a following section.

Observing

Looking and *observing* are not the same thing. Teachers need to provide guidance in observation techniques. Children can be encouraged to look carefully for specific actions or information. For example, children can be encouraged to observe the behavior of a bird on the ground—does it walk or hop? Observation is certainly not limited to visual input; it should involve all the senses—seeing, hearing, smelling, tasting, and feeling.

Classifying and Comparing

Classifying is a basic process skill used in organizing information. In order to classify objects or information, children must be able to compare and contrast the properties of objects or information. Very young children begin to classify by function, color, or shape. Older children can classify on the basis of specific characteristics or properties, but multiplicative classifications, in which objects fit into multiple categories, are difficult for children in the early childhood years. Children must be able to think in concrete operational terms before they can think of objects as belonging to several categories at once, and most children are not concrete thinkers in the early childhood years. Teachers can encourage children to classify objects and to explain how objects have been grouped. Children can classify blocks by shape, group the materials that are stored in the art area, or sort buttons, leaves, shells, or other collections.

Measuring

Measuring is a basic process skill necessary for collecting data. Measurement does not refer only to using standardized measures.

Children can measure the hamster's food by scoops, cut a piece of string the height of their bean plant, compare the sizes of seeds or rocks, or use a beaker to collect snow and observe the amount of water produced when the snow melts.

Communicating

Communicating is another basic process skill. Children can be encouraged to share their observations and their data collections through a variety of means. They can talk about their findings, make pictorial records, produce charts and graphs, or write narratives in order to share information, data, and conclusions. The communication process is important, as children begin to understand how knowledge is created in the field of science.

Experimenting

Experimentation is not a new process for young children. They have been experimenting since they first picked up a rattle or threw a cereal bowl off the high chair tray. In the scientific process, experimenting means controlling one or more variables and manipulating conditions. Teachers can help children think of their play activities as experiments by skillful questioning and encouraging children to reflect on their actions and the results of their actions. When children try to balance one block on a tower of blocks, drop food coloring into glasses of water, or plant several seeds in different soils, they can be guided to think of these activities as experiments.

Relating, Inferring, and Applying

Young children will use the process skills of relating, inferring, and applying only in very informal ways. *Relating* is the process of drawing abstractions from concrete evidence. For example, children who observe water freezing may not be able to relate that observation to the abstract idea that given liquids become solids at given temperatures. *Inferring* is the ability to determine cause-and-effect relationships or explanations for phenomena when the processes are not directly observable. Examples of such unobservable phenomena include electricity and magnetism. *Applying* is using information from experiences to invent, create, solve new problems, and determine probabilities. Children can be involved in applying scientific knowledge but not in a formal, analytical sense. For example, if children can observe the behavior of water when it is dropped on waxed paper, blown across waxed paper with a straw, or left outside on a winter night, they can apply some of these observations to other liquids and make predictions about what will happen to other liquids under the same conditions. It is unreasonable, however, to expect children to analyze results and apply them without concrete experiences to think about.

PLANNING AN EARLY CHILDHOOD SCIENCE PROGRAM

Goals

The goals of science education in the early childhood classroom include:

1. Having children explore and investigate a wide variety of materials and phenomena
2. Getting children actively involved in using the process skills of science
3. Encouraging children's curiosity and interest and an attitude of "let's find out"
4. Helping children acquire some factual knowledge
5. Helping children understand how the work of scientists is related to their own lives and investigations

All these goals are very broad. None talks about learning specific scientific facts or being able to perform specific tasks because children participating in the scientific process—engaging in activities, reflecting on those activities, and learning about what other scientists do—are "doing science."

Planning Content and Balance

Children's interest in biological science is so strong that teachers often emphasize it and fail to help children explore the areas of physical or earth sciences. But the basics of all areas of science can be developed in the early childhood years.

With guidance, children learn about botany as they sow seeds, eat plants, pull weeds, and smell flowers. They learn about zoology as they observe animals at the zoo, feed a puppy, hold a snake, and bury a goldfish. They learn about physics as they try to lift a heavier friend on the other end of the teeter-totter, observe the gears in a clock, watch someone jack up the family car, throw balls at targets, and feel the heat of a city side-walk. They learn about chemistry as they watch sugar disappear in lemon-ade and feel the fizz when they place lozenges in their mouths. They learn about geology as they fill their pockets with stones, find fossils in rocks, pour water on sand, and mark the sidewalk with a rock. They learn about astronomy as they observe the sun, the moon, the stars, and the seasons.

The rule for planning a balanced science program for early childhood is simple: Do not try to teach children concepts about phenomena that can-not be touched, tasted, seen, or heard. If children cannot explore a concept through real materials, then the concept is too abstract and is not appro-priate for the early childhood years. Children develop concepts over many experiences and explorations.

Vygotsky (1962) supports this notion, stating that "practical experi-ence . . . shows that direct teaching of concepts is impossible and fruitless. A teacher who tries to do this usually accomplishes nothing but empty ver-balism, a parrotlike repetition of words" (p. 83). Howe (1993) agrees: "The effort to teach concepts that are not accessible to children through their own experience and thinking is inappropriate in preschool and the pri-mary grades" (p. 232).

Smith (1981) explains that "concepts of natural phenomena must be developed through manipulation of items within children's immediate environment and observation of children's reactions under varying cir-cumstances. Abstract concepts outside the realm of immediate experience should not be included in an early childhood science curriculum" (pp. 5–6). Smith (1987) recommends that teachers ask the following questions in selecting science experiences:

Are the materials selected those that:

- *children will naturally gravitate to for play?*
- *provide opportunities for the development of perceptual abilities through total involvement of the senses (perception of color, size, shape, texture, hardness, sound, etc.)?*
- *encourage self-directed problem solving and experimentation?*
- *children can act upon—cause to move—or that encourage children's observations of changes?*

Do the experiences that evolve from children's play with the materials:

- *provide opportunities for the teacher to extend the child's learning by ask-ing questions or making suggestions that stimulate children's thinking?*

- *allow for additional materials to be introduced gradually to extend children's explorations and discoveries?*
- *allow for differences in ability, development, and learning style?*
- *allow children to freely interact with other children and adults?*
- *encourage children to observe, compare, classify, predict, communicate?*
- *allow for the integration of other curriculum areas? (p. 36)**

Electricity is an example of a topic often presented in early childhood classrooms. However, the outcomes of experiences involving electricity usually reflect the child's preoperational thinking and often are not what is expected when the experiences are planned. Usually, children are supplied with batteries, small bulbs, and wires. The goal is to attach the wire to the battery and light the bulb. The expected outcomes are that children will develop an understanding that electricity is energy and that energy can be stored in a battery, channeled through a conduit (the wire), and released as the bulb lights.

What usually happens is that the teacher must verbalize these concepts. The children may learn to repeat them, but their explanations of why the bulb lights up include that it wants to light up or that it lights up because we want light or that it is magic. Electricity is a very abstract concept; even when children can be active in attaching the wires to the battery, what they learn from manipulating the objects is rarely what teachers expect them to learn (Good 1977). Unless an abstract concept can be made concrete, it is not appropriate for study by young children.

In planning experiences that will help children develop concepts, teachers must also examine the materials they select to make sure that the concepts children learn with them are not erroneous. For example, if all the tall containers in the water play area hold more than the short containers, children might assume that tall containers always hold more. The same sort of erroneous reasoning might result if children who were exploring floating and sinking found that all the materials that floated were small and all that sank were large (Benham et al. 1982).

A science program, like a math program, consists of the children's everyday experiences supplemented by some planned experiences that will spark their interest and help them explore new materials and objects. Children's everyday observations would make them aware of what happens to milk when a carton is inadvertently left out overnight; to a carrot when it is left out in the room for a few days; to the volume of rice when

*From Robert F. Smith, "Theoretical Framework for Preschool Science Experiences," *Young Children* 42 (January 1987): 34–40. Reprinted by permission of the author.

it is cooked; to water left outdoors on a freezing night; to a snowball when it is brought into the classroom; and so on.

Planned experiences to supplement these observations require some preparation by the teacher. Planned experiences might involve bringing various animals into the classroom; bringing in assortments of natural materials for sorting and classifying; or providing levers and gears for children to explore. In each case, the teacher would help the children observe, hypothesize, collect data, and draw conclusions. A balanced science program, then, includes both types of experiences and activities to help develop concepts in the life sciences, physical sciences, and earth sciences.

In addition to thinking about the concepts that are appropriate for children to learn, teachers who are planning for science experiences must provide an environment that is safe for exploration, teach children how to explore and investigate safely, and encourage them to enjoy science and learn some basic concepts and attitudes that are not specific to any one experience.

Providing a Safe Environment

It is the responsibility of the teacher to examine the environment for any hazards to young children. As children mature and become more skillful, safety rules may change. The following are some general safety rules:

1. Equipment should be sturdy and in good repair. Although glass may be the best choice for some activities (such as making an aquarium), most materials provided for the children should be unbreakable. Metal materials should not have torn places or rough edges. Tubs and bins should not be cracked or torn.

2. Use of all heat sources should be well supervised. All electric outlets should have safety covers; electric cords should be taped against walls.

3. Plants in the classroom should be nonpoisonous.

4. Tubs or pools of water should be closely supervised.

5. Tools such as knives and hammers should be in good condition, and their use should be supervised carefully.

Teaching Children to Explore and Investigate Safely

Once the environment has been made safe, teachers need to think about rules to help children explore materials, objects, animals, and plants safely. The following general guidelines will help ensure safe explorations:

1. No material should be tasted or eaten unless the children know that it is edible or safe to taste. If, for example, the teacher provides powder for the children to explore, children must be taught not to taste the powder without instruction to do so. Children should be taught never to taste any unfamiliar substance.

2. Plants also should not be tasted or eaten unless the children know what they are or an adult says they are safe to eat. For instance, children should never eat leaves, berries, or roots unless they know they are safe. Children should be aware of safety precautions even when eating commercially obtained foods.

3. Children should be taught how to smell any unfamiliar substance. Plunging one's face into a container can result in irritation of the eyes or nose. Teachers can demonstrate how to hold and sniff any substance without danger of inhaling the substance or burning membranes.

4. Children should be taught not to touch or handle unknown animals. Every child should know not to touch wild animals and how to hold any pet or classroom animal without hurting or frightening the animal.

The art is in teaching children to be properly cautious without dimming their enthusiasm. Teachers should make sure that children understand the necessity for these precautions while encouraging safe explorations and discoveries.

Encouraging Children to Enjoy Science

Children delight in their scientific discoveries. They may be cautious about touching a toad for the first time, but once they have, they will not be able to wait to share that experience with their families. Teachers of young children may need to relearn some attitudes about science themselves in order to enjoy and guide children's explorations.

Science should be nonbiased. Many adults feel that science is more appropriate for boys than for girls. In fact, all children should be encouraged to participate in a variety of activities and their interests should be respected, regardless of their sex or socioeconomic status. Children involved in a science-based curriculum gain observation skills and classification skills. They may also be encouraged to pursue careers in science. This encouragement is especially important for girls and children from ethnic and cultural minorities, who are underrepresented in the science professions (Iatridis 1981).

Science can be the hub around which other learning experiences are organized. One first-grader refused to read about hats and bears in his basal reader but would struggle to read anything about science. He dictated the following story:

> I like science. I'll tell about science. If you want to know about making sparklers. You need some aluminum filings and you need charcoal powder. You need sulfur and potassium nitrate. You buy these things at a pharmacy. You mix all these chemicals together to make sparklers. You put the stuff on wires like those in plant holders. You wait a night and a day.

This boy's story illustrates the interest many children have in learning about the world and the importance of building curriculum experiences around those interests. The point is not to make sparklers but to build on children's interests while teaching them literacy and other skills.

"Messing about" can be extremely important in developing scientific concepts. Not everything about science is neat and tidy. Sometimes, children's explorations do not end with neat answers. When a four-year-old beats the soap bubbles in a tub of water with a rotary beater until they get smaller and smaller, she doesn't necessarily come up with answers about how the bubbles get smaller, but her curiosity to try things out is sustained. Many discoveries have been made when specific outcomes were not planned.

Finally, teachers must be flexible in planning so that unexpected events can be appreciated. If a child brings in a pet iguana, the teacher should be able to leave his carefully planned study of tree rings for another day.

Teaching Basic Concepts and Attitudes

Some concepts and attitudes are important as children learn about science:

- *Conservation*—Children should begin learning early about the importance of conserving the world's limited resources. Most of this teaching can be done through modeling. For example, teachers should arrange for children to wash vegetables in a pan of water rather than under running water. By recycling all paper used in the classroom, teachers will help children learn not to waste paper. Lights should be turned off when they are not needed. Food should be used only to eat; use junk for printing, rather than potatoes or other vegetables. Collages can be made with inedible weeds rather than edible seeds (Holt 1977).

- *Respect for life*—Teachers can help children learn to respect life and not destroy it. For example, insects and spiders can be captured and released outdoors, rather than killed. Care should be taken that proper food and habitats are provided for any animal visitor to the classroom.
- *Respect for the environment*—Children can become aware of pollution, including litter. They can be taught not to litter and to recycle the materials used in the classroom.

Planning the Sequence of Activities

Kamii and DeVries (1978) have outlined some principles to follow in planning activities through which children can develop physical and logico-mathematical understandings. They suggest that teachers consider various levels of acting on objects when selecting activities.

- *Acting on objects to see how they react*—Young children engage in actions such as rolling, squeezing, and pushing objects. Teachers can ask children what will happen if they squeeze an object, and so on.
- *Acting on objects to produce a desired effect*—Children also act on objects not simply to explore them but intentionally to make things happen. They may pour the milk from their cup onto the high chair tray so they can splash it. The teacher might ask children to blow on a spool to move it across the floor and so on.
- *Becoming aware of how an effect is produced*—Many children can produce effects without knowing how they achieved the results. The teacher might ask a child to tell someone else how an effect was achieved. If the child is unable to do so, the teacher will know that the request was inappropriate for the child's level of development.
- *Explaining causes*—Most young children cannot explain the causes of many effects that they observe and should not be asked to give explanations.

Introducing the Activity
- *Principle I*—The teacher should introduce the activity in a way that maximizes children's initiative. An activity can be introduced by putting out material to which children will naturally gravitate; by presenting the material and telling them "See what you can think of to do with these things"; or by proposing a specific problem to be solved with the materials.

- *Principle II*—The teacher should begin with parallel play. Because teachers want children to do things with materials, they must make sure that each child has her own materials. (If, however, several children want to play together, they should of course be encouraged to help each other with questions, comparisons, and so on.)

During the Activity
- *Principle I*—The teacher should figure out what the child is thinking and respond sparingly in his terms. Figuring out what the child is thinking is sometimes quite difficult. The teacher may get clues from the child's actions or from his questions. The direction to "respond sparingly" may force the teacher to drop his own agenda and follow the child's, at least for the time being. Teachers can help children with practical problems to facilitate experimentation and observation, offer materials to encourage comparisons, or model new comparisons.
- *Principle II*—The teacher should encourage children to interact with other children.
- *Principle III*—The teacher should offer the child activities that increase her physical knowledge and that exercise her current social, moral, and motor abilities.

After the Activity
Teachers should encourage children to reflect on activities briefly after they have been completed. This can be accomplished through questions about what they did, the results of what they did, what they noticed, what other children did, the problems they encountered, and so on. The point is not to get all children to arrive at one right answer but to allow children to think about what they did.

Wasserman (1988) describes a model for science instruction that incorporates the same principles as the Kamii and DeVries model. She calls it *play-debrief-replay*. In this model, the children engage in investigative play with selected materials. Following the play, the teacher guides their reflection through questions and sets the stage for replay, in which the children play with the same materials again, either to duplicate their previous results or to explore further.

An example of these principles in action might be a bubble-blowing activity for young children. Since most children are fascinated by bubbles, just making the materials available will be motivational. To begin, each child should have his own bubble wand and access to bubble solution. As

Think about what you have read and what you have experienced in regard to science instruction as you reflect on these questions:

- What elements of a science program are essential for DAP? Why?
- In comparison to traditional science programs, will developmentally appropriate programs produce more people who are scientifically literate? Why?
- Why are some teachers more successful at traditional science instruction than others? Is it

motivation? intelligence? experience? Are any of the reasons for that success relevant to developmentally appropriate practice? If so, how?
- Should learning scientific facts ever be part of a developmentally appropriate program? If so, for what age group?

the children blow bubbles, the teacher should try to get them to think about the force needed to make bubbles. After a time, the teacher should offer the children bubble wands that are not round but square, triangular, or rectangular and perhaps of different sizes, as well. The children should be guided to observe the sizes and shapes of the bubbles blown with different wands and then to draw conclusions about those observations. To follow up, the children might make bubbles again but be encouraged to find different materials to use in the bubble solution—their hands, cheesecloth, and so on. In this replay activity, the children can apply what they learned from the first bubble activity.

An example of a play-debrief-replay scenario with primary-grade children might involve mechanics. Children could be invited to take apart an old toaster and observe the mechanical parts. As they worked, the teacher would try to determine what they were thinking about how the machine worked. After the children had a chance to examine the materials carefully, the teacher could provide other levers, springs, and gears for investigation. After reflection on the activity, the children could play with the materials again and perhaps invent their own simple machines.

SUGGESTIONS FOR EXPERIENCES IN THE CLASSROOM

Many science experiences can also be labeled math, art, or language arts experiences. In reading the following suggestions for appropriate science activities, keep in mind the discussion of an integrated model of curriculum in Chapter Five and remember that science should not be separated from ongoing classroom experiences.

Many experiences help children develop process skills in observation.

Biological Science

Threes and Fours

Science experiences for three- and four-year-olds should be playful experiences. Teachers should be very alert to the discoveries that children are making as they play and should be ready to guide the children's thinking as they participate in the following kinds of activities:

- Observing animals—Small animals that can be held are ideal, such as rabbits, guinea pigs, or snakes. Teachers may want animals to visit for short periods of time rather than be permanent residents. Fish, birds, insects, spiders, and reptiles are also interesting to children.
- Observing simple ant farms or beehives—Some schools have specially prepared beehives that attach to windows so that children can observe the bees safely from inside the room.
- Observing spider webs, bird nests, or other animal homes
- Providing some care for classroom pets, such as feeding the fish or filling the rabbit's water container
- Collecting and observing tadpoles from the local pond

- Observing the life cycles of butterflies or moths
- Examining the different textures found in natural items such as tree bark
- Sprouting sweet potatoes, pineapple and carrot tops, grapefruit or orange seeds, and so on—With care (and a little luck), the children may actually be able to eat the results of their work.

Fives and Sixes

Science experiences for five- and six-year-olds should continue to be based primarily on play experiences. Teachers will want to record or encourage children to record their discoveries on charts and in reports. Many print materials can be provided to extend children's interests in science topics, and more planned experiences are appropriate as children mature. Activities for fives and sixes can include the following:

- Making a collection of seeds to sort—Most seeds sold commercially are treated with substances that are poisonous when ingested, so if the class uses commercially prepared seeds, the teacher should ensure that children do not put them in their mouths and that they wash their hands carefully after handling the seeds.
- Conducting an ongoing study of animals—During the course of the year, many different animals can be introduced into the classroom: hamsters, goldfish, lizards, gerbils, crayfish, turtles, garter snakes, and land snails. With some guidance (and some good library resources), children can help construct habitats for these animals, study their life cycles, and focus reading and writing experiences around these visitors. Teachers are cautioned not to use a human family analogy when studying animals. The animals should be referred to as "male" and "female" rather than as "Mommy" and "Daddy." If a family analogy is used and the male gerbil eats the offspring, the teacher will have some explaining to do about what daddies do! The important concepts that children should learn are that it takes a male and female of the same species to produce offspring, that the amount of care animals provide for their young varies, and that each animal needs food, water, and protection in order to survive.
- Starting and maintaining a class garden—If creating one is possible, a garden plot outdoors is ideal. If weather and space limit outside gardening options, an inside garden can be planted in tubs or old wading pools. Children can help prepare the garden with pebbles or sand for drainage, soil for planting, and organic material for fertilizer. Children can learn about appropriate plants, plant seeds, and sprouts and care for the plants. They can also cook and eat the products of a garden.

- Conducting an intensive study of the life cycles of selected insects or amphibians—To learn about life cycles, children might study silkworms, butterflies, moths, frogs, or other creatures. The life cycles must be readily observable in the classroom, so that children can record changes and keep scientific records of the stages.
- Hatching eggs—Many classrooms hatch eggs in the spring. Ideally, eggs should be hatched by a mother hen at school, but an incubator is the next best choice. Hatching eggs can stimulate many reading and writing projects. Children can describe the development of the embryo or care of the eggs. Teachers should keep in mind that no hatching experiences should be undertaken without planning for what will be done with the baby animals after they have been hatched. It is not appropriate to teach children that life is expendable.
- Making collections of natural materials for sorting and classifying, such as leaves, pine cones, and seashells—What to choose depends on the environment and the children's experiences. Print materials such as posters, books, and magazines can be added to displays of natural materials, and experiences can be extended from these collections.

Sevens and Eights

Experiences for sevens and eights should continue to be based on their interests and their home and school environments. More of their experiences should involve experimenting and employing the scientific process. Activities for children of this age include the following:

- Studying plants—Children might learn the names and purposes of parts of plants and seeds and experiment with different conditions for sprouting seeds and growing plants while controlling environmental elements (light, soil conditions, amount of water, and so on). The teacher could introduce children to some plants that are not green (fungi, mushrooms) and plants that reproduce without seeds (ferns).
- Studying the life requirements of different animals—Children might carry out studies of animal growth and behavior, for example, by feeding two hamsters different diets (both healthy) and comparing their growth. The teacher can emphasize the importance of keeping careful scientific records and can extend children's interests to reading and writing experiences.
- Studying the characteristics of different animals and performing simple classifications based on these characteristics
- Studying birds in the local environment—Activities might focus on adaptations in feet, bills, wings, and so on to meet environmental demands and on the place of birds in ecosystems.

Physical Science

Threes and Fours

Physical science experiences, like all school experiences for very young children, must be based on play experiences and everyday classroom activities. Some possibilities include:

- Manipulating modeling clay and observing its properties—Can it be rolled? stretched? pushed? Children can compare the properties of Silly Putty and Play Doh to those of clay.
- Using pull toys with removable wheels to discover the difference between moving toys with wheels and moving toys without them
- Painting with tempera paints—Children can observe how paint drips and runs, what consistencies paints have, and how colors mix.
- Playing with water—Teachers should provide a variety of containers, tubes, funnels, and so on for explorations with water (Bird 1983).
- Playing with blocks—Children learn about gravity, balance, and support as they build structures.
- Blowing activities with straws—Children can explore wind and air pressure (blowing) as forces to move different objects.
- Rolling balls toward targets from various distances and angles (Kamii and DeVries 1978)
- Using rollers and boards for moving materials, balancing themselves, and so on (Kamii and DeVries 1978)
- Observing light and shadows—Very young children often believe that shadows are parts of the objects that cast them. Activities need not include technical explanations of shadows.

Fives and Sixes

Teachers of fives and sixes can begin to introduce some activities to help the children develop specific concepts and can extend their experiences through reading and writing tasks. Children might share some of what they learn orally as a way of evaluating their daily activities in addition to recording some of their discoveries in their journals. Several activities are appropriate for this age group:

- Playing with water—Children can explore floating and sinking with a variety of materials. They can sort the materials into categories and then try to modify the materials that float so that they sink and vice versa. Modifications might include adding materials or making boats out of different materials.

- Moving objects across water by blowing on them through straws—Children can have races (Kamii and DeVries 1978).
- Blowing bubbles—Children can mix and compare bubble solutions and record the best mixtures. They can also experiment by dipping different shapes into bubble solutions and record their findings (shapes of bubbles, which bubbles last longer, which shapes produce the most bubbles, and so on).
- Finding gears, levers, and planes in the environment—Children can take apart old appliances to examine their parts.
- Learning about clamps, vises, and levers at the woodworking table (Schiller and Townsend 1985)
- Creating elevators during block play; using pulleys
- Experimenting with different weights in different positions on balance scales or teeter-totters
- Experimenting with sound using different materials and different ways of vibrating the materials
- Controlling the variables for some physical changes in matter—Is there a way to make ice or snow melt faster or water evaporate more quickly?
- Making paper airplanes and paper helicopters—Do different folds in the paper produce different results?
- Cooking—Children can observe changes in matter (melting, hardening, expanding, shrinking, and so on).

Sevens and Eights

The physical science exploration of sevens and eights can be extended by reading and writing tasks associated with keeping careful records and recording discoveries:

- Playing with water—Experiences should be extended to exploring the properties of water and beginning activities that focus on water cycles. Children can record the results of rate-of-flow experiments on sand in the sandbox or changes in evaporation rates of water and other liquids.
- Dissolving and heating substances—Children can observe different reactions of matter by finding substances that dissolve in water or testing the effects of heat and cold on different materials.
- Changing states of matter (solid, liquid, vapor)—Children can observe matter in these states, record their observations, and form hypotheses about the causes of the changes.
- Inventing machines—Children can invent machines using gears, levers, inclined planes, or pulleys. Kuehn (1988) suggests that humorous inventions (balloon poppers, dog feeders, and so on) are appropriate

because the children learn invention strategies without having to produce serious inventions.

- Exploring magnets—Children can explore magnets by creating structures with magnetic building pieces and testing which materials will or will not be attracted by magnets. They can also explore magnetic forces using different materials: Will iron filings be attracted through paper? plastic? wood? thin metal (Harlan 1980)?

- Studying sources of light and shadows—Children can measure the shadows of the same object at different times of day and record the results. Children can also create shadow plays or make silhouettes from shadows of children.

- Cooking experiences—More complex activities are appropriate, during which time children can explore the reactions of different combinations of ingredients, temperatures, or other conditions of cooking. An example is separating biscuit dough into two portions, adding baking powder to one portion only, and then cooking and comparing the two portions.

Earth Science

Threes and Fours

As in other areas of science, basic concepts of scientific thinking about the earth and the universe are developed while young children play. For threes and fours, such concepts are developed when they play with different mixtures of sand and water and different textures and colors of sand; observe rain, snow, or other precipitation; or watch snow melt or water freeze or evaporate.

Fives and Sixes

Earth science experiences for fives and sixes might include:

- Classifying rocks by size, shape, color, density, and hardness—Children can experiment with rocks by scratching them with nails, using eye droppers to drop vinegar on their surfaces, weighing rocks of approximately equal size, chipping rocks with a rock pick (if safety goggles are supplied), or comparing polished and unpolished rocks of the same kind. The teacher can read *Everybody Needs a Rock* (Baylor 1974).

- Making simple maps of the school property that show all the different surface coverings (grass, asphalt, gravel, and so on)

- Examining the different compositions of soil collected in the children's yards or from different places on the school grounds—Are there differences in color, smell, texture? What happens when water is added?

INTEGRATING THE CURRICULUM

Extending the theme of patterns, the following activities are a few of many possibilities:

➤ Look for patterns in how the leaves are arranged on stems (evenly? on opposite sides? on alternating sides?).

➤ Find the patterns in leaves (lobes, smooth edges, serrated edges, and so on).

➤ Observe the growth patterns of needles and cones in coniferous trees.

➤ Look for coloration patterns in any group of animals (stripes, spots, masks, and so on).

➤ Look for patterns of legs and body parts in identifying insects.

➤ Examine closely patterns in the wings of butterflies and moths.

➤ Create patterns with gears of various sizes (and perhaps print the patterns with tempera paint).

➤ Observe the pattern produced when a pebble is dropped into still water.

➤ Using an overhead projector, observe the patterns created when drops of paint are added to small, flat dishes of water.

➤ Experiment with different patterns of shapes used to hold up bridges, and determine which is strongest.

➤ Explore the patterns that work best for creating a pinwheel that turns easily or patterns of windmill or waterwheel blades.

➤ Find and observe rock samples that illustrate the patterns of the deposits that created the rocks.

➤ Observe and record the patterns of sunrise and sunset or of tides.

➤ Observe the seasonal patterns of the year (if appropriate for the region), and relate these patterns to patterns of the earth and sun.

Children can put each sample through a screen and compare what they find or plant seeds in each sample and record the results.

• Recording weather daily over the course of the year—What is the most common type of weather in any given month? Some children may be able to start taking some weather measurements with a large thermometer, a wind sock, and a rain gauge.

• Observing the change of seasons by noting the weather, plants, and animals in the local environment during each season

• Exploring the wind with kites, pinwheels, bubbles, and their own bodies

Sevens and Eights

The following activities are appropriate for seven- and eight-year-old children:

• Learning about air and air pressure through experiments such as blowing up balloons, creating bubbles in water, or moving materials with air

• Observing the weather—A simple weather station allows children to take their own measurements and record them.

- Becoming familiar with the relationship of the earth, the moon, and the sun—Children might make models or observe the position of the moon in the sky for one complete phase.
- Learning about land features in the region—Children might observe land features such as ponds, lakes, mountains, rivers, or deserts and study the characteristics of these features as habitats for people and animals.
- Comparing temperatures in full sun and in the shade, holding other conditions constant
- Placing different materials in the sun and measuring their temperatures to begin understanding the differential heat absorption rates of different materials

USING TEXTBOOKS

Many science programs for primary children are based primarily on materials in textbooks. A more appropriate approach would be to organize science experiences for children and then use science textbooks as resources, much as one would choose other appropriate books to enhance study of a topic. For example, suppose a teacher organizes classroom activities around the theme of insects. If a science textbook included information about insects or photographs that could help children, then it should be used. But students should not study insects simply because the topic is in the textbook.

LEARNING ABOUT THE WORK OF SCIENTISTS

One of the goals of science instruction is for children to understand the applications of science to their daily lives and to value the work of scientists. Teachers need to create opportunities to help children develop this knowledge and attitude.

Teachers of very young children must remember that they lack a stable concept of time. Young children often ask adults if there were cars or telephones or electric lights when they were children. These questions demonstrate the difficulty young children have in understanding when discoveries were made. As children mature, they will be able to understand the time frames within which inventions and discoveries changed people's lives. It is the teacher's job to lay the groundwork for this kind of understanding.

In helping children understand the application of science to their own lives, teachers might have them consider a process such as the pasteurization of milk by comparing raw milk and pasteurized milk as it sours. Children might also list all the items in the classroom or in their homes that depend on electricity. Field trips can also help children learn about science in their daily lives. A trip to a water treatment plant might help children appreciate the work of those who keep water supplies safe for drinking. Some planetariums and museums provide special programs for young children, including hands-on experiences and exhibits that are appropriate and interesting. Field trips to forests, rivers, fish hatcheries, farms, ranches, and construction sites also provide good opportunities to see science in action.

Finally, classroom visitors can talk with children about science. Teachers might introduce children to someone who supervises restaurants and other facilities for cleanliness; someone who is working to preserve forests or grasslands or to protect endangered species of animals or birds; or someone who has invented a labor-saving device. Biographies of scientists can be included in read-aloud programs or provided for independent reading.

INTEGRATING SCIENCE THROUGH THE DAY

Science is so much a part of the youngest children's play experiences that teachers rarely need help in integrating science. Teachers of primary children are often required to teach a certain number of minutes of science each day and to document that they have planned and implemented science instruction.

One strategy for meeting the requirements for science instruction while integrating it with the other classroom activities is to plan thematic units that lend themselves to interesting science activities. Many themes that are appropriate for primary children emphasize science. In selecting a theme, the teacher must remember that it should be interesting to both children and himself, important enough to be taught, and appropriate to the children's level of development and environment. Science themes include trees, fish, birds, minibeasts, patterns, and cycles, among others, as well as the traditional themes of senses, colors, and seasons. Table 9.1 lists science activities for primary grades that revolve around the theme of insects and activities that can be used in other subject areas to complement the science activities. A list of selected references about insects is also included at the end of the References.

Table 9.1 Science Activities for Insect Theme

SUBJECT AREA	ACTIVITIES
Language Arts	• Read aloud a variety of story and information books about insects. What did the authors need to know to write the books? How did the authors obtain the information? What are the authors' backgrounds? • Write reports, scientific observations, and poetry about insects. (Carle's *Very Hungry Caterpillar* [1990] is an example of a life-cycle story; Fleischman's *A Joyful Noise* [1988] is an example of poetry about insects. These books and others listed in the References for this chapter can be used as models for the children's writing.) • Learn to use reference books to find information about insects.
Science	• Study the characteristics of insects. Chart information needed to classify insects. • Study the life cycles of butterflies or moths and grasshoppers. Compare and contrast the changes in these insects. • If possible, observe the activity of bees in a beehive. Identify each type of bee. • Observe the homes of different types of insects (wasp nests, mud dauber nests). Compare the material used to make the homes. • Study the places of several specific insects in the food chain. What do they eat? What eats them? • Study the contributions of particular insects to their ecosystems. How do insects help people? • Study the ways insects protect themselves: camouflage (color, shape patterns); exoskeleton (in some areas, cicada shells are common; they are excellent examples of exoskeletons); odors or taste; stings or bites. • Discuss appropriate safety precautions for avoiding stings and bites; then go on an insect hunt. Supply children with a magnifying glass, a length of rope or a hula hoop, and a clipboard and paper. Have each child select an area of the playground or a park, place the rope or hula hoop on the ground, and find all the insects within the boundaries of the rope or hoop. Record the numbers and kinds of insects and where each is located (in grass, soil, taller plants). Have children compare observations when they return to the classroom. • If your area includes their habitat, compare several water insects. What adaptations do they have for living in the water?
Social Studies	• Study insect pests. Why is it necessary to control them? List the environmental impacts of various methods of control (for example, spraying for mosquitoes versus importing birds or destroying mosquito breeding grounds). • Invite a local gardener to discuss control of harmful insects through nonchemical means, such as with plantings that discourage insects or the introduction of other insects to control pests.
Art and Crafts	• Make models or drawings of appropriate habitats for particular insects. What does each insect need to have in its habitat? • Compare drawings and photographs of insects in books. Are there times when using a drawing is better than using a photograph and vice versa? • Create drawings to illustrate reports or poetry related to insects.
Music and Movements	• Ask the music specialist to help you find songs and music about insects (for example, Rimsky-Korsakov's "The Flight of the Bumble Bee"). • Study the methods used by insects to produce sounds. • Dramatize some insect movements (water striders gliding, grasshoppers jumping, and so on).

THE READING AND WRITING CONNECTION

As science is taught throughout the day, children will "learn to read for information, interpret graphs, compare charts, and keep journals as a natural part of their school day" (Fine and Josephson 1984, p. 29). Skills in language arts will be developed through meaningful activities, and children will learn science because it is interesting and exciting.

If teachers choose to organize science experiences around themes, reading and writing experiences can and should be integral parts of the theme. Many topics of interest will emerge from classroom incidents, classroom visitors, or trips. Teachers will want to extend the interests of the children through their developing literacy skills. The following examples may give you other ideas of ways to help children use reading and writing in meaningful ways.

Class Pets

The class might acquire a pet when a child brings his turtle to the class for a few weeks. (Laws have changed about keeping and selling turtles. Check the laws in your area.) The teacher might incorporate some of the following reading and writing experiences into her plans in order to expand on the children's interest in the turtle:

- The children might learn "The Little Turtle" (a fingerplay).
- The teacher might find a large copy of the fingerplay, prepare a large chart, print the words to be used with a pocket chart, or find some other way to present the print in a large format. The teacher could read the words aloud several times, then the children could read chorally, and finally the children could read independently.
- After the children have read the words to the fingerplay many times, they might be given small booklets containing the words and then make their own illustrations. These booklets might be read independently.
- Children might write about turtles. The teacher could help children structure reports about turtles that contain factual information, records of observations of the class turtle, and narratives about personal experiences with turtles.
- The teacher might read aloud stories that feature turtles. "The Tortoise and the Hare"; *Timothy Turtle* (Davis 1940); *I Wish I Could Fly* (Maris 1986); *Turtle Tale* (Asch 1978); and *The Foolish Tortoise* (Buckley 1985) are all good choices.
- The teacher might read aloud information books about turtles and their habitats. Examples include *Green Turtle Mysteries* (Waters 1972); *Nature's Children: Turtles* (Switzer 1986); and *Turtle Watch* (Ancona 1987). The

illustrations in Holling's *Minn of the Mississippi* (Holling 1951) might also be useful. *A Turtle in the House* (Navarra 1968) and *The Total Turtle* (Reeves 1975) supply information about the details of keeping a turtle as a pet. (Children might enjoy some of the illustrations in these latter two books, but the text is too complicated for reading aloud.)

- Children might keep a chart of the turtle's care. The chart should include columns for food, water, who cleans the container, who baby-sits on weekends, and whatever else is required in caring for the turtle.
- The children might dictate facts about turtles while the teacher records them (Laminack 1987).

Machines

For a study of simple machines, a teacher might plan reading and writing activities such as the following:

- Read *Mike Mulligan and His Steam Shovel* (1939) and *Katy and the Big Snow* (1943), both by Virginia Burton.
- Read directions for putting together a simple household device. Discuss the structure of the directions. Children might write directions for putting together an invention of their own in two or three steps.
- If possible, take a walk to a construction site, and have the children write descriptions of one or more of the machines they see at work there.
- Have children write reports of what they find when they dismantle a household appliance.
- Have children write invitations to parents to come to class to talk about the machines they use in their work.
- Children might use Maccaulay's *The Way Things Work* (1988) as a reference book for finding information about machines.

Plants

For a study of plants, children might participate in the following activities:

- Find information about specific plants in references books.
- Read the planting directions on seed packages and the directions for plant care on tags from a florist.
- Keep records of plant growth, amount of water, fertilizers, and any other information that can be charted or graphed.
- Write reports of classification experiences with seeds or leaves.
- Invite someone who sells seeds or plants to visit the class and talk about her work.

- Invite a guest whose hobby is gardening to talk about plants and gardening techniques most suitable for the area.
- Write invitations and thank-you letters to these speakers. Write reports as a group or as individuals of the information gained.

Clearly, any topic in science can be expanded by reading and writing experiences that are real and meaningful to the children. Science experiences can also be extensions of literature experiences. Butzow and Butzow (1988) argue that scientific and technological literacy are becoming increasingly important and that the issues related to science and technology should be introduced early in a child's experience. Many issues can be introduced through literature experiences, and follow-up activities can be planned to help children gain information and develop problem-solving skills along with increasing literacy skills.

CHILDREN WITH SPECIAL NEEDS

Some adaptations of materials may be necessary to help children with disabilities develop concepts in science. Some possible adaptations include:

- Helping children with visual impairments sort and classify objects using tactile cues
- Helping children with hearing impairments experience sound through tactile means—For example, children can feel the vibrations of tuning forks, guitar strings, or rubber bands stretched across cigar boxes.
- Arranging materials so that children with physical disabilities can work with them easily and as independently as possible

As in other areas of study, teachers will want all children to participate fully and will adapt materials when necessary to make that possible. "Multisensory instruction with a variety of activities provides the experiential background necessary for concept formation for all students. It also allows students with sensory limitations to profit from more activities" (Cain and Evans 1984, p. 233).

Multisensory activities are also appropriate for children who are gifted. Follis and Krockover (1982) recommend that programs for such children be discovery based and designed to foster independent learning. Teachers of children who are gifted must be careful not to emphasize the verbal facility of these children so much that they fail to involve them in manipulative learning experiences.

CHAPTER SUMMARY

- Science *is* process, thinking, and an attitude of curiosity and interest in the world. Science *is not* memorizing facts and formulas.

- The scientific process is a cycle that includes forming hypotheses, collecting data, confirming or rejecting the hypotheses, making generalizations, and repeating the cycle. Process skills for young children include observing, classifying and comparing, measuring, communicating, and experimenting. Other process skills that are used less often by young children include relating, inferring, and applying.

- One goal of science instruction is to get children actively involved in exploring and manipulating a variety of materials or phenomena. Other goals include helping children acquire factual knowledge and encouraging their curiosity and interest.

- A balanced science program includes the everyday, playful activities of children that can lead to scientific understandings as well as experiences planned by the teacher. Science instruction should include activities that focus on biological science, physical science, and earth science.

- Concepts in science must be constructed by the learner. Very little knowledge in science can be simply transmitted from teacher to learner.

- Teachers planning science experiences must provide a safe environment for exploration, must help children learn to investigate safely, and must help children enjoy science.

- Topics in science can easily be extended to promote literacy by having children create and read charts, reports, journals, and literature.

- Most topics in science can be the focus of a thematic organization; classroom experiences in all subject-matter areas can revolve around the science topic.

- Children with special needs can benefit from a multisensory, hands-on approach to teaching science. Teachers may have to make minor adaptations in materials to meet the needs of special learners.

WHAT WOULD YOU DO?

Reflect on your reading and your own experiences with young children as you think about the following situations:

1. You find a book of hands-on science activities for preschoolers. One of these activities suggests having each child experiment with dissolving sugar cubes in hot and cold water. The purpose of the activity is to demonstrate that the sugar cube dissolves more quickly in the hot water because heat makes the molecules move faster. Would the children learn this concept from doing this experiment? Why?

2. A kindergarten teacher in another school has a unit each year on outer space. The children in her class memorize information such as the distance from Earth to the nearest star. A parent of one of your kindergarten students asks you why you do not teach this information. What would you tell him?

3. You have just visited a school in which there is a room for art, another room for science, another room for reading stories, and a library. Some of your peers are really impressed with this arrangement. What would you think of it? Why?

4. You are the student representative on the university curriculum committee that has been charged with creating a new science course for early childhood majors. What would you suggest should be in the course? Why?

THEORY INTO PRACTICE

1. Observe in a preschool program for threes and fours or in a primary classroom. Record all the activities that involve learning basic science concepts. Compare lists with your classmates. Do you agree on what could be labeled "science"? Why?

2. Develop a theme using a science topic that would be suitable for preschool or primary children. Discuss your reasons for including the amount of instruction in science that you recommend.

3. Choose a topic in science for young children, and find reference and story books related to the topic. Prepare a plan for reading and writing activities based on the topic.

4. Prepare a science experience that involves hands-on exploration in which a group of your classmates can participate. What would you do differently when planning the experience for young children? What would you do similarly?

5. Prepare a plan for a first-grade science activity using materials found in an average kitchen or home. This activity should involve no commercial materials.

6. Survey your community for resources that would contribute to science education, including sites for field trips and resource people.

RECOMMENDED FOR FURTHER READING

Harlan, Jean. *Science Experiences for the Early Childhood Years.* 2d ed. Columbus, OH: Merrill, 1980.

> *Although this book includes some topics that might be better for older children, it is an excellent resource. For each topic, the author suggests activities ranging from small-group experiences to dramatic play, field trips, visits by resource people, and music and literature experiences. Resources for children and teachers are listed, as well.*

Holt, Bess-Gene. *Science with Young Children.* Rev. ed. Washington, DC: National Association for the Education of Young Children, 1989.

> *This expanded edition contains the same useful information as the first edition—practical ideas about science in early childhood programs, such as teaching children to investigate safely; thoughts about conservation; and sensible attitudes about science. In addition, this edition has many more activities that are appropriate for young children. Especially useful are the three chapters on curriculum content.*

Kamii, Constance, and Rheta DeVries. *Physical Knowledge in Preschool Education: Implications of Piaget's Theory.* Englewood Cliffs, NJ: Prentice-Hall, 1978.

> *Kamii and DeVries explain what Piaget meant by* physical knowledge *and the importance of physical knowledge in the child's development. Most of the book is devoted to descriptions of activities that are easily incorporated into the classroom.*

McIntyre, Margaret. *Early Childhood and Science.* Washington, DC: National Science Teachers Association, 1984.

> *This book is a collection of articles reprinted from the journal* Science and Children. *It contains two- and three-page articles on a vast array of topics; most of these are practical articles describing ideas teachers of young children can use to help children explore science. All the articles are very readable and contain helpful information.*

Scott, Johanna, ed. *Science and Language Links: Classroom Implications.* Portsmouth, NH: Heinemann, 1993.

> *Teachers who are interested in making strong connections between the language arts and science will want to read this book. The authors of various chapters*

discuss talking, writing, and reading about science in their classrooms. They stress that children learn both science content and language arts from participating in talking, writing, and reading about science. The chapter on second-language learners will be especially important for many teachers, and the samples of children's work will be inspirational.

Taylor, Barbara. *Science Everywhere: Opportunities for Very Young Children.* Fort Worth, TX: Harcourt Brace Jovanovich, 1993.

This book contains a thorough explanation of how children learn science. The author stresses the development of the learner, the curiosity of the child, play, and motivation in preparing science activities for young children. A very useful section of activities on such topics as air, animals, body, food, health, machines, water, weather, and others is included; these topic suggestions include references to literature to enhance learning.

REFERENCES

General Sources

Benham, Nancy Barbour, Alice Hosticka, Joe D. Payne, and Catherine Yeotis. "Making Concepts in Science and Mathematics Visible and Viable in the Early Childhood Curriculum." *School Science and Mathematics* 82 (January 1982): 45–55.

Bird, John. *Science from Water Play.* London: Macdonald Educational, 1983.

Butzow, Carol, and John Butzow. *Science, Technology and Society as Experienced through Children's Literature.* ERIC Document Reproduction Service 294141. 1988.

Cain, Sandra E., and Jack M. Evans. *Sciencing: An Involvement Approach to Elementary Science Methods.* 2d ed. Columbus, OH: Merrill, 1984.

Fine, Edith H., and Judith P. Josephson. "Footprints, Fireflies and Flight: Primary Science Magic." *Childhood Education* 62 (September/October 1984): 23–29.

Follis, Helen, and Gerald Krockover. "Selecting Activities in Science and Mathematics for Gifted Young Children." *School Science and Mathematics* 82 (January 1982): 57–64.

Forman, George E., and David S. Kuschner. *The Child's Construction of Knowledge: Piaget for Teaching Children.* Washington, DC: National Association for the Education of Young Children, 1983.

Good, R. G. *How Children Learn Science: Conceptual Development and Implications for Teaching.* New York: Macmillan, 1977.

Harlan, Jean. *Science Experiences for the Early Childhood Years.* 2d ed. Columbus, OH: Merrill, 1980.

Holt, Bess-Gene. *Science with Young Children.* Rev. ed. Washington, DC: National Association for the Education of Young Children, 1989.

Howe, Ann C. "Science in Early Childhood Education." In *Handbook of Research on the Education of Young Children,* edited by B. Spodek, 225–235. New York: Macmillan, 1993.

Iatridis, Mary. "Teaching Science to Preschoolers." *Science and Children* 19 (October 1981): 25–27.

Kamii, Constance, and Rheta DeVries. *Physical Knowledge in Preschool Education: Implications of Piaget's Theory.* Englewood Cliffs, NJ: Prentice-Hall, 1978.

Kuehn, Christine. "Inventing: Creative Sciencing." *Childhood Education* 65 (Fall 1988): 5–7.

Laminack, Lester. "Mr. T Leads the Class: The Language Experience Approach and Science." *Science and Children* (February 1987): 41–42.

McIntyre, Margaret. *Early Childhood and Science.* Washington, DC: National Science Teachers Association, 1984.

McNairy, Marion R. "Sciencing: Science Education for Early Childhood." *School Science and Mathematics* 85 (May/June 1985): 383–393.

Perry, Gail, and Mary Rivkin. "Teachers and Science." *Young Children* 47 (May 1992): 9–16.

Piaget, Jean, and Barbel Inhelder. *The Psychology of the Child.* Translated by Helen Weaver. New York: Basic Books, 1969.

Raper, George, and John Stringer. *Encouraging Primary Science: An Introduction to the Development of Science in Primary Schools.* London: Cassell, 1987.

Schiller, Pam, and Joan Townsend. "Early Childhood:

Science All Day Long: An Integrated Approach." *Science and Children* 23 (October 1985): 34–36.

Smith, Robert F. "Early Childhood Science Education: A Piagetian Perspective." *Young Children* 35 (January 1981): 3–10.

Smith, Robert F. "Theoretical Framework for Preschool Science Experiences." *Young Children* 42 (January 1987): 34–40.

Towsley, Ann, and Burton Voss. "What the Science Education Literature Says About Elementary School Science." In *The Third Sourcebook for Science Supervisors*, edited by LaMoine Motz and Gerry M. Madrazo. Washington, DC: National Science Teachers Association, 1988.

Vygotsky, Lev. *Thought and Language*. Cambridge: MIT Press, 1962.

Wasserman, Selma. "Play-Debrief-Replay: An Instructional Model for Science." *Childhood Education* 64 (April 1988): 232–234.

Ziemer, Maryann. "Science and the Early Childhood Curriculum: One Thing Leads to Another." *Young Children* 42 (September 1987): 44–51.

Children's Books

Ancona, George. *Turtle Watch*. New York: Macmillan, 1987.

Asch, Frank. *Turtle Tale*. New York: Dial Press, 1978.

Baylor, Byrd. *Everybody Needs a Rock*. New York: Atheneum, 1974.

Buckley, Richard. *The Foolish Tortoise*. Natick, MA: Picture Book Studio, 1985.

Burton, Virginia. *Katy and the Big Snow*. Boston: Houghton Mifflin, 1943.

Burton, Virginia. *Mike Mulligan and His Steam Shovel*. Boston: Houghton Mifflin, 1939.

Davis, Alice V. *Timothy Turtle*. New York: Harcourt Brace Jovanovich, 1940.

Holling, Holling C. *Minn of the Mississippi*. Boston: Houghton Mifflin, 1951.

Maccaulay, David. *The Way Things Work*. Boston: Houghton Mifflin, 1988.

Maris, Ron. *I Wish I Could Fly*. New York: Greenwillow, 1986.

Navarra, John Gabriel. *A Turtle in the House*. Garden City, NY: Doubleday, 1968.

Reeves, Martha E. *The Total Turtle*. New York: Crowell, 1975.

Switzer, Merebeth. *Nature's Children: Turtles*. New York: Grolier Educational, 1986.

Waters, John F. *Green Turtle Mysteries*. New York: Crowell, 1972.

Selected References for Insect Theme

Allen, Gertrude E. *Everyday Insects*. Boston: Houghton Mifflin, 1963.

Armour, Richard. *Insects All Around Us*. New York: McGraw-Hill, 1981.

Brouillette, Jeanne S. *Insects*. Chicago: Follett, 1963.

Carle, Eric. *The Very Hungry Caterpillar*. New York: Putnam, 1981.

Carle, Eric. *The Very Quiet Cricket*. New York: Putnam, 1990.

Coldrey, Jennifer. *The Silkworm Story*. London: Andre Deutsch, 1983.

Cole, Joanna. *Cockroaches*. New York: Morrow, 1971.

Conklin, Gladys. *When Insects Are Babies*. New York: Holiday House, 1969.

Dewey, Jennifer. *Can You Find Me? A Book About Animal Camouflage*. New York: Scholastic, 1989.

Fleischman, Paul. *A Joyful Noise*. New York: Harper and Row, 1988.

Graham, Ada and Frank Graham. *Busy Bugs*. New York: Dodd, Mead, 1983.

Greenland, Caroline. *Nature's Children: Ants*. New York: Grolier, 1985.

Hess, Lilo. *The Praying Mantis, Insect Cannibal*. New York: Charles Scribner's Sons, 1971.

Hutchins, Ross E. *Hop, Skim, and Fly: An Insect Book*. New York: Parents' Magazine Press, 1970.

Johnson, Sylvia. *Chirping Insects*. Minneapolis, MN: Lerner, 1986.

Kelsey, Elin. *Nature's Children: Bees*. New York: Grolier, 1985.

Norsgaard, E. Jaediker. *How to Raise Butterflies*. New York: Dodd, Mead, 1988.

O'Hagan, Caroline. *It's Easy to Have a Caterpillar Visit You*. New York: Lothrop, Lee and Shepard Books, 1980.

Parker, Nancy W., and Joan R. Wright. *Bugs*. New York: Greenwillow, 1987.

Shuttlesworth, Dorothy. *The Story of Flies*. Garden City, NY: Doubleday, 1970.

Stevenson, Carla. *Insect Pets: Catching and Caring for Them*. New York: Greenwillow, 1978.

Chapter Ten

Encouraging the Creative Arts

Today, you visited a school where there were a class of four-year-olds, a kindergarten, and a first grade. You were assigned to observe creative experiences in these different age groups. The four-year-olds sang to themselves as they played with blocks and rode on the tricycles. They also spent a short time listening to music, and one activity they could choose today was finger painting. Most of the children painted, but some chose to play with clay instead. In the kindergarten class, you saw some children painting at easels while other children were making vases from orange juice cans to give as gifts. The first-graders were scheduled to have a music lesson for thirty minutes. The teacher explained that they have music three times a week, art twice a week, and physical education daily with specialists. You chose to observe the music lesson. The children sang some familiar songs, moved to various rhythms that the music specialist played on the piano, and listened for repeating melodic phrases in several pieces of music.

When you returned to class, you were surprised to find that many of your classmates' observations were not at all similar to yours. One visited a school where no art was taught; the teacher at that school explained that next quarter, the art teacher would come and the children would have art once a week for a nine-week period. In another school, one of your classmates found a kindergarten teacher presenting lessons on perspective. He was using the model of a children's book and trying to get the children to copy the illustrator's use of perspective. In another school, fine arts seemed to be the focus of the curriculum. Children were involved in arts activities for most of the day.

Now you have questions about planning and evaluating creative experiences. You also wonder how teachers ensure that the time spent with building specialists in art, music, and physical education and movement is most productive for a given group of children. What is the purpose of creative arts in the curriculum? Should teaching art be left to art teachers? Likewise, should only music and physical education/movement specialists teach those subjects? How do teachers plan and evaluate creative arts experiences?

· ·

The arts are important in an early childhood program. Not only do they encourage self-expression and imagination, but they are pleasant for both children and teachers. In creative experiences, children reveal what they know and how they think. Children also learn problem-solving strategies as they create ways of moving or ways of representing what they have observed (Lasky and Mukerji 1980). The creative arts also provide opportunities for helping children learn content from the sciences, social studies, and other subject-matter areas.

In a position statement supporting every child's right to involvement in the expressive arts, prepared for the Association for Childhood Education International, Jalongo (1990) notes these benefits:

- *The expressive arts foster "learning from the inside out," authentic learning that changes behavior and encourages reflection.*
- *The expressive arts enhance the child's ability to interpret symbols.*
- *The expressive arts are associated with growth in all areas of development, including academics.*
- *The expressive arts regard the child as a meaning-maker and constructor, a discoverer and an embodiment of knowledge rather than a passive recipient of someone else's ready-made answers. (p. 196)*

An early childhood program would be much the poorer without music, art, and drama.

Definitions of **creativity** vary considerably. For the purposes of this chapter, *creativity* is defined as "the proactive, purposeful impulse to extend beyond the present, characterized by originality, imagination, and fantasy" (Edwards 1990, p. 8). To foster creativity, the teacher of young children must help the children express themselves and avoid teaching children that their interpretations of their world are not "correct" or "good." Young children are willing to draw and sing and dance without self-consciousness. They do not worry that the colors they use are not the colors of the things they are representing in real life. Nor do they worry that what they have drawn does not look like what they say it is. They believe in themselves and their abilities. The challenge is to maintain their belief in themselves while working in a group setting.

Creativity
Purposeful behavior or ideas that extend beyond the present and are original and imaginative.

The National Education Association (NEA 1990) has passed a resolution stating that

> *artistic expression is basic to an individual's intellectual, aesthetic, and emotional development. The Association further believes that fine arts transcend cultural barriers and foster multicultural understanding. The Association therefore believes that every elementary and secondary school curriculum must include a balanced, comprehensive, and sequential program of fine arts. (p. 17)*

The arts provide us with several more ways of seeing and of expressing ourselves; children are the poorer if their education does not include a wide diversity of experiences with art (Haskell 1979). Art is also a way of expressing feelings when other language is inadequate. Dancer Isadora Duncan was once asked what a dance meant. She replied that if she could tell what it meant, she would not need to dance it (Bateson 1977). Thomas Kean (1989/90), former governor of New Jersey, believes strongly in arts education. In addition to other reasons for including the arts in the curriculum, he believes that arts education contributes to success in the workplace:

> *Creativity and expressiveness will be valuable commodities in an economy that places a premium on adaptability. As a recent report on "workplace basics" put it, "Increasingly, skills such as problem solving, listening, negotiation, and knowing how to learn are being seen as essentials." The "frill" of art may well provide the best career training a solicitous parent could hope for. (p. 5)*

The arts can serve as an integrating force that helps children make connections with their experiences. The arts help young children put together what they know about topics in science, social studies, health, math, literature, and so on. The arts are also important for personalizing education. "There is an increasing awareness among educators that the development of instructional approaches that integrate the student's affect and unique personal experiences with course content can increase student motivation, participation, and learning" (Edwards 1990, p. 5).

Probably the most discussed early childhood programs in the world in recent years are the preschools of Reggio Emilia in northern Italy. Arts are the major focus of the school experience in these programs, and the curriculum is project based. Projects generally grow out of children's play and interests, although some are initiated by teachers in response to observed needs of the children. Children express what they are learning and observing in their environment through the arts. For example, children might be encouraged to create images of themselves using many different media. These images and the discussions about them might lead to explorations of body movements. The environment is also visually stimulating in ways that encourage pondering, wondering, and remembering.

The goal of these preschools is to enhance children's creative and intellectual development, and the arts are believed to be central to that development (New 1990). Gandini (1993) states that teachers in Reggio Emilia view art as only one of the child's means of expression: "Children's expression through many media is not a separate part of the curriculum but is inseparable from the whole cognitive/symbolic expression in the process of learning" (p. 8).

VISUAL ARTS

The term *visual arts* usually refers to graphic arts, such as using crayons, chalk, and paint and creating sculpture or collage. From the developmentalist point of view, as children grow and develop, their representations with graphic materials change in predictable and unvarying stages. Every child moves through the same sequence of stages, but every child moves through them at an individual rate. As teachers observe these stages, they can make inferences about the child's cognitive development and thinking processes. The following are brief descriptions of the stages in drawing.

Stages in Development

Lowenfeld and Brittain (1982) have identified the stages in children's drawings as scribbling, preschematic, schematic, and drawing realism. The first stage, *scribbling*, usually begins at about thirteen months of age.

Before that age, children put the crayons or pencils in their mouths. At about thirteen months, children begin to mark with crayons and pencils. The first scribbles are generally zigzags, not distinct shapes. Kellogg (1970) has examined children's scribbles and concludes that they usually fall into distinct patterns, which can be identified by an educated observer. By around three years of age, children begin to include distinct shapes, mostly circles, in their scribbling. Figure 10.1 is an example of scribbling.

FIGURE 10.1 Scribbling

At about four years of age, children begin to make attempts to represent objects that are familiar in their environment. This stage is the *preschematic* stage. Children in this stage typically draw human figures with very large heads and legs coming out of heads. Kellogg (1970) points out that these first drawings of humans derive from the circles and lines that children have created in their scribbles. Children may also draw other objects that are part of their experience, such as animals, using basically the same forms. Colors used in children's drawings are not realistic, and

FIGURE 10.2 Preschematic Drawing

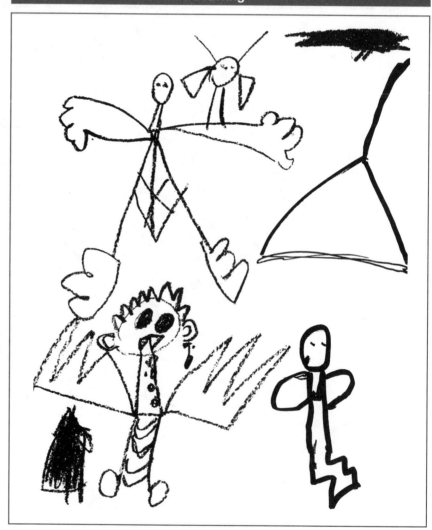

figures tend to be placed randomly on a page. Figure 10.2 is an example of a drawing by a child in the preschematic stage.

At about seven years old, children move into the *schematic* stage, in which definite forms are developed, representing the child's environment. Children will repeat basically the same forms, again and again—drawing people or trees or birds with the same forms or symbols. Figures or objects are often arranged on a baseline, rather than placed at random on the page; however, the baseline itself may be placed randomly or at an angle to the edge of the paper. Children in this stage often represent objects in space from a point of view that is much different from the adult point of view. Children may use an "X-ray" perspective so that viewers can see the inside and outside of a house at the same time. They may also draw objects from

FIGURE 10.3 Schematic Drawing

different views in one picture. The drawing in Figure 10.3 on page 323 is representative of the schematic stage.

At around nine, children enter the stage of *drawing realism*. They begin to make their drawings much smaller and include much more detail; they are also no longer eager to share their work with adults. Some children in early childhood classrooms may be making the transition into this stage. The drawing in Figure 10.4 is typical of the drawing realism stage. Observe the large outline of the firefighter that has been partially erased and replaced with a person more in proportion to the truck and building.

How young children draw does not seem to reflect training. Brittain (1969) reported his experience in trying to teach nursery school children to draw squares. After many experiences with squares, the children began to

FIGURE 10.4 Drawing Realism

draw squares at around four years of age. As Brittain put it, "Those children who were not so lucky as to be taught square making abilities also accomplished the task successfully at the age of four" (p. 46).

Even though instruction may not result in changes in drawing, children can learn the vocabulary of art. Dixon and Tarr (1988) demonstrated that children could be taught to recognize elements of art. In a unit on lines, the children moved to music to create lines with their bodies; looked at examples of lines in art; and used lines in their own art with straws, strips of paper, and markers. After these experiences, the children could identify lines as elements of art. Schirrmacher (1986) recommends that teachers point out the elements of color, line, mass or volume, pattern, shape or form, space, and texture when discussing art with young children.

Davis and Gardner (1993) suggest that teachers respond to children's art not by asking the children to tell about their pictures and then writing on them (usually just labeling the components) but by demonstrating their own perceptions. For example, the teacher might say "Look at the action in this line; this figure is indeed scribbling around on this page" or "This is a nicely balanced drawing; see how you have placed these large figures over here; it makes your drawing very strong" (p. 202). Such statements help children realize that the symbols of art can indeed communicate and that the symbols need not be accompanied by words in order to be valuable.

Goals of Visual Arts Experiences

The expected outcomes of art instruction are much more process oriented than product oriented. In other words, goals are likely to be general—involving children in art experiences and helping children become aware of the elements of art—and are unlikely to include having each child achieve a certain product. Other important goals of visual arts experiences in the early childhood classroom include:

1. Encouraging children to explore a wide variety of materials
2. Providing activities that give sensory pleasure to the participants
3. Allowing children to make discoveries about color, shape, and texture
4. Helping children gain control of fine muscles and practice eye-hand coordination
5. Helping children feel comfortable with their ability to express themselves through art
6. Introducing children to the work of the world's artists

Clearly, these goals are very broad; they do not focus on specific skills, such as mastering perspective. The purpose of art in the early childhood years is to help children express what they know and feel and to begin to recognize how others express themselves through art.

Colbert (1991) reminds us that "the goal of the visual arts in early childhood settings is not to make children into artists. The goal is to enhance those abilities children bring to us, their perceptions, memories, feelings and observations about their own worlds" (p. 25).

Suggested Visual Arts Experiences

Graphic Art

Children can draw with pencils, crayons, chalk, and markers. A variety of papers of different colors, surface textures, and shapes can add interest to drawing activities. Patterns, dittos, or coloring books carry the message that the child cannot produce acceptable representations for herself; these should therefore be avoided. If the goal is for a child to learn to control the marker or chalk in order to fill in spaces, the child can fill in her own spaces, achieve the goal, and maintain a feeling of competence by drawing her own shapes and figures.

Painting

Young children can paint with tempera at easels or on tables, or they can finger paint. Children painting at easels have freedom to move their arms and can use more muscles than they can sitting at tables, where the muscular movements tend to be confined to the hands. When painting at easels, children can learn to control the paint drips, explore the results of using paints of different thicknesses, and stand back to look at their work from eye level more easily than when painting at tables. Finger paint invites children to explore texture and to risk the messiness. Children can be encouraged to use the sides of their hands and their palms as well as their fingers in the paint.

Teachers may want to offer other paint experiences such as rolling paint from a roll-on bottle; spatter painting; blowing paint with a straw; dropping paint on paper; using objects other than a brush to apply paint (sponges, crumpled paper, aluminum foil, and so on); or rolling a small ball or marbles in paint and then on paper placed on the bottom of a box.

Printing

Printing can range from quite simple experiences, such as dipping a sponge or a piece of junk into paint and then pressing it onto paper, to

Painting at an easel offers the opportunity to solve problems and to express oneself.

complex projects, such as preparing a print form, rolling ink on it with a brayer, and then printing with it. Most kindergarten and primary children can make simple prints. Younger children tend to smear the paint when they try to press objects on paper. In addition to junk prints, kindergartners and primary children can make prints by gluing yarn, fabric scraps, or pieces of natural material onto cardboard or cylinders and then printing with these. Or they can combine media by doing a crayon rubbing and then printing over it.

Sculpture

Children enjoy sculpting with a variety of media; modeling clay is most commonly used. Clay should be available to children regularly. Clay experiences can be varied by using potter's clay that will harden; then children can paint their creations. Other variations include mixing clay with collage materials so that objects are embedded in the clay to achieve three-dimensional creations. Paper is another popular medium for sculpting—it can be folded, torn, crumpled, or glued into three-dimensional forms. Cardboard tubes and small boxes are useful, too. Wood sculpture is also popular; children can glue wood scraps to create extraordinary shapes and designs.

(Cabinet shops will often save wood scraps for teachers. Hardwood scraps usually have interesting shapes.)

Collage

Collages can be made with tissue paper; natural materials, such as bark and seeds; fabrics; and a variety of found materials. Collage gives children opportunities to develop an appreciation for texture and appealing arrangements of objects that are not possible with other media. Another advantage of collage is the use of glue. Paste and glue offer unique sensory experiences, and children will want to explore the stickiness, adhesive qualities, and spreadability of different adhesives.

Sewing and Weaving

Very young children can sew on styrofoam trays with holes punched in them or on net stretched in a frame. Kindergartners can sew on burlap with yarn. If children have trouble tying knots, the ends of the yarn can be taped on the back of the burlap with masking tape. Older children can sew with a variety of fabrics, either to create soft sculptures or to decorate the fabrics. Primary children can produce simple projects on circular or straw looms. They can also weave paper or fabric strips into interesting designs.

Combining Techniques

Teachers will think of many other experiences that are appropriate for young children and many ways to combine basic techniques. For example, children might paint on fabric; dye fabric; create simple batiks using crayons and dye on fabric; create puppets using paper, clay, or fabrics; use yarn to create a string design on cardboard and then print with the cardboard; finger paint on a table top and then make a print of the design by covering it with paper and rubbing lightly; create a crayon resist by drawing with wax crayons and painting over the drawing with tempera; or color with crayons, cover the colors with black crayon, and then scratch a design through the black crayon. The list of ideas is almost endless. Keep in mind, however, that as Wachowiak (1977) notes, children often do not enjoy or appreciate a new process or media until they become involved in it.

Art versus Crafts

Art and craft activities are not the same. *Art*, as it is being defined in this chapter, is an opportunity for children to explore media with no external product goals. Although children may indeed create products as part of an art experience, they have control of their products, and the process of creating is more important than the products that result. *Craft* activities, on the other hand, generally require that children produce something, and most of the products will be very similar or even exactly the same. Some craft activities, such as making pencil holders for gifts, are acceptable if children have a choice about whether to participate. Such craft activities can be made more appropriate for children if the materials and designs for decorating the cans are selected by the children rather than dictated by the teacher. The planning, decision making, and self-expression that are so important in art are rarely found in craft experiences, in which the outcome is predetermined.

Many activities presented to young children as art are neither art nor craft. When children are given patterns for making owls or spiders at Halloween or flowers in the spring, what they learn from these cut-and-paste activities is to follow the teacher's directions, to wait until they are told what to do with materials, and to make their products look exactly like the teacher's model. Such activities meet none of the goals of art. Justifying these experiences with the claim that they teach children to follow directions is questionable—children can learn to follow directions in other activities. The negative learning and frustration that often accompany these projects outweigh any advantages in learning to follow directions.

Edwards and Nabors (1993) describe several examples of what is and what is not art. They describe *art* as becoming "absorbed in what the *process* has to offer rather than in how their *products* will be evaluated" (p. 79, italic in the original).

MUSIC

Music, like art, is a basic way of learning, experiencing, and communicating. All children deserve a rich musical environment in which to learn to sing, to play music, to move, and to listen. Music is also a valuable tool for helping children gain content knowledge and make sense of their experiences.

Music is a pervasive influence in our lives. We hear music when we worship, exercise, relax, drive, and attend baptisms, weddings, and funerals (Merrion and Vincent 1988). Planned musical experiences should not be delayed until children can participate in group singing or until they can keep an accurate beat. Since research indicates that children respond to music very early, McDonald (1979) suggests that "the starting time for learning about music is the same as the starting time for any learning. Music is one facet in the total education of the child. It must emerge with the nature and needs of the child, from birth onward" (p. 4).

Goals of a Music Program

The goals of a music program include:

1. Teaching children to sing tunefully
2. Encouraging children to experiment with tempo, volume, and quality of sound
3. Encouraging children to express themselves through singing, movement, and playing simple instruments
4. Giving children opportunities to listen to music
5. Exposing children to a wide variety of types of music

For very young children, music need not necessarily be a group experience, although very short group experiences may be successful. More frequently, music is an individual or small-group activity. As children go about the day's activities, they and their teachers can sing about what they are doing. Also, music need not be limited to actual songs—it is *sound* that brings pleasure and helps children express feelings or thoughts. A child crooning a lullaby while rocking a doll or splashing rhythmically in water is making music a part of everyday experience.

Singing

Children learn to sing tunefully over a period of time. Young children need a supportive and encouraging environment for singing. Their ability to sing is closely related to their growing abilities in other areas of development. McDonald (1979) distilled the following information from research on children's singing:

- *By age two most children sing as we generally recognize the skill. Much of their singing is self-generated and spontaneous, occurring as individual exploratory experiences with melody or playing with language.*
- *The pitch range of their spontaneous singing can be quite extensive. From A flat below middle C to the C# an octave above middle C has been reported. However, when learning songs by imitation, a limited range from D to A (above middle C) seems to be their most comfortable, usable range.*
- *Many spontaneous songs grow out of motor activities or play with language and vocabulary, and language development may be enhanced by creating simple songs containing repetitive words or phrases.*
- *Their spontaneous songs frequently use the "teasing chant" melodic configuration (as in "Rain, Rain, Go Away"). Songs with large melodic intervals are more difficult to sing than those with smaller ones. When melodies*

contain intervals larger than a fifth or sixth, young children often compress them so that they fit into their easily used pitch range.

- *Very young children are not attentive to the necessity to match pitch or tonality when singing with others. Rather, they choose their own pitch range. You may match your pitch to those of the children and in this way introduce the concept of singing in unison.*
- *Two- and three-year-old children often sing only snatches of songs. Between the ages of two and three, there is considerable progress in the ability to reproduce songs in their entirety. Many three-year-olds are able to sing whole songs accurately and develop a large repertoire of songs.*
- *Many young children regard group singing experiences as opportunities to listen without joining in. When they do sing, they often lag behind a bit. Sometimes they begin participating by whispering the words. Often they sing only parts of songs—perhaps a repeated phrase that has caught their attention. They enjoy listening to favorite songs over and over and need many opportunities to listen before they become participants in group singing. (pp. 13–14)**

Primary children increase their repertoire of songs, continue to grow in their ability to sing in tune and to recognize the expressive qualities of a song, and may be able to sing an individual part while others sing related parts.

Research indicates that children learn songs in a predictable pattern, beginning with words and moving to rhythms, phrases, and contour (McDonald and Simons 1989). As children gain more control of vocal pitches, they become more able to produce melodies of songs. Beginning singing instruction should include rhythmic speech—chants and rhymes—to help children gain control of their voices. Older children who are not able to sing in tune can also be helped by speech-to-song instruction. Gould (1969) recommends that teachers focus first on activities that include tone-matching exercises. The teacher matches tones produced by the children and then introduces short melodic patterns that match individual children's pitch. When these melodic patterns are mastered, the teacher can introduce short melodic patterns in the singing range. Children's singing voices develop in response to the environment—opportunities and encouragement are very important.

Selecting Songs

In choosing songs for children, teachers must consider the pitch range, the intervals, and the subject of the song. The range must be one in which most

---

*From Dorothy T. McDonald, *Music in Our Lives: The Early Years* (Washington, DC: National Association for the Education of Young Children, 1979). Reprinted with permission of NAEYC.

children are comfortable singing, which includes approximately the A below middle C to the G or A above middle C. As children mature, the range can be increased; children in the primary grades who are comfortable singing can be introduced to songs with greater range. Songs with descending intervals and few wide skips in the melody are more easily sung by young children. Songs should also be repetitious, both in melody and rhythmic patterns. Children enjoy a wide variety of songs about animals, themselves or their friends, and some nonsense rhymes and jingles (McDonald and Simons 1989).

Gilbert (1981) lists the following points to consider when choosing songs to teach:

1. *The song should* appeal to the children. *It may be the tune itself or the rhythm that is attractive; whatever it is, if children like the song and can remember it easily, they will enjoy singing it.*
2. *The song should* not be too *long and, in general, the younger the child the greater the need for repetition and for a predictable pattern within each verse.*
3. *Songs with* a chorus *encourage even shy children to join in.*
4. *Songs which lend themselves to* movement *often have greater potential with young children.*
5. *Avoid tunes with* very high notes *or difficult leaps.*
6. *Choose songs with words that the children* understand. *Sometimes it is necessary to explain a particular word; at other times it is better to substitute another word or phrase. Always try out new words to see how they "sing." (p. 16)*

A surprising number of songs fit the criteria described above. Some examples include "Go Tell Aunt Rhody," "Twinkle, Twinkle Little Star," "Where Is Thumpkin?" "Baa, Baa Black Sheep," and many other nursery songs. Older children will enjoy folk songs ("Michael Row Your Boat Ashore" and "This Land Is Your Land"), humorous songs (such as the songs from *Mary Poppins*), and songs from other cultures. Teachers will know that songs are good choices if the children sing them spontaneously or ask to sing them in group music times.

Presenting Songs

Teachers who are not confident of their singing voices can begin by learning a few simple folk songs and singing them with individual children or small groups before singing with the whole group (Jalongo and Collins 1985). What children need most is a teacher who loves music and shares that interest and enthusiasm; young children are very appreciative of the teacher's singing and are not music critics.

Teachers who play the piano or feel comfortable about their own singing voices usually introduce songs by playing or singing them several times for the children and then encouraging children to sing along with them. Teachers who cannot play the songs can use recordings to introduce music quite successfully. After presenting the whole song several times, the teacher may want to sing a line if the children are having difficulty learning it, but each experience should end with the children singing the whole song through again. This routine will need to be repeated several times over a period of days before the children are comfortable with a new song.

Musical experiences can be opportunities for problem solving, as children invent new words to songs or new ways of moving to music. Singing games such as "Hokey Pokey" and "Punchinella" lend themselves naturally to problem solving, as children must create their own movements. Children can also create new words to familiar songs. They might substitute any five-letter name in "B-I-N-G-O" and make up a verse about that person. Problem solving is encouraged when children are free to explore and play and when their efforts are supported (Hitz 1987).

Chants such as "The Bear Hunt" are also valuable in the music program, as children learn the rhythms and patterns of language. Many chants lend themselves to instrumentation or body percussion sounds: children can add claps, snaps, or clicks to the rhythm of the chant.

Playing Instruments

Today's approach to playing instruments with young children focuses on children's exploration of sound and rhythm. Even very young children like to produce sounds by banging on pots and pans. Such interest usually continues, and they are eager to explore sound with drums, bells, xylophones, and shakers. Even though the focus is on exploration, the teacher can help individuals or small groups with instruction in how to hold an instrument or how to strike it to get a more satisfactory sound. As children become able to keep a beat, they can invent simple accompaniments to familiar songs. Primary children can begin to learn to play simple instruments such as recorders.

Studies of children's use of musical instruments and the implications for teachers can be summarized as follows:

1. Children should have many opportunities for free exploration with instruments before any structured activities are attempted.
2. Teachers should attend to the child's interest and needs when providing any instruction on how to play an instrument.

3. Children need to express rhythm through physical movement before instruments are introduced.
4. Exploration with instruments can help children learn about pitch, timbre, rhythm, and melody.

Teaching should be focused on helping children achieve the technical skills needed to express creative ideas (McDonald and Simons 1989).

Listening Experiences

Children can be encouraged to listen to a variety of music. Guided listening experiences for younger children should be very short. As children mature, the pieces of music selected for listening can be longer and the children can be expected to hear more complex patterns. Teachers should select classical music, folk music, and music from a variety of cultures and ethnic groups. Listening experiences are most effective if the children are comfortable, both physically and psychologically, and if the experiences are based on the children's previous experiences. Children also need guidance in what to listen for, such as repeated phrases or passages that create moods or images.

Listening experiences can be created through games and other everyday experiences. Children can be encouraged to listen to environmental sounds, both inside and outside the room. Games can include guessing what produced a given sound, clapping back a pattern produced on a drum by the teacher or another student, or recognizing voices (as in "Doggie, Doggie, Who Has the Bone?").

Older preschoolers and primary children can benefit from listening to short, live performances. Often, local symphony orchestras or high school groups prepare special programs for young children. Some of these programs introduce the instruments of the orchestra and help children listen for their sounds; others present musical stories that children will enjoy.

Whether to use music in the background when children are engaged in other activities is a question that teachers will have to answer for themselves. Some teachers argue that children ignore background music; this makes it difficult for them to learn to listen to music attentively. Others argue that providing carefully selected background music at quiet times of the day can be a way of exposing children to music when there might otherwise be no time to do so. No one advocates playing music that adds to the noise level when the children are engaged in noisy activities. Many teachers do choose to make records and tapes available for children to use at listening stations during the activity times of each day. Such stations allow children who wish to listen to music the opportunity to do so without disturbing other children.

Movement and Dance

Movement to music begins very early—children often sway and nod to music they hear. Emile Jaques-Dalcroze (1865–1950), a Swiss composer and teacher, believed that movement was the best way to help children learn to love and appreciate music. He believed that training in moving in response to music should begin in the first year of life (Jaques-Dalcroze 1921). (We will return to Jaques-Dalcroze in a following section on "Dalcroze Eurhythmics.")

Fundamental motor abilities are learned and mastered during the preschool years; it therefore makes sense to focus on the *process* of movement instruction during this time, rather than on the *product*. Most children have mastered the basic movements by the time they enter first grade, but as Malina (1982) notes, "The quality of performance continues to improve as the fundamental patterns are refined and integrated into more complex movement sequences" (p. 215). Seven- and eight-year-olds continue to gain skill and control in motor development. They can add a beat to music, keep a beat with an instrument while singing, and learn simple folk dances. Table 10.1 on page 336 presents Bayless and Ramsey's (1991) review of the basic sequence of motor development and implications for instruction in movement.

Movement experiences should be planned to include both creative and more structured movements. Creative movement activities are those in which children interpret instructions in their own ways; their movements may not necessarily match the beat of the music. Examples of creative movement activities are having children move in a given direction and then change direction when the music changes; use movements that are heavy or light; move fast or slow; and so on. More structured movement experiences include asking children to learn to keep a beat and move to a beat.

Weikart (1982) suggests that movement exercises to help children learn to feel and move to a beat should begin with speech activities and progress to keeping the beat to music. She recommends the following sequence in teaching children to keep a beat:

Step One: *Say. No music is used. The learner is asked to repeat single words ("knee, knee, knee" or "walk, walk, walk") which will be matched with movements in the next step.*

Table 10.1	Listening and Moving to Music
Birth to four months	**Awareness of music starts almost immediately.** The baby may show his early awareness by responding differently to different kinds of music; he quiets himself to a soothing lullaby and becomes more active when lively music is played.
Four to eight months	**Musical awareness becomes more active.** The baby now enjoys listening intently to all types of sounds in his environment. He begins showing more active awareness of musical sounds by turning his head or face toward the source of the music.
Ten to eighteen months	**Expression of musical preferences begins.** The infant may begin indicating the types of music he likes best—many at this age prefer vocal to instrumental—as well as showing clear displeasure at music he does not like. He rocks or sways his hips to a familiar tune, although not necessarily in time with the music, and claps his hands to a pleasing song.
Eighteen months to two years	**Exploration of musical sounds increases.** Sounds in her environment continue to captivate the toddler. Her developing language skills and increasing mobility allow her to seek out sounds that please her most. She may especially enjoy music on daily TV or radio programs or commercials, and may watch with fascination as a family member plays a musical instrument.
Two to three years	**Dance begins.** The toddler now attempts to "dance" to music by bending his knees in a bounding motion, turning circles, swaying, swinging his arms, and nodding his head. He especially likes a marked rhythm, so band music, nursery songs, or catchy TV jingles may be favorites. He shows an increasing ability to keep time and to follow directions in musical games, which he loves. You'll also notice that he can now pay attention for longer periods. While easily distracted in the past, he can now lie or sit down quietly and listen for several minutes at a time.
Three and one-half to four years	**Self-expression through music increases.** At this stage, a very significant change takes place. As the child listens, she is increasingly aware of some of the components that make up her favorite music. She may love to dramatize songs and may also enjoy trying out different ways of interpreting music (for example, experimenting with different rhythms). She shows marked improvement in keeping the beat, although she is still not always entirely accurate. Music is now an important means for her to express and communicate ideas and emotions that may be beyond her developing language skills.
Four to five years	**Ability to discuss musical experiences expands.** By now the child can talk about what a piece of music suggests to him, and he is able to tell you in greater detail what he is hearing. This is the stage of the "active listener." With encouragement, the child's desire to listen to music will increase.
Five to six years	**Actual coordinated dance movements begin.** The child's increased motor control and ability to synchronize his movements with the rhythm of the music are evident as one watches his attempts to dance. He can actually synchronize hand or foot tapping with music and can skip, hop on one foot, and make rhythmic dance movements to music. This is the time when he may begin to show an interest in dance lessons.

Source: Reprinted with the permission of Macmillan College Publishing Company from *Music: A Way of Life for the Young Child,* 4/e by Kathleen M. Bayless and Marjorie E. Ramsey. Copyright © 1991 by Macmillan College Publishing Company, Inc.

Step Two: *Say and do. Learners are asked to match the chant with motions so that both occur simultaneously. The beat is kept by the chant of the words.*

Step Three: *Whisper and do. Learners are asked to whisper the chants while continuing the motions. After they are proficient, music is added.*

Step Four: *Do. Learners are asked to think the chant while continuing the move-ment. Music must have a strong beat that can be clearly understood. (pp. 18–19)*

A typical structured movement experience is clapping to simple rhythms. Teachers often have children clap the syllables in their own and their classmates' names. Teachers might also ask children to walk to a drum beat or walk to the beat of music played on the piano or a recording. As children gain more control and are able to keep the beat more accu-rately, they may be asked to learn simple dance steps.

Sullivan (1982) recommends another simple movement exercise, "Clap, Clap, Clap Your Hands." With the children sitting down, the teacher plays:

C   C   G   F   E   C   C   D   E D   low G

Clap, clap, clap your hands. Clap your hands to-geth-er.

C   C   G   F   E   E   E   D   D D   C

Clap, clap, clap your hands. Clap your hands to-geth-er.

Children can be encouraged to think of other movements, such as tap-ping their knees, tapping their elbows, shaking their hands, shaking their heads, and so on.

Primary children can be encouraged to keep the beat and explore movement through such exercises as "Copycat." The children find their own space. The leader improvises a movement on the count of 1, and the children imitate the movement on the count of 2. A drum may be used to help keep the beat. In another exercise, the children stand in a long line across the room and are numbered off by threes. Together, they walk for-ward for eight counts, backward for eight counts, and then turn in their original spot for eight counts. When this pattern has been mastered, the "1's" perform the routine alone, followed by the "2's" and then the "3's." The whole pattern is repeated several times (Findlay 1971).

Approaches to Music Instruction

Four approaches to musical instruction for young children will be described briefly in the following sections: Dalcroze Eurhythmics, the Kodály method, the Orff approach, and Education Through Music.

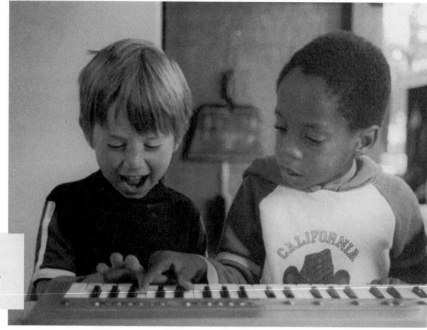

Music is a joyful learning opportunity for children.

Dalcroze Eurhythmics

Emile Jaques-Dalcroze developed an approach to teaching music based on the belief that rhythm was the fundamental force in music and that children should develop an awareness of music through body movement. Jaques-Dalcroze believed that sequence was very important in teaching children music and that the simplest of rhythmic experiences should be first, followed by more difficult and complicated activities, followed by instrumental study. This method—called *eurhythmics*—emphasizes the importance of an immediate physical response to music and of having children dramatize music with their bodies.

Findlay's *Rhythm and Movement: Applications of Dalcroze Eurhythmics* (1971) is a good source for teachers; it contains a brief explanation of the child's need for a rhythmic response and a wealth of ideas and activities that any teacher of young children will find interesting and helpful. Dalcroze training for teachers is also available at many universities across the United States.

The Kodály Method

Zoltán Kodály (1882–1967), a Hungarian composer, was a contemporary of Jaques-Dalcroze. He believed that the most important instrument in a child's music education was her own voice. Kodály relied heavily on children's games, nursery songs, and folk music in helping children learn to sing. He believed that accompaniments to songs should be very simple and that a child should learn to "appreciate music as a pure, unadulterated melody emanating from himself, this appreciation being achieved through ear-training exercises" (Bayless and Ramsey 1991, p. 218). The Kodály method is not complicated, and most teachers can implement the program without special training or special equipment.

The Orff Approach

Carl Orff (1895–1982), a German composer, developed his method from work with young dance students in his school. Orff is most commonly associated with the pitched instruments that bear his name. (Most catalogs of musical instruments for children include the Orff instruments.) The Orff program involves structuring a musical environment and then helping children improvise within the environment. Important elements of the Orff method include rhythm, body percussion (stamping, slapping the thighs, clapping, and finger snapping), dramatic movement, melody, and the use of instruments (both percussion instruments and pitched instruments). Orff advocated that activities progress from speech to rhythmic activities to song and then to playing musical instruments. Although they are fairly expensive, many schools use Orff instruments, and Orff training is available to teachers who are interested in learning the approach (McDonald and Simons 1989).

Education Through Music

Mary Helen Richards developed the Education Through Music (ETM) program, which combines learning music, movement, singing, and exploration. As Richards (1969) explains, "Music is a catalyst and a leaven in the development of beautiful human beings. It is through the children's songs and games of our folk culture and through the children's natural love of movement that we can reach them with music" (p. 1). The approach advocates teaching children carefully selected songs; guiding them to understand the music (by discussing lyrics, analyzing rhythm patterns, and becoming familiar with melody patterns); and teaching other content areas, especially language arts, through music. Children sing, move to music, create patterns to represent music, and learn to listen carefully—what Richards calls "inner hearing."

Harper et al. (1973) report that kindergarten students who were exposed to the ETM program for twenty minutes each day showed growth on tests of auditory discrimination and on a screening measure when compared to children in a control group who received more traditional music

INTEGRATING THE CURRICULUM

Patterns are very evident in the creative arts. To extend our theme of patterns, the following are a few examples of activities:

➤ Create patterns with sponge printing.
➤ Create patterns using collage materials.
➤ Create patterns using geometric shapes.
➤ Create patterns using textile scraps.
➤ Find the patterns in wallpaper.
➤ Find the patterns used on wrapping paper.
➤ Find the patterns used on household textiles.
➤ Find the patterns used on pieces of clothing.
➤ Find the patterns in music of different beats, and then recreate them.

➤ Record rhythmic patterns, first in vertical lines and then in musical notation.
➤ Find the patterns in repeating musical phrases.
➤ Find the patterns in musical scales.
➤ Find the patterns in simple dance steps (for instance, three steps to the right, heel and toe, three steps to the left, heel and toe, and so on).
➤ Create a system for recording the patterns in simple dances.

instruction. ETM training is available through workshops and seminars for teachers wishing to learn the approach.

DRAMA

Drama in the early childhood classroom is defined as experiences in which children play, pretend, role-play, or create characters or ideas. McGregor, Tate, and Robinson (1987) state that the essential characteristic of drama is acting out. In acting out,

> there is an agreement to suspend the normal social roles with each other in identifying with the new imagined roles. There is an agreement to make a different use of the environment. In this case a desk becomes a dining table laden with food, a chalk box becomes a cigar box, and so on. This different use of the environment includes a shift in the conventions of time. Events may be telescoped to give them greater or less significance. The usual conventions of space and time may be suspended during acting out. (p. 12)

Drama in early childhood education is not the production of plays in which children memorize lines and act given roles. Such productions are often appropriate for older children but are not appropriate for the early childhood years. Creative drama usually refers to spontaneous productions in which children create or recreate stories, moods, or incidents without learning lines or practicing their roles.

Other aspects of drama include children's theater and participatory theater. *Children's theater* refers to productions designed for an audience of children. The performers may be adults or children, but the production is aimed at the children in the audience. A newer form of theater for children is *participatory theater,* in which the audience is encouraged to participate in the production by contributing ideas or sounds or sometimes even by participating in the play.

Drama in the classroom can contribute to the general goals of early childhood programs in a variety of ways. It can foster:

1. the development of critical thinking and problem-solving skills
2. an ability to work cooperatively with others
3. an increased ability to understand the perspective of others
4. an ability to communicate more effectively
5. the integration of ideas from many sources into a meaningful whole

Of course, drama experiences provide another avenue for self-expression and developing creativity that is as important as their contributions to other curriculum goals.

Encouraging Drama

Most experiences with drama occur spontaneously in children's play or in response to music, songs, stories, or other experiences. Teachers will want to encourage and support these dramatic activities, but they may also plan for specific experiences in drama. Teachers can encourage children's play and help them add or extend dramatic elements. For example, a teacher observing children choosing roles for dramatic play might help a child think of a role or imagine how someone might act in a given role or provide a prop or costume to help the child conceptualize the role more fully.

Most teachers of young children have observed that drama, like other creative arts experiences, is a natural response that arises in a supportive classroom environment with teacher encouragement. Children returning from a trip to the zoo often assume the roles of the people or animals they encountered at the zoo. After hearing a story, children will often act out the role of one of the characters. Even very young children can be heard imitating voices or observed pretending to be as sad or as scared as one of the characters in a story.

Planned drama experiences may be incorporated into movement, music, or literature experiences. If the children are exploring movement patterns, they might be asked to move in a way that represents a given character or mood—to tiptoe quickly to represent the movement of mice, for example. Children might also use drama to demonstrate their understanding of the lyrics of songs they are learning. (If they are asked to glide and they flap their arms, the teacher can assume that they do not understand the term *glide*.) After listening to a story, children often want to retell it through dramatic representations. If, after listening to *Where the Wild Things Are* (Sendak 1963), they can act out Max's anger, the power of the wild things, and Max's relief when he returns to his very own room, there will be no need to ask them comprehension questions.

Other planned drama experiences can extend children's concept knowledge. Fox (1987, pp. 59–60) describes a dramatic activity that she calls "Caterpillars and Butterflies." (If the class were studying insects or caterpillars, these activities would not only add interest but would give the teacher a chance to observe the children's understanding of concepts.) Fox suggests that children begin by observing how real caterpillars move. After these observations, the children crawl around, imitating the movements of the caterpillars (perhaps to music). After hearing the teacher read *The Very Hungry Caterpillar* (Carle 1970), some children can form a tight circle to create an orange, and others can crawl through the orange (eating a hole in the orange). Then the children can think about what happens to the caterpillar after it has eaten all the food. They can curl themselves into cocoons and then pretend to nibble out and spread their butterfly wings. It is helpful if the children can observe the movements of a real butterfly or watch a film of a butterfly in slow motion before they imitate the butterfly movements. Children might also create butterfly wings with scarves or tissue paper and use them in their movements.

In other planned drama experiences, children might act out eating hot soup in a hurry; holding an angry cat while a dog is barking at it; putting on a sweater that is too small; ripping one's clothing while climbing over a fence; blowing up a balloon until it bursts; or being a robin pulling a worm from a hole (Zimmerman 1984). Teachers should consider the children's experience when thinking about episodes for them to dramatize. Without experience and observation, one cannot dramatize effectively. Sometimes children will need to participate in the real experience or observe it (on film or in reality) before they will be able to recreate it.

ROLES OF SPECIALISTS

Teachers who are privileged to teach in schools that have specialists in art, music, or physical education on staff should not hesitate to call on these people. They can be excellent resources.

Specialists do not relieve classroom teachers of the responsibility for teaching art, music, or movement. The best situation is for specialists and classroom teachers to work together to achieve mutual goals. Because art, music, and movement are integral to most content-area instruction, the classroom teacher's role is to inform the specialist of the concepts that she is seeking to help the children develop; the specialist's role is to advise the teacher of activities that would be appropriate for those concepts. For example, if the focus in the classroom is on small animals, an art specialist might suggest having children create torn-paper collages of animals or tempera paintings of animals.

An art specialist can help the classroom teacher not only by suggesting appropriate activities but also by helping the teacher recognize the language of art that is important for the children to learn and by helping the teacher develop other concepts. The art specialist is also a good resource person for the teacher who wants to present the works of other artists to young children. Exposure to fine art can serve as a stimulus to creative experiences and can increase awareness of aesthetic elements (Bowker and Sawyer 1988). The art specialist can also aid the classroom teacher in helping children learn to look at and talk about art. Unless the teacher and art specialist provide opportunities for this kind of art appreciation, it may never occur (Cole and Schaefer 1990).

Similarly, the music specialist can help the classroom teacher incorporate music into daily classroom activities. He can help the teacher select songs that are appropriate for the group and provide guidance in choosing movement experiences or instruments appropriate for the specific theme the teacher is using. For a theme of small animals, the music specialist might help the children learn songs about the small animals in the classroom; listen to animal sounds; distinguish pitch in animal sounds; and produce rhythm patterns to represent various animals.

The physical education specialist can also provide assistance for the classroom teacher of young children. The specialist can help select appropriate movement experiences and provide opportunities for motor activities that can contribute to children's learning in other areas. To extend the theme of small animals, the physical education specialist might help children reproduce the movement patterns of the animals in the classroom. These movements could further the objectives of the physical education program by promoting body control and integrating patterns of motor abilities.

The classroom teacher can take advantage of the expertise of specialists by keeping them informed about topics of interest in the classroom and needs that have been observed. Each specialist has much to offer that will expand children's experiences and further the collaborative development of the best program possible for each child.

CONNECTING THE ARTS
AND OTHER SUBJECT-MATTER AREAS

Although the goals and objectives of a creative arts program are important enough to stand alone, the arts also contribute to other curriculum areas in powerful ways. Children learning concepts in science, math, health, and social studies can express their understandings through art, music, movement, and drama. The following sections provide a few examples of the many possible ways the arts can be integrated into different themes or subject-matter areas.

- *Shadows*—Movement possibilities include having children attempt to make their shadows move in certain ways, move without touching the shadows of the other children, and so on. Primary children can make shadow characters and produce a shadow play. Children might also create a stage for the shadow play from a large carton and decorate it. Children can select or create background music for their shadow plays.
- *Birds*—Children can imitate the movements of different birds on the ground and in the air. They can listen to bird songs and learn to recognize a few distinctive calls as well as melodic or repeating patterns. Birds can be represented through graphic art, collage, or sculpture. Bird nests can be made from natural materials. Primary children can note color patterns of birds and perhaps chart common colors or patterns.
- *Seashells*—Children can notice ocean sounds and the regularity of waves. Children can be challenged to represent the movements of different sea

---

DEVELOPMENTALLY
APPROPRIATE
PRACTICE

It is hard to conceive of a developmentally appropriate program that fails to include the creative arts. For young children, the arts provide many opportunities to explore materials and techniques, to make choices, to express themselves, and to gain social and cognitive skills. Think about the arts in terms of:

- Allowing each child to choose her own activity and within that activity, to choose how to complete the activity—For example, a child might choose to paint at the easel and then choose which colors to use, how to place the elements of the composition on the paper, and how long to work on the painting.
- Providing intellectual challenge—A child can continue to learn new techniques and continue to explore new media. The arts are never learned in the sense of learning facts;

every experience with the arts is new and challenging.
- Providing opportunities for growth in all domains—While participating in the arts, children gain physical skill (control of body and fine motor skills), grow intellectually (making decisions, planning, organizing), gain social competence (work with others, have responsibility for materials, share space and materials), and develop emotionally (expressing feelings, gaining empathy for the feelings of others, and so on).

creatures, such as anemones or snails. They can sort shells by shapes and note the patterns of seashells. Paintings and drawings of seashells as well as objects (buttons, jewelry) made from seashells can be introduced. (Note, however, that the craft of making creatures from seashells is not art.)

- *Literature*—Children can dance like Sendak's "wild things"; recreate Peter's movements in *The Snowy Day* (Keats 1962); create costumes and make up a dance like the *Song and Dance Man* (Ackerman 1988); move as silently as the owl in *Owl Moon* (Yolen 1987); and dramatize folk tales.
- *Reading and writing*—After children have learned the lyrics to a song, they can put them on a chart or on sentence strips. Primary children can write new lyrics or substitute words in the lyrics. In *Rhythms to Reading* (1972), Wood includes many examples of reading and writing activities to accompany children's songs.

CHILDREN WITH SPECIAL NEEDS

Many experiences in the arts can be modified or adapted to make participation by children with special needs possible. Children with developmental delays may not be ready for group work or for some of the cognitive tasks in the arts program. Teachers will have to determine which experiences are developmentally appropriate for individual children and provide alternative experiences when necessary.

Because most art activities are planned for individuals, most children can participate in art at their own level without adaptations; work surfaces or materials may have to be adapted for children with orthopedic disabilities. Examples of adaptations include providing work surfaces that are accessible for children in wheelchairs and providing sturdy materials that are easy to grasp so that children can draw and paint. Some children who do not have much control of their arms and hands might benefit from creating computer art; a computer program allows them to control color and so on. Children with visual impairments can paint, finger paint, create collages, and sculptures.

Teachers may need to seek expert advice about planning activities for children with specific types of hearing impairments. Some children are able to hear or feel many sounds—especially percussion or rhythmic elements. Gfeller (1989) provides several recommendations for adapting activities for children with hearing impairments:

1. Children who use hearing aids may hear better if background noises can be minimized.

2. If children use sign language, incorporate signing into singing activities.

3. Use visual aids to help children recognize patterns and other musical information that they may not be able to hear.

4. Placement in the group should make lip reading or watching or feeling instruments possible.

5. Using quality sound equipment that does not distort the sound helps children with some residual hearing.

6. Some children can hear better in the lower frequencies; therefore, instruments with lower pitches should be selected.

7. Rhythmic and percussive elements should be emphasized.

Children with delays in motor development may require instruments that do not have to be grasped, such as bells on a strap that can be fastened around the child's wrist or ankle; stands that hold instruments so that the child can play them are also helpful. During group movement sessions, children can be encouraged to move heads, arms, legs, or whatever body parts they can control; they need not feel left out just because they cannot manage whole-body movements.

Singing may be difficult for some children with speech disabilities, and teachers may need to use more chants and rhythmic speech experiences with them. The teacher may need to consult with a speech specialist to determine the best course of instruction for such children.

Brown (1991) suggests that signing can be added to many drama activities. She recommends that teachers use the following techniques for adapting drama for children with special needs:

1. *Use pictures to visually represent new vocabulary and concepts.*
2. *Break the drama lesson up into a series of short segments.*
3. *Use repetition to reinforce new language and concepts.*
4. *Allow children to imitate as a starting point.*
5. *Sequence the activities, building from the simple to more complex.*
6. *Begin the activities with warm ups and end with a closing.*
7. *Introduce techniques to maintain focus and control. (pp. 173–174)*

Brown (1991) goes on to suggest that signing during drama can help to involve those children who cannot physically participate in activities:

While some children become frogs hopping from log to lily pad, other children may carry out the action with a puppet-frog and environment created from signs and gestures. Give children in wheelchairs a special role by using

the chair as an integral part of the activity. Wheelchairs make great space-
ships and train engines. Children with limited movement can be given the
role of the tree in the middle that the other children's hand/leaves fall from,
or the Indian chief who must call back braves from a hunt. (p. 178)

Creative arts also offer children with language differences opportunities to be successful. Difficulties with a dialect or learning a second language will not affect a child's ability to create a painting or sculpture.
Cultural and ethnic differences can be honored in musical and dance experiences and in sharing art from many cultures. The creative arts are for
everyone.

As with all children, exposing children with special needs to the arts is
a matter of thinking about what the children can do, providing materials
that are appropriate for them, and providing guidance in helping each
child achieve his own goals.

CHAPTER SUMMARY

- The arts are very important in early childhood programs. Children need to learn to express themselves and what they know in a variety of ways; the arts provide multiple avenues for expression.
- Children's drawing develops through predictable stages: scribbling, preschematic, schematic, and drawing realism.
- Program goals in the visual arts include helping children explore a wide variety of materials, engage in pleasurable activities, gain control of fine muscles, express themselves, and learn about the work of other artists.
- Music is a basic mode of learning, experiencing, and communicating. The goals of a music program include helping children learn to sing and encouraging them to experiment with tempo, volume, and quality of sound; express themselves; listen to music; and appreciate many kinds of music.
- Young children's singing ability develops over time, as they gain control of their voices and learn to match the pitch of others.

- Songs selected by the teacher must be evaluated in terms of range of pitch, musical intervals, and content.
- Children should have many opportunities to explore simple musical instruments. Instruction in playing instruments should focus on helping individual children achieve their own musical objectives.
- Listening experiences are an important component of a music program. Children need guidance in listening and opportunities to listen to many types of music.
- Movement experiences should include both creative and more structured movements. Movement experiences can be planned to help children feel and move to a musical beat and to allow children to express their ideas.
- Drama in the early childhood classroom is a creative activity in which the children act out their ideas, impressions, or moods.
- Drama contributes to the overall goals of a program by helping children develop critical thinking and problem-solving abilities, helping them

work cooperatively with others, increasing their ability to understand the perspective of others, learning to communicate more effectively, and helping them integrate concepts from subject-matter areas.

- Specialists in art, music, and physical education can help classroom teachers achieve objectives in subject-matter areas and can collaborate with

teachers in promoting goals specific to art, music, and physical education.

- Activities in the arts can help integrate topics of study from the sciences and the social studies and can extend literary experiences.
- Activities in the arts can be modified so that children with special needs can participate and benefit from the experience.

WHAT WOULD YOU DO?

Reflect on your reading and your own experiences with young children as you think about the following situations:

1. The local school board has proposed cutting the art and music teacher positions in order to save money. How would you respond to this proposal?
2. Some parents of your first-graders want you to spend more time teaching basic subjects and less time facilitating creative arts activities. What would you tell them about how time is allotted for different subjects and activities?
3. The art specialist in your district only has time to offer instruction to your second-grade class

once every month. As the classroom teacher, what would you do to develop art activities?
4. The director of the school wants the building decorated for spring with cute art projects. How would you respond to this request?
5. You have been asked to explain the value of creative arts in terms of children's intellectual development at the next parent group meeting. What information would you present?

THEORY INTO PRACTICE

1. Observe a three-year-old and a primary child as they paint at easels. Record their conversation, if any. Compare the paintings created and the language used by the children.
2. Plan an appropriate introduction to a new art medium for a group of five-year-olds.
3. Choose a topic usually taught in the primary grades, and plan several appropriate arts experiences to enrich the topic.
4. Consult with a specialist in art, music, or physical education in the primary grades. Determine

how much of his planning is done in cooperation with classroom teachers. Would he prefer to work more closely with classroom teachers? Discuss some ideas for facilitating teamwork between classroom teachers and specialists.
5. Plan an appropriate experience in drama or movement for a group of four-year-olds.
6. Choose a children's book, and plan an arts experience to deepen the children's understanding or appreciation of the book.

RECOMMENDED FOR FURTHER READING

Bayless, Kathleen M., and Marjorie E. Ramsey. *Music: A Way of Life for the Young Child.* 4th ed. Columbus, OH: Merrill, 1991.

The authors discuss musical experiences for children from infancy to the early primary grades and provide good examples of songs appropriate for children of each age. The book includes chapters on children with special needs and on integrating music through the child's day.

Edwards, Linda Carol. *Affective Development and the Creative Arts: A Process Approach to Early Childhood Education.* Columbus, OH: Merrill, 1990.

This book contains chapters on music and movement, creative drama, art, and literature. Each chapter describes many examples of activities that are useful for a teacher planning to include creative arts in the classroom. This book is especially useful for primary-grade teachers.

Fox, Mem. *Teaching Drama to Young Children.* Portsmouth, NH: Heinemann, 1987.

Fox begins with a very brief justification for including drama in an educational program. The remainder of the book is devoted to descriptions of activities, which are coded based on the approximate amount of time required and labeled for appropriate age groups. The activities are arranged in categories that will aid the teacher who wants to use them in an integrated program.

Hoffman, Stevie, and Linda L. Lamme, eds. *Learning from the Inside Out: The Expressive Arts.* Wheaton, MD: Association for Childhood Education International, 1989.

In this collection of original writings, each author supports the importance of the creative arts in the curriculum; topics include developmentally appropriate practice, the integration of learning, and the importance of the arts in a child's development as a learner. This work has been described as a crusade to include expressive arts in the classroom.

Lasky, Lila, and Rose Mukerji. *Art: Basic for Young Children.* Washington, DC: National Association for the Education of Young Children, 1980.

The core of this book is practical information for the classroom teacher. The authors discuss development in art, how to set up an art center, and how to evaluate art experiences. They provide many examples of art experiences and include an amazing amount of information in a short, easy-to-read book.

McDonald, Dorothy T., and Gene M. Simons. *Musical Growth and Development: Birth Through Six.* New York: Schirmer Books, 1989.

The authors provide a wealth of information about musical development and instruction in music for young children. Even though the title says "birth through six," teachers of primary-grade children would benefit from this book. It contains chapters on research, integrating children with disabilities into music activities, and program evaluation that are especially useful.

Overby, Lynnette Y., ed. *Early Childhood Creative Arts: Proceedings of the International Early Childhood Creative Arts Conference.* Reston, VA: American Alliance for Health, Physical Education, Recreation and Dance, 1991.

This collection of papers covers a broad range of topics—such as the need for creative arts, assessment of creative arts, and descriptions of arts programs—and also includes specific papers on art, music, dance, and drama. The papers are very readable and aimed at an audience of practicing teachers and teachers in training.

Sullivan, Molly. *Feeling Strong. Feeling Free: Movement Exploration for Young Children.* Washington, DC: National Association for the Education of Young Children, 1982.

This book has two major sections—one is a description of a movement program for threes and fours and the other is a description of a program for fives to eights. The author discusses the implementation and management of movement activities and the teacher's role in movement experiences. The suggested activities are manageable and would be enjoyable for both children and teachers.

REFERENCES

General Sources

Bateson, G. *Steps to an Ecology of Mind*. New York: Ballantine, 1977.

Bayless, Kathleen M., and Marjorie E. Ramsey. *Music: A Way of Life for the Young Child*. 4th ed. Columbus, OH: Merrill, 1991.

Bowker, Jeanette E., and Janet K. Sawyer. "Influence of Exposure on Preschoolers' Art Preferences." *Early Childhood Research Quarterly* 3 (1988): 107–115.

Brittain, W. L. "Some Exploratory Studies of the Art of Preschool Children." *Studies in Art Education* 10 (1969): 14–24.

Brown, Victoria. "Integrating Drama and Sign Language: A Multisensory Approach to Learning for Children with Special Needs." In *Early Childhood Creative Arts: Proceedings of the International Early Childhood Creative Arts Conference*, edited by L. Overby. Reston, VA: American Alliance for Health, Physical Education, Recreation and Dance, 1991.

Colbert, Cynthia. "Connecting with Art in the Classroom." In "Nurturing the Expressive Arts," edited by Stevie Hoffman, Larry Kantner, Cynthia Colbert, and Wendy Sims. *Childhood Education* 68 (Fall 1991): 23–26.

Cole, Elizabeth, and Claire Schaefer. "Can Young Children Be Art Critics?" *Young Children* 45 (January 1990): 33–38.

Davis, Jessica, and Howard Gardner. "The Arts and Early Childhood Education: A Cognitive Developmental Portrait of the Young Child as Artist." In *Handbook of Research on the Education of Young Children*, edited by B. Spodek, 191–206. New York: Macmillan, 1993.

Dixon, Glen T., and Patricia Tarr. "Extending Art Experiences in the Preschool Curriculum." *International Journal of Early Childhood* 20 (June 1988): 27–34.

Edwards, Linda C. *Affective Development and the Creative Arts: A Process Approach to Early Childhood Education*. Columbus, OH: Merrill, 1990.

Edwards, Linda C., and Martha L. Nabors. "The Creative Arts Process: What It Is and What It Is Not." *Young Children* 48 (March 1993): 77–81.

Findlay, Elsa. *Rhythm and Movement: Applications of Dalcroze Eurhythmics*. Evanston, IL: Summy-Birchard, 1971.

Fox, Mem. *Teaching Drama to Young Children*. Portsmouth, NH: Heinemann, 1987.

Gandini, Lella. "Fundamentals of the Reggio Emilia Approach to Early Childhood Education." *Young Children* 49 (November 1993): 4–8.

Gfeller, Kate. "Integrating the Handicapped Child into Music Activities." In *Musical Growth and Development: Birth Through Six*, edited by Dorothy T. McDonald and Gene M. Simons, 113–140. New York: Schirmer Books, 1989.

Gilbert, Jean. *Musical Starting Points with Young Children*. London, England: Ward Lock Educational, 1981.

Gould, A. O. "Developing Specialized Programs for Singing." *Council for Research in Music Education* 17 (1969): 9–22.

Harper, Andrew, Marty Flick, Karen Taylor, and Renee Waldo. "Education Through Music: A Breakthrough in Early Childhood Education?" *Phi Delta Kappan* 54 (May 1973): 628–629.

Haskell, Lendall L. *Art in the Early Childhood Years*. Columbus, OH: Merrill, 1979.

Hitz, Randy. "Creative Problem Solving Through Music Activities." *Young Children* 42 (January 1987): 12–17.

Jalongo, Mary Renck. "The Child's Right to the Expressive Arts: Nurturing the Imagination as Well as the Intellect. A Position Paper of the Association for Childhood Education International." *Childhood Education* 66 (Summer 1990): 195–201.

Jalongo, Mary Renck, and Mitzie Collins. "Singing with Young Children! Folk Singing for Nonmusicians." *Young Children* 40 (January 1985): 17–21.

Jaques-Dalcroze, Emile. *Rhythm, Music and Education*. Translated by L. F. Rubenstein. London, England: Hazell Watson and Viney Ltd. for the Dalcroze Society, 1921.

Kean, Thomas H. "The 'Imperative' of Arts Education." *Excellence in Teaching* 7 (Winter 1989/90): 4–5.

Kellogg, Rhoda. *Analyzing Children's Art*. Palo Alto, CA: National Press Books, 1970.

Lasky, Lila, and Rose Mukerji. *Art: Basic for Young Children*. Washington, DC: National Association for the Education of Young Children, 1980.

Lowenfeld, Viktor, and W. Lambert Brittain. *Creative and Mental Growth.* 7th ed. New York: Macmillan, 1982.

Malina, R. M. "Motor Development in the Early Years." In *The Young Child: Reviews of Research,* vol. 3, edited by S. G. Moore and C. R. Cooper, 11–229. Washington, DC: National Association for the Education of Young Children, 1982.

McDonald, Dorothy T. *Music in Our Lives: The Early Years.* Washington, DC: National Association for the Education of Young Children, 1979.

McDonald, Dorothy T., and Gene M. Simons. *Musical Growth and Development: Birth Through Six.* New York: Schirmer Books, 1989.

McGregor, Lynn, Maggie Tate, and Ken Robinson. *Learning Through Drama.* Portsmouth, NH: Heinemann, 1987.

Merrion, Margaret Dee, and Marilyn Curt Vincent. *A Primer on Music for Non-Musician Educators.* Fastback 270. Bloomington, IN: Phi Delta Kappa Educational Foundation, 1988.

National Education Association. "Resolution C-27." *National Education Today* 9 (September 1990): 17.

New, Rebecca. "Excellent Early Education: A City in Italy Has It." *Young Children* 45 (September 1990): 4–10.

Richards, Mary Helen. *Mary Helen Richards Teaches: The Child in Depth.* Portola Valley, CA: Richards Institute of Music Education and Research, 1969.

Schirrmacher, Robert. "Talking with Young Children About Their Art." *Young Children* 41 (July 1986): 3–7.

Sullivan, Molly. *Feeling Strong, Feeling Free: Movement Exploration for Young Children.* Washington, DC: National Association for the Education of Young Children, 1982.

Wachowiak, Frank. *Emphasis Art.* 3d ed. New York: Harper and Row, 1977.

Weikart, Phyllis S. *Teaching Movement and Dance.* 2d ed. Ypsilanti, MI: High/Scope Press, 1982.

Wood, Lucille. *Rhythms to Reading: Picture Songbook.* Glendale, CA: Bowmar, 1972.

Zimmerman, Marilyn P. *State of the Art in Early Childhood Music and Research.* ERIC Document Reproduction Service 250068. 1984.

Children's Books

Ackerman, Karen. *Song and Dance Man.* New York: Knopf, 1988.

Carle, Eric. *The Very Hungry Caterpillar.* New York: Scholastic, 1970.

Keats, Ezra Jack. *The Snowy Day.* New York: Viking, 1962.

Sendak, Maurice. *Where the Wild Things Are.* New York: Harper and Row, 1963.

Yolen, Jane. *Owl Moon.* New York: Philomel Books, 1987.

Chapter Eleven

Living Together
The Social Studies

reading-writing connection

multicultural education

definition

SOCIAL STUDIES

holidays and themes

planning programs

experiences

goals

This week, you observed in kindergarten and first-grade classrooms. In the kindergarten class, you observed children celebrating the birthday of George Washington by coloring silhouettes of Washington, cutting them out, and mounting them on construction paper. Before they colored the silhouettes, the children learned some facts about George Washington and repeated those facts in response to the teacher's questions. The teacher in the first-grade class explained to you that she does not teach social studies specifically because the children are learning social studies as they learn to share materials and to get along in social groups.

When you returned to class, you had many questions about social studies in early childhood programs, as did your classmates. Some of them saw activities similar to the Washington assignment that you observed; some talked to teachers who said that they were teaching democracy and freedom in the way the classroom was organized and managed; some classmates talked to teachers who said they had a peace curriculum.

What *is* social studies? Is it learning to recite facts about historical figures? Is it learning to interact successfully with social groups? Is it learned from planned experiences? Is it absorbed from the social milieu of the classroom?

....

Programs for young children use several approaches to social studies. One approach is to integrate social studies into the daily lives of the children. Proponents of this approach believe that social studies need not be a content area for young children. They believe that as children learn to settle disputes, work out systems for taking turns, and establish other arrangements for living and working together responsibly, they are learning the most important concepts of social studies. Another approach is to treat social studies as a content area with a body of knowledge that should be learned by all young children. Proponents of this view believe that social studies content is important and that young children could be learning much more than is commonly taught in preschools and primary grades. A third approach combines these two views of social studies, so that children learn content in social studies but do so while learning the skills of interacting in groups.

Proponents of all three views believe that social studies is important because world conditions are changing and citizens must be prepared to participate effectively in government and society. Education for participation in a democracy is not a new idea. The focus of American schools during the period following the Revolutionary War was on educating citizens to participate in the new democratic government. Thomas Jefferson (1743–1826) stated, "If a nation expects to be ignorant and free, in a state of civilization, it expects what never was and never will be" (Butts 1960). To be successful, a representative democracy requires a citizenry capable of examining the issues and making decisions that will benefit the nation.

John Dewey (1859–1952) also emphasized the importance of learning to live in a democratic society. He believed that classrooms should be democratic and that children should learn to participate in the decision-making process as part of their school experience (Dewey 1916). His thinking was considered to be radical in his time because schools of that era were so authoritarian.

The organizational pattern for social studies in elementary schools— called the **expanding curriculum**—was developed from the ideas of Lucy Sprague Mitchell. The expanding curriculum typically begins in kinder-

Expanding curriculum
An organizational pattern for social studies in which the focus of activities moves from the individual to the family, the neighborhood, the city, the state, the nation, and the world.

garten or first grade with a focus on the individual; the focus then moves to the individual in a group, a community, a state, a nation, and finally, the world. Mitchell believed that children learn social studies by participating in real experiences. She described how children learn geography, for example, from field trips during which they can examine the real features of the region around them (Mitchell 1928). Mitchell believed that in order to learn, children must have experiences, see relationships, and make connections and generalizations. She expected teachers not merely to supply information but to arrange activities that would enable children to gain information through experience.

In recent years, the teaching of social studies has been widely criticized in the popular press. Critics have pointed to the lack of factual knowledge and skills exhibited by students, especially high school graduates, who lack geographic knowledge and often cannot even locate North America on a map. Critics also find that very few Americans have what they consider an adequate knowledge of U.S. history. According to some analysts, these problems have arisen in part because of the expanding curriculum. Former Secretary of Education William Bennett has been very critical of the expanding curriculum concept; he believes that it has no content (Bennett 1988). According to Bennett, children starting school already know the information presented to them in social studies, and much more content should be introduced much earlier.

It is not the expanding curriculum itself that has caused problems, however. Rather, over the years, some teachers of young children have lost sight of Mitchell's emphasis on thinking and intellectual development and have presented so-called units on the home, school, and neighborhood. Critics have reason to be concerned with any curriculum that relies on units presented without active involvement by children and without consideration of what children already know.

DEFINITION OF SOCIAL STUDIES

What is social studies, and what is appropriate social studies instruction for young children? *Social studies* includes all the social sciences—anthropology, sociology, psychology, history, geography, political science, and economics—but neither teachers nor children should be expected to separate learning experiences into these categories. Social studies in early childhood classrooms should help children gain knowledge, skills, and attitudes that are important in the social sciences. Social studies, like other subject-matter areas, is best taught through an integrated approach that uses activities appropriate for the age and development of the children and is best learned through active participation.

In a position statement defining appropriate practice in the education of preschool children, the National Association for the Education of Young Children (NAEYC) describes social studies as integrated when children participate in meaningful activities: "build with blocks; observe changes in the environment; sing and listen to music from other cultures" (Bredekamp 1987, p. 56). The same document describes appropriate social studies instruction for the primary grades as follows:

Social studies themes are identified as the focus of work for extended periods of time. Social studies concepts are learned through a variety of projects and playful activities involving independent research in library books; excursions and interviewing visitors; discussions; the relevant use of language, writing, spelling (invented and teacher-taught), and reading skills; and opportunities to develop social skills such as planning, sharing, taking turns, and working in committees. The classroom is treated as a laboratory of social relations where children explore values and learn rules of social living and respect for individual differences through experience. Relevant art, music, dance, drama, woodworking, and games are incorporated in social studies. (p. 71)

The National Council of Social Studies (NCSS) has also issued a position statement (NCSS Task Force 1989) that defines social studies and presents a rationale for including it in the curriculum:

The social studies are the study of political, economic, cultural, and environmental aspects of societies in the past, present, and future. For elementary school children, as well as for all age groups, social studies have several purposes. The social studies equip them with the knowledge and understanding of the past necessary for coping with the present and planning for the future, enable them to understand and participate effectively in their world, and explain their relationship to other people and to social, economic, and political institutions. Social studies can provide students with the skills for productive problem solving and decision making, as well as for assessing issues and making thoughtful value judgments. Above all, the social studies help students to integrate these skills and understanding into a framework for responsible citizen participation, whether in their play group, the school, the community, or the world. (p. 15)

It is clear that teachers do have responsibilities in the area of social studies instruction other than to help children learn to interact in groups, but it is equally clear that social studies need not be a separate subject or divorced from other activities in children's experiences. An early childhood teacher must plan for experiences in which the children can be active and that will help children gain meaningful knowledge, skills, and attitudes important in the social studies.

PLANNING SOCIAL STUDIES EDUCATION

Goals

The position statement of the NCSS supports social studies programs for young children in which they gain knowledge, skills, and attitudes (NCSS Task Force 1989):

- *Knowledge goals*—Knowledge goals focus on concepts, including concepts that reflect the content of the social studies, such as:
  —Each person is unique.
  —People are interdependent.
  —The earth is covered with water and land.
  —Land forms determine where people live and affect how they live.
  —Social groups must solve problems.
  —Each person has responsibilities.

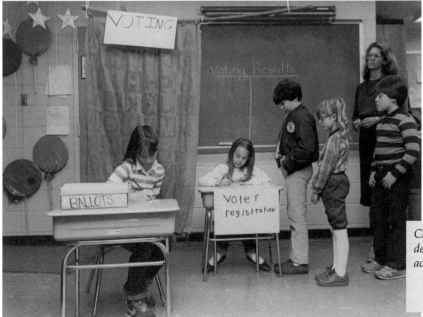

Children can learn about democracy through many activities.

Other knowledge goals focus on concepts based on the structure of the social science disciplines, such as:

—We can learn about the past from evidence left by others.

—Records can help us recall what has happened.

—Groups can make decisions that affect each individual.

—Individuals can help determine how problems are solved.

Finally, some knowledge goals focus on concepts based on children's interests, such as:

—Change is continuous.

—Different social groups solve problems differently.

—People in neighborhoods help each other.

- *Skill goals*—Skill goals are furthered by activities that emphasize the ability to record and communicate simple data; the ability to interact in socially acceptable ways with family, peers, and adults; and the ability to solve problems of a social nature.

- *Attitude goals*—Attitude goals emphasize helping children recognize the importance of each individual; respect the feelings of other individuals; and cultivate a continuing interest in learning about the people, places, and systems that are integral to the social studies.

A relatively new concept in social studies for young children is *conflict resolution*. The goals of conflict resolution overlap several of the knowledge, skill, and attitude goals listed above. Drew (1987) identifies the major concepts of conflict resolution as "accepting self and others, communicating effectively, resolving conflicts, and understanding intercultural differences" (p. 1). Teachers who focus on conflict resolution will help children learn alternate responses to social situations, learn about other people, and learn how to communicate their feelings and expectations in ways that lead to peaceful solutions to problems. Proponents of conflict resolution skills hope that more people will learn to apply them and that eventually even nations will use the techniques to solve problems rather than resorting to violence or war.

Classroom Experiences

Threes and Fours

Appropriate experiences in the social studies, like any experience for children who are three or four, cannot be separated from play. Just as in math and science, teachers will want to provide not only play materials that help children learn some social studies concepts but also time to use them. In developing themes for organizing curriculum, teachers should make sure that social studies concepts are included when they are appropriate. The following descriptions may suggest other possibilities:

- Toys related to methods of transportation can be included in play areas. Trucks, cars, buses, trains, airplanes, and helicopters can be added to the block area, and boats and barges can be added to the water play area. The teacher can help children focus on the concept of the necessity of transporting goods and people.
- Children can take short walks in their neighborhood and identify structures (houses, businesses, churches, and so on).
- Children can be led to observe changes in their immediate environments, such as changes in the room, on the playground, or in the school building.
- Children can be encouraged to create structures with blocks that represent what they know of their neighborhood or community. They might construct a fire station if they live near one or if the school is near one, an airport if it is part of their experience, a gas station, a harbor, or other structures.
- Children can work together to move toys or materials that need to be moved or to clean up the materials and play areas.
- Teachers can keep a large scrapbook with records of important events in the children's experiences. Reviewing it with the children will teach them that we can keep records of events and that these records help us to recall the events accurately.
- Teachers can help children appreciate their growing skills and abilities by pointing out, for example, that they can run, throw a ball, walk on tiptoe, share materials, control the crayon when drawing, or use language more effectively than they could earlier.

Fives and Sixes

Social studies for the school beginner should continue to be based on play experiences and meaningful activities. The teacher will want to plan some experiences that help children develop specific concepts, but this does not imply that lessons in social studies should be isolated from other experiences. Suggested activities include the following:

- Children can continue to learn about change by observing any changes in the neighborhood or community (such as buildings being constructed or torn down). The children can record their observations in their journals, or the teacher can help them record their observations on experience charts. Photographs of the sequence of the changes can help children keep records. Children can also learn about change in themselves by bringing in baby pictures or baby clothes and comparing them with their current looks and clothing.

- Children can learn about the world of work by visiting workplaces in the neighborhood and then making models of the neighborhood. They can use hats and other pieces of clothing to create the roles of various workers. The teacher can then develop themes around different businesses or jobs (Borden 1987). The children's parents can be invited to class to describe their work and the tools they use. Teachers are urged to use their imaginations and invite workers of all kinds to the classroom—not just dentists or doctors. The parent workers who created the most long-term interest in one kindergarten (role-play, block play, sociodramatic play) were an athletic trainer, a telephone line person, and a shoe salesperson. People who work in the school can be asked to visit class and describe their work. Children will learn that the school cannot operate without many people making contributions.

- Children can celebrate the diversity of family structures in which they live. The teacher can find pictures to represent the family structures in the class, and the children can write or dictate lists of common features and positive attributes of families.

- Children can begin to explore racial and ethnic differences by examining differences in skin color, hair texture, and eye shape. After selecting paint chips or mixing paint to match their individual skin colors, they can create a chart illustrating the range of colors in the class. They can create another chart of hair textures and eye colors. With guidance from the teacher, kindergarten children can discuss the advantages of physical characteristics under different environmental conditions—for example, dark skin provides more protection from the sun (Derman-Sparks and ABC Task Force 1989).

- Children can begin to categorize objects or goods as "wants" or "needs." They can develop the concept that people are paid for their work and that the money is used to acquire goods.

- Children can create three-dimensional maps of the classroom and of their neighborhood. Photographs can be attached to models of buildings or other structures in the neighborhood. These maps can be created with blocks, milk cartons, cereal boxes, and so on.

- Children can locate and label different kinds of homes in the neighborhood. They can look for single-family homes, apartment buildings, condos, homeless shelters, or whatever is part of their experience. They can compare and contrast living in each kind of house.

- Children can trace the route taken by the milk that is served every day in the classroom from the dairy farm to the dairy, the distributor, the delivery truck, and the cafeteria. They can make books of their observations and learn about the animals that provide milk and the people who process and deliver it.
- Children can survey the school neighborhood for problems. If they find litter, for example, they can try to find out who is contributing to the litter problem, find solutions to the problem, and report their findings to others at school or in the community. They could also pick up litter on a regular basis, thereby performing a valuable community service and contributing in a meaningful way to community life.
- Children can trace the route of a piece of mail. They can address a brightly colored envelope to themselves and then visit the post office and trace its progress: through the sorting machines, as it is sorted again by the postal worker on the delivery route, as it reaches the school, and as it is sorted yet again in order to reach their classroom.
- Children can invite their families to talk about family and cultural customs or holiday celebrations, food, clothing, or other cultural experiences with the class.

Sevens and Eights

Sevens and eights can do more with maps and learn more about economics and politics than younger children; however, they still need real experiences. Teachers should not expect sevens and eights to learn from textbooks or be able to handle abstract concepts that are not part of their experience. Activities for this age group include the following:

- Children can map their school and perhaps their neighborhood by constructing three-dimensional maps and then transferring the information to a two-dimensional form. They can create legends for the two-dimensional maps.
- Children can learn about elections and voting. They can visit a polling place and see how the records are kept and how the ballots are marked. They can invite people who are running for local office to visit and explain why they want to be elected. They might interview several different people to determine how people make decisions about voting or why they do or do not vote. They can participate in classroom and school elections and make classroom decisions by voting.
- Children can survey others in school to find out what kinds of jobs their parents hold. This information can be presented on charts and graphs. (The teacher can use the work done by parents as a source of themes— for example, factory production or service industries.) If some parents

INTEGRATING THE CURRICULUM

To continue our theme of patterns, think about the following possibilities in planning social studies activities:

- Find patterns in the United States flag.
- Find patterns in the house numbers, street numbers, and street names of the community. (In many communities, streets run alphabetically or are named for names of trees, presidents, states, or some other pattern.)
- Find street patterns on a map. Are they square? Are they curved in some areas?
- Look for patterns in the ways different kinds of houses are grouped in neighborhoods.
- Find patterns in bus routes (and trolley or train routes, if appropriate).

- Look for patterns in the organization of the schoolday and the schoolyear.
- Find patterns on the calendar for days, weeks, months, and years.
- Find family patterns represented in your class group.
- Find work patterns in your school. (For instance, how many parents do what kinds of work, or if they are not working, what kind of work would they like to do?)
- Find population patterns in your neighborhood (urban, suburban, rural or mixed).

are unemployed, on welfare, on strike, or laid off from their jobs, teachers can help children learn some of the reasons for these conditions in their neighborhoods.

- The class can survey the community to determine local natural resources and how they are used. They can determine who in the community makes decisions about resources and interview those people about their long-term goals. The teacher can help children obtain information on conserving natural resources from books, speakers, films, and so on. Children can make lists of what they can do to conserve resources.
- Children can determine who is responsible for all the services provided in the community and create Venn diagrams of government and private responsibilities.
- Current events can provide learning experiences for this age group if they are related to the children's interests and experience. Interesting pictures or stories from newspapers can be posted on a bulletin board as a catalyst to spark discussion or further explorations.

CELEBRATING HOLIDAYS

Some teachers of young children center their social studies instruction around holidays. Many teachers move from one holiday to another, justifying the emphasis on holidays as important to the cultural heritage of the children. Such a rationale is logical only if the children share the culture in which the holiday originated. It is acceptable to celebrate holidays appropriately with young children, but social studies should certainly be more than completing worksheets about Lincoln's birthday.

Holiday instruction is complicated by the fact that many holidays are religious in nature and cannot be celebrated in public schools. When the religious meaning is removed from holidays, only the secular elements are left—a lot of red and green art and Easter bunnies. Another objection to the "curriculum-by-holiday" approach is the frenzy that surrounds most holidays. By the time children do holiday art for a month, see all the advertisements on TV, and see all the displays in the stores, the holiday itself seems rather anticlimactic. Finally, too often, teachers do not consider the meaning of the holiday for individual children in a program, particularly in today's multicultural society. One has to wonder, for example, what meaning Native American and Hispanic children get from a week of cutting and pasting shamrocks and similar St. Patrick's Day activities.

Given all the problems just mentioned, teachers may begin to wonder whether to celebrate holidays at all—and if so, how. The following guidelines may be helpful:

1. Consider what the children will learn if the holiday is acknowledged in the curriculum. Each holiday should be evaluated in terms of the curriculum goals of the program (Timberlake 1978; Dimidjian 1989).

2. Determine what the children think the holiday means and what they know about it.

3. Remember that the children should have the most important role in deciding how the holiday should be celebrated. Involve the children in planning and implementing the celebration. Is the celebration something they can really do themselves, or is it so elaborate that an adult must do it for them?

4. Reduce the amount of hype over holidays to a minimum. One or two meaningful art projects should be enough—it is not necessary to plan fifteen.

5. Celebrate holidays of all the cultural groups in your class. Involve children's families, and learn about some of their traditions. Find common elements in how people celebrate holidays: food, family visits, religious ceremonies, gifts, and so on. Recognize different cultural views of holiday celebrations. Native Americans, for example, probably do not have the same view of Thanksgiving as those in the mainstream culture (Ramsey 1979).

6. Present information that is age appropriate for the children. Do not try to make children memorize and repeat meaningless information. For

example, on President's Day, children often have to repeat lists of facts about Washington or Lincoln. It may be worthwhile to show pictures of Washington and Lincoln and explain that they were great presidents, especially if the children initiate the conversations, but fours and fives have no need to know many details about these men. Sixes, sevens, and eights may know more about the current president, be able to understand that past presidents were very important, and be able to listen to short biographies of these men. Children who demonstrate interest in learning more about past presidents or other historical figures should be encouraged to do so, but having children memorize facts isolated from their reality is not appropriate.

The following suggestions for specific holiday celebrations are based on ideas in two books: *Anti-Bias Curriculum: Tools for Empowering Young Children* (Derman-Sparks and ABC Task Force 1989) and *Teaching and Learning in a Diverse World* (Ramsey 1987).

Thanksgiving

- The children can focus on the harvest aspects of the holiday by visiting a farm, harvesting their own garden, or finding evidence of harvest in the community.
- The teacher can help the children find information about other harvest festivals and how they are celebrated.
- The teacher can help the children relate the eating of a meal to the celebration of the harvest.
- The teacher should supply *accurate* information about contemporary Native Americans using books, pictures, and guest speakers. The teacher can help children critique greeting cards and TV specials for images of Native Americans and the authenticity of the portrayals of the first Thanksgiving. In the words of author and Native American rights activist Michael Dorris, "It must be communicated to educators that no information about Native peoples is truly preferable to a reiteration of the same old stereotypes, particularly in the early years" (cited in Derman-Sparks and ABC Task Force 1989, p. 88).
- The children can help cook some foods typical of Thanksgiving celebrations such as cornbread, squash, and cranberries.

Halloween

- The teacher can help children recognize the harvest aspects of Halloween (scarecrows, pumpkins, and so on).
- Children can learn to recognize the similarities between jack-o'-lanterns and other cultures' representations of human figures with food. They

Making masks and learning how masks are culturally important are appropriate activities for celebrating Halloween.

can create some "vegetable people" from squash, turnips, or ears of corn. The vegetable people can be washed and eaten after the activity.

- Children can explore costumes for different purposes (theater, other entertainment). Younger children can be encouraged to explore the concept of being the same person even though they look different in costumes.

- A maker of masks can be invited to share his collection and help the children understand some of the cultural uses of masks or show slides of different masks from around the world. Involve the children in mask-making. In order to avoid having them associate the color black with scary things, children can be encouraged to make masks that are scary but not black and others that are black but not scary.

- Teachers can help children explore scary feelings. Children can create paintings, songs, or dances that help them express their feelings. They can find scary things in books such as *Where the Wild Things Are* (Sendak 1963) and *There's a Nightmare in My Closet* (Mayer 1968) and talk about how the characters responded to being scared.

DEVELOPMENTALLY
APPROPRIATE
PRACTICE

Achieving DAP in social studies instruction, where topics are fairly abstract, may seem more complicated than in math or science instruction, where real things can be manipulated and observed. Teachers of young children will be especially challenged in planning appropriate social studies activities. In deciding what is developmentally appropriate, teachers should consider the following:

- Can children understand the concepts to be learned? If the concepts depend on being able to understand historical times or places far from children's experience, then children will not likely understand them.
- Are the concepts related to children's real-life experiences? Learning about a harbor may not be appropriate for children who live far inland.
- Can meaningful activities in which children are involved be planned around the concept? Field trips, resource people, and real objects to explore may bring concepts to life for young children; completing dittoed worksheets and coloring pages, however, will not promote concepts.
- Can the concept be integrated into other areas of the curriculum? For example, can the concept be developed through activities in which children sing songs, learn dances, read stories, and create art?
- Do the activities honor the diversity of the children and their families?
- Will stereotypes be reduced rather than increased through participation in social studies activities?

- Children in communities that still maintain the tradition of going from house to house at Halloween can explore how that tradition is carried on in other celebrations. Teachers can help children understand the trick in *trick or treat* by sharing "trickster" stories from the southwestern Native American tradition and inviting children to plan some tricks.
- Older children can trace the origins of symbols used in Halloween celebrations.

SOCIAL STUDIES THEMES

As with other subject-matter areas, a thematic approach to social studies offers opportunities for children to do meaningful tasks that can help them acquire important knowledge, skills, and attitudes. A list of possible themes that would be useful for developing social studies concepts would be nearly endless. Teachers could focus on the family; justice; change; the neighborhood; the city; celebrations; historical places in the community; parks; interdependence; workplaces; bread—and this is by no means an exhaustive list. Suggestions for developing two such themes are described in the following sections.

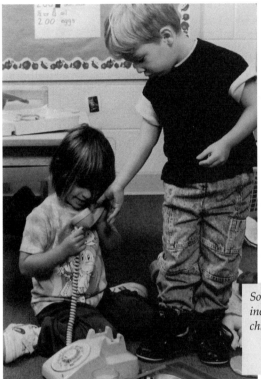

> *Social studies instruction must include experiences in which children can participate actively.*

Activities for a Supermarket Theme

- Learn vocabulary words: *shopping, bakery, produce, dairy, meat, canned goods, paper goods, cereals, spices* (and other words related to each of these categories).
- Have children write signs, shopping lists, advertisements for products, descriptions of new products, directions for using products, or an ABC book of the supermarket.
- Visit a local supermarket. List departments. Observe signs on aisles, shelves, and products. Observe workers and find out what each does: delivery people, stock people, butchers, bakers, custodians, checkers, manager, deli clerk, florist. Purchase unfamiliar fruits or vegetables to taste later.
- Set up a supermarket in the classroom using as many props as possible: aprons, name tags, jackets, bags, shelves, a scanner or a cash register. Classify foods into departments (meat department, dairy case, frozen foods, and so on). Group foods that go together (Mexican foods, Chinese foods, and so on). Find other ways food items can be grouped.

- Use a map to find countries where imported products originate: crackers, cheeses, exotic fruits, and the like.
- Learn money concepts. Observe as the teacher pays for purchases. Discuss the concept "change." Depending on children's math skills, look at the costs of items in grocery ads. Compare costs at different stores. Give each child an amount of play money: What can she buy with the money? Will she get change? Discuss how families get money to purchase food. Talk about why packaged foods cost more than foods prepared at home by consumers. Compare the costs of making bread or applesauce, for example, versus buying it.

Activities for a Theme of Changes around Us
- Take a walk and observe changes in the neighborhood (houses being painted, new plants, new stores, new street signs, and so on). Observe a new house or other building under construction. Observe seasonal changes in the neighborhood.
- Visit a museum or an antique store. Find old-fashioned household articles or appliances, such as washing machines, vacuum cleaners, brooms, stoves, telephones, bathtubs, toys. Find changes in school-related items, such as desks and school bags, or find items that are no longer used, such as ink bottles and slates. Invite a local antique car buff to bring an old car to school. Find toys that change (for example, transformers or reversible dolls). Talk or write about the different ways they change.
- Read about change in literature: *Shaker Lane* (Provensen and Provensen 1987); *Mike Mulligan and His Steam Shovel* (Burton 1939); *The Little House* (Burton 1942); *The Mountain* (Parnall 1971); *Changes, Changes* (Hutchins 1971).
- Expand the theme of change by focusing on personal changes (growth and development) or changes in the plant and animal worlds (life cycles, plant growth).

Multicultural education
An approach to education that encourages children to understand and respect all people and cultures.

Antibias curriculum
A curriculum aimed at eliminating bias of all types by teaching children to respect people regardless of their sex, age, race/ ethnicity, or other traits.

MULTICULTURAL EDUCATION

Multicultural education and **antibias curriculum** are terms used to describe educational programs that attempt to teach children respect for all people and their cultures. Multicultural education involves learning about one's own and other cultures in an integrated way. A multicultural or antibias curriculum is not achieved by superficial lessons; it is achieved by sensitive and knowledgeable teachers who help children learn in a context in which all cultures are appreciated.

The National Council for Accreditation of Teacher Education (1987) defines *multicultural education* as a perspective that recognizes "(1) the social, political, and economic realities that individuals experience in culturally diverse and complex human encounters and (2) the importance of culture, race, sex and gender, ethnicity, religion, socioeconomic status, and exceptionalities in the education process" (p. 57).

The effort to eliminate racism and prejudice by making students and teachers more aware and accepting of the cultural diversity in the United States is relatively new. Recent U.S. demographic information indicates that cultural and ethnic minority populations are growing rapidly; consequently, multicultural education is also gaining importance.

Whaley and Swadner (1990) argue for beginning multicultural education in infant and toddler programs. Very young children learn to discriminate differences and classify things and feelings; they can also learn to be more empathetic than was once believed. Programs that support multicultural education are important as very young children begin to learn about people other than family. Teachers of preschoolers can make sure that materials (books, music, dolls, and so on) represent a variety of cultures, use pictures of different cultural and ethnic groups involved in a variety of experiences, and take every opportunity to help children learn to care for each other.

The basic assumptions of multicultural education have been articulated by Hernandez (1989):

1. It is increasingly important for political, social, educational, and economic reasons to recognize that the United States is a culturally diverse society.
2. Multicultural education is for all students.
3. Multicultural education is synonymous with effective teaching.
4. Teaching is a cross-cultural encounter.
5. Traditionally, the educational system has not served all students equally well.
6. Multicultural education is synonymous with educational innovation and reform.
7. Next to parents, teachers are the single most important factor in the lives of children.
8. Classroom interaction between teachers and students constitutes the major part of the educational process for most students (pp. 9–11).

Several classroom implications follow from these assumptions. One is that lessons limited to teaching children about a single aspect of one other culture are inappropriate. For example, teachers sometimes attempt to teach about Hispanic culture by making and serving tortillas. More appropriate experiences would continue over a period of several days, during which children would discover that each cultural group has bread of some kind and participate in making and eating bread from each cultural group represented in the classroom. These experiences could reveal to children that people of all cultures buy bread at markets, that some cultures do not have traditional breads at all, and that others bake traditional breads only on special occasions. Finding the common elements in how people from different cultures cook, eat, dress, live in families, and carry on daily activities is an important goal.

Multicultural education is not just learning about other cultures. Facts alone will never erase stereotypes and prejudice. As Phillips (1988) stresses:

We must struggle to truly understand how culture is a source of group power and strength, and to examine how to allow groups to retain their cultural integrity while they gain the skills to function in the larger society. This perhaps is the central struggle we face as adults responsible for preparing today's children and tomorrow's leaders in a society that may de-value them by demanding that they give up their culture in order to achieve. (p. 46)

For too many children, success in school depends on learning in only one way and giving up other ways of learning and acting. Many Native American educators believe that Native American students drop out of school as soon as they can legally do so because they have to be "White" in order to succeed at school. Teachers of young children can provide students with many choices of learning activities and with many avenues for expressing what they know and are learning.

Another implication of Hernandez's (1989) assumptions is that effective teaching must be individualized, based on the child's development and relevant to the child's experience. Memorizing facts about other cultures, pasting a sombrero on a ditto sheet of a Hispanic man sitting under a cactus, and learning about Native Americans of long ago are activities that do not meet the criteria for effective teaching. Children will develop concepts about other people as they interact with real people at school and in their neighborhoods. Thomson (1989) suggests that experiences in which children can actively participate are the most valuable for helping them develop understanding and tolerance. She suggests that experiences such as role-playing Rosa Parks or discussing children's feelings upon encountering discriminatory signs foster the active learning that is necessary for young children.

A third implication of Hernandez's assumptions is that teachers must take individual responsibility for learning about the children in the class and for helping all children learn to appreciate each other. Children learn how to appreciate others from observing and participating in interactions with the teacher. No commercial multicultural education program can relieve the teacher of learning about the children, including their cultural backgrounds, and planning experiences that will help them learn about each other in positive ways.

Education that is multicultural will be reflected in the teacher's choices of books and literature, in the signs posted in the classroom, in holiday celebrations, and in planned activities—in short, throughout the curriculum. For example, children can learn about different languages and different systems of writing through language arts activities (Saracho and Spodek 1983). They can learn about foods contributed to their diets by North and South American cultures (corn), Eastern cultures (rice), or European cultures (wheat).

Teachers must plan all activities with an eye for including a multicultural dimension. Table 11.1 on page 372 is a checklist designed to help teachers analyze their classrooms and provide education that is multicultural. Another useful resource for teachers is an extensive bibliography of materials about cultural diversity in the United States, which can be found in the March 1993 issue of *Young Children* (see the References, "General Sources," National Association for Education of Young Children 1993).

The ability of children now in early childhood classes to cope with life in the twenty-first century may well depend on the quality of their educational experiences. Quality education must include multicultural experiences.

CONNECTING SOCIAL STUDIES WITH READING, WRITING, AND LITERATURE

Social studies topics are interesting to children; they want to know about people and relationships in their world. Topics of interest can be introduced, explored, and summarized through meaningful literacy experiences using stories and poetry. Topics of interest in the social studies often emerge from reading aloud. The books and stories listed on page 373, for example (adapted from Hennings 1982), relate to the themes of freedom, justice, interdependence, and power.

Table 11.1   Multicultural Checklist

This checklist will help you focus on individual aspects of your classroom environment, take a closer look at your curriculum, and highlight areas that need improvement. Try to answer each question as it pertains to your classroom.

CURRICULUM AREA	QUESTIONS
Language Arts	1. Does your classroom have a wide variety of age-appropriate and culturally diverse books and language arts materials? Look for examples. 2. Are the cultures in your class and community represented in your books and materials? 3. Are there any books that speak of people of diverse cultures in stereotypic or derogatory terms? What are they? Should they be removed, or is there a way to use them with children to broaden their concepts and encourage them to share their experiences? 4. Are the pictures of people on the walls representative of a multicultural community?
Social Studies	5. Does the curriculum help children increase their understanding and acceptance of attitudes, values, and lifestyles that are unfamiliar to them? If so, how? If not, what can you do to change it? 6. Are materials and games racially or sex-role stereotypic? If so, how can you change your collection to give strong, positive images?
Blocks	7. Are the accessories in the block area representative of various cultural groups and family configurations? If not, how can you change them? 8. Are the people block accessories stereotypic in terms of sex roles? If so, how can you change them?
Dramatic Play	9. Is there a wide variety of clothes (everyday garments, not exotic costumes) from various cultural groups? 10. Are the pictures on the walls and the props representative of a diversity of cultures? 11. Are the dolls representative of the major racial groups in our country, not just in colors but in features?
Music and Games	12. Do music experiences reinforce children's affirmation of cultural diversity? How? 13. Do you use fingerplays, games, and songs from various cultural groups?
Cooking	14. Do cooking experiences encourage children to experiment with foods they aren't familiar with? 15. Are these experiences designed to give children a general notion of the connections between cultural heritage and the process of preparing, cooking, and eating food? If so, how?

Source: Adapted from Frances E. Kendall, Ph.D., "Creating a Multicultural Environment," *Pre-K Today* (November/December 1988): 34–39. Reprinted with permission of the author.

Freedom

Hawk, I'm Your Brother (Baylor 1976)
Hansel and Gretel (Lesser 1984)
Jorinda and Joringel (Grimm 1970)

Justice

Why Mosquitoes Buzz in People's Ears (Aardema 1975)
Once a Mouse (Brown 1961)
The Three Little Pigs (Zemach 1988)
Goldilocks and the Three Bears (Brett 1987)
The Three Billy Goats Gruff (Galdone 1973)
Roland the Minstrel Pig (Steig 1968)
Strega Nona (de Paola 1975)
Mufaro's Beautiful Daughters (Steptoe 1987)
The Talking Eggs (San Souci 1989)
Lon Po Po (Young 1989)

Interdependence

The Big Snow (Hader and Hader 1948)
Ox Cart Man (Hall 1979)
Building a House (Barton 1981)
Truck (Crews 1980)

Power

Fisherman and His Wife (Jarrell 1980)
The Stonecutter (McDermott 1981)
The Mouse Couple (Malotki 1988)

Table 11.2 on page 374 lists guidelines adapted from those of the Council on Interracial Books for Children (1974), which teachers may find helpful in evaluating literature for the classroom.

In addition to read-aloud experiences, there are many other opportunities for meaningful literacy experiences as children explore social studies topics of interest. For example, if children are studying the work of their parents or of school personnel, they could write reports of their findings from their surveys, read more about some of the occupations that especially interest them, write entries for an ABC book of jobs, write letters inviting speakers to class and thank-you notes to speakers who have shared information, and so on. The children might also create charts, reports, books of various kinds, narrative stories, and poetry. For example,

Table 11.2   A Checklist for Analyzing Bias in Children's Books

GUIDELINES	POINTS TO CONSIDER
Check the illustrations	a. Look for stereotypes. Some illustrations are blatantly stereotypical; others may be more subtle in ridiculing characters based on their race/ethnicity or sex.
	b. Look for tokenism. Check to be sure that the illustrator has not simply colored in characters who have White features and that all people of color do not look alike.
	c. Examine who's doing what. Are only White men active or in leadership roles? Are women and people of color in subservient or passive roles?
Check the story line	Watch for subtle bias in the following areas:
	a. Standards for success—Do people of color have to exhibit so-called White behavior in order to succeed? Must people of color be extraordinary in order to succeed?
	b. Resolution of problems—Are problems solved by White people? Are societal problems explained, or are they treated as inevitable? Are minority people considered to be the problem?
	c. Role of women—Are achievements of women and girls based on their looks? Could the same story be told if the sex roles were reversed and the characters were men or boys?
Look at the lifestyles	Are the contrasts between people of color and Whites negative? Are people of color presented in settings other than barrios or ghettos? Does the author sincerely present an alternative lifestyle without negative value judgments?
Weigh the relationships among people	Are the Whites in the story in control? Are the family structures stereotypical?
Note the heroes	If the heroes or heroines are persons of color, do they avoid all conflict with Whites? Are they admired for the same qualities as White heroes or heroines?
Consider the effects on a child's self-image	Are standards established that limit the child's aspirations and self-esteem? Are there positive and constructive role models for children of color and girls?
Consider the author's or illustrator's background (if possible)	If the book is about people of color or women, does the author or illustrator have the experience and knowledge necessary to create nonbiased descriptions or discussions?
Check the author's perspective	Is the author's or illustrator's personal perspective limited? Does this view distort the story in any way?
Watch for "loaded" words	Some words carry insulting or derogatory connotations. Does the author avoid the use of such words as *savage, treacherous,* and *primitive* when describing people of given ethnic, cultural, or social groups?
Look at the copyright date	The copyright date is no guarantee that a book is nonbiased, but more recent books generally present a more authentic view of people of color and women than those published in the 1960s and before.

Source: Adapted from Council on Interracial Books for Children 1974.

if the children have been exploring the cultures of the children in their class, they could create journals in which they record their responses to foods they have tried, pictures of articles of clothing, or their personal responses to something they learned. The class might create a "big book" with photographs and reports they have dictated, which could be reviewed often.

There are many ways of recording and summarizing what children learn. Such documentation allows children to present and reflect upon what they learn. It is also useful to teachers in reporting to parents and administrators the concepts that children are developing and their growing literacy abilities and understandings in the social studies.

CHAPTER SUMMARY

- Several approaches to social studies can be found in programs for young children. Some approaches stress learning facts, and some stress learning to live together successfully in group settings. Others attempt to combine these two approaches.
- Goals of social studies instruction focus on strengthening knowledge, skills, and attitudes. Children's experiences should help them develop concepts related to social studies, skills in collecting and presenting data, and attitudes that are important in a democracy.
- Teaching social studies as a series of lessons is not as effective as integrating it into a variety of classroom activities.
- Holidays are often the basis of the curriculum in social studies. When celebrating holidays, teachers should examine what children will learn from celebrations; include different cultural perspectives; involve the children in making decisions about holiday celebrations; reduce the amount of stress surrounding holidays to a minimum; and choose appropriate learning experiences for the age and developmental level of the children.
- An important strategy for integrating social studies with other curriculum areas is to use themes.

As always, teachers should select themes that are meaningful to the children and that provide real reasons to apply skills.
- Education that is multicultural is more important than ever in the United States and the world. Ethnic and cultural minority populations are becoming larger; it is imperative that groups work together.
- A multicultural point of view should permeate all instruction and not be limited to isolated lessons designed to teach one cultural group about another group.
- Multicultural education should begin with infants and toddlers and should help children learn to respect and care for each other.
- Multicultural education is synonymous with effective teaching. Teachers must plan experiences that are appropriate to children's ages and developmental abilities.
- Social studies topics are interesting to children. Literacy experiences are a natural way of introducing, exploring, and concluding topics related to the social studies.

WHAT WOULD YOU DO?

Reflect on your reading and your own experiences with young children as you think about the following situations:

1. The social studies curriculum guide for your school district suggests that a study of the president's family would be a suitable topic for primary children. How would you respond to this suggestion?

2. Some parents of your preschoolers are impressed with the extensive holiday art done in a preschool across town. What would you tell them about your approach to celebrating holidays with preschoolers?

3. You find a children's book about the first Thanksgiving, which tells a simple story about how the Pilgrims and Native Americans celebrated. How would you determine whether to use the book in your kindergarten classroom?

4. In your second-grade classroom, you emphasize having the children make decisions all through the schoolday. Would this be teaching and learning social studies? Why?

THEORY INTO PRACTICE

1. Plan an experience that will help threes and fours develop a concept in social studies. (Remember that this will not be their last opportunity to learn this concept.)

2. If possible, observe the same holiday celebration at a preschool and in a primary grade. Could you determine the goals of each celebration? Could you determine if the children actually learned what they were intended to learn? Use the guidelines in this chapter to evaluate each celebration.

3. Select a social studies experience that you think is appropriate for preschool children, and determine one or two ways that you could broaden the activities to include a multicultural dimension.

4. Plan activities for a specific age of young children around a theme related to social studies. You may want to work together in small groups and help each other brainstorm ideas for themes.

5. Choose a social studies concept that you would like to introduce through literature to a specific age group. Find at least three books you could use to introduce the concept. Create a plan for using them. Will you read the books aloud, one by one? Will you present a media version of one or all of them? How will you guide the children in relating the books to the concept?

RECOMMENDED FOR FURTHER READING

Derman-Sparks, Louise, and the ABC Task Force. *Anti-Bias Curriculum: Tools for Empowering Young Children.* Washington, DC: National Association for the Education of Young Children, 1989.

This publication is a must for teachers of young children. The chapters cover such topics as creating an antibias environment, learning about racial/ethnic differences and similarities, learning about cultural differences and similarities, and planning holiday activities. Especially important are the chapters on helping children learn to recognize and resist stereotyping and discrimination and helping children become activists.

Pagano, Alicia L., ed. *Social Studies in Early Childhood: An Interactionist Point of View. National Council for the Social Studies Bulletin 58.* Washington, DC: National Council for the Social Studies, 1978.

Although this bulletin is older than other books that have been recommended for further reading, it is useful because it gives action-oriented approaches to helping children develop concepts in the social studies. Two especially useful chapters describe the importance of parents in children's experiences and ways of helping children understand the influence of the media in modern American culture.

Ramsey, Patricia G. *Teaching and Learning in a Diverse World: Multicultural Education for Young Children.* New York: Teachers College Press, 1987.

Ramsey describes the goals of education with a multicultural perspective and provides many examples of how to implement multicultural education in the early childhood classroom. Topics include adapting the physical setting of the classroom and adding multicultural elements to different activities.

Schreiber, Joan E. *Using Children's Books in Social Studies: Early Childhood Through Primary Grades. National Council for the Social Studies Bulletin 71.* Washington, DC: National Council for the Social Studies, 1984.

This booklet provides a rationale for including children's books in the social studies. The author has prepared bibliographies of books on themes such as careers, change, feelings, geography, history, biography, interdependence, relationships, rules, similarities and differences, and world cultures. These bibliographies should serve as excellent starting points for teachers who want to strengthen social studies concepts through literature programs.

Seefeldt, Carol. *Social Studies for the Preschool-Primary Child.* 3d ed. Columbus, OH: Merrill, 1989.

The author describes various approaches to social studies for young children. There are excellent chapters on planning, resources, and concept formation. The descriptions of appropriate activities related to the major topics covered in social studies are very helpful.

REFERENCES

General Sources

Bennett, William J. *James Madison Elementary School: A Curriculum for American Students.* Washington, DC: U.S. Department of Education, 1988.

Borden, Esta J. "The Community Connection—It Works!" *Young Children* 42 (May 1987): 14–23.

Bredekamp, Sue, ed. *Developmentally Appropriate Practice in Early Childhood Programs Serving Children From Birth Through Age 8.* Washington, DC: National Association for the Education of Young Children, 1987.

Butts, R. Freeman. "Search for Freedom—The Story of American Education." *National Education Association Journal* (March 1960): 33–48.

Council on Interracial Books for Children. *10 Quick Ways to Analyze Books for Racism and Sexism.* ERIC Document Reproduction Services 188852. 1974.

Derman-Sparks, Louise, and the ABC Task Force. *Anti-Bias Curriculum: Tools for Empowering Young Children.* Washington, DC: National Association for the Education of Young Children, 1989.

Dewey, John. *Democracy and Education.* New York: Free Press, 1916.

Dimidjian, Victoria Jean. "Holidays, Holy Days, and Wholly Dazed." *Young Children* 44 (September 1989): 70–75.

Drew, Naomi. *Learning the Skills of Peacemaking: An Activity Guide for Elementary-Age Children on Com-*

municating, Cooperating, Resolving Conflict. Rolling Hills Estates, CA: Jalmar Press, 1987.

Hennings, Dorothy Grant. "Reading Picture Storybooks in the Social Studies," Reading Teacher 35 (December 1982): 284–289.

Hernandez, Hilda. Multicultural Education: A Teacher's Guide to Content and Process. Columbus, OH: Merrill, 1989.

Kendall, Frances E. "Creating a Multicultural Environment." Pre-K Today (November/December 1988): 34–39.

Mitchell, Lucy S. "Making Young Geographers Instead of Teaching Geography." Progressive Education 5 (July/August/September 1928): 217–223.

National Association for the Education of Young Children. "Educating Yourself About Diverse Cultural Groups in Our Country by Reading." Young Children 48 (March 1993): 13–16.

National Council for Accreditation of Teacher Education. NCATE Standards, Procedures, and Policies for the Accreditation of Professional Units. Washington, DC: NCATE, 1987.

National Council of Social Studies Task Force on Early Childhood/ Elementary Social Studies. "Social Studies for Early Childhood and Elementary School Children: Preparing for the 21st Century." Social Education 53 (January 1989): 14–23.

Phillips, Carol Brunson. "Nurturing Diversity for Today's Children and Tomorrow's Leaders." Young Children 43 (January 1988): 42–47.

Ramsey, Patricia G. "Beyond 'Ten Little Indians' and Turkeys: Alternative Approaches to Thanksgiving." Young Children 34 (1979): 28–32, 49–52.

Ramsey, Patricia G. Teaching and Learning in a Diverse World: Multicultural Education for Young Children. New York: Teachers College Press, 1987.

Saracho, Olivia N., and Bernard Spodek, eds. Understanding the Multicultural Experience in Early Childhood Education. Washington, DC: National Association for the Education of Young Children, 1983.

Thomson, Barbara James. "Building Tolerance in Early Childhood." Educational Leadership 47 (October 1989): 78–79.

Timberlake, Pat. "Classroom Holidaze." Childhood Education (January 1978): 128–130.

Whaley, Kimberlee, and Elizabeth Blue Swadner. "Multicultural Education in Infant and Toddler Settings." Childhood Education 66 (Summer 1990): 238–240.

Children's Books

Aardema, Verna. Why Mosquitoes Buzz in People's Ears. New York: Scholastic, 1975.

Barton, Byron. Building a House. West Caldwell, NJ: Greenwillow, 1981.

Baylor, Byrd. Hawk, I'm Your Brother. New York: Aladdin Books, 1976.

Brett, Jan. Goldilocks and The Three Bears. New York: Dodd, Mead, 1987.

Brown, Marcia. Once a Mouse. New York: Atheneum, 1961.

Burton, Virginia L. The Little House. Boston: Houghton Mifflin, 1942.

Burton, Virginia L. Mike Mulligan and His Steam Shovel. Boston: Houghton Mifflin, 1939.

Crews, Donald. Truck. West Caldwell, NJ: Greenwillow, 1980.

de Paola, Tomie. Strega Nona. Englewood Cliffs, NJ: Prentice-Hall, 1975.

Galdone, Paul. Three Billy Goats Gruff. New York: Clarion Books, 1973.

Grimm, W. Jorinda and Joringel. New York: World, 1970.

Hader, Berta, and Elmer Hader. The Big Snow. New York: Collier Books, 1948.

Hall, Donald. Ox Cart Man. New York: Penguin Books, 1979.

Hutchins, Pat. Changes, Changes. New York: Aladdin Books, 1971.

Jarrell, Randall. Fisherman and His Wife: A Tale from the Brothers Grimm. New York: Farrar Straus and Giroux, 1980.

Lesser, Rika. Hansel and Gretel. New York: Dodd Mead, 1984.

Malotki, Ekkehart. The Mouse Couple: A Hopi Folktale. Flagstaff, AZ: Northland, 1988.

Mayer, Mercer. There's a Nightmare in My Closet. New York: Dial Books, 1968.

McDermott, Gerald. The Stonecutter. New York: Penguin Books, 1981.

Parnall, Peter. The Mountain. Garden City, NY: Doubleday, 1971.

Provensen, Alice, and Martin Provensen. Shaker Lane. New York: Viking Kestrel, 1987.

San Souci, Robert. *The Talking Eggs.* New York: Dial Books, 1989.

Sendak, Maurice. *Where the Wild Things Are.* New York: Harper and Row, 1963.

Steig, William. *Roland the Minstrel Pig.* New York: Simon and Schuster, 1968.

Steptoe, John. *Mufaro's Beautiful Daughters.* New York: Lothrop Lee and Shepard Books, 1987.

Young, Ed. *Lon Po Po.* New York: Philomel Books, 1989.

Zemach, Margot. *The Three Little Pigs.* New York: Farrar, Straus and Giroux, 1988.

Chapter Twelve

·····················

Wellness for the Young Child
Motor Development, Health, and Safety

goals

encouraging
motor development

children with
special needs

activities

MOTOR DEVELOPMENT,
HEALTH, AND SAFETY

integrating health/
safety education

health, nutrition,
and safety

Your classroom observations this week were at a local child-care center where the children ranged in age from two to five. The children were grouped by age. The center had a playground with equipment for climbing and sliding and areas for riding toys. You observed the threes and fours while they were outside. You saw the teacher help several children walk on a balance beam; he held most children's hands, but one or two walked alone. You also saw several children jumping over two ropes that the teacher had placed on a flat, grassy area. Others were climbing on a large dome-shaped climber, running up and down a slope in the play area, or playing catch with a large ball.

Some of your peers visited primary schools and reported seeing a variety of activities that were labeled "physical education." One of your classmates observed a second-grade class that played dodge ball for the entire physical education period. Another observed a second-grade class involved in noncompetitive activities that were set up in stations: hula hoops that the children could move around in various ways, bean bags to be tossed at targets, balls for throwing and bouncing, and a station for modified pushups. When the teacher blew the whistle, the children moved from station to station. The class ended with a whole-class activity in which the children performed various tasks with a parachute.

Clearly, physical education means different things to different teachers. Both you and your classmates are concerned about the goals of physical education and the guidelines for planning activities.

•••

In this era when physical fitness is of such concern to many adults, newspapers continue to report that U.S. children are neither as fit as they once were nor as fit as they should be. Many more children than ever before are obese, have limited capacity to perform physical tasks, or suffer from hypertension and cardiovascular disease. The solution to this problem lies in educating children to make more healthful choices in their lives—choices that include active exercise and a healthy diet. The list of fitness facts in this chapter emphasizes the need to develop the habit of healthy exercise in young children.

Fundamental motor skills
Basic motor skills such as moving, running, jumping, throwing, and so on.

Young children need the opportunity to develop **fundamental motor skills.** That does not mean that they need a workout program that will make them physically fit as adults. Seefeldt (1984) advises caution in devising a program designed to develop fitness in young children, because not enough is known about the relationship between physical fitness and overall health at this age; obviously, young children are different from other populations on which fitness data have been collected. However, Seefeldt does suggest that a planned program of physical education can be beneficial to young children.

ENCOURAGING MOTOR DEVELOPMENT

Young children need a variety of enjoyable experiences to give them both a broad range of physical skills and a disposition to continue to participate in physical activities. Grineski (1988) states that a physical education program can accomplish the following:

1. *Provide movement opportunities for children to explore and experiment with and in doing so allow them to express their pleasure in being a player or mover*

Teachers can encourage motor development through a variety of activities.

2. *Develop the psychomotor domain through a planned sequence of learning experiences designed to enhance body awareness, spatial awareness, balance, and fundamental motor skills*
3. *Promote the development of self-concept by providing more accurate perception of self through participation in a wide variety of success-oriented and appropriate physical education experiences*
4. *Develop minimal levels of physical fitness competence*
5. *Stimulate the development of imagination through game play, dramatic play, use of apparatus, tumbling, rhythmic expression, and movement exploration experiences*
6. *Promote the development of thought processes through participation in guided discovery and problem-solving activities*
7. *Facilitate the development of language skills through the use of movement-related terms*
8. *Enhance the development of social skills through experiences designed to promote positive interpersonal interactions with playmates (i.e., cooperative games) (pp. 92–93)*

Teachers know that motor development is important and can contribute to children's development in other areas. The psychomotor domain is stimulated by activities that require thought and deliberate movement, such as bouncing a ball, hitting a target with a ball, or hitting a ball with a bat. This area of development includes fundamental motor skills such as walking and running, which are necessary for participation in games and sports throughout life. Seefeldt (1984) notes that "the rudimentary skills which make up the components of our games and sports can be learned by children in an enriched environment before they are six years of age" (p. 35). He goes on to state that both opportunities for practice and motivation are at their highest levels in the early childhood years.

Although physical fitness for young children is more difficult to define than fitness for older populations (Seefeldt 1984), with a minimal level of physical fitness, young children will be able to perform physical tasks such as walking and running. Fitness is also defined by cardiorespiratory function, relative leanness, abdominal endurance, lower-back flexibility, and upper-body strength and endurance (Gober and Franks 1988; Leppo 1993; Ross and Pate 1987). Because children younger than age ten have been included in national studies of children's fitness only recently (Ross and Pate 1987), fitness for young children cannot be measured against a national standard; it can, however, be encouraged by teachers.

Teachers must not overlook physical education activities in their efforts to balance a program so that every area of a child's development is fostered. Physical education activities can contribute to a child's social and intellectual development as well as to physical development. For example, through sports or games, children learn to interact with others in positive ways. Children may learn the importance of interdependence and the feeling of belonging that being part of a team can offer. A child's self-concept may be enhanced as the child becomes physically skillful. Children gain intellectual skill by creating games and movements, expressing themselves as they negotiate in games, and solving problems related to physical goals. Working puzzles, cutting, and pushing buttons to operate teaching equipment all require not only thinking but physical skills, as well. Omwake (1971) reminds us that children need both physical skills and cognitive abilities to feel good about themselves. Emphasizing only cognitive abilities may strengthen a child in one area while undermining his ability in another.

Goals of Physical Development Programs

The goals of physical development programs for young children include having children participate in a variety of activities that will foster motor development; helping children develop gross motor skills; helping children develop a positive attitude toward active movement experiences; and helping children develop fine motor skills. These goals, like goals in other areas of curriculum, are broad and can best be met by a balance of planned and spontaneous activities. Activities designed for specialized skill development should never overshadow, replace, or serve as the primary purpose of general physical education (Gallahue 1981). However, teachers must make a concerted effort to involve children in active physical experiences. One study (Miller 1978) found that children in free-play situations often spent the time playing quietly and spent very little time in vigorous physical activities. Participation in vigorous activity can be increased through planned activities, teacher modeling and participation, and careful observation of children to ensure their involvement.

A developmentally appropriate program of physical education is based on three principles: "(1) motor skill development is sequential and age-related; (2) children progress through similar sequences of motor development; and (3) the rates at which children progress through sequences of motor development varies" (Grineski 1992, p. 33). Primary-age children should be involved in activities designed to help them develop movement awareness and basic motor skills. As in any other area of the curriculum, the teacher has to observe the children carefully in order to know when to increase the difficulty of the task and when to provide more time for development of individual skills.

Planned Activities

Physical education programs should include experiences with movement and games and activities that help to foster skill development. In each of these areas, activities must be matched to children's developmental levels and to the needs of individuals. Some children will be able to jump from a standing position or catch a ball while others will still be learning to walk backward or to go down steps by alternating feet.

When planning for individual differences, teachers can accommodate a wide variety of skill levels in the way that directions are given. For example, rather than asking all children to do headstands, teachers could ask all children to "find a way to balance using three parts of your body" (Petersen 1992, p. 37). As you read the following ideas for planned experiences, keep in mind that all activities must be evaluated in terms of their appropriateness for individual children.

Movement
In planning movement activities, emphasize the exploration of space and how one's body can move in space. Many movement activities can be enhanced with the addition of music or rhythmic accompaniment.

Jumping

Lay two ropes on the ground about ten inches apart, and allow children to practice a standing broad jump over them; as children's skills increase, move the ropes farther apart. Place hula hoops in a pattern across the floor or on flat ground so that children can jump from one to another. Position a sturdy bench or box so that children can jump off it safely. Encourage children to explore how they can turn while jumping or how they can stretch their bodies or make them as small as possible while jumping.

Climbing on Apparatus

Encourage children to think of different ways to hang, move, stretch, or curl and to find different ways to get on and off the apparatus safely.

Following an Obstacle Course

Build an obstacle course with materials in the classroom. For example, create a path to follow that requires children to crawl under a table, climb over a sturdy bench, jump through a series of hula hoops placed on the floor, and crawl through a tunnel created with a quilt and chairs. Invite children to move over, around, under, and through in as many ways as possible.

Rolling and Tumbling

If you have a grassy slope that children can roll down, use it. If not, encourage children to roll and find ways to turn their bodies on mats.

Using a Parachute

Preschool children can enjoy stretching a parachute and moving it up and down. They also enjoy getting under it. Older, more well-coordinated children can enjoy games in which they bounce objects on the parachute, take turns running under it, and use it in stretching and rhythmic activities.

Games

Games such as circle games in which only one person is "it" often require all other participants to sit or stand and wait for most of the play period. Better choices are games that involve the whole group. Teachers can invent games of Tag with multiple "its" for kindergarten and primary children.

For preschool children, one game that keeps everyone moving is Soap Bubbles, in which all the children move within a marked space without touching anyone else. If children touch, they "burst" and must make themselves as small as possible. (Children who have been touched can move outside the space and continue moving.) The game begins with a very large space, but the teacher moves the space markers so that there is less and less space until most children have been touched. This game can be accompanied by music (Pangrazi and Dauer 1992).

Many games for primary children involve an entire group in movement activities. One example is Back-to-Back, for which there must be an uneven number of children. Children pair off and stand back-to-back; the child left over claps her hands and calls out a movement ("run," "hop," "skip," "slide," "gallop," or "jump"). Following the command, each child must move forward a certain distance and then turn and find a new partner; the one left over becomes the leader for the next round. In a similar game called Stop and Start, the children are spaced far enough apart to move freely. The leader calls out a movement, such as "skip." All the children move until the leader signals them to stop. Any child who moves after that must wait on the sidelines for one round.

Skill Activities

Throwing and Catching

Very young children should practice throwing with relatively large, soft balls. Balls about six inches in diameter are easiest to catch. Threes and fours can begin to catch with their arms extended. A yarn ball or a Nerf ball is good for these children. Children can be encouraged to throw a ball as high as possible, to roll it on the ground, and to stop the ball with their feet or other body parts while it is rolling. Children can also toss the ball with two hands, with one hand, and play catch with a partner. Tossing bean bags or tossing or rolling small balls at a target (a bowling pin or an empty bleach bottle) are also appropriate activities.

Kicking and Batting

Primary children can begin to learn to kick a ball. To learn how, they should begin with a stationary ball and be encouraged to tap the ball with their feet, to tap it so that it goes to a partner, and to kick the ball to a target area. Batting a ball should also begin with the ball stationary, perhaps on a cone. Children should be encouraged to think of as many ways to hit the ball as possible.

CHILDREN WITH SPECIAL NEEDS

Children with special needs can participate in outdoor play and physical education activities with some adaptations in equipment and in activities. The teacher must consider the developmental level of the individual child and the child's abilities when planning for physical experiences. Children with mental retardation can participate in most outdoor activities, but they may need more encouragement and more praise than other children. Teachers may have to help children with retardation establish motor patterns by moving them into positions or by modeling behaviors over and over. These children may also make less rapid progress, and teachers should be aware that children may have to repeat activities many times before mastering them.

Children with visual disabilities can participate in many climbing, swinging, and sliding experiences without adaptations. For skill activities for these children, the teacher will need to be attentive to lighting conditions and equipment choices. For example, Pangrazi and Dauer (1981) recommend that when teaching a child with visual limitations to catch a ball, the area should be well lighted and a yellow ball should be used. In certain games, children with visual limitations can get help from other children; the teacher can make sure that tactile information is provided to help children identify home base, boundary lines, and so on.

Auditory disabilities rarely prevent children from participating fully in physical activities. Such children should be placed in front of the teacher so they can read lips and have the best opportunity for hearing directions. Children with auditory disabilities may need interpreters in order to follow the directions in games and may need visual signals to supplement some auditory signals. For example, if children were playing Stop and Start, described earlier, the teacher could wave a flag when the group was to stop moving.

Teachers who want to involve children with orthopedic disabilities in programs of physical education should first consult with the child's physician or case manager to determine the level of activity recommended. A physical education specialist can help the teacher make the adaptations that will benefit each child. Some will need modified equipment, for example, a bat with straps that enable the child to hold it. Others will need to use larger or softer balls or to participate in activities that involve upper-body strength if their legs are immobile. Every child needs to interact as much as possible with other children, and physical education should not be inaccessible to children with disabilities.

Pangrazi and Dauer (1992) recommend that teachers think about modifications for youngsters lacking strength and endurance by lowering or enlarging goals, softening balls, reducing the distance balls must be thrown, and using lighter balls and bats. If coordination is a problem, teachers should have children begin with stationary objects when learning to strike an object; throw for velocity without concern for accuracy when learning to throw; and use soft, lightweight objects for catching, such as beach balls and balloons. For children who lack ability in balance, teachers might increase the width on balance beams; suggest learning to balance with as many body parts touching the floor as possible; provide assistance with balance, such as a cane or chair; and think about play surfaces so that children are not playing on slick floors with slick shoes (pp. 133–134).

HEALTH, NUTRITION, AND SAFETY

Helping children develop their physical abilities and encouraging them to be physically active is certainly important. It is also important to help children learn to make good choices in health practices, nutrition, and safety. Young children, of course, do not make these choices without guidance from parents and teachers, but they can begin to develop healthy habits.

Health Education

Historically, health care was an important goal of early preschool programs. In today's world of more personal responsibility for health, education for healthful choices continues to be important; however, it tends to be overlooked in many programs (Bruhn and Nader 1982). Because children and young adults do not perceive themselves as vulnerable to illness (Gochman and Saucier 1982), health educators have recommended that programs in health education be developed and implemented for children as young as two or three (Kingsbury and Hall 1988).

Personal Routines

Health education is not a lesson to be taught on a schedule. It must be integrated throughout the day and made a part of many activities. Children learn about good health habits in many ways: observing parents and teachers (especially those who take time to explain why they are making the decisions that they make); listening to stories; and making regular visits to the doctor and dentist. For example, as children wash their hands after using the toilet and before eating, the teacher can mention the importance of cleanliness in staying healthy; as children brush their teeth after eating, the teacher may demonstrate how to hold the brush and point out that brushing down over the teeth is best. Brushing teeth can be encouraged if the children can reach their own toothbrushes and the sink so that they can be independent about the task. A visit by a dental hygienist to demonstrate the correct procedures for brushing and flossing will remind children to brush on a regular basis. The children might also visit a dentist's office and get a chance to sit in the chair and look at the tools and equipment. A flashlight and a chair will probably be all the children need to play "dentist" after such a visit. When a child loses a tooth, the teacher is given a perfect opportunity for discussing and reading about teeth—how they grow and the importance of caring for them.

A significant portion of health education in early childhood programs will be taught as daily routines are established. Children will learn to wash their hands after using the toilet or blowing their noses or before eating and to brush their teeth after eating. As they participate in these routines, they can be taught the reasons these behaviors are important. Although young children are not able to understand the causal relationships between germs and disease, they can understand that regular hygiene routines contribute to their staying well and feeling healthy.

Teachers also must be aware of sanitary procedures that will help prevent illness. Teachers of infants and toddlers must be careful to wash their hands thoroughly after diapering or assisting children at the toilet. Often teachers of young children must help them blow their noses or clean their faces after a sneeze. Teachers should scrub their hands after every such incident. Teachers must also model the importance of washing their hands carefully before either serving or cooking food. Changing tables and tables where food is served should be scrubbed and disinfected regularly.

Medical Procedures

The health education program should also include helping children become more comfortable and accepting of medical procedures, health care professionals, and hospitals. Parents should be involved in planning these particular activities, as they can provide specific information about their children's experiences and possible fears. Many activities in the classroom—such as playing with puppets, listening to stories, playing with toy medical equipment (or real equipment, if that is possible and appropriate), and meeting health care professionals—can help children understand and feel more positive about medical care. Field trips to the offices of health care professionals and to hospitals can also be arranged. These trips must be planned carefully, but most hospitals have programs for educating even very young children about being in the hospital.

Children can learn some simple first aid procedures. One program uses puppets to dramatize stories in which first aid is required (Marchand and McDermott 1986). Children learn first aid procedures and why they are necessary. They also learn to select the most appropriate procedure from the alternatives available and how to use the telephone to get help in an emergency.

Substance Abuse and AIDS

Two relatively new facets of health education for young children are substance abuse programs and programs to educate children about AIDS (acquired immune deficiency syndrome). In many public schools, such programs are now required. With so much about drugs and AIDS on television and in the conversations of adults, teachers in preschool settings must be able to answer children's questions and understand their fears. Early childhood educators are in a unique position to contribute to preventing drug abuse and educating the public about AIDS, because both problems affect many children's lives directly and because early childhood educators can work with parents in ways that have positive results over long periods of time.

In a longitudinal study that followed a group of children from the time they were five until they were eighteen, Shedler and Block (1990) found that young adults who were frequent users of drugs were relatively maladjusted as children of seven years old. The frequent users were described at age seven as

> *not getting along well with other children, not showing concern for moral issues (e.g., reciprocity, fairness), having bodily symptoms from stress, tending to be indecisive and vacillating, not planful or likely to think ahead, not trustworthy or dependable, not able to admit to negative feelings, not self-reliant or confident, preferring nonverbal methods of communication, not developing genuine and close relationships, not proud of their accomplishments, not vital or energetic or lively, not curious and open to new experience, not able to recoup after stress, afraid of being deprived, appearing to feel unworthy and "bad," not likely to identify with admired adults, inappropriate in emotive behavior, and easily victimized and scapegoated by other children. (p. 618)*

Based on these findings, Shedler and Block (1990) recommend that resources for prevention of drug abuse be focused on intervening in the development of the personality syndrome that underlies drug use, rather than on campaigns such as "Just Say No." The research highlights the importance of positive experiences for children at home and at school that will develop stronger self-concepts, more skill in social interactions, and more prosocial behaviors.

Even young children know about AIDS and may fear that they or people close to them will catch the disease. Children see programs, news stories, and commercials on television aimed at educating the public about AIDS, but they rarely understand what they see and hear. Teachers who feel the need to provide information about AIDS must consider the children's cognitive development and needs when making decisions about what to say. As Skeen and Hodson (1987) remind us:

> We do not want young children (who, as we all know, muddle the most carefully correct sex information) to get it into their heads that sex will kill you. We do not want young children (many of whom fear when they see blood oozing from a small cut that they will deflate like a balloon losing its air and cease to exist) to begin worrying about poisoned blood inside them. We do not want young children, for whom it is overridingly important to trust that grownups, most especially parents, will protect them, to be told that babies can be given AIDS through their mothers' blood! Information is not always good. (p. 69)

Teachers of young children can be prepared to answer children's questions in positive ways. For example, they can say that AIDS is a disease but that children who do not have it are not likely to catch it and that children cannot get it from touching a person who has it. Most children asking such questions are seeking reassurance that they are safe; they do not need a lesson on adult sexual behavior or drug use. Parents also may need guidance in what to say when children ask them questions. Primary-grade children are likely to encounter some sort of planned instruction that is aimed at making children aware of the dangers of AIDS. The goals of most programs for primary children are limited to having the children understand that they cannot contract AIDS by being with or touching someone who has AIDS.

When making a decision about what to tell children when one of their classmates has AIDS, teachers will have to exercise their own judgment, based on knowledge of the children and how much they have heard from parents. If the children know that a child is ill and ask questions, the teacher should answer as honestly as possible while helping children feel safe from the disease.

Even though young children do not need to know much about AIDS, teachers *do* need to know. The National Education Association has published a handbook of information entitled *The Facts About AIDS* (Bauer et al. undated). Because many teachers will have children who have AIDS in class or will know of parents who have AIDS, they will be faced with providing information to other parents; thus, teachers need accurate, up-to-date information. They also need to work together to determine the best alternatives for teaching children about AIDS and the best information to provide to parents (Fetter 1989).

Nutrition Education

Food is not only basic to life; it is closely related to people's social and cultural lives. Food is an integral part of family, religious, and cultural celebrations. Many aspects of food are culturally determined: what people think is appropriate to eat; how they eat it (with fingers, pieces of bread, chopsticks, or forks); with whom they eat (with other men, with women and children, or in family groups); and when they eat during the day. How food is used socially is also culturally determined. Many people offer guests something to eat or drink as soon as they are in their homes, and food is often central to social gatherings. For years, business was conducted over lunch—now people even have "power breakfasts"! Teaching children to make healthy choices in the food they select is certainly a worthwhile goal and one that will affect their lives through adulthood.

Nutrition education is important because children commonly have problems related to nutrition. Although children do not often have control over what they are offered to eat, they do make choices from the food offered to them. The choices provided for them in a school setting should be nutritious and should help them learn about food and nutrition. Physical problems related to nutrition include tooth decay, obesity, iron deficiency anemia, and hypersensitivity to foods. Teachers need to focus on providing nutritious snacks; controlling the amounts of sugar, salt, and fiber in children's school diets; and establishing good food habits.

The following conceptual framework for teaching children about nutrition is based on the findings of the White House Conference on Food, Nutrition, and Health (1969):

1. *Nutrition is the process by which food and other substances eaten become you. The food you eat enables you to live, to grow, to keep healthy and well, and to get energy for work and play.*
2. *Food is made up of certain chemical substances that work together and interact with body chemicals to serve the needs of the body.*
3. *Each nutrient has specific uses in the body.*
4. *The nutrients needed by the body are usually available through food.*
5. *Many kinds and combinations of food can lead to a well balanced diet.*

6. *No food, by itself, has all the nutrients needed for full growth and health.*
7. *The way food is handled influences the amount of nutrients in the food, its safety, appearance, taste, and cost.*
8. *Throughout their lives, all humans need about the same nutrients, but in varying amounts.*
9. *Food use relates to the cultural, social, economic, and psychological aspects of living. (p. 151)*

Appropriate goals for nutrition education with young children based on this framework would include helping children learn to eat a variety of foods; increasing children's awareness of their reasons for selecting certain foods; and helping children develop positive attitudes about food.

Notice that these broad goals do not include teaching children to recite the four food groups on cue. Primary children might find it meaningful to classify foods according to their contributions to a healthy diet, but Herr and Morse (1982) believe that classifying foods into four groups requires more skill in generalization than should be expected from young children. They recommend that foods be categorized into ten groups: milk, meat, dried peas and beans, eggs, fruits, vegetables, breads, pastas, cereals/ grains/seeds, and nuts.

The goals of teaching children sound eating habits can be achieved in the classroom by offering nutritious snacks and meals and through food preparation experiences. Teachers are responsible for the quality of food that children are offered; children can then choose if and how much they are going to eat. The following is a list of foods appropriate for snacks:

Raw Vegetables

Celery	Cauliflower flowerets
Peas in pod	Turnip sticks
Cucumber wedges	Jicama sticks
Tomato slices	Broccoli flowerets

Fresh Fruits

Apple wedges	Pineapple cubes
Orange segments	Pear or peach slices
Banana slices	Kiwi
Strawberries	Papaya
Blueberries	Mango

Other Snacks

Unsweetened fruit juice	Cottage cheese
Dried fruit	Peanut butter
Milk	Muffins
Milkshakes made from milk and fruit	Dry cereals (unsweetened)
Lowfat yogurt	Whole-grain crackers
Cheese	

In programs where children are offered lunch or both breakfast and lunch, teachers should follow the guidelines of the U.S. Department of Agriculture (USDA 1986) or the guidelines in the accreditation standards of the National Association for the Education of Young Children (NAEYC 1984) describing the nutritional and caloric requirements for children.

Teachers of children younger than three will want to be especially careful not to offer children food they cannot chew easily, such as raw carrots or peanuts, or bite-sized pieces of food that they can swallow without chewing. Foods such as raisins and popcorn can easily cause choking. Unless the children can be supervised carefully while they eat, other foods are better choices.

Teachers and parents must work together in order to achieve the goals of nutrition education. If parents know what teachers are trying to do with nutrition information, they can help reinforce the ideas. For example, teachers who work in schools where children bring their own snacks to school can ask parents to cooperate in sending only nutritious snacks for the children. A letter explaining the importance of reducing the sugar in children's diets (Rogers and Morris 1986) and a list of suggested snacks will aid parents in choosing snack foods that are appropriate.

One strategy for helping children learn to eat a variety of foods is to offer new foods at snack time. Rothlein (1989) suggests the following ways to make adding new foods to a child's diet relatively easy:

1. *Introduce only one new food at a time.*
2. *Serve the new food with familiar foods.*
3. *Serve only small amounts of the new food—begin with one teaspoon.*
4. *Introduce new foods only when the child is hungry.*
5. *Talk with the child about the new food—taste, color, texture, and shape.*
6. *Encourage the child to taste the new food but do not force the child to eat it. If the food item is rejected, accept the refusal calmly and try again in a few weeks. As foods become more familiar, children more readily accept them.*

7. If the child rejects the food, try to determine why she didn't like it. Often children will accept a food if it is prepared and presented in a different way. For example, raw carrots may be accepted although cooked carrots are refused.

8. Provide cooking experiences. When children are involved in preparing the food, they have more of an interest in tasting it.

9. Be a model! If children observe adults eating and enjoying new foods, they are more likely to enjoy them. Remember that young children often imitate the eating habits of their parents, and that the child's food habits—likes and dislikes—frequently reflect the parents'. Children can learn to accept foods disliked by a parent if they are presented positively and if Mom and Dad take a few bites themselves! Help parents see the wisdom of doing this. As a caregiver or teacher, model a curious approach to new foods yourself.

10. Finally, keep trying. . . . A child's fear of a new food can be reduced by simply increasing exposure to the food. (p. 34)*

To help older children learn to appreciate new foods, involve them in cooking experiences as part of their social studies or science studies, ask parents or volunteers to share special cultural or ethnic dishes, and taste foods that are mentioned in stories that they read or hear. For example, if the teacher reads the Paddington books aloud to the class, he could have children taste marmalade and could explain its place in a healthy diet.

Cooking Experiences

Many teachers involve children in preparing foods for snacks or meals to be eaten at school. Even very young children can spread peanut butter or cheese on their crackers, sprinkle topping on their toast, or make simple sandwiches. Older children can peel vegetables, cut fruit, squeeze oranges to make juice, make English muffin pizzas with cheese and pizza sauce, and cut up apples for applesauce. Kindergarten and primary children can read and follow simple recipes for a variety of foods. Teachers should be aware of certain guidelines for cooking experiences:

1. Cook only nutritious foods.
2. Let the children do the cooking. Watching while the teacher measures the ingredients and then getting to stir does not give children a feel-

*From Liz Rothlein, "Nutrition Tips Revisited: On a Daily Basis Do We Implement What We Know?" *Young Children* 44 (September 1989): 30–36. Reprinted with permission from NAEYC.

ing of being involved. In planning a cooking experience, consider the maturity and skills of the children. Can they do what is required—measure, cut, mix, and so on? How many children can participate in the activity? Experiences should be planned for individuals or very small groups.

3. Plan for the children's safety, particularly if an experience involves heat or cutting. Make sure children are carefully supervised when using sources of heat. Tape electrical cords of appliances to the wall so that children cannot trip over them and pull appliances off the table; position appliances so that spills land on the table rather than on the floor. Make sure that children understand how to use cutting tools and sources of heat safely.

4. Be attentive to cleanliness. Are the children's hands and the utensils clean? In some areas of the United States, hepatitis has been a problem and teachers have been asked not to cook at school. Check local policies before cooking in the classroom.

Teachers will of course want to anticipate the learning outcomes that will be possible from a cooking experience. Children will be able to relate content from other subject-matter areas to cooking experiences. The following are only a few examples of the possibilities:

- *Science*—Observing changes in matter such as melting, congealing, shrinking (greens before and after cooking), expanding (rice before and after cooking), and transformation of water into steam
- *Language*—Learning cooking vocabulary, such as *boil, simmer, roll, knead, dice, shred,* and *grate,* as well as the names of foods and utensils
- *Mathematics*—Comparing quantities, measuring
- *Social Studies*—Working cooperatively, learning about people involved in food production, preparing or tasting ethnic or cultural foods, and learning about food customs
- *Literacy*—Reading recipes or charts, connecting food experiences to stories (for example, making blueberry muffins after reading *Blueberries for Sal* [McCloskey 1948]), writing shopping lists, writing recipes, collecting and illustrating booklets of favorite recipes

Teachers can find many cookbooks containing nutritious and practical recipes for cooking experiences. The picture recipes in Figures 12.1 and 12.2 are from *Cook and Learn: Pictorial Single Portion Recipes* (Veitch and Harms 1981).

FIGURE 12.1 Picture Recipe

Source: From *Cook and Learn* by B. Veitch and T. Harms. Copyright © 1981 by Addison-Wesley Publishing Company, Innovative Division. Reprinted by permission.

FIGURE 12.2 Picture Recipe

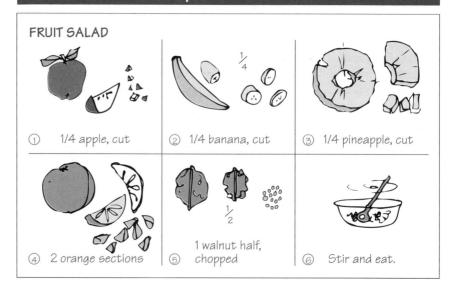

Source: From *Cook and Learn* by B. Veitch and T. Harms. Copyright © 1981 by Addison-Wesley Publishing Company, Innovative Division. Reprinted by permission.

Safety Education

Teachers of young children need to address questions of fire safety, traffic safety, water safety, poison safety, and personal safety. The teacher is responsible for checking the classroom and the play yard for any safety hazards, planning for emergencies, teaching children safe behaviors and what to do in an emergency, and supervising children closely. Pickle (1989) demonstrated that even preschoolers can benefit from instruction in safety education; primary children can also benefit from such instruction.

Fire Safety

Most elementary schools have a fire safety program that includes visits from local firefighters, poster contests about fire prevention, instruction about what to do if there is a fire, and regular fire drills. A fire safety program should help children recognize the danger of fire and learn to treat fire with caution; prepare children to respond appropriately during a fire through regular fire drills; and teach children how to call the fire department.

Every classroom should have a written plan of action in case of fire, which specifies the duties and responsibilities of each person (who will check the restroom, who will be responsible for children who are disabled, who will carry the class list, and so on), the exits to be used, and the point of assembly outside. Every teacher should practice fire drills on a regular basis. In some drills, selected exits should be blocked; drills should be planned to occur at unpredictable times such as meal times or nap times. Near each exit, teachers should post a map showing all exits and routes for evacuating the building and a class list to be used to account for the children after the building has been evacuated. Finally, teachers should provide parents with information about the fire drill procedures at school and encourage parents to plan regular fire drills at home.

Asking a local firefighter to visit the classroom can help promote children's awareness of fire safety. Most fire departments have an educational specialist who is responsible for teaching children fire prevention and fire safety. These people are usually talented in communicating with young children; they can teach children the "stop, drop, and roll" technique and demonstrate the pieces of equipment used by firefighters. Some firefighters encourage children to touch or try on equipment so that it does not frighten them when they see it on a firefighter. If children do try on firefighting gear, the firefighter can talk to the children about how different they look when they wear it. It is important that children recognize and not be afraid of firefighters in full gear in case they should ever have to be rescued from a fire. Teachers should preview any presentation to assure that it is appropriate for their children.

All children should be taught that in the case of a fire, they should leave the building or house first and then call the fire department. In the dramatic play area, a toy telephone and a large poster with the numbers to be dialed can help children practice dialing "0" or "911" to call the fire department in an emergency. Primary children might benefit from reading *The 9 Lives of El Gato the Cat* (Consumer Product Safety Commission 1983), a comic book that reviews the most common causes of fires and burns and explains what to do in case of fire. *Protect Someone You Love from Burns* is another publication of the Consumer Product Safety Commission (1978) that reviews fire safety.

Traffic Safety

Teachers must share with parents the responsibilities for teaching children about traffic safety. The most frequent accidents involving children are those in which the child darts into the street, usually in the middle of the block. Goals of a traffic safety program include teaching children to stop

Teachers and parents can help children learn traffic safety.

before entering a street; teaching children how to cross a street safely; and teaching children to interpret traffic signals.

With repetition and the cooperation of parents, teachers can impress upon children the importance of stopping at every curb. If there are no curbs on local streets, children should be taught to identify the boundary of the street and to stop there every time.

Children need direct experience in looking and listening for traffic and then walking—not running—across the street. Often, very young children do not know what to look and listen for when they approach a street. With guidance from teachers and parents, they can learn to look and listen for approaching traffic and to cross carefully after the traffic has cleared. Children also must learn to make sure that drivers of stopped vehicles have seen them before crossing in front of the vehicles. Children may also need help understanding directions from crossing guards at school crossings. It may be prudent to teach children younger than four not to cross the street at all unless an adult tells them it is safe to do so.

Street crossings can be simulated in the dramatic play area so children can practice stopping, looking and listening for traffic, and walking carefully across the street. An area outdoors can be marked as a street, especially where children are riding wheel toys, and with guidance, the children can practice crossing these "streets" carefully. The teacher might also mark some streets on the floor inside with masking tape and have the children role-play pedestrians and drivers of vehicles as they practice traffic safety. Teachers can make or purchase replicas of traffic signals for the block center and help the children set up their own streets, complete with signals, and practice safety procedures.

The third goal, teaching children to interpret traffic signals, can be furthered by constructing paper traffic signals or wiring a simple signal to a battery. Games such as Mother, May I? help children learn to move when the signal is green and stop when the signal is yellow or red. Teachers can invent other games based on Follow the Leader or Tag in which children must respond to traffic signals.

With help from a police officer and volunteers, the children can be taken to an intersection and helped to cross the street with the signals provided. At intersections in some communities, children must learn to read symbols or the word WALK, rather than traffic signals. Pictures or posters of these words and symbols will teach the children to interpret them.

Involve parents by explaining what you are trying to teach in traffic safety and seek their help in reinforcing the same rules when they are with their children. Both parents and teachers must model safe traffic behavior if children are to learn it.

NAEYC (1990) has published a curriculum package called *Walk in Traffic Safely*. The kit contains two story books, one for twos and threes and one for fours and fives; a teacher's guide that suggests discussion questions and learning concepts; a brochure for parents; and a poster to remind children about traffic safety. Two other NAEYC curriculum packets also relate to traffic safety. One is entitled *We Love You—Buckle Up!* and the other is called *Children Riding on Sidewalks Safely* (both NAEYC 1987).

Water Safety

Discussions of water play in this book have stressed that such play should be carefully supervised. Water play is enjoyable and important for meeting program goals, and teachers should not hesitate to include water play in their programs—but it must be supervised. In some areas where backyard swimming pools are very popular, drowning has become the leading cause of death for young children. Children should never be left unsupervised when near swimming pools, lakes, or ponds. Even children in wading pools must have constant supervision.

No child should ever be allowed to swim alone, even if she is a capable swimmer. Swimming lessons do not make a child immune to danger, and supervision should not be relaxed simply because a child has had swimming lessons. The American Academy of Pediatrics (AAP) (1988) recommends that only children three and older be given swimming lessons. The AAP's view is that the risk of contracting infectious disease or swallowing dangerous amounts of water during swimming lessons are too great for children younger than three.

Poison Safety

Teachers have a responsibility to make sure that school environments are poison free. Anything poisonous, including ornamental plants, should be removed. Cleaning compounds or other hazardous materials must be stored in locked cabinets, out of children's reach. All such materials must be carefully marked with poison symbols and never stored in food containers.

Children must learn that they are never to eat any unknown substance or anything that is not food. Children younger than three or four cannot be expected to remember not to put objects in their mouths. Teachers of children this young need to take extra precautions to remove any dangerous items and to supervise the children closely.

Children should be taught to recognize the symbol for poison and to avoid containers that show it. Teachers should keep in mind that many household chemicals, such as automatic dishwasher detergent, are very dangerous if ingested yet are not marked with the poison symbol. Children must learn to recognize these dangerous items.

Helping children learn about safety is the responsibility of many people in the community.

Personal Safety

Periodically, horror stories in the news remind us that the world is not always a safe place for children. Children must learn some rules of personal safety. In many police departments, officers are specially trained to communicate to children the importance of not talking to, accepting rides with, or taking treats from strangers. Many young children do not know what the word *stranger* means—they must be given practice in distinguishing strangers from people they know.

Identifying strangers might be made into a game, using pictures of familiar people and unfamiliar people so that children develop the concept that an unknown person is a stranger. Children might also role-play what to do if approached by a stranger offering treats or rides. Parents might be alerted to the dangers of having their child's name displayed on clothing or backpacks, which makes children identifiable; young children will be confused if a stranger knows their name.

Teaching children about "safe touching" from people they know is also very important. In many communities, groups present puppet plays that help children understand the difference between "good touching" and "bad touching." Films can also help teachers convey these messages to children, and children might role-play how to tell the appropriate person if they have been touched inappropriately.

Many primary-grade children are *latchkey children,* meaning that they stay alone after school until their parents return from work. Many communities offer special programs for helping these children learn rules for safety and for feeling more secure while they are alone. In the best of worlds, young children would not be left alone, but if they are, they need some guidance in answering the telephone and the door and in practicing fire safety and first aid. Efforts to keep children safe must involve the parents, the school, and the community.

INTEGRATING HEALTH AND SAFETY EDUCATION

Many health and safety concepts can best be taught by establishing healthy routines, modeling healthy choices for the children, and incorporating discussions about health or safety procedures into the normal activities of the day. Children will learn nutrition lessons at snack and meal times by what is served and through conversations with the teacher. Traffic safety can be reviewed every time children go on a walk, although instruction should not be limited to these reviews. Some safety lessons can also be incorporated into other experiences. For example, if the focus in literacy were on reading environmental print, then poison signs and traffic signs could be incorporated into the experience. However, some safety instruction should be included in the curriculum even if it cannot be integrated

DEVELOPMENTALLY APPROPRIATE PRACTICE

Think about your readings, your observations, and your experiences as you respond to the following statements about developmentally appropriate practice in physical education and health:

- A developmentally appropriate physical education program offers children a challenge at the level of their individual abilities.
- An outside play period is sufficient for physical education in a developmentally appropriate program.

- Some areas of health education require direct instruction, which does not normally fit a developmentally appropriate program.
- The guidelines for DAP state that teachers of young children are responsible for children's total development, not just academic or intellectual development.

INTEGRATING THE CURRICULUM

Think about the many patterns that occur in physical activities:

- Step, step, hop in skipping
- Left, right, left, right in marching
- Heel, toe, heel, toe in walking the balance beam
- Up, down, up, down in bouncing

In health education, children can find patterns in many topics:

- Food groups
- Safety signs
- Surface coverings that show ends of sidewalks, beginnings of streets
- "STOP," "GO," and "WALK" of traffic signals
- Toothbrushing patterns

with other classroom experiences. Teachers may choose to present short lessons on safety once a week or so throughout the year; this approach is more effective than focusing on a safety theme and concentrating all the instruction in a one- or two-week period.

Physical education and nutrition experiences are easier to integrate into the classroom routine than safety instruction. If, for example, the current theme were animals, children could imitate animal movements, learn what animals need to eat to be healthy, compare human food to animal food, and so on. If the theme focused on the neighborhood, children could determine how food is obtained and distributed in the neighborhood and identify facilities for physical activities (parks, jogging trails, exercise stations, courts for basketball or volleyball, and so on). Science activities can include growing food and observing changes in foods as they cook. Social studies experiences can include visiting producers or distributors of food; learning about what manners are considered appropriate in different cultures (in some cultures, people eat with their fingers; in other cultures, people do so only with certain foods or at specific times, such as at picnics); and learning about who prepares food in different cultures (men, women, or both).

Physical education and nutrition education can easily be integrated into literacy experiences. In addition to tasting foods mentioned in stories, children can create ABC books or reference books of healthy foods, learn to read recipes, find foods mentioned in stories, write stories about special times when food is served in their homes, and find food words used in conversation (for example, "That's peachy," "He's a ham," "That car is a lemon"). They can create movements to tell stories, describe movements after they do them, write about how exercise makes them feel, keep records of their exercise, and find examples of movements or exercise in the books they hear or read.

CHAPTER SUMMARY

- Planned physical education programs should include movement, games, and activities to foster skill development.
- Physical activities can be adapted to allow children with special needs to participate. Adaptations might include modifying equipment and structuring experiences so that children can achieve goals.
- Children learn health concepts best when they are integrated with daily classroom routines, such as washing hands and brushing teeth.
- Children need to learn the importance of cleanliness and to become more comfortable with medical procedures and health professionals.

- Today's teachers must be prepared to help children resist substance abuse, to communicate with parents, and to answer children's questions about drug abuse and AIDS.
- Children can begin to learn about healthful foods through snacks and meals served at school. They can also learn about nutrition through cooking experiences.
- Teachers of young children must incorporate lessons on fire safety, traffic safety, poison safety, water safety, and personal safety into their programs. Parents should be involved in these efforts.

WHAT WOULD YOU DO?

Reflect on your reading and your own experiences with young children as you think about the following situations:

1. The physical education teacher has no experience with DAP. What would you tell him are the significant criteria for a developmentally appropriate program for young children?
2. A child in your first-grade class wants to stay inside every day, rather than go outside for physical education. What would you do to encourage this child's participation?

3. Your preschool does not have a physical education specialist. Some of the parents would like the children to have lessons in tumbling. What would you tell them about the possibility of tumbling lessons?
4. You are asked to speak at the parent-teacher association meeting about the need for physical education for young children. What would you tell parents?

THEORY INTO PRACTICE

1. Plan experiences in movement and physical skills development for a group of four-year-olds and for a group of seven-year-olds.
2. Find a recipe for a nutritious snack. Plan for a certain age group to prepare this snack. Be sure to think about the skills necessary for success with this experience, given the age of the group. Construct an outline that would help a volunteer supervise this experience. What steps

should be followed? What skills and vocabulary should be emphasized?
3. Make a list of the resources in your community that can assist in providing safety instruction for young children. What programs do the fire and police departments have to offer? Do any other community groups offer safety programs?
4. Plan a literacy experience that incorporates physical education or nutrition activities.

RECOMMENDED FOR FURTHER READING

Engstrom, Georgianna, ed. *The Significance of the Young Child's Motor Development*. Washington, DC: National Association for the Education of Young Children, 1971.

   Even though this book is somewhat older than the resources usually recommended, it has some up-to-date information. It is a collection of papers delivered at a conference of the American Association for Health, Physical Education, and Recreation and the National Association for the Education of Young Children. One of the most useful chapters for new teachers is on observing young children's motor experiences.

McCracken, Janet Brown. *Keeping Healthy: Parents, Teachers, and Children*. NAEYC Brochure 577.

Washington, DC: National Association for the Education of Young Children, 1988.

   This brochure reviews health practices and is a good resource for sharing with parents.

Wanamaker, Nancy, Kristin Hearn, and Sherrill Richarz. *More Than Graham Crackers: Nutrition Education and Food Preparation with Young Children*. Washington, DC: National Association for the Education of Young Children, 1979.

   In addition to containing nutritious recipes for cooking experiences, this book provides information about nutrition education and teaching nutrition through cooking experiences.

REFERENCES

General Sources

American Academy of Pediatrics. *Safe Swimming for Your Young Child*. Washington, DC: AAP, 1988. (This leaflet is one in a series called "TIPP: The Injury Prevention Program.")

Bauer, Nancy, Martin Botel, Helen O. Dickens, Kenneth D. George, Sol Levin, Aaron H. Katcher, and Irving E. Sigel. *The Facts About AIDS: A Special*

Guide for NEA Members. Washington, DC: National Education Association Health Information Network, no date.

Bruhn, John G., and Philip R. Nader. "The School as a Setting for Health Education, Health Promotion, and Health Care." *Family and Community Health* 4 (1982): 57–59.

Fetter, M. Patricia. "AIDS Education: Every Teacher's Responsibility." *Childhood Education* 65 (Spring 1989): 150–152.

Gallahue, David L. "Fundamental Movement Experiences for Children: A Developmental Skill Theme Approach." ERIC Document Reproduction Service 211459. Paper presented at the annual conference of the Indiana Association for Health, Physical Education, Recreation, and Dance, Lafayette, Indiana, 1981.

Gober, Billy E., and B. Don Franks. "Physical and Fitness Education of Young Children." *Journal of Physical Education, Recreation, and Dance* 59 (September 1988): 57–61.

Gochman, David S., and T. F. Saucier. "Perceived Vulnerability in Children and Adolescents." *Health Education Quarterly* 9 (1982): 46–59.

Grineski, Steven. "Teaching and Learning in Physical Education for Young Children." *Journal of Physical Education, Recreation and Dance* 59 (May/June 1988): 91–94.

Grineski, Steven. "What Is a Truly Developmentally Appropriate Physical Education Program for Children?" *Journal of Physical Education, Recreation and Dance* 63 (August 1992): 33–35, 60.

Herr, Judith, and Winifred Morse. "Food for Thought: Nutrition Education for Young Children." *Young Children* 39 (November 1982): 3–11.

Javernick, Ellen. "Johnny's Not Jumping: Can We Help Obese Children?" *Young Children* 43 (January 1988): 18–23.

Kingsbury, Nancy M., and Joan C. Hall. "Provision of a Health Education Program for Preschoolers: A Demonstration Project Using Volunteers." *Early Child Development and Care* 36 (July 1988): 91–100.

Leppo, Marjorie L. *Healthy from the Start: New Perspectives on Childhood Fitness.* Teacher Education Monograph 15. ERIC Document Reproduction Service 352357. 1993.

Marchand, Nancy E., and Robert J. McDermott. "'Mouse Calls': A Storytelling Approach to Teaching First Aid Skills to Young Children." *Journal of School Health* 56 (December 1986): 453–454.

Miller, S. "The Facilitation of Fundamental Motor Skill Learning in Young Children." Doctoral dissertation. East Lansing, MI: Michigan State University, 1978.

National Association for the Education of Young Children. *Accreditation Criteria and Procedures of the National Academy of Early Childhood Programs.* Washington, DC: NAEYC, 1984.

National Association for the Education of Young Children. *Children Riding on Sidewalks Safely.* Washington, DC: NAEYC, 1987.

National Association for the Education of Young Children. *Walk in Traffic Safely.* Washington, DC: NAEYC, 1990.

National Association for the Education of Young Children. *We Love You—Buckle Up!* Washington, DC: NAEYC, 1987.

Omwake, Eveline B. "We Know So Much—We Know So Little." In *The Significance of the Young Child's Motor Development*, edited by Georgianna Engstrom. Washington, DC: National Association for the Education of Young Children, 1971.

Pangrazi, Robert P., and Victor P. Dauer. *Dynamic Physical Education for Elementary School Children.* 10th ed. New York: Macmillan, 1992.

Pangrazi, Robert P., and Victor P. Dauer. *Movement in Early Childhood and Primary Education.* Minneapolis, MN: Burgess, 1981.

Petersen, Susan C. "The Sequence of Instruction in Games: Implications for Developmental Appropriateness." *Journal of Physical Education, Recreation and Dance* 63 (August 1992): 36–39.

Pickle, Barbara. "Increasing Safety Awareness of Preschoolers through a Safety Education Program." ERIC Document Reproduction Service 310880. 1989.

Rogers, Cosby S., and Sandra S. Morris. "Reducing Sugar in Children's Diets: Why? How?" *Young Children* 41 (July 1986): 11–16.

Ross, James G., and Russell R. Pate. "The National Children and Youth Study II: A Summary of Findings." *Journal of Physical Education, Recreation and Dance* 58 (November/December 1987): 51–56.

Rothlein, Liz. "Nutrition Tips Revisited: On a Daily Basis Do We Implement What We Know?" *Young Children* 44 (September 1989): 30–36.

Seefeldt, Vern. "Physical Fitness in Preschool and Elementary School-Aged Children." *Journal of Physical Education, Recreation and Dance* 55 (November/December 1984): 33–37.

Shedler, Jonathan, and Jack Block. "Adolescent Drug Use and Psychological Health: A Longitudinal Inquiry." *American Psychologist* 45 (May 1990): 612–630.

Skeen, Patsy, and Diane Hodson. "AIDS: What Adults Should Know About AIDS (and Shouldn't Discuss with Very Young Children)." *Young Children* 42 (July 1987): 65–71.

U.S. Department of Agriculture. *Nutrition and Your Health: Dietary Guidelines for Americans.* Bulletin 232-8. Washington, DC: USDA, 1986.

Veitch, Beverly, and Thelma Harms. *Cook and Learn: Pictorial Single Portion Recipes.* Menlo Park, CA: Addison-Wesley, 1981.

White House Conference on Food, Nutrition, and Health. *Final Report.* Washington, DC: U.S. Government Printing Office, 1969.

Children's Books

Consumer Product Safety Commission. *The 9 Lives of El Gato the Cat.* Washington, DC: CPSC, 1983.

Consumer Product Safety Commission. *Protect Someone You Love from Burns. Project Burn Prevention.* Washington, DC: CPSC, 1978.

McCloskey, Robert. *Blueberries for Sal.* New York: Viking, 1948.

Chapter Thirteen

Guiding Behavior
Encouraging Self-Control

Your assignment as you visited in a school yesterday was to observe the discipline techniques employed by teachers. You were in a first-grade class. When you entered the class, you could not find the teacher at first. She was on the floor in the back of the room, helping a small group plan a mural. You stayed in the room for most of the morning and observed only one interaction between the teacher and the children that could be categorized as discipline. The teacher asked two girls to find another place to do their work because they were disturbing a small-group discussion.

You thought all the talk about the difficulties of discipline was exaggerated until you got back to your class and discovered that most of your classmates had witnessed many more examples of teachers disciplining students. Some of your peers observed a system of discipline in primary classrooms in which the teacher wrote down children's names when they violated rules and added checkmarks for further violations. Each checkmark carried specific consequences. One classmate reported observing a first-grade class in which all the children's names were posted on a large chart; below each name was a pocket with a card in it, similar to those in library books. Children who were "being good" had a card with a green dot on it; children who had committed one transgression had a card with a yellow dot; and children who had committed more than one transgression had a card with a red dot. A red dot meant that the child was excluded from recess and all activities other than academic work.

Obviously, there are clear contrasts in the ways teachers choose to handle discipline. How does a teacher make discipline decisions? What is good discipline?

· ·

GUIDANCE, DISCIPLINE, AND PUNISHMENT

Discipline
Guidance aimed at helping children gain self-control of their behavior.

Punishment
Removal of privileges or physical punishment designed to change children's behavior.

Corporal punishment
Physical punishment such as spanking, pinching, or slapping.

Discipline and **punishment** are not synonymous terms. Often, members of the public and even teachers use the word *discipline* when what they are referring to is *punishment* designed to enforce obedience to those in authority. Table 13.1 contrasts discipline and punishment.

The title of this chapter uses the word *guiding* because the best discipline consists of guiding children in developmentally appropriate ways to achieve self-control and eventually become self-disciplined individuals. Guidance is not punishment—it is helping children learn. Teachers must consider carefully how to guide and discipline children's behavior. Just as teachers would think about children's needs and developmental levels in planning for growth in literacy or any subject-matter area, they must think about how children can best learn to achieve self-control.

Corporal punishment is physical punishment; when the term is used in schools, it almost always refers to spanking. The Association for Childhood Education International issued a position paper supporting a ban on corporal punishment (Cryan 1987). The paper traces the historical and legal perspectives on corporal punishment and then briefly cites the research on the effects of such punishment. The effects are so negative, especially over the long term, that it is clear that corporal punishment is not an effective method of discipline and does not help children learn self-control.

Punishment is not always corporal punishment, however. Children can be punished by being confined to their rooms, by having privileges restricted, or by a variety of other means. Some punishments are natural

Table 13.1	Discipline versus Punishment		
DISCIPLINE		**OR**	**PUNISHMENT**
Children are *disciplined* when . . .			Children are *punished* when . . .
they are shown positive alternatives rather than just told "no" . . .			their behavior is controlled through fear . . .
they see how their actions affect others . . .			their feelings are not respected . . .
good behavior is rewarded . . .			they behave to avoid a penalty or get a bribe . . .
adults establish fair, simple rules and enforce them consistently.			the adult only tells them what not to do.
Children who are disciplined . . .			Children who are punished . . .
learn to share and cooperate . . .			feel humiliated . . .
are better able to handle their own anger . . .			hide their mistakes . . .
are more *self*-disciplined . . .			tend to be angry and aggressive . . .
feel successful and in control of themselves.			fail to develop control of themselves.

Source: From *Helping Children Learn Self-Control* (brochure), 1986, Washington, DC: National Association for the Education of Young Children. Copyright © 1986 by the National Association for the Education of Young Children. Excerpted by permission.

consequences of behavior. If a child breaks the crayons, then he will not have any when he wants to draw. If a child bullies her friends, no one will want to play with her. A later section of the chapter will discuss the use of natural consequences in a system of discipline (see "Dreikurs Model"). This section covers a punishment commonly meted out by early childhood teachers to control children's behavior: being confined to the "time-out" chair.

The original theory behind *time out* was sound: Taking time out gives children an opportunity to gain control of their own behavior and to choose when they are ready to return to the group. Unfortunately, that is not the way time out is used in most classrooms. In many classrooms, the time-out chair is clearly punishment that is overused to obtain obedience. Clewett (1988) believes that there are hazards associated with using a time-out chair. One is that its use tends to place emphasis on conformity and does nothing to teach children different strategies for behavior. There is also the strong possibility of diminishing children's self-concepts when they are threatened with time out and removed from the group.

Miller (1984) also has concerns about the use of time out as a punishment technique. She recommends the following principles for using time out:

> *Time out is not a punishment. Children should not be threatened with or fearful of a time out.*
> *Time out should not be humiliating. Consequently, there should not be a predetermined time-out chair or place.*

> *Time out should last as long as the child feels is needed to calm down. If children underestimate the length of time they need, they can be asked to try to calm down again in time out.*
>
> *Time out can be a time for the adult and child to talk about feelings—after the child has calmed down. An adult's presence can help calm an angry child, but only after calm has been restored will it be productive to talk. (pp. 17–18)*

Punishment may stop a behavior temporarily, but it may also interfere with teaching children appropriate behavior (Schickedanz, Schickedanz, and Forsyth 1982). Punishment may reduce children's initiative if they do not know which behaviors will be punished, and it may result in children's avoiding new situations in order to avoid punishment (Clewett 1988).

Classroom discipline is a continual topic of interest. One Gallup Poll (Gallup 1985) reported that discipline was perceived by the public to be the number-one problem in U.S. schools. An indication of the concern teachers have about discipline is the number of articles in professional journals and the number of sessions at professional conferences that focus on discipline. Discipline is important—how teachers respond to children's behavior is crucial in helping them grow and feel competent. No one would suggest that discipline be ignored; chaos in the classroom is not healthy for children or for teachers. Neither would anyone be naive enough to suggest that discipline is easy.

There are no clear-cut rules to follow, because every situation and every child are different. The same behavior from two different children might (and probably should) elicit different responses from the same teacher. So much depends on the child's age, development, previous experience, and present situation that no rules will ever apply to all situations. Good discipline helps children gain self-esteem, learn to be cooperative, and gradually learn the skills necessary for taking responsibility for their own behavior.

TEACHERS AND DISCIPLINE

Every teacher has faced or will face situations in which children's behavior is inappropriate or hurtful. It would be unrealistic to expect children who are still growing and learning to behave in ways that always please the other people around them. A professional teacher knows that some behavior management will be required when working with children and thinks about how different situations can be handled most successfully.

Teachers must consider the long-term effects on children's self-esteem rather than just the immediate results when making discipline decisions.

Providing appropriate curriculum experiences and materials is a good preventive measure in terms of achieving good classroom discipline.

Teachers must also think of discipline situations as teaching opportunities—opportunities to help children learn how to solve problems, how to negotiate differences, how to handle frustrations, and so on. Effective discipline requires thinking and planning, not only to prevent problems but also to prepare reactions that will be most appropriate when problems do occur.

A knowledgeable teacher also understands what is normal behavior for children of different ages and does not have unrealistic expectations. For example, very young children may scream or throw tantrums; four-year-olds may use foul language; five-year-olds may call each other cruel names; and eight-year-olds may form tight groups that gang up on outsiders. Children in one kindergarten class were often punished for lying. A sound knowledge of child development would have helped the teacher understand that many five-year-olds do not have well-developed concepts of truth and that most will deny any deed to protect themselves. Teachers have to think about what lying and other behaviors mean to the children they are teaching.

Guiding the behavior of young children is related to building self-concept, to curriculum planning and organization, and to teachers' beliefs about how children learn best. Guidance requires that teachers make decisions about individual and group behaviors. In some teaching situations, guidance may also require that teachers make decisions about discipline plans that are adopted by the school. The goal of all of this decision making is to plan carefully in order to prevent as many problems as possible.

Children's development of a healthy self-concept is greatly enhanced by caregiver responsiveness.

GUIDANCE AND SELF-CONCEPT

Self-concept is a broad term usually referring to the "perceptions, feelings, and attitudes that a person has about himself or herself" (Marshall 1989, p. 45). Self-concept includes perceptions of one's physical characteristics, gender, personality traits, ethnic identity, and so on. *Self-esteem* is a much more specific concept that refers to feelings of self-worth. Most of these perceptions are shaped initially by one's parents or other significant adults. As children mature, their self-esteem is shaped more and more by their evaluation of the responses of their peers. High self-esteem is developed when children believe that significant people in their lives view them as valuable and worthwhile. Self-esteem is also increased when children feel competent, capable, and in control. High self-esteem is important; research has shown that low self-esteem is related to a number of problems, including lack of academic achievement, delinquent behavior, and poor mental health (Zigler and Finn-Stevenson 1987).

Social context is extremely important in children's development of self-concept. Caregiver responsiveness can help children learn that they are valuable and that they can influence their environment (Harter 1983).

Freedom to explore the physical environment and materials that provide children with challenges and successes are also important (Bredekamp 1987). Sears (1970) found that children of parents who were authoritative (as opposed to authoritarian or permissive) had more positive self-concepts. *Authoritative* parents are in charge but do not make unreasonable demands; provide reasons for expecting given behaviors rather than asserting their authority; and help children make decisions about behavior. *Authoritarian* parents demand obedience because of their authority position, and *permissive* parents fail to set and enforce limits for their children.

For the early childhood teacher, several implications arise from the research on self-concept. One is that children need to feel competent; teachers must select materials and experiences thoughtfully to ensure both challenges and successes. Another implication is that children need to feel in control; therefore, as much of the day as possible should be spent in self-selected activities. Finally, teachers should approach discipline from an authoritative point of view, not an authoritarian or a permissive point of view.

PREVENTING PROBLEMS

Often, when teachers are having discipline problems, they look at the children to determine what is wrong with them. At times, teachers may need to look at the programs instead, to see if they are meeting children's needs—not just academic needs, but also social, emotional, and physical needs.

Preschool children need an environment in which they are safe to explore, in which they have enough materials to minimize conflicts, and in which they face very few demands to sit still or attend to teacher-directed instruction. Primary children also need to be able to move about the room and to have activities available that are interesting and appropriate for their level of development. Both age groups need a minimum number of rules. Nothing is harder than trying to make a group of children do something that is inappropriate for their level of development *and* be good while they are doing it. Appropriate curriculum activities, room arrangements, and routines will help prevent many discipline problems.

Curriculum activities need to be interesting and engaging for children. When caught in dull or boring situations, adults can play mental games, plan what they are going to do later, do something else (as when college students study for upcoming tests during boring lectures), or at least pretend not to be bored (as when we chat politely with the boss at a dull office party). But children simply do not have the skills to look attentive while they are doing something else. When bored or frustrated, they pinch their neighbors, fall out of their chairs, or get out of their seats. In one second-grade classroom, two children were disrupting the teacher's lesson on the four food groups. Their behavior resulted in being removed from the classroom. Later, the teacher admitted that these boys were gifted and already knew all the information being presented. If the curriculum had been more individualized, these two boys would have done their own experiment involving food, which would have engaged them intellectually and eliminated their disruptions and the need for punishment.

In addition to examining curriculum activities for appropriateness, teachers also need to examine materials and classroom arrangements. If, for example, only two wheeled toys are available for a large group of children, there will be disputes because of the unreasonable amount of time children must wait for a turn. Similar problems will arise if there are not enough blocks for several children to be building with them at one time. Children become extremely frustrated when they start a project and then find they do not have enough materials to complete it or when storage areas are so congested and unorganized that they cannot get the materials they need.

Room arrangements are also important in preventing discipline problems. If the blocks are in an area through which children must walk to get from one part of the room to another, the teacher will spend an inordinate amount of time mediating disputes over toppled structures. In primary classrooms, the pencil sharpener often seems to be a source of contention. The pencil sharpener should be located where users will disturb other children and disrupt the class as little as possible yet allow children to sharpen their pencils when needed. Nagging and making rules about such little things as using the pencil sharpener seems a waste of teacher energy in comparison to the time it would take to prevent the problem in the first place.

One technique to discover traffic patterns or areas of congestion is to make a map of children's movements. The teacher should make a copy of the floorplan of the classroom and draw lines to show the paths children take during given five-minute periods; observations should be repeated every thirty minutes to show patterns throughout the day. These traffic maps will help teachers make decisions about where to locate storage and program areas.

Once the teacher has examined the curriculum and the room arrangements in an effort to prevent problems, another step is to establish routines so that children feel safe and know what to expect. We would all be exhausted if we had to start from scratch to organize our time each day. We know that most of what we do is routine, and we do not have to put energy into deciding about most of our activities (eating, working, sleeping, and so on). Children also need routines in which activities are predictable but not rigidly set. Children need to know that there will be play time, snack time, outdoor play time, and other basic elements in their day. A mentally healthy person can change daily routines without undue stress. When they are secure about basic routines, children, too, can adjust to changes—the arrival of a guest speaker, a field trip, and so on. Complete lack of routine, however, leads to frustration, insecurities, and behavior problems.

Teachers might also need to examine their attitudes and feelings about autonomy and what constitutes obedient behavior from children. Kamii (1982) describes *autonomy* as the ability to make decisions for oneself. She believes that schools generally reinforce children when they obey without thinking and therefore "unwittingly prevent them from developing autonomy" (p. 85). Having autonomy does not mean that children do not have to obey rules or respect other people and their property. It does mean that children learn to make decisions and think clearly about their behavior and their learning.

GUIDANCE AND TEACHING SKILLS
....

In *More Talks with Teachers,* Lilian Katz (1984) suggests that professional teachers respond to problem situations by analyzing what can be taught in them. She categorizes what can be taught as social skills, verbal skills, social knowledge, and dispositional learning.

Social skills include taking turns, negotiating, and coping. Taking turns is not limited to sharing toys but is important in all social situations. During language activities, for example, children must learn to read the signals from a speaker that tell them when they can have a turn talking—eye contact, body language such as inclining the head, and so on. Children must also learn when the speaker is not willing to give up the floor—when he says "ah, ah, ah," avoids eye contact, and so on (Wells 1981). A similar kind of reading of the situation is helpful when one child wants a toy that another child has. The teacher might suggest that the child who wants the toy observe the child who has it and look for signs that he is tiring of it and might be ready to give it up. The teacher might help by modeling language to be used in negotiation, such as "I'll pull you in the wagon later if you'll let me have the truck now." Children also need to learn coping skills because not every request that they make will be honored. The teacher might say "Well, perhaps you can play with the truck tomorrow. For now, you might want to listen to a record or draw a picture." We have all seen adults who cannot cope with not getting what they want, when they want it. Teaching children to cope gives them a valuable life skill.

Verbal skills that can be taught in problem situations include making appropriate assertive statements and talking about disagreements. For example, a child who has just had a toy snatched from her can learn to say firmly "I was not finished playing with that boat. Please give it back." Being able to be assertive without being aggressive is a skill that will serve the child well for the rest of her life. Carrying on conversations about disputes is often difficult for children because they lack the words to continue the discussion. Teachers may have to model the conversations by speaking for both children, as described by Katz (1984):

> *Using this technique, the teacher might say to Leslie, "Robin really wants a turn," to which Leslie might grunt a refusal. The teacher might then say to Robin something like, "Leslie does not want to give up the tricycle yet." Robin might respond to this with a whining protest, in which case the teacher can paraphrase to Leslie what Robin is feeling by saying, "Robin really would like a turn now," and so on. In short, the teacher keeps up the conversation, verbalizing to each child what she infers to be the feelings of the other. (p. 31)*

Social knowledge includes the ability to put incidents into perspective and an initial understanding of the concept "justice." If one child fails to get a turn on the swing, the teacher might say "I know that you are disappointed, but there are other things you can do." The tone of voice should be empathetic but not tragic. Children who hit learn about justice when they are restrained from hitting and told "I won't let you hit anyone. If anyone else hits, I will stop them from hitting, too." The child then begins to feel safer and to feel that the environment is a just one.

Dispositional learning in discipline situations includes learning to be more empathetic, to try different techniques, and to avoid negative dispositions (sulking, temper tantrums, whining, and the like). Children can be taught to be more empathetic (Honig 1985; Marantz 1988). One of the best strategies for teaching empathy is modeling accompanied by discussion. For example, if one child grabs a toy from another, the teacher can return the toy while asking the grabber how she feels when someone grabs a toy from her. Concern for the feelings of others must be a priority in the early childhood classroom.

Children can also learn that problem-solving strategies can be applied in conflicts with others. The teacher might recommend a strategy to a child and then follow the recommendation by saying "If that doesn't work, come back, and we'll think of something else to try." Children must learn to accept that their first efforts may not always be successful while realizing that they can try again. Sometimes, a child may have adopted a negative behavior that the teacher would like to help him change—for example, tattling or complaining. The teacher must make a decision about how best to respond to a child's complaints to help him learn that complaining is not always successful and to learn when an adult should be told about an incident. Children are usually six or seven before they can understand the difference between tattling to get someone in trouble and telling the teacher about something that it is important for an adult to know.

GUIDING GROUPS

Children in groups must be given some rules. The fewer and more flexible these rules are, the better. As soon as children are old enough, they should have a part in making group rules. Some children as young as three can be involved in rule making.

Rules must be clearly stated. Leatzow, Neuhauser, and Wilmes (1983) observe that many early childhood educators have only one rule: "You may not hurt yourself or anyone else" (p. 83). This kind of rule covers many situations and is understood by the children. Other teachers add a rule that children cannot destroy property.

Sometimes, the teacher must manage the group in addition to guiding individual children. The younger the children, the fewer group-management techniques that should be needed. As children are able to participate in more group activities, group-management techniques will become more useful to the teacher. One rule for group management is not to call attention to an individual child. For example, a teacher might say "You all need to sit on your bottoms so that everyone can see the pictures while I read the story," rather than "Julian and Hope must sit down so that others can see." It also helps in this particular situation to reassure some children that they will get to see a book later if they are very excited about it. The teacher might say "You all need to sit flat on your bottoms now, but after I read the story, I'll leave the book here on the table if you want to look at the pictures more closely." With older children who are anxious to see something, the teacher might say "When you leave this table, put your name on the list if you want to see the book again later." Just as public criticism is to be avoided, so, too, is public praise inappropriate in group-management situations. For example, the teacher might say "Almost everyone is ready for the story; in just a minute, we will begin," rather than "Sara and Randy are sitting nicely, waiting for the story."

In using group-management strategies, teachers must be careful to preserve children's self-esteem and to use techniques that help children learn acceptable behaviors—the same concerns that apply when guiding individual behavior. Gartrell (1987b) acknowledges that learning these techniques takes commitment and practice on the part of teachers. Teachers must "deal with the young child's need to feel safe and secure, through personal acceptance, sensible limits, gentle correction, and genuine encouragement" (p. 55).

The same considerations of appropriateness of activity must also be applied to group-management situations as to individual guidance situations. When children are in group situations too long or when group activities are inappropriate, behavior problems will result. One teacher of five-year-olds had a group lesson on the beginning sound of "r." The teacher had twenty-three children sit in a circle to listen to a recording about the letter *r*. The teacher held an inflatable figure representing *r*. During the thirty-minute lesson, the teacher had to discipline children many times— "Stop leaning back in your chair," "Don't pull her hair," "Pay attention," and so on. Clearly, this activity was inappropriate for five-year-olds, and the time spent on it was too long. The teacher could have saved much frustration for himself and the children by choosing other teaching strategies.

Planning for Key Points in the Schedule

Experienced teachers will agree that discipline problems are more likely at certain times of day than others, including arrival times, transition times, and departure times. Planning for these key times is essential.

For arrival time, the teacher might ask that children wait until everyone has arrived or until a set time has been reached before activities begin. The fact is, though, that children are not good at waiting. Alternatives to waiting might be to plan an activity to occupy children who arrive early or to allow these children to begin working in learning areas.

Music and fingerplays can be used to help children make transitions from one activity to another without nagging and reminding by the teacher. Often, children will put away toys and materials if the teacher helps and makes up a simple song ("This is the way we put blocks on the shelf" or "This is the way we wash the paint brushes"). Playing a record or tape of a march song will encourage the children to march around the room until they come to the area for group activities; while marching, they will have no time to become bored and get into trouble. If the children are old enough, one child can begin to lead either a song or a fingerplay, and each child can join when she is ready. Fingerplays led by the teacher can encourage children to do what is necessary without being reminded. For example, the fingerplay "Two Little Hands Go Clap, Clap, Clap" ends with the line "And one little child sits quietly down." By the end of this fingerplay, all the children will be sitting, and the teacher will not have nagged anyone to do so.

Departures also need to be planned. Teachers need to think about how to distribute notices and work at the end of the day so that children do not have to wait too long. A routine of getting coats, distributing materials to take home, and delivering some short closing message can help keep children on track during departures.

On occasion, an activity might be appropriate for most of the group but not for an individual child. If a child is having difficulty, it is usually appropriate to allow him another choice. The teacher might whisper to a child "You can stay here if you choose, or you may work quietly with the puzzles or books if you want." Individualizing curriculum means attending to the needs of different children. The sensitive teacher is usually aware of when a child may need to leave a group and tries to arrange for that before an incident happens.

In sum, many discipline problems can be avoided by anticipating when they are likely to occur and planning to circumvent them. Crosser (1992) uses the acronym BASIC to describe such planning:

Before school begins
Arrival and departure times
Schedule transitions
Interactions with equipment and materials
Conflict management (p. 23)

In other words, the teacher plans the environment, plans for special times in the day, plans to help children learn to work with classroom equipment and materials, and teaches children how to settle conflicts that arise.

GUIDANCE DECISIONS

When teachers are confronted with misbehavior, they must make decisions about whether to respond, how to respond, and how to evaluate the growth of the children involved.

Weighing the Situation

In some situations, the most effective response is no response at all. Children sometimes behave in ways that are not appropriate but are not harmful to anyone and are not disruptive if they are ignored. For example, suppose the teacher asks the children to come to group time and sit on the floor for a story. Jennifer comes to the group but stands instead of sits. The teacher comments to the group that she is almost ready to start reading and makes eye contact with Jennifer, who remains standing. Rather than call her name and force her to sit, the teacher should do nothing and begin reading, as if Jennifer were sitting quietly. Jennifer may soon sit down and join the group, or she may keep standing, but as long as she is not interfering with others, little will be gained from making her sit. If Jennifer continually refuses to do anything that she is asked, the teacher needs to take steps privately to find out what makes Jennifer feel so defiant.

Effective teachers know when to ignore behavior and when to deal with it. No rules determine what to ignore and when—only professional judgment provides the answers. In weighing a given situation, the teacher should ask herself these questions: What will be gained in terms of teaching and increased self-control by responding to the behavior? What will be lost in terms of the child's self-concept or feeling of autonomy?

Making the Choice to Respond

Once a teacher has decided to respond to a child's behavior, he must decide how. In this case, there are certain rules to follow:

1. The response should be private, if at all possible. A child who is hitting another child will have to be restrained immediately, but then he can be removed and the behavior can be dealt with privately.

2. The response should be developmentally appropriate, for example, redirecting a toddler; appealing to the empathetic feelings of a five-year-old; or explaining rationally to an eight-year-old.

3. The response should be aimed at helping the child increase her self-control. The teacher should express acceptance of the child's feelings and provide guidance in finding a socially acceptable way of expressing them.

4. The response should demonstrate caring for the child but firmness in rejecting the behavior. "I'm sorry that you are frustrated because you can't have the doll now, but you cannot spit on anyone. You can spit in the sink."

5. The response should involve as much knowledge about the child and her situation as the teacher can summon in the split second that is often available for making a decision. For instance, suppose that the teacher knows that Sylvia's father has just moved out and that her family

Good discipline offers children an opportunity to learn how to control their own behavior.

is under stress. When Sylvia behaves in a way that is not typical for her, such as throwing sand on a friend, the teacher can quietly take her aside and explain gently that he knows that she feels like throwing something, that she can tell him how she feels if she wants to, but that she cannot hurt other children.

Withitness is a term that has become popular in the literature on discipline; it was derived from the work of Jacob Kounin, a well-known educational researcher (Charles and Barr 1989). Withitness is knowing what is going on in the classroom at all times. If students observe that the teacher chooses to correct the wrong child's behavior, they assume that the teacher does not know what is going on. Teachers with withitness also know to stop misbehavior before it spreads to others; timing such as this requires that teachers observe carefully.

Examples of Effective Responses

The following scenarios demonstrate effective responses to real-life problems in the classroom:

- You are reading a story to a small group. Several children start to whine that they do not like the story. One child puts her hands over her ears. Others notice and start to put hands over their ears. You could ignore the behavior and do a little editing of the story to finish it quickly. Or you could stop reading and say "I know that some of you like other books better. Perhaps we will read a book that you like better tomorrow. But some people like this book, so I'm going to finish reading it now. You can wait quietly for the few minutes that it will take."
- You find several children in the bathroom exposing themselves. You could say "I see that you are interested in the differences between boys and girls. Would you like to have me read this book to you that explains some of the differences?"
- One child pulls all the blocks off the shelf and refuses to help put them away. You might say "I know that it is much more fun to pull these blocks off the shelf than it is to put them away. We all have to do things that are not much fun sometimes. I'll help you begin, and you can finish." If the child still refuses to help, you could say "I'm going to put away these blocks now. Then you and I must talk about why you are not feeling like helping today."
- A child bites another child. First, you must restrain the child so that no more biting can occur. Then you might say "You cannot bite Sidney. You know that biting hurts very much, and the rule is that you cannot hurt anyone. I will not let you hurt anyone, and I will try not to let anyone hurt you. I know that you are angry, and I know that Sidney grabbed your toy. You must tell Sidney that you do not like it when he grabs your toy. Use words to tell him how angry you are."

Evaluating Growth

Evaluating children's growth in handling conflicts and in managing their own behavior requires that teachers keep anecdotal records of children's behavior over time and be able to document their growth in behaving in more acceptable ways. Gartrell (1987b) recounts the story of a visitor in a class of young children who overheard a child say "Damn it to hell." The visitor was astounded to hear the teacher say "Good for you, Arthur" and watched as she went to talk to Arthur. When she returned, the teacher explained to the visitor that Arthur's previous responses to being upset included hitting and kicking and that she had been trying to get him to use words—which he finally did. The teacher did not want Arthur to swear, but she had chosen to work on hitting behaviors first; she will deal with Arthur's

<table>
<tr><td>

DEVELOPMENTALLY **A**PPROPRIATE **P**RACTICE

</td><td>

Reflect on the connections between discipline and developmentally appropriate practice as you respond to the following questions:

</td></tr>
</table>

- Can discipline be developmentally appropriate if it is not based on understanding the child and what is normal behavior for her given stage of development? Why?
- Should a system of discipline be instituted without considering the match between the child and the curriculum? Can discipline be appropriate if the curriculum is not? Explain your answers.

- Discipline must be considered as an opportunity for teaching. If it is not, can it be developmentally appropriate? Why?
- If you read about a conference presentation called "Developmentally Appropriate Discipline," what information would you expect to be covered?

language later. Growth usually takes time and comes in little steps, but teachers need to be able to see the changes, even when they are small.

Teachers must also evaluate their own growth in responding to children's behavior. Teachers must remember that both children and adults get tired and become angry. If teachers occasionally respond in ways that are less than professional, they should forgive themselves and learn from their experience.

BEHAVIOR-MANAGEMENT SYSTEMS

Several behavior-management systems have been designed to help teachers control children's behavior. The following sections will describe assertive discipline, the Glasser model, the Ginott model, and the Dreikurs model.

Assertive Discipline

Designed by Lee Canter (1976), *assertive discipline* is a system in which the rules for classroom behavior are established by the teacher and posted in the classroom. The consequences for breaking any of the rules are also posted. If a child breaks the rule against speaking out in class, for example, her name is written on the chalkboard. (In recent publications, Canter has recommended that the names be written on a clipboard or in a book, rather than on the board [Hill 1990].) Another offense results in a checkmark being placed after the child's name. Usually, the consequence of receiving two checkmarks is being sent to the principal's office or having the teacher call the child's parents.

Because disruptions prevent teachers from teaching effectively, Canter believes that use of the assertive discipline system enables teachers to be more effective and solves the management problems in any classroom. This system is in use in many elementary schools, which means that many early childhood teachers are required to follow assertive discipline. Administrators who believe that the system helps teachers feel more comfortable about discipline are likely to promote its use.

One of the first things any teacher of young children must do is assess the validity of the assumptions of any behavior-management program. Canter based the assertive discipline system on the assumption that children want to disrupt the teacher and prevent teaching (Canter 1988; Hitz 1988). Teachers who believe that children have an inherent desire to learn and who have observed the eagerness with which young children approach learning will deem this an invalid assumption.

Another problem with assertive discipline is that it assumes that young children can operate according to rules. Experienced teachers know that young children can learn that some behaviors are acceptable at school and others are not. They also know that this learning usually takes time, guidance, and repeated experience. The assertive discipline system assumes that telling children that there is a rule and punishing them for breaking the rule will prevent unacceptable behavior. This approach may prevent the behavior at a given moment, but children will not know why the behavior is unacceptable nor will they learn to make better judgments about how to behave in future situations.

Behavior-management systems that enforce rules established by adult authority do not help children learn to be responsible. Such systems do, however, teach children to obey authority that is exercised through "power assertion" (Hitz 1988). There are situations in which adults must assert their power and demand instant obedience—for example, in order to prevent injury or cope with an emergency, such as a fire. Adults exert such control until children are old enough to learn rational reasons for controlling their own behavior in like situations. However, controlling children by power and demanding instant obedience should not be typical means of behavior management. Gartrell (1987a) expresses concerns that assertive discipline damages children's self-concepts and turns teachers into "managing technicians" (p. 11). Perhaps a larger concern is the danger that children will not be able to determine appropriate behavior and to develop a sense of responsibility for their actions.

The assertive discipline model also fails to examine the causes of disruptive behavior. The system is applied regardless of the curriculum, the room arrangements, or the schedule. No system of discipline should ever be applied without careful assessment of all the factors and individuals involved in a teaching situation.

Jones and Jones (1990) report that some schools that began assertive discipline programs several years ago have moved away from them, for several reasons:

> *Many teachers are frustrated because problem students seem to be relatively unaffected by the procedures, and students who do not need such repressive methods tend to find the method insulting or anxiety provoking. Our own concern is that too frequently the method creates a "sit down, shut up, or get out" philosophy in classrooms in which teaching methods are failing to meet students' basic personal and academic needs. Too often teachers use the Assertive Discipline procedures rather than examining their own teaching methods to consider how to prevent disruptive behavior. (p. 412)*

Glasser Model

The Glasser model (Glasser 1985) is based on providing good choices for children and handling disruptions that do occur in a calm and logical manner. Glasser believes that good choices produce good behavior and bad choices produce bad behavior. He believes that behavior represents individuals' attempts to meet their needs and that if schools are to have better discipline, they will have to become places where fewer children and teachers are frustrated in getting what they need. Some of the important needs that Glasser identifies are the needs to belong, to be free, and to have fun. Schools in which children do not feel a sense of belonging or have no power to make choices are schools in which discipline problems are common.

Glasser recommends that teachers structure learning experiences so that children have high motivation to work on behalf of the group and that stronger students help weaker students, thus fulfilling the stronger students' need for power and the weaker students' need to contribute to the group. One of the hallmarks of Glasser's model is the class meeting, in which students discuss class rules and behavior. Although Glasser's model is used more often with older students than with young children, his focuses on problem solving, on the choices provided by teachers, and on teachers' persistence in helping children with problems is appropriate for young children.

Ginott Model

The Ginott model (Ginott 1972) is based on setting up a classroom climate that is conducive to good discipline through effective communication between teachers and children. Ginott believes that discipline is an ongoing process that is achieved over time. One of the principles of his model is that corrective messages to children should attack the problem and not the child. Ginott uses the term *congruent communication* to describe responses that are in harmony with children's feelings about situations or themselves. He also advocates inviting cooperation, not demanding it. Teachers applying Ginott's recommendations do not label children and communicate their willingness to help children solve problems.

Charles and Barr (1989) report that even teachers who are sympathetic with Ginott's views feel that more structured management is needed in many teaching situations. Nonetheless, Ginott's emphasis on the ability to communicate well with children is of value to early childhood teachers. Another component of Ginott's model that is of value to early childhood teachers is its emphasis on the self-esteem of the child and the importance of the teacher's behavior.

Dreikurs Model

The Dreikurs model (Dreikurs 1982) is best known for its emphasis on logical consequences. Dreikurs defines *discipline* as teaching students to impose limits on themselves. He believes that all children want to belong and that their behaviors represent efforts to achieve a sense of belonging. Misbehaviors are the result of mistaken goals such as seeking attention, power, or revenge or seeking to display another child's inadequacy. Dreikurs suggests that the best method of discipline is encouraging positive behavior.

When teachers encounter behavior problems, Dreikurs recommends that they point out to students the logical consequences of their actions. In describing *logical consequences*, Charles and Barr (1989) use examples that apply to older children, but their explanation will suggest applications for younger children, as well:

> *Logical consequences must be differentiated from punishment. Punishment is action taken by the teacher to get back at misbehaving students and show them who is boss. Punishment breeds retaliation and gives students the feel-*

ing that they have the right to punish in return. Logical consequences, on the other hand, are not weapons used by the teacher. They teach students that all behavior produces a corresponding result: good behavior brings rewards and unacceptable behavior brings unpleasant consequences. If a student throws paper on the floor, that student must pick it up. If a student fails to do work as assigned, that student must make up the work on his or her own time. (p. 83)

In evaluating different models for managing behavior, Charles and Barr (1989) state that "Dreikurs' views have the greatest potential for bringing about genuine attitudinal change among students, so that they ultimately behave better because they consider it the proper thing to do" (p. 85).

Assessing Behavior-Management Systems

It is the teacher's responsibility to assess any management system or discipline policy based on the following criteria:

- *Respect for children*—Not every teacher will love every child, but each child deserves respect as a human being. If it is hard to respect the child because of constant problems, the teacher should seek help from co-teachers, counselors, parents, or administrators. Using a behavior-management system that does not respect the individual child will cause more harm than it attempts to address.
- *Knowledge of individual children*—Discipline cannot be applied fairly if it is applied without knowledge of the individual child. For example, enforcing a rule against bad language with Arthur (discussed earlier), who said *damn* instead of hitting, would leave Arthur without an acceptable way to express his frustration. Later, when Arthur has shown more growth, the teacher will help him find more acceptable classroom words for expressing anger. Behavior-management systems often make it easy for teachers to gloss over the need to know each child.
- *Knowledge of normal growth, development, and behavior*—Children who are behaving in ways that are normal for their age may be helped to learn more acceptable responses to be used at school. But such behavior will not be irritating to the knowledgeable teacher because he will realize that it is a normal part of working with this particular age group.
- *Willingness to accept discipline as an opportunity for teaching*—Discipline is not punishment. Teachers sometimes have to work hard at helping

children control their behavior in ways that teach them new strategies for interacting successfully in groups or with individuals.

- *Avoidance of judgmental words*—Calling children *good* or *bad* does not help them learn alternative ways of behaving. More appropriate descriptions of behavior guide children without judging them.
- *Limited but cooperative rule making*—Being well-behaved in a classroom where there are long lists of rules is difficult for children, because too many things are against the rules. As soon as children are old enough, they can begin to help teachers decide on rules that the group will follow.

CHAPTER SUMMARY

- Discipline is a major concern of teachers. It is perceived by the general public to be the most important problem in schools.
- The professional teacher views discipline as integral to the teaching process. Discipline must be based on knowledge of children's normal development, and the teacher must be aware of the effects of disciplinary decisions on children's self-esteem.
- The curriculum may contribute to discipline problems if activities are not appropriate for children. Children need both challenges and successes. They also need interesting, engaging activities that they select themselves.
- Room arrangements may be a source of discipline problems. Too little space to work, traffic through play areas, and spaces that are difficult to supervise may be sources of frustration to both teachers and children.
- Teachers who view discipline as a teaching opportunity can help children learn social skills, verbal skills, coping skills, and the disposition to use positive strategies in relating to others.
- Good group-management techniques require that

- the teacher avoid calling attention to individual children for either positive or negative behaviors.
- Often, teachers have the choice of ignoring inappropriate behavior. The decision to respond to behavior must be based on the teacher's professional assessment of the situation and what a child can learn from it.
- When teachers decide to respond to behavior, their responses should be private, developmentally appropriate, aimed at helping children achieve self-control, expressive of concern for children, and based as much as possible on knowledge of the individual children involved.
- In the last few years, many schools have adopted behavior-management systems that all teachers, even those in early childhood, must apply. In assessing any such system, teachers should examine the assumptions on which the system is based, its effects on children's self-esteem, and the cognitive requirements the system makes of young children.
- *Discipline* and *punishment* are not synonymous terms. Punishment often has long-term negative effects and does not teach children self-control.

WHAT WOULD YOU DO?
....

Reflect on your reading and your own experiences with young children as you think about the following situations:

1. A child hits another child with a block. What would you do in response to this behavior?
2. A parent brings his child to school for the first time and says, "Just hit him if he doesn't behave." What would you tell this parent about your philosophy of behavior management?
3. The faculty of the school where you teach is considering whether to adopt assertive discipline for schoolwide application; this idea is to be discussed in an upcoming faculty meeting. What viewpoint would you present regarding the use of assertive discipline?
4. A child in your class insists on using bad language to express her anger. What would you do in response to this behavior?

THEORY INTO PRACTICE
....

1. Interview four different early childhood teachers about their discipline problems and solutions. What are their most common problems? What are their solutions to the problems?
2. Write a description of a behavioral situation in which a teacher must decide whether to respond. Exchange descriptions among a small group of classmates, and discuss how you would respond to each situation and why.
3. In a small group, discuss your own feelings about discipline. Do you feel comfortable about managing individual and group behavior? Have you had opportunities to observe many positive models of behavior management? Describe your observations.
4. Make a list of ways in which discipline must reflect the developmental level of the child.

RECOMMENDED FOR FURTHER READING
....

Charles, C. M., and Karen Blaine Barr. *Building Classroom Discipline.* 3d ed. New York: Longman, 1989.

 The authors summarize eight models of discipline that are commonly discussed in the literature. Each model is described in terms of its philosophy and classroom applications. This information will be especially helpful to teachers who must use specific systems or must help evaluate models of discipline.

Honig, Alice S. *Love and Learn: Discipline for Young Children.* NAEYC Brochure 528. Washington, DC: National Association for the Education of Young Children, 1985.

 This brochure contains good sections on discipline for infants and toddlers. The author suggests setting reasonable expectations, respecting children's feelings, preparing a safe environment, and having faith in children. Solutions are suggested for some typical problems, such as expressing anger or fear inappropriately and stealing. This is an excellent brochure to share with parents.

Leatzow, Nancy, Carol Neuhauser, and Liz Wilmes. *Creating Discipline in the Early Childhood Classroom.* Provo, UT: Brigham Young University Press, 1983.

This book includes excellent chapters on the relationship of curriculum and the physical environment to discipline and group management. Other helpful chapters discuss the role of creative problem solving in building trust with children and parents and preventing as many discipline problems as possible.

National Association for the Education of Young Children. *Helping Children Learn Self-Control.* NAEYC Brochure 572. Washington, DC: NAEYC, 1986.

This brochure summarizes positive techniques for discipline. It reminds readers to model the skills that

children need in coping with their world, to prepare a good environment, and to schedule activities with children's needs in mind. It also outlines basic techniques of distraction, "time out," ignoring inappropriate behavior, noticing good behavior, and helping children see the consequences of their actions. This brochure would be excellent to share with parents when explaining the discipline choices teachers make.

Stone, Jeannette Galambos. *A Guide to Discipline.* Rev. ed. Washington, DC: National Association for the Education of Young Children, 1978.

This is a book that should be in every early childhood teacher's professional library. The author provides some philosophical explanations of discipline, but most of the book is devoted to examples of common classroom problems and suggestions for dealing with them. The examples of language to use in discipline situations are especially useful and will help teachers think of more positive responses to children when they are faced with problems in the classroom.

REFERENCES

Bredekamp, Sue, ed. *Developmentally Appropriate Practice in Early Childhood Programs Serving Children from Birth Through Age 8.* Washington, DC: National Association for the Education of Young Children, 1987.

Canter, Lee. *Assertive Discipline.* Seal Beach, CA: Canter and Associates, 1976.

Canter, Lee. "Assertive Discipline and the Search for the Perfect Classroom." *Young Children* 43 (January 1988): 24.

Charles, C. M., and Karen Blaine Barr. *Building Classroom Discipline.* 3d ed. New York: Longman, 1989.

Clewett, Ann S. "Guidance and Discipline: Teaching Young Children Appropriate Behavior." *Young Children* 43 (May 1988): 26–31.

Crosser, Sandra. "Managing the Early Childhood Classroom." *Young Children* 47 (January 1992): 23–29.

Cryan, John R. "The Banning of Corporal Punishment." *Childhood Education* 63 (February 1987): 146–153.

Dreikurs, R., B. Grunwald, and F. Pepper. *Maintaining Sanity in the Classroom.* New York: Harper and Row, 1982.

Gallup, Alec M. "The 17th Annual Gallup Poll of the Public's Attitudes Toward the Public Schools." *Phi Delta Kappan* 67 (September 1985): 35–47.

Gartrell, Dan. "Assertive Discipline: Unhealthy for Children and Other Living Things." *Young Children* 42 (January 1987a): 10–11.

Gartrell, Dan. "Punishment or Guidance?" *Young Children* 42 (March 1987b): 55–61.

Ginott, Haim G. *Teacher and Child.* New York: Macmillan, 1972.

Glasser, William. *Control Theory in the Classroom.* New York: Perennial Library, 1985.

Harter, S. "Developmental Perspectives on Self-Esteem." In *Handbook of Child Psychology: Vol. 4. Socialization, Personality, and Social Development,* 4th ed., edited by E. M. Hetherington, 275–386. New York: Wiley, 1983.

Hill, David. "Order in the Classroom." *Teacher Magazine* (April 1990): 70–77.

Hitz, Randy. "Assertive Discipline: A Response to Lee Canter." *Young Children* 43 (January 1988): 25–26.

Honig, Alice Sterling. "Compliance, Control, and Discipline." *Young Children* 40 (January 1985): 50–58.

Jones, Vernon F., and Louise S. Jones. *Comprehensive Classroom Management: Motivating and Managing Students.* 3d ed. Boston: Allyn and Bacon, 1990.

Kamii, Constance. *Number in Preschool and Kindergarten.* Washington, DC: National Association for the Education of Young Children, 1982.

Katz, Lilian. *More Talks with Teachers.* Urbana, IL: ERIC Clearinghouse on Elementary and Early Childhood Education, 1984.

Leatzow, Nancy, Carol Neuhauser, and Liz Wilmes. *Creating Discipline in the Early Childhood Classroom.* Provo, UT: Brigham Young University Press, 1983.

Marantz, Mady. "Fostering Prosocial Behavior in the Early Childhood Classroom: Review of the Research." *Journal of Moral Education* 17 (January 1988): 27–39.

Marshall, Hermine H. "The Development of Self-Concept." *Young Children* 44 (July 1989): 44–51.

Miller, Cheri Sterman. "Building Self-Control: Discipline for Young Children." *Young Children* 40 (November 1984): 15–19.

National Association for the Education of Young Children. *Helping Children Learn Self-Control.* Washington, DC: NAEYC, 1986.

Schickedanz, J. A., D. I. Schickedanz, and P. D. Forsyth. *Toward Understanding Children.* Boston: Little, Brown, 1982.

Sears, R. "Relation of Early Socialization Experiences to Self-Concepts and Gender Role in Middle Childhood." *Child Development* 41 (1970): 267–289.

Wells, Gordon. *Learning Through Interaction: The Study of Language Development.* Cambridge, England: Cambridge University Press, 1981.

Zigler, Edward F., and Matia Finn-Stevenson. *Children: Development and Social Issues.* Lexington, MA: D. C. Heath, 1987.

Chapter Fourteen

Assessment and Reporting

definition

reporting

types of tests

ASSESSMENT AND REPORTING

standardized tests

other techniques

You were scheduled to visit a primary class this morning, but when you arrived, you found signs on the classroom doors that read "Do Not Disturb." All the children were taking achievement tests. According to the schedule posted in the hall, these tests were to continue over the next several days, occupying most of the morning hours. You remembered taking achievement tests when you were in elementary school and wondered if the tests today are similar.

One of your friends teaches a mixed group of four- to six-year-olds and has explained that the children in her group neither take achievement tests nor get report cards. She feels strongly that these measures are inappropriate for young children. You know of a preschool, however, where even four-year-olds get report cards to take home. And another friend has told you that the district she teaches in puts enormous pressure on teachers to have children do well on achievement tests. Test results are published in the local paper, and the administration wants the district to post higher scores than neighboring districts.

You also noticed a sign in the hall about dates of screening tests for children who would enter kindergarten in the fall. You wondered what skills and behaviors kindergartners could be expected to have and how they could be determined.

On your way out of the building, you asked the secretary for a copy of the report card used by the school. You found that it looked very much like the report cards you received as a child. Yet classmates who visited other schools brought back a variety of report cards.

At this point, you are confused about assessment. You would like to know more before rescheduling your visit to the primary school. You have many questions: Should young children take achievement tests? Should children be screened before they enter kindergarten? How do parents know how their children are progressing in school? What should report cards show?

DEFINITION OF ASSESSMENT

Assessment and *testing* are not synonymous terms. Although testing is only one of several components of assessment, in recent years, testing seems to be have been misused and to have become the major determinant of the value of schools and the abilities of children.

Assessment
Use of a comprehensive evaluation system to determine the quality of a program or the progress of a child.

Assessment is more than just testing, however; it is using a variety of strategies in an effort to uncover the understanding and determine the development of individual children. Teachers assess children's social, emotional, and physical development as well as their intellectual growth—just as a pediatrician assesses a child not only by weighing and measuring him, checking his visual acuity, his hearing, and his reflexes but also by observing his ability to walk and his relationship to his parents. Similarly, programs are assessed by measuring not only the success of the children enrolled in them but also parents' satisfaction with their children's progress and teachers' feelings of accomplishment. Assessment is sometimes formal and sometimes informal. In contrast to testing, assessment is ongoing. A test is a sample of behavior or knowledge taken at a specific time. Assessment covers a much longer time frame and attempts to sample a much broader spectrum of behavior or knowledge.

Assessment is vital to good teaching; it is necessary to assess both the program and the progress of individual children. Good teachers would be involved in assessment even if there were no external requirements to do

DEVELOPMENTALLY **A**PPROPRIATE **P**RACTICE	*To determine whether assessment of individual children is developmentally appropriate, teachers should ask the following questions:*

1. Is the assessment procedure based on the goals and objectives of the specific curriculum used in the program?

2. Are the results of assessment used to benefit children, i.e., to plan for individual children, improve instruction, identify children's interests and needs, and individualize instruction, rather than label, track, or fail children?

3. Does the assessment procedure address all domains of learning and development—social, emotional, physical, and cognitive—as well as children's feelings and dispositions toward learning?

4. Does assessment provide useful information to teachers to help them do a better job?

5. Does the assessment procedure rely on teachers' regular and periodic observations and record keeping of children's everyday activities and performance so that results reflect children's behavior over time?

6. Does the assessment procedure occur as part of the ongoing life of the classroom rather than in an artificial, contrived context?

7. Does the assessment procedure evaluate performance rather than only testing skills in isolation?

8. Does the assessment relay on multiple sources of information about children, such as collections of their work, results of teacher interviews and dialogues, as well as observations?

9. Does the assessment procedure reflect individual, cultural, and linguistic diversity? Is it free of cultural, language, and gender biases?

10. Do children appear comfortable and relaxed during assessment rather than tense or anxious?

11. Does the assessment procedure support parents' confidence in their children and their ability as parents rather than threaten or undermine parent's confidence?

12. Does the assessment examine children's strengths and capabilities rather than just their weaknesses or what they do not know?

13. Is the teacher the primary assessor, and are teachers adequately trained for this role?

14. Does the assessment procedure involve collaboration among teachers, children, administrators and parents? Is information from parents used in planning instruction and evaluating children's learning? Are parents informed about assessment information?

15. Do children have an opportunity to reflect on and evaluate their own learning?

16. Are children assessed in supportive contexts to determine what they are capable of doing with assistance as well as what they do independently?

17. Is there a systematic procedure for collecting assessment data that facilitates its use in planning instruction and communicating with parents?

18. Is there a regular procedure for communicating the results of assessment to parents in meaningful language, rather than letter or number grades, that reports children's individual progress?*

*From "Assessment in Context—Teachers and Children at Work" by T. W. Hills, 1993, Young Children, 48(5), p. 24. Copyright © 1993 by the National Association for the Education of Young Children. Excerpted by permission.

so; they want to know about how well children are doing, and they want to know about the effectiveness of their programs.

Assessment alone does not improve children or programs—just as measuring a child's height and weight does not make the child grow. Only when assessment has a purpose and is used to help make decisions about curriculum, about individual children, and about programs can it help a child or program grow.

Hills (1993) summarizes a strong assessment program when she states:

Assessment will serve the best interests of children when it is carried out as an integrated part of an overall program, when it contributes positively to children's self-esteem and developmental progress, and when it recognizes children's individuality and respects their family and community backgrounds. Assessment that will accomplish these ends is continuous, broadly focused on child development and learning, sensitive to children's diversity, integrated into their day-to-day activities, and designed to reap benefits for them, through teachers' knowledgeable planning and teaching and through clear communication between school and home. (p. 28)

TYPES OF TESTS

Tests vary considerably in the purposes for which they were designed. The following definitions are based on the National Association for the Education of Young Children's (NAEYC) "Position Statement on Standardized Testing of Young Children 3 Through 8 Years of Age" (1988):

Achievement test—A test that measures the extent to which a person has mastery over a certain body of information or possesses a certain skill after instruction has taken place

Criterion-referenced test—A test that evaluates a test taker in relation to a specified performance level (as distinguished from a test that compares the test taker's score to the performance of other people, which are norm-referenced tests)

Developmental test—An age-related, norm-referenced assessment of a child's skills and behaviors compared to those of children of the same chronological age; sometimes used incorrectly as screening tests

Norm-referenced test—A test that compares the test taker's performance to the performance of other people in a specified group

Readiness test—A test that assesses a child's level of preparedness for a specific academic or preacademic program

Reliability—The degree to which test scores are consistent, dependable, or repeatable; that is, the degree to which test scores can be attributed to actual differences in test takers' performance rather than to errors of measurement

Screening test—A test used to identify children who may be in need of special services; such a test focuses on the child's ability to acquire skills and may also called a *developmental screening test*

Standardized test—A test composed of empirically selected items that is to be used in a specific way, is based on adequately defined norms, and is backed by data on reliability and validity

Validity—The degree to which a test measures what it is supposed to measure; also, the degree to which a certain inference from a test is appropriate or meaningful (p. 45)*

Think about these definitions in terms of your own testing experience. In many states, before you are allowed to take professional education courses, you must pass a standardized test of basic skills. The basic skills test is an achievement test; its purpose is to determine your mastery of reading, writing, and mathematics. Additionally, in many states, you must pass the National Teacher's Examination in order to obtain a teaching credential. This is also an achievement test to measure what you have learned about teaching and its theoretical underpinnings.

Such achievement tests are norm-referenced tests; they measure your performance against the performance of other people in a specific group. Test designers administer these tests to representative samples of the population the tests are aimed at. The idea is that if a test is accurately designed, the scores of those in the sample population will form a bell-shaped curve. The average score on a 100-point test, for example, would be 50; most of the scores would cluster in the middle, and a few higher and lower scores would appear on either end of the curve.

If you were so inclined, you could find out the characteristics of the populations on which basic skills tests and professional credentials tests are normed. (This information is provided to your college or university with the tests themselves and is not usually made available to test takers.) The more closely the populations reflected your own background in terms of culture and experience, the more likely the tests would accurately measure your individual skills.

In contrast, the tests your instructors give in class are criterion-referenced tests. Your instructors determine the correct answers to the test items, and in theory, everyone could pass with a perfect score. You also took a criterion-referenced test when you took the test to get your driver's license.

*Based on "NAEYC Position Statement on Standardized Testing of Young Children 3 Through 8 Years of Age" by the National Association for the Education of Young Children, March 1988, *Young Children*, 43, pp. 42–47. Copyright © 1988 by NAEYC. Adapted by permission.

At some time in your school experience, you may have taken another type of norm-referenced test—an *intelligence test*. The score on an intelligence test is supposed to indicate your potential intellectual ability compared with that of others. One reason for giving an intelligence test would be to determine if a person were achieving as much as possible in school. Keep in mind, however, that many students have achieved much more than was predicted by their intelligence test scores. Moreover, many people believe that innate intelligence cannot be measured and that intelligence tests actually measure learning, not intelligence. Such tests tell nothing about an individual's motivation, incentives, or determination. Because their usefulness and validity may be questionable, intelligence tests are not given as often as they once were.

OTHER TECHNIQUES FOR ASSESSMENT

Anecdotal Records

Anecdotal records are observations of children's behavior and verbalizations. Kept over a period of time, they are likely to reveal patterns of behavior that will suggest strategies for helping an individual child become more competent or supporting the child's obvious growth. Irwin and Bushnell (1980) state that anecdotal records help teachers "test hunches about reasons for a child's behavior or learning style, . . . identify what conditions may be reinforcing behavior, and . . . gain feedback about what children have learned from a particular curriculum unit or presentation" (p. 23).

One key to making an anecdotal record is to record the information without interpretation—just the facts, please! For example, if the teacher observes Sally push Leon so hard that he falls backward into the sandbox, then the teacher should record the act, not make a statement such as "Sally was aggressive." This may be the only incidence of pushing all year—Sally may be reacting to the fact that Leon pulled her hair. If Sally pushes several children and each incident is noted in the anecdotal record, then the teacher might interpret from the series of observations that Sally needs help in controlling her impulse to push people. A record that states that Sally was aggressive does not help the teacher focus on her behavior and find its causes. Any interpretation of behavior included in anecdotal records must be clearly labeled as such.

If possible, the teacher should record what happens just prior to an observation and also what happens after it. For example, if Leon pulls

Recording children's behavior in anecdotal records and keeping samples of the products children create are components of a good assessment system.

Sally's hair, that should be noted as part of the observation. What Sally does next should also be part of the recording. Knowing whether Sally runs away after pushing Leon, apologizes and helps him up, or sits down to play with him is valuable for the teacher in assessing Sally's behavior.

The bias of the observer is always an issue in anecdotal records. Even though the observer may record an incident exactly as it happened, with no evaluative or interpretive comments, the choice of incidents to record, the frequency of recordings, or the lack of recordings may all reflect the bias of the observer.

Another key to making helpful observations is to observe children in many different situations and activities. Children who never initiate conversation inside the classroom may talk nonstop outdoors and single-handedly organize half the class for an activity. Observations should also focus on the total development of the child. Records of the child's physical, social, emotional, and intellectual development help the teacher put together a clear picture of the whole child. Katz (1984) suggests looking at preschoolers in terms of their range of affect, variations in play, curiosity, response to authority, friendship, interest, spontaneous affection, and enjoyment of life.

Various educators' guidelines for collecting anecdotal records (Irwin and Bushnell 1980; Boehm and Weinberg 1987; Bentzen 1985) are summarized here:

1. Record the incident as soon as possible after it occurs.
2. Include the setting, time, and activity.
3. Record the exact words of the participants when possible.
4. Record the actions and words of other people in the incident.
5. Make each record as objective, accurate, and complete as possible.

Boehm and Weinberg (1987, p. 17) further recommend limiting discussion to one incident; recording incidents as soon as possible after they occur; separating interpretive comments from factual reporting; and considering supportive information in order to accumulate the most useful records.

Making anecdotal records is time consuming. Unfortunately, this kind of information often stays in the teacher's head, rather than being put on paper. One technique for making collecting notes easier is to prepare a loose-leaf notebook, with a page for each child. The teacher might carry a pad of Post-it notes or computer labels in her pocket and jot down observations on individual notes; at the end of the day, these notes can be stuck on the appropriate child's page and the teacher won't have to recopy the information. Additional notes can be added as trends or patterns are observed (Reardon 1991).

Teachers should make an effort to observe two or three children daily. Over time, they will have accomplished observations on every child. (Sometimes, a teacher may choose one or two children and observe them for a week or two. Usually, these are children the teacher feels need special help because they have either behavior or learning problems.)

If teachers develop the habit of observing carefully, they will have much information that is useful for planning and for sharing with parents. One study investigated the match between teacher assessments of children and the children's performance on tests. The teacher assessments were found to be very accurate predictors of children's performance on tests (Stoner and Purcell 1985). It is not surprising that qualified teachers are capable of making good assessments of young children.

Checklists and Rating Scales

Teachers can use checklists to make quick notes of what children actually do in the classroom. This information is valuable for determining which children are interested in which activities or which children have accomplished given tasks. Teachers can use the information obtained from checklists for evaluating learning areas and for reporting to parents.

Most checklists are constructed by teachers and used in a variety of activities, although some may be supplied by the district, state, or other administrators. Consider a checklist of children's physical skills. The skills to be observed would be listed across the top of the page and the children's names down the side of the page. If skipping were one of the skills listed and a teacher observed a child skipping, she would enter the date beside the child's name. Other abilities are also relatively easy to record on a checklist: working puzzles, constructing patterns with beads or pattern blocks, cutting with the right or left hand, using counting as a problem-solving strategy, choosing a book and looking at it for five minutes, playing in a group for ten minutes, and so on. Most teachers who use checklists find that it is most helpful to have a variety of such lists in the areas where the activities would be most likely to be observed. Table 14.1 on pages 446–447 identifies possible skills or abilities that can be noted on checklists.

Checklists are appropriate for gathering factual information, not for determining the curriculum of the program. Some checklists include items such as counting to 10, tying shoes, and naming the letters of the alphabet. It is useful to know that children can do these things, but it is inappropriate to base the curriculum on a list of such skills and to engage the child in drill-and-practice exercises to master them.

Rating scales are similar to checklists except that the behavior is marked in terms of frequency (always, sometimes, never) or quality (above average, average, or below average). Rating scales can also provide useful information for teachers as they plan learning experiences. It is most appropriate to use rating scales to compare a child's current behavior to his previous behavior. Teachers can get caught in the trap of comparing children to each other if they are not judicious in their use of rating scales. Figure 14.1 on page 448 shows an example of a rating scale.

Attitude and Interest Inventories

Information about how children feel about different activities and the things that interest them most is usually obtained by asking questions

Table 14.1	Skills or Abilities That Can Be Noted on Checklists
Physical Development	• Develop large muscles: Run, hop, skip, gallop, balance, walk backward, throw and catch a ball • Develop small muscles: Cut, paste, clap, button, zip, tie, stack • Manipulate tools • Copy simple shapes • Assemble puzzles • Draw, pretend write, write • Play games • Wash, use the toilet, dress without assistance • Visually follow a line of print form left to right and top to bottom and return • Distinguish sounds and symbols
Social-Emotional Development	• Experience success at school • Interact with other children • Listen, follow directions • Make choices • Initiate and complete activities • Accept responsibility • Express thoughts in a variety of ways • Show appreciation for, sensitivity to others • Explore and experiment • Practice social skills • Enjoy school • Maintain self-control • Talk • Play • Respond positively to adult authority • Share • Help clean up • Approach tasks positively, stay with tasks • Work independently

through an attitude or interest inventory. Often, these questions are intended to be open ended. For example, the teacher might ask "What is your favorite thing to do in the classroom?" or "What is your favorite thing to do outdoors?" Some inventories are designed to gather information by asking children to mark responses to given questions.

Figure 14.2 on page 448 shows an example of the type of form a teacher might complete during an open-ended interview with a child. Figure 14.3 on page 449 is an example of one page of a five-page commer-

Table 14.1	*(continued)*
	• Cooperate
	• Respond to humor
Intellectual Development	• Know and recite personal information: First and last name, age, address, birthdate, telephone number
	• Explain simple pictures
	• Show an interest in print and a desire to read and write
	• Differentiate between fantasy and reality
	• Speak in sentences of five or more words
	• Recognize colors
	• Recognize numbers
	• Count
	• Demonstrate one-to-one correspondence
	• Recite the alphabet
	• Recognize upper- and lowercase letters
	• Write first name
	• Draw a picture of a person with ten recognizable body parts
	• Solve problems
	• Demonstrate resourcefulness and independence
	• Continue to expand vocabulary based on experiences
	• Identify patterns and basic shapes
	• Recognize likenesses and differences
	• Measure
	• Paraphrase
	• Ask questions
	• Relate new information to previous knowledge
	• Brainstorm
	• Make lists
	• Remember a sequence or pattern
	• Classify objects and topics
	• Use reasoning skills
	• Participate in activities for aesthetic development

cial attitude survey that would be used during an interview with a child; the format of the questions prompts the child to choose a response.

Attitude and interest inventories can help teachers make planning decisions. If the teacher determines that children are feeling uncomfortable about certain learning experiences, then those can be modified so that the children's attitudes about school might be improved. Interest inventories provide teachers with clues about experiences that would be of interest to the children and would therefore be likely to be successful learning experiences.

FIGURE 14.1 Rating Scale

Name	Frequently	Sometimes	Not yet
Uses language effectively			
Solves problems in arithmetic with sums to 10			
Participates in group discussions			
Participates in singing experiences			

FIGURE 14.2 Form for Open-Ended Interview

Name _____   Date _____

1. Do you have a pet? Tell me about your pet.

2. What is your favorite toy?

3. What do you like to do best when you play outside?

4. Who do you like to play with?

5. What do you like to do best here at school?

6. Tell me about your favorite books (stories).

FIGURE 14.3 Elementary Reading Attitude Survey

School   **Grade**   **Name**

1. How do you feel when you read a book on a rainy Saturday?

GARFIELD:
© 1978 United Feature Syndicate, Inc.

JIM DAVIS

2. How do you feel when you read a book in school during free time?

3. How do you feel about reading for fun at home?

4. How do you feel about getting a book for a present?

Source: GARFIELD reprinted by permission of UFS, Inc.

FIGURE 14.4 Time-Activity Record

9:15 a.m.	Reading	Writing center	Sand/Water play	Art	Science
Juan	X				
Sara		X			
Addie			X		
Robert		X			

Time-Activity Samples

Another assessment technique is to record on a regular schedule the activities in which children are engaged. For example, for an entire day, the teacher would record each child's activity every thirty minutes. After a given period (a week, a month), the teacher would repeat the observation. These records would provide information about the child's choices over time and help the teacher determine each child's interests. Time-activity samples can also provide some clues as to the quality of the child's involvement but are most useful when accompanied by other information, as well. Figure 14.4 is an example of a time-activity record.

Self-Evaluation

Even very young children can begin to evaluate themselves. They can describe orally what they learned while they were involved in the activities of the day, or they can tell how they learned to do something. Older children can decide with the teacher which things they are learning are most important and record those in a booklet or on a checklist that they have constructed.

Primary children might be encouraged to complete short, written evaluations of selected pieces of their work to share with others. For example,

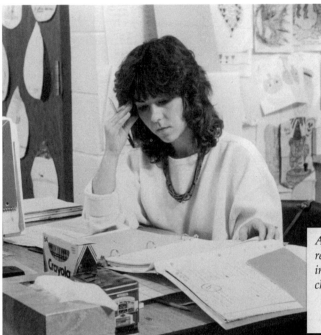

A variety of assessment records help teachers plan instruction for individual children.

they might complete the sentence "I think this is my best writing because
_____" or "I want to share this art because _____."

Part of the process of self-evaluation should include what needs to come next, so as children think about what they have done well, they should be encouraged to think about what they need to learn, too. For instance, if a child has learned to print his first name, he should be acknowledged for that achievement and then asked if he wants to learn to print his last name (or perhaps the name of a friend or some other word of interest). If a child can read a given text successfully, then he might be encouraged to read a more difficult text or a text from a different genre. Self-evaluation should be linked to personal goal setting.

Portfolio Assessment

Of the many types of alternative assessment, **portfolio assessment** seems to be the most popular with teachers. Paulson, Paulson, and Meyer (1991) define a *portfolio* as "a purposeful collection of student work that exhibits

Portfolio assessment
Assessment based on an evaluation of a collection of artifacts and anecdotes.

the student's efforts, progress, and achievements in one or more areas. The collection must include student participation in selecting contents, the criteria for selection, the criteria for judging merit, and evidence of student self-reflection" (p. 60).

Purpose

Before teachers decide to use a portfolio system, they must decide the purpose the portfolio will serve: Will it be used to communicate with parents? Will it be used to determine the child's individual progress? Will it be used for teacher accountability? Will it be used for all these purposes?

In deciding purpose, teachers should understand that a portfolio alone is not an assessment; rather, it is a collection of materials that can be used to assess progress. Thus, a portfolio is not especially useful until the materials have been evaluated by the teacher or others. A collection of materials such as writing samples and artwork, for instance, is only that—a collection. It becomes an assessment tool when it has been used to determine a child's progress and needs.

Graves (1990) suggests that teachers take an experimental stance toward portfolios, rather than treating them as permanent records. In this view, a portfolio is a dynamic, ongoing collection created by both teacher and child—either can contribute or remove items.

Portfolios can be invaluable in communicating with parents. When a child receives a letter grade of A or C for an entire year's performance in a subject, parents have no way of knowing exactly what the child has learned or how much progress she has made since the beginning of the term. Flood and Lapp (1989) suggest a comparison portfolio strategy that is especially helpful in communicating a child's growth to parents. They suggest selecting writing samples, reading samples, and other pertinent information (such as the number of books read, how often reading is chosen as a free-choice activity, changes in attitudes, and so on) that will demonstrate the child's growth in an area. Teachers should make sure that parents are aware of how pieces were selected for a portfolio: Are they the child's best work? work that demonstrates a particular competency? work that is in progress? Parents also should be invited to offer suggestions for portfolio entries or deletions.

Sometimes, portfolios are used to provide evidence for teacher accountability. For instance, items in portfolios could be used to document that given activities were provided for children. Teachers might also exchange three or four portfolios with peers in order to validate their own opinions about the instruction provided and the children's achievement. If teachers choose to exchange portfolios, the selection of the portfolios for examination should be clearly understood. For example, if four were to be exchanged, one might be from a child showing outstanding performance, two from children showing average performance, and one from a child having difficulties of some kind. Teachers might even want to submit portfolios of selected children's pieces to their administrators in order to demonstrate effectiveness in fostering children's achievement.

Content and Organization

Portfolios can be valuable for documenting children's growth, for communicating with parents, and for validating the quality of instruction. However, their usefulness depends on how and what materials are selected and how they are organized.

A variety of items could be included in a portfolio—drawings or paintings the child has made, photos of block constructions he has made, photos or videos of him climbing on outdoor equipment, notes about or videos of him throwing or catching a ball, records of books he has read (or listened to the teacher read), stories he has written or dictated, samples of his classification activities, and notes about his social growth.

Of course, portfolios may also contain teacher observations and notes. If, for example, a piece of writing is selected for inclusion in a child's portfolio, then the teacher might add some observation about the selection—perhaps noting that the child worked on the piece over a period of four days but was reluctant to make any changes after a conference with the teacher. The same sort of comment might accompany art samples or other work. Work samples, when used along with other information collected by the teacher, clearly demonstrate the child's growth and the effectiveness of the program.

The most logical organization for a portfolio that will be used to determine a child's individual progress is to create a section of the portfolio to match each of the major program goals. For example, Meisels (1993, p. 36) suggests the categories of personal-social development, language and literacy, mathematical thinking, scientific thinking, social studies, art and music, and physical development.

The High/Scope program (Schweinhart 1993) recommends the following categories:

- *Initiative*—expressing choices, engaging in complex play
- *Creative representation*—making, building, pretending
- *Social relations*—relating to adults, making friends
- *Music and movement*—exhibiting body coordination, imitating movements to a beat
- *Language and literacy*—showing interest in reading, beginning reading, beginning writing

• *Logic and mathematics*—sorting, counting objects, describing time sequences (p. 32)

Teachers of younger children might find different categories more appropriate for their students, whereas teachers of eight-year-olds might need more specific categories for mathematics, reading, and writing.

Once the major categories have been determined, one or two core items can be collected and dated in fall, winter, and spring. *Core items* are work samples that are common to all children. For example, all children in the first grade would be expected to complete some writing and reading. Other items can be added in each category that reflect the child's individual interests or activities.

Another useful means of organizing a portfolio is to provide a table of contents or summary sheet, listing the materials included and the dates they were collected. Two or three times a year, it will be helpful to summarize the data in the portfolio. Such a summary will serve to help teachers determine where their information is too thin and to use what information they have more fully in planning learning experiences. Including some sort of summary will also help prevent the portfolio from becoming a jumble of materials over time.

Most teachers prefer to collect portfolio items in large, expandable folders or loose-leaf binders. However the materials are collected, they should be stored in a place that is easily accessible to both children and teachers. Often, children like to review what they have done already and add items that are especially significant to them. And teachers will certainly want to add to the portfolios on a regular basis.

Although portfolios will differ from child to child and teacher to teacher, Paulson, Paulson and Meyer (1991) offer some guidelines for creating powerful portfolios:

1. *Developing a portfolio offers the student an opportunity to learn about learning. Therefore, the end product must contain information that shows that a student has engaged in self-reflection.*

2. *The portfolio is something that is done by the student, not to the student. Portfolio assessment offers a concrete way for students to learn to value their own work and, by extension, to value themselves as learners. Therefore, the student must be involved in selecting the pieces to be included.*

3. *The portfolio must convey explicitly or implicitly the student's activities: for example, the rationale (purpose for forming the portfolio), intents (its goals), contents (the actual displays), standards (what is good and not-so-good performance), and judgments (what the contents tell us).*

4. *The portfolio may serve a different purpose during the year from the purpose it serves at the end. Some material may be kept because it is instructional, for example, partially finished work on problem areas. At the end of the year, however, the portfolio may contain only material that the student is willing to make public.*

5. *A portfolio may have multiple purposes, but these must not conflict. A student's personal goals and interests are reflected in his or her selection of materials, but information included may also reflect the interests of teachers, parents, or the district. One purpose that is almost universal in student portfolios is showing progress on the goals represented in the instructional program.*

6. *The portfolio should contain information that illustrates growth. There are many ways to demonstrate growth. The most obvious is by including a series of examples of actual school performance that show how the student's skills have improved. Changes observed on interest inventories, records of outside activities such as reading, or on attitude measure are others ways to illustrate a student's growth.*

7. *Finally, many of the skills and techniques that are involved in producing effective portfolios do not happen by themselves. By way of support students need models of portfolios as well as examples of how others develop and reflect upon portfolios. (pp. 61–62)**

Standardized Tests

Young children are routinely given **screening tests.** Screening tests vary considerably, but most attempt to determine a child's ability to learn skills. Many of these tests ask children to identify objects, words, or numerals that are common in some environments. Developmental screening tests are designed to determine what children can do compared to other children their age. These tests often involve drawing geometric figures, bouncing balls, balancing on one foot, and repeating series of numerals or words. Readiness tests ask young children to recognize letters and numerals, to find objects that go together, or to recognize objects that are not the same as other objects in a set. These tests are supposed to predict a child's success in coping with an instructional program.

> **Screening test**
> A test designed to determine whether a child is eligible for a particular program or needs special attention.

Meisels (1987) argues that in most cases, screening tests lack reliability and validity. Further evidence of the problems of reliability and validity comes from a large-scale study conducted in Minnesota (Thurlow, O'Sullivan, and Ysseldyke 1986), in which every preschool child in the state was given a developmental screening test. Some districts found a problem

---

*From F. Leon Paulson, Pearl R. Paulson, and Carol A. Meyer, "What Makes a Portfolio a Portfolio?" *Educational Leadership* 48 (February 1991): 60–63. Reprinted with permission of the authors.

with every child, and some found no problems at all. These results probably reflect the inadequacies of the tests themselves, the way in which they were administered, or the way in which the results were interpreted. In sum, the study makes clear one of the real dangers of using standardized tests, which is that decisions may be made on the basis of faulty information.

STANDARDIZED TESTS AND YOUNG CHILDREN

Questionable reliability and validity are not the only problems associated with standardized tests. Meisels (1989) contends that testing changes teachers' perceptions of children, education, and instruction and allows test makers to control curriculum decisions. According to this view, if test results indicate that an individual child is not as capable as some other

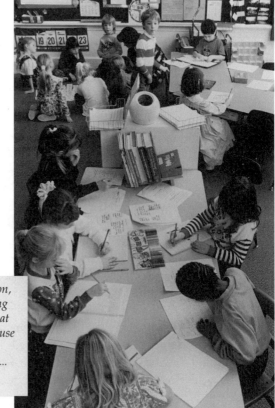

To help plan future instruction, teachers and schools are trying to find ways to determine what children know and how they use that knowledge.

child, then teachers will treat the child differently. The child might not be invited to participate in some activities or might be stigmatized by being assigned tasks to help remediate the deficiency uncovered by the test. In some school districts, test scores are published in the local newspapers, which compounds the problems. This practice is deplorable; it motivates some teachers to teach the information that will be tested so that their children's test scores look good.

For example, one first-grade teacher had been teaching reading using literature and a whole-language approach that involved reading and writing. After some months, she was pressured by parents to tell them at which levels their children could read in the basal readers. She gave the children the basal tests and put them into three reading groups. She discovered after a month or two not only that the children felt differently about learning to read and about their abilities as readers but that she began to perceive the children differently. Before the tests, her perception was that all the children were capable of learning to read. After the tests, she began to feel that some were much less capable of learning to read. Happily, she realized what was happening, learned from her experience, and reverted back to her original strategies for teaching reading.

Standardized tests should be considered one of many avenues available for collecting information about a child, not the only avenue. Kamii and Kamii (1990) argue that standardized achievement tests encourage teachers to teach in ways that do not promote autonomous learning and that the tests do not tap children's thinking processes. Martin (1988) disapproves of the use of standardized screening tests to homogenize the children in any program. She maintains that a flexible program "can accommodate a wide diversity in children's backgrounds, maturity, temperaments, interests, talents, abilities, and skills" (p. 489). Screening tests, she believes, are symptoms of the schools' refusal to accept differences.

The report of a task force of the National Association of State Boards of Education (NASBE 1988) echoes this view. The authors state that "developmental or readiness tests should not be used to determine placement in what may be perceived as homogeneous groups. We think that early childhood classrooms should contain a heterogeneous mix of children with various levels of skills and abilities" (p. 14). It is true that pressures on schools to achieve are enormous and that some schools try to limit differences so that they can show more gains on tests. Only knowledgeable teachers, administrators, and parents can break this cycle.

Before administering any standardized test, a teacher must think carefully about the purpose of the test and how the information from the test will be used. Standardized tests should *never* be used to deny services to any child or as the basis for placement decisions (retaining a child in grade, placing a child in special programs). Perrone (1990) states, "I cry when I read about young children 'held back' on the basis of a test, or placed in one or another of the schooling tracks that support various judgments about children's potential. And I wonder about those who believe that testing young children, then making placement, promotion, or retention decisions on the basis of such testing, leads to any constructive ends" (p. 1).

The following guidelines, which are based on NAEYC's "Position Statement on Standardized Testing of Young Children 3 Through 8 Years of Age" (1988), will help teachers determine if and when a standardized test should be used with young children:

1. Standardized tests must be used only for the purposes for which they were intended.

2. The use of standardized tests must be restricted to situations in which testing provides information that will clearly contribute to improved outcomes for children.

3. Test content should *not* determine the school's curriculum. Rather, the school's curriculum should guide teachers and others in the selection of tests.

4. Test givers must be qualified to administer the tests and sensitive to the developmental needs of young children.

5. Teachers and administrators must be knowledgeable about testing and able to interpret test results accurately and cautiously to parents, school personnel, and the media.

6. The younger the child, the more difficult it is to design tests that are reliable and valid. Nevertheless, all standardized tests used must be reliable and valid according to technical standards of test development.

7. Day-to-day instructional decisions must depend primarily on teacher observation. Standardized tests cannot provide information for planning day-to-day instructional activities.

8. Since standardized tests are not useful for day-to-day instructional decisions and student appraisal, taking time to administer the tests takes away from instructional time. Therefore, before teachers devote substantial classroom time to administering standardized tests, they should establish the purposes of the test data and determine whether the time and expense involved are warranted.

9. Student appraisal decisions should be based primarily on teacher observation and should reflect the goals of the classroom.*

*Based on "NAEYC Position Statement on Standardized Testing of Young Children 3 Through 8 Years of Age" by the National Association for the Education of Young Children, March 1988, *Young Children,* 43, pp. 42–47. Copyright © 1988 by NAEYC. Adapted by permission.

There are some valid reasons for using standardized tests, such as to collect data for research studies that allow broad-based comparisons that can help make schools better places for children. Some tests may also help in diagnosing children who need special services. The responsibility for using tests in ways that benefit children lies with teachers and administrators.

REPORTING

Reporting to parents is an important aspect of the job of the early childhood teacher. Parents have a right to know about their child's performance and behavior in school. The teacher has an obligation to be as honest as she can with parents, but this honesty must be leavened with tact and sensitivity. Nothing is as important to a parent as his child; honesty does not have to be brutal or hurtful. Reports to parents usually take the form of report cards, conferences, narratives, telephone calls, casual conversations, newsletters, or videotapes.

Report Cards

Although many schools require report cards for children in kindergarten or the primary grades, report cards are frustrating to both parents and teachers of young children. Many parents and most educators question the information conveyed on report cards: What does a grade mean? Does an A in mathematics mean that the child knows a given set of concepts or that the child can complete a given number of computations correctly?

Many schools have done away with letter grades on report cards for kindergarten (and some for primary grades), but often letter grades have been replaced by checklists of skills mastered, such as "Speaks in complete sentences" or "Counts to 100." These checklists have some of the disadvantages of letter grades and leave the impression that the program consists of isolated skills.

A report card is not the best choice for reporting to parents. If teachers must use report cards, however, they should try to mediate the information for parents by enclosing written summaries of children's progress or at least comments that help parents understand the grades. Some schools have adapted their report cards so that they reflect more about what the child can do and depend less on letter grades. For example, rather than posting a grade in reading, some parts of a developmental checklist might be on the report card, such as "Self-corrects errors that change meaning." A report card might also have spaces for the child, teacher, and parents to record their goals for the next grading period. Another strategy is to have a conference with the parents to discuss the child's progress and to review the report card.

Conferences

The most effective way of reporting to parents is face to face, in a conference. A conference should not be conducted so that the parents sit passively while the teacher tells them about their child. Both parents and teachers (and sometimes children) should participate; each should learn from the other, and both should have the opportunity to share information.

Effective conferences require advance preparation. All the anecdotal records, information gathered from checklists, information from inventories or interviews, and portfolios of work will need to be assembled and organized. Teachers must not withhold information from parents; all records should be open to them. Preparation should also include writing a summary of the child's progress in all areas of development and thinking about the implications of assessments for future planning for the child. The teacher's role is also to seek information from the parents by asking for their observations and their plans and expectations for their child.

During a conference, the teacher should be prepared to answer questions from parents. Parents will likely want to know what they can do at home to help their child, what interests and abilities the teacher has observed in their child, how their child gets along with other children, who are their children's friends at school, and what kinds of things are difficult for their child.

A conference may allow the teacher to share information about the program with parents as well as information about their child. The inverse of this sharing is eliciting the feelings and understandings of the parents about the program. A well-planned conference provides for sharing information and for keeping the lines of communication open between teachers and parents (Gelfer and Perkins 1987).

Effective follow-up to a conference will be helpful in planning the next conference and will increase the parents' trust. All agreements made during a conference should be summarized in writing, and copies should be made for both the teacher and the parents. If the conference ends with an agreement that the teacher will perform certain tasks, then these tasks should be completed promptly and the information should be entered in the conference file. For example, if the parents request that the teacher observe their child for a specific behavior in the next two weeks and report to them, then the teacher should make the observations, record them, and share them with the parents.

Evaluation of the conference is a component of follow-up activities. Canady and Seyfarth (1979, pp. 49–50) suggest some questions that will assist in evaluating the conference: Could the conference be described as a problem-solving session? Was there an equal distribution of power among all persons present during the conference? Was the emotional climate of the conference positive? Was the tone of the conference constructive? Were the goals of the conference understood by all persons present? Were the goals met? Were facts and all information related to the conference adequately handled? Follow-up should be considered as carefully as preconference planning.

Narrative Reports

The next most effective way of reporting to parents is through a narrative report. Narratives include basically the information that the teacher would share with parents in a conference. Statements in a narrative should be supported by evidence from the various records that the teacher has accumulated. One method of organizing the information is to focus on each area of development (intellectual, social, emotional, and physical). The narrative should also include what the teacher considers to be implications of the information and plans for the future.

A good narrative is a summary of the information from other records. For example, in summarizing a child's growth in social abilities, the narrative might read: "Since the beginning of the year, Denise has gained in her ability to communicate her needs and wants with words most of the time. On three occasions, she has been observed asking a child for a toy that she wanted. She is also able to share classroom materials. She has been observed willingly sharing toy trucks and blocks with other children. "

Note the objectivity of these remarks. They are specific observations, not judgments or generalizations. Statements such as "Jediah is unhappy" or "Samantha does not function at the level of her peers" have no place in a narrative report.

Telephone Calls

Generally, telephone calls are most useful for sharing with parents information about specific incidents. If, for example, Carly used words to express her frustration for the first time rather than hitting people, a telephone call to report that progress would be appropriate. Telephone calls should not be used to relay negative information about a child unless there is absolutely no alternative. Telephone calls should be brief and to the point and made at times that likely will be convenient for parents.

Casual Conversations

Sometimes, parents prefer to have casual conversations with the teacher when they are picking up or delivering their child. These conversations do not substitute for conferences, but teachers can help keep parents informed by reporting on progress or interesting anecdotes from the day. Again, these are not the times to report negative information. If a problem needs to be shared, a conference should be scheduled.

Newsletters

Although newsletters are not commonly listed as a means of reporting to parents, they can help keep parents informed about what is going on in the program. Some newsletters use reports that children write or dictate about field trips, visitors, or other events to provide interesting information to parents. Newsletters need not be formal productions that require a lot of time. Kindergarten and primary children can write items to be included in newsletters. Even threes and fours can write items (these may need to be translated for the parents) or dictate items to be shared with families. A review of the week's events and a list of plans for the next week will help parents know what their children are learning and doing. Many parents will engage their children in activities at home that relate to topics at school if they are kept informed through a newsletter.

Videotapes

Another general means by which teachers can keep parents informed about the school program is to make a videotape of a typical schoolday and encourage parents to check it out. After everyone has had a chance to view the video, the teacher should make a new one. The first video might provide general information about the program, and later videos might concentrate on specific topics: new themes, areas added to the classroom, classroom pets, storytime, music and movement activities, and so on. The teacher should ensure that every child is included in class videos.

ASSESSMENT AND REPORTING

Assessment and reporting go together like graham crackers and milk. It is hard to fathom why any educator would bother to institute a comprehensive assessment program if the information was not to be shared with others—administrators, parents, and other teachers. It is also difficult to imagine attempting to report to parents about their children without having a strong, ongoing assessment program.

In the process of collecting information and preparing for reporting, teachers can evaluate their assessment programs: Are some pieces of information missing? Are there areas in the child's development about which more information is needed? Are there more effective ways of gathering the needed information? Parents, too, will offer assessment information. They may let the teacher know that the child is transferring the information being learned in school to other situations. Effective reporting and effective assessment go hand in hand.

CHAPTER SUMMARY

- Assessment is much more than testing; it involves ongoing data collection that leads to curriculum and planning decisions.
- Program assessment is achieved by looking at the progress of individual children, the opportunities for learning, and the curriculum. Like assessment of children, program assessment should be ongoing and should contribute to decision making about the program.
- Assessment of children should reflect as much information about them as possible, should serve

a clear purpose, should be age appropriate, should be as much like the everyday work that children do as possible, should reflect the teacher's knowledge, and should be ongoing.
- Keeping anecdotal records is one method of collecting information about children. Such records should record exactly what happened and should be collected over time and in a variety of settings.
- Checklists and rating scales are quick ways of collecting limited information on children's skills. They can be used to document children's behav-

ior in play situations, their physical skills, and a variety of other kinds of information.

- Attitude or interest inventories help teachers know more about what children are thinking and feeling. They can be open ended or require more structured responses.
- Time-activity sampling is a technique for periodically recording the location of each child (or selected children) and the activity in which he is engaged. These records provide information about how long children stay with activities and how often they choose the same activity.
- Portfolios of children's work are some of the most important assessment tools. These portfolios can include written work, video- and audiotapes, and photographs.
- Standardized tests are another tool for gathering assessment information about children. However, such tests should never be used to deny services to or make placement decisions about a child.
- The most common standardized tests given to young children are screening tests and readiness tests. These tests are often used inappropriately; critics of such tests also argue that they are not as valid and reliable as they should be.
- When testing young children, teachers should use tests only for the purposes for which they were intended and only when their use will clearly benefit children; select tests that are appropriate for the curriculum; allow only qualified people to administer tests; ensure that they and the school's administrators are knowledgeable about tests; choose only reliable and valid tests. Careful consideration should be given to the value of the tests in terms of the time consumed in administering them.
- Reporting to parents is an important component of the job of the early childhood teacher. The most common reporting methods include report cards, conferences, narrative reports, telephone conversations, casual conversations, newsletters, and videotapes.
- Report cards do not provide very meaningful information. The best choice for effective communication between the teacher and parents is a conference. If conferences are not possible, written narratives are the next best choice.
- Telephone calls, casual conversations, newsletters, and videotapes can keep parents informed about day-to-day happenings and the general nature of the school program, but they are not appropriate for sharing in-depth information about individual children.

WHAT WOULD YOU DO?

Reflect on your reading and your own experiences with young children as you think about the following situations:

1. Your school has eliminated traditional report cards and substituted parent conferences. A parent wants to know how she can compare her child to other children in such a system. What would you tell her?
2. One of the directors of your school insists that children should never be tested. How would you respond to this statement?
3. The local paper publishes achievement test scores by school and encourages parents to compare the scores of their children's school to those of other community schools. What would you tell your students' parents if they called you for an explanation of the scores?
4. The teachers in your school are debating about what should be done with student portfolios at the end of the schoolyear. What would you recommend?

THEORY INTO PRACTICE

1. Interview two or three teachers of young children about how they assess children's progress and report to parents. Do they have control of these decisions? Are they required to use some specific techniques? Explain your findings.
2. Examine a screening test and a readiness test. Study the information about reliability and validity that is furnished by the publisher of each test. Could the information that is gathered from each test be gathered in other ways? Why?
3. Observe a class of young children taking a standardized test. What behaviors do they exhibit? Then read *First Grade Takes a Test* (Cohen 1980). How does the author describe the children's responses to the test? Do you think her interpretation is accurate? Why?
4. Review the brochure *Testing of Young Children: Cautions and Concerns* (NAEYC 1989). How can better information be disseminated to the public?
5. Participate in a simulation of a parent-teacher conference. Play the role of the teacher of a child with learning or behavior problems that must be communicated to the parent. What kinds of information would you gather before the conference? How would you arrange the physical setting for the conference? How would you conclude the conference?

RECOMMENDED FOR FURTHER READING

Grace, Cathy, and Elizabeth Shores. *The Portfolio and Its Use: Developmentally Appropriate Assessment of Young Children.* Little Rock, AR: Southern Association on Children Under Six, 1992.

   This book helps teachers understand why portfolios are appropriate in classrooms for young children and what teachers need to know in order to use them well. The authors provide many practical examples of checklists and other records that can be helpful to teachers who want to align their assessments with their curriculum more successfully.

Kamii, Constance, ed. *Achievement Testing in the Early Grades: The Games Grown-Ups Play.* Washington, DC: National Association for the Education of Young Children, 1990.

   Kamii and the other authors represented in this book describe the dilemmas of testing young children. Points of view include those of principals, superintendents, and teachers. Especially thought provoking are the chapters on why achievement testing should be discontinued and the negative effects of achievement testing in mathematics. Reading this book could provide some teachers with the information they need to bring about change in testing young children and others with ammunition to continue to resist testing.

National Association for the Education of Young Children. *Testing of Young Children: Concerns and Cautions.* NAEYC Brochure 582. Washington, DC: NAEYC, 1989.

   This brochure provides excellent information in a brief form for sharing with parents and administrators. It suggests some solutions to the problems of increasing testing.

National Association of State Boards of Education Task Force on Early Childhood Education. *Right From the Start.* Alexandria, VA: NASBE, 1988.

   This document discusses assessment in the larger context of changes that must be made to curriculum and other elements of early childhood education programs in the public schools.

REFERENCES

Bentzen, Warren. *Seeing Young Children: A Guide to Observing and Recording Behavior.* New York: Delmar, 1985.

Boehm, Ann E., and Richard A. Weinberg. *The Classroom Observer: Developing Observation Skills in Early Childhood Settings.* 2d ed. New York: Teachers College Press, 1987.

Canady, Robert Lynn, and John T. Seyfarth. *How Parent-Teacher Conferences Build Partnerships.* Fastback 132. Bloomington, IN: Phi Delta Kappa Educational Foundation, 1979.

Cohen, Miriam. *First Grade Takes a Test.* New York: Dell, 1980.

Flood, James, and Diane Lapp. "Reporting Reading Progress: A Comparison Portfolio for Parents." *Reading Teacher* 42 (March 1989): 508–514.

Gelfer, Jeffrey I., and Peggy G. Perkins. "Effective Communication with Parents: A Process for Parent/Teacher Conferences." *Childhood Education* 64 (October 1987): 19–22.

Graves, Donald. Presentation at a conference of the International Reading Association, Atlanta, Georgia, May 1990.

Hills, Tynette W. "Assessment in Context—Teachers and Children at Work." *Young Children* 48 (July 1993): 20–28.

Hills, Tynette W. "Reaching Potentials Through Appropriate Assessment." In *Reaching Potentials: Appropriate Curriculum and Assessment for Young Children,* vol. 1, edited by S. Bredekamp and T. Rosegrant. Washington, DC: National Association for the Education of Young Children, 1992.

Irwin, D. Michelle, and M. Margaret Bushnell. *Observational Strategies for Child Study.* New York: Holt, Rinehart and Winston, 1980.

Kamii, Constance, and Mieko Kamii. "Why Achievement Testing Should Stop." In *Achievement Testing in the Early Grades: The Games Grown-Ups Play,* edited by Constance Kamii, 15–39. Washington, DC: National Association for the Education of Young Children, 1990.

Katz, Lilian G. *More Talks with Teachers.* Urbana, IL: Eric Clearinghouse on Elementary and Early Childhood Education, 1984.

Martin, Anne. "Teachers and Teaching." *Harvard Educational Review* 58 (November 1988): 488–501.

McKenna, Michael C., and Dennis J. Kear. "Measuring Attitude toward Reading: A New Tool for Teachers." *Reading Teacher* 43 (May 1990): 626–639.

Meisels, Samuel J. "High-Stakes Testing in Kindergarten." *Educational Leadership* 47 (April 1989): 16–22.

Meisels, Samuel J. "Remaking Classroom Assessment with the Work Sampling System." *Young Children* 48 (July 1993): 34–40.

Meisels, Samuel J. "Uses and Abuses of Developmental Screening and School Readiness Testing." *Young Children* 42 (January 1987): 4–6, 68–73.

National Association for the Education of Young Children. "NAEYC Position Statement on Standardized Testing of Young Children 3 Through 8 Years of Age." *Young Children* 43 (March 1988): 42–47.

National Association for the Education of Young Children. *Testing of Young Children: Concerns and Cautions.* NAEYC Brochure 582. Washington, DC: NAEYC, 1989.

National Association of State Boards of Education. *Right From the Start: The Report of the NASBE Task Force on Early Childhood Education.* Alexandria, VA: NASBE, 1988.

Paulson, F. Leon, Pearl R. Paulson, and Carol A. Meyer. "What Makes a Portfolio a Portfolio?" *Educational Leadership* 48 (February 1991): 60–63.

Perrone, Vito. "How Did We Get Here?" In *Achievement Testing in the Early Grades: The Games Grown-Ups Play,* edited by Constance Kamii, 1–14. Washington, DC: National Association for the Education of Young Children, 1990.

Reardon, S. Jeanne. "A Collage of Assessment and Evaluation From Primary Classrooms." In *Assessment and Evaluation in Whole Language Programs,* edited by Bill Harp. Boston: Christopher Gordon, 1991.

Schweinhart, Lawrence J. "Observing Young Children in Action: The Key to Early Childhood Assessment. *Young Children* 48 (July 1993): 29–33.

Stoner, Sue, and Karyn Purcell. "The Concurrent Validity of Teachers' Judgments of the Abilities of

Preschoolers in a Daycare Setting." *Educational and Psychological Measurement* 45 (Summer 1985): 109–116.

Thurlow, Martha L., Patrick J. O'Sullivan, and James E. Ysseldyke. "Early Screening for Special Education: How Accurate?" *Educational Leadership* 44 (November 1986): 93–95.

Chapter Fifteen

Teachers, Parents, and Paraprofessionals

As you observed a class of five-, six-, and seven-year-olds this morning, you noticed that in addition to the teacher, two other adults were working in the classroom. One of them took a small group of children outside, where she helped them mark off a circle in the grass and begin investigating and recording what they found there. The other adult worked with a small group of children who were exploring patterns with math manipulatives. Meanwhile, the teacher listened as two children read the stories they had written. During your visit, you observed these adults as they read to individual children, helped a group dramatize a story, and assisted individuals with solving problems related to their projects.

As you were preparing to leave, you were introduced to the other adults and learned that one was a parent volunteer and the other was a paid teacher aide. Based on what you saw, you felt that the children really benefited by having these extra adults in the class. Yet you wondered how the teacher made sure that they knew what to do and what made the relationships among these adults so positive.

· ·

The previous chapter discussed communication with parents as it relates to reporting on the progress of their children and activities in the program. This chapter will further explore the relationship between families and teachers and expand on the theme of communicating with parents. The teacher's goal must be to forge a partnership with parents that results in the best possible educational experience for the children.

NEED FOR PARENT INVOLVEMENT

There are good reasons for teachers to want parents to be involved in the education of their children (Olson 1990). Greenberg (1989) believes that encouraging parent involvement aids teachers in building children's self-esteem, reduces discipline problems, and increases children's regard for themselves as learners. Parents teach their children much that cannot be taught in school. Teachers who view parents as important partners in the children's education will appreciate parents more and be more open to parental involvement.

Research indicates that children achieve more when parents are involved in their schooling. The major findings from the research on parent involvement have been summarized by Henderson (1988):

- *The family, not the school, provides the primary educational environment for children.*
- *Involving parents in their children's formal education improves the children's achievements.*
- *Parent involvement is most effective when it is comprehensive, well-planned, and long-lasting.*
- *Involving parents when their children are young has beneficial effects that persist throughout the child's academic career.*
- *Involving parents with their children's education at home may not be enough to improve schools; a school's average level of achievement does not appear to improve unless parents are involved in the school.*

- *Children from low-income and minority families benefit the most when parents are involved in the schools, and parents do not have to be well-educated to make a difference. (p. 153)*

When parents are involved in their children's school experiences, they are as likely to be affected positively as the children. A study of parents who worked in Head Start programs found that they "gained significantly in their positive attitudes about the importance of education" (Systems Development Corporation 1972). Leik and Chalkey (1990) report that Head Start parents who were involved in an enrichment program (involving more parental activities than the minimum required by Head Start) were more likely to see their children as competent than were parents who did not participate in the enrichment program. However, both groups of parents functioned more effectively after being involved in parental activities.

Parent involvement also affects the family, as the parent gains skill in interacting with all the children in the family, not just the child in school. Many parents who have become involved with their children's schools have even used the skills learned there to improve their job opportunities (Kagan 1982).

In reviewing what we know and do not know about parent involvement programs, Epstein (1991) offers these conclusions:

- Parents and teachers are more similar than different—they have many goals in common and a need to share information.
- Programs must continue through the elementary and high school years, not stop after the early childhood years.
- Programs must include all families.
- Programs make the teacher's job easier.
- Program development takes time.

REALITIES OF PARENT-TEACHER RELATIONSHIPS

Parent-teacher relationships are not as simple as many articles lead us to believe. New teachers could mistakenly come to think that parent volunteers are common and that all parents will attend parent conferences if they are invited to do so. However, as teachers of young children, you need to recognize that although parent involvement is very important, it is not always easy for the teacher, the school, or the parents to facilitate. The irony, expressed by Lightfoot (1978), is that *families and schools are engaged in a complementary sociocultural task and yet they find themselves in great conflict with one another. One would expect that parents and teachers would be natural allies, but social scientists and our own experience recognize their adversarial relationship—one that emerges out of their roles as they are defined by the social structure of society, not necessarily or primarily the dynamics of interpersonal behaviors. (p. 20)*

Pressures on parents today are tremendous. Changing family structures, economic conditions, and lack of support for the nuclear family contribute to the stress. Family structures have changed radically from the 1950s; only 5.9 percent of Americans have a "Dick and Jane" family (Cline 1990), in which the father works outside the home and the mother stays at home to care for the children. More and more children live with single parents, in two-parent working families, or in blended families created by remarriages. Many children also live with relatives other than their parents. Families today may consist of stepparents, foster parents, grandparents, single mothers, single fathers, or any number of other configurations.

The number of homeless children and the number of children living in poverty in the United States increases daily. Children in families headed by someone younger than thirty, minority children, and children in single-parent families are more likely to be poor than other children. "More than one-third of all children living in young families are poor; nearly one out of two black children is poor; more than half of all children who live in female-headed families are poor" (Children's Defense Fund 1990, p. 25). These figures have not improved. "Nearly 25 percent of children younger than six were living in poverty in 1991" (Children's Defense Fund 1992, p. 17).

More than half the mothers of children under six are employed outside the home, and that number is constantly rising (Children's Defense Fund 1990, p. 152). This enormous number of mothers in the workforce reflects economic conditions that make it ever more difficult for a family to survive economically. Many mothers work because they are the sole source of support for their children. These economic stresses in turn make it more difficult than ever before for parents to have choices about child care, to spend energy nurturing and educating their children rather than just trying to survive, or to become involved in the formal education of their children.

In addition to these pressures on the family, today's nuclear family does not have the support from the extended family that was available to past generations. Families often live long distances from other relatives and must depend on outsiders for child care and advice or support. Many parents are isolated; they have no one to help them cope with all the demands of caring for children and maintaining their daily lives.

In a review of research on changing demographic trends, Halpern (1987) found that:

1. *families with young children are increasingly dependent on agencies outside their informal social networks for the emotional, informational, and material support underlying nurturant childrearing;*
2. *our sense of collective responsibility for other people's children, never strong to begin with, is deteriorating further;*
3. *the stress on parents of trying to provide both adequate economic support and adequate care and nurturance for children is likely to intensify; and*
4. *we as a society face the urgent task of renewing and redefining our social contract with each other, and with young families in particular; the early childhood care and education community has a central responsibility with respect to this task. (p. 34)*

Implications for Teachers

One of the first rules for teachers who want to establish good relationships with all parents is to adopt a **nonjudgmental attitude** toward them. Most parents care desperately about their children. There are many reasons why parents do not get involved in school, but lack of concern about their children is usually not one of them. Some parents may have had negative experiences in school, so that any contact with the school revives their own feelings of inadequacy; others may be overwhelmed with the pressures in their lives and unable to cope with one more demand; still others may not know what they can do to help their child in school. For some parents, it would be culturally inappropriate to be other than passive in their involvement with the school. (In some cultures, teachers are highly respected figures of authority. For parents from such cultures to take an active role in school would be perceived as an infringement on the teacher's authority.)

Nonjudgmental attitude
An attitude of acceptance; a refusal on the part of a teacher to criticize parents.

There are many other reasons why parents may not get involved. The fundamental principle that should guide teachers in working with parents is that parents need help, understanding, and support, not criticism (Hranitz and Eddowes 1987). It is imperative that teachers persist in efforts to involve parents in their children's education.

The Maryland State Department of Education (1983) has drawn up some recommendations for establishing contact with parents who do not respond to the usual invitations to participate in school activities:

- *Meet the family at its present level of need, no matter how different from your own its values or motivation may be.*

- *Develop obtainable goals and realistic expectations for change. This will decrease frustration for families and staff. Through interagency contact, help families meet their basic needs for food, shelter, medical care, and a sense of self-worth before focusing on the less basic needs for education, child development, and parenting skills.*
- *Try to be aware of personal expectations when working with special families. When expectations are realistic they can motivate achievement; when they are not realistic they can overwhelm and defeat. (p. 7)*

New teachers must expect to be involved in major efforts to restructure family and school relationships. Expecting all families to meet middle-class standards for involvement in schools is unrealistic. It is also unrealistic to believe that only one model for family involvement is possible. Families and schools must learn new ways of interacting. Karr and Landerholm (1991) state the goal well: "Programs must meet the needs of the parents they serve rather than demand that the parents meet the needs of the program" (p. 6).

Teachers of young children must be especially sensitive to the needs of children from different family structures, and this sensitivity should be reflected in the language used to discuss families. The phrase *broken home*, for example, is inappropriate. A child's parents may be divorced and she may be living in a single-parent family, but there is nothing inherently wrong or deprived about such a family structure. Similarly, teachers must avoid planning activities in which the child is to make gifts for parents or events that are labeled "father-son" or "mother-daughter." Activities involving gifts or family events should be presented as opportunities to share with someone special in a child's life—a foster mother, a grandparent, or any other relative—rather than being specifically labeled for mothers and fathers. When using photographs of families, teachers should make sure that a variety of family structures are illustrated and that discussions are not limited to families made up of Mother, Father, and children.

ENCOURAGING PARENT INVOLVEMENT

Many educators have developed strong relationships with even hard-to-reach parents. Greenberg (1989) summarizes the characteristics of a teacher in a successful parent outreach program. Such a teacher:

- *shows equal, warm welcome and respect to all parents;*
- *truly listens to parents, knowing that they don't always agree with teachers and that teachers aren't always right, . . . seeks to elicit from parents*

Parents play a variety of roles in their children's schools, from passive to very active.

knowledge about the child, the child's culture, and the parents' views and values, and then customizes the child's school experience accordingly and works with parents, starting where they are;

- *holds meetings at varying times of the day and evening to permit parents who work various shifts and parents who live far away to be able to attend;*
- *implements a regular policy of reaching out to hard-to-find parents through home visits; . . .*
- *provides a reason for low-income parents to bother to come to school [for example, by offering transportation and escorting to more specialized services or programs in which they can learn about childrearing or other subjects] (p. 73)**

Teachers should encourage parents to visit frequently and to drop in without an appointment. Teachers can also provide guidance to parents in how to help young children learn at home.

*From Polly Greenberg, "Parents as Partners in Young Children's Development and Education: A New American Fad? Why Does It Matter?" *Young Children* 44 (May 1989): 61–75. Reprinted with permission of the author.

Teachers and schools must make the effort to work with parents. Teachers who have not worked with parents may think that parents who have less than a high school diploma are unwilling or lack the ability to work with their children. Research indicates, however, that teachers who use home-learning activities are able to involve parents, regardless of their educational backgrounds. Reporting on the results of their research, Epstein and Dauber (1989) assert:

> If schools don't work to involve parents, then parent education and family social class are very important for deciding who becomes involved. But if schools take parent involvement seriously and work to involve all parents, then social class and parents' level of education decrease or disappear as important factors. (p. 21)

Parent Roles

Parents may take on a variety of roles in the school. Figure 15.1 illustrates the levels of parent involvement along a continuum, from very passive to very active. At the "low" end of the continuum are parents who never participate in any school activities, although they are active in the sense of sending their children to school; one level higher are parents who participate in very passive roles that only require them to listen. Further along the continuum are parents who participate by attending events at school or volunteering their time to help teachers in the classroom; even further along are those parents who get involved in decision making at the school or district level and who assist in teaching. Parents of children in cooperative schools usually are at this point. Some parents take total responsibility for their children's education and make the commitment to educate their children at home.

Many parents do not see how their involvement at school could possibly benefit their children. Teachers need to supply specific information about why parent involvement is important. For example, teachers often suggest that parents read to their children but do not share with the parents why reading will help the children become more literate. Parents who have specific information are much more likely to become involved.

Parents who choose not to be involved in their children's school cite as reasons health problems, economic differences between themselves and teachers, and work responsibilities. Some teachers, on the other hand, believe that parents are not more involved because of their unrealistic expectations of the school's role; an attitude that school is not important

FIGURE 15.1 Continuum of Parent Involvement

HIGH

↑

- Parents, trained by teacher, assist in classroom in such learning activities as reviewing writing samples, assisting at learning centers, or helping with computer use.
- Parents in classrooms reinforce processes and concepts introduced by teachers.
- Parents in classrooms practice with children on vocabulary words, number facts; help them enter answers on computer cards.
- Parents read to children in the classrooms.
- Parents make classroom presentations or present hands-on activities in areas of expertise.
- Parents participate in committees that directly influence school curricula and policies. Committees consist of parents, teachers, and administrator(s).
- P.T.A. parents work on sponsorship and implementation of curriculum-related and family-oriented activities, e.g., cultural arts contests, displays, Family Fun Night.
- Parents make instructional materials for classroom use, as directed by teachers.
- Parents assist in school library, checking out and shelving books.
- Parents participate as room mothers or room fathers.
- Parents supervise on class trips or chaperone at school functions.
- Parents visit classrooms during American Education Week or Back-To-School Night.
- Parents attend classroom plays, presentations.
- Parents attend school assembly programs.
- Parents attend competitive games, athletic events at school.
- Parents attend promotion ceremonies.
- Parents attend parent-teacher conferences.
- Parents are encouraged to help children with homework at home.
- Parents are involved in P.T.A. fundraising activities.
- Parents are asked to join P.T.A.
- Parents are encouraged to read school's handbook for parents.

↓

LOW
- No parental involvement.

Source: Harlene Galen, "Increasing Parental Involvement in Elementary School: The Nitty-Gritty of One Successful Program," *Young Children* 46 (January 1991): 19. Reprinted with permission of NAEYC.

FIGURE 15.2 Parent Interview Form

1. Would you like to work with the children in the classroom?
2. What would you prefer doing in the classroom if you were to come?
3. Name something special that you can do or make or something you know about that you would be willing to share with the children.
4. I'm going to read a list of items to you. Tell me if you have ever felt a need to know more about any of these items by answering either yes or no. (Interviewer: Please check appropriate category.)

		Yes	No
a.	How to teach my preschool children		
b.	Whether my child is developing appropriately		
c.	Services provided by community agencies to which I have a right		
d.	How to communicate better with my children		
e.	How to help my children interact better with others		
f.	How to discipline my children		
g.	How to make toys and other things for my children		
h.	How to tell whether my child is progressing in school		
i.	What to do when my children do things that I do not consider proper (temper tantrums, thumb sucking, bad manners)		
j.	How to play with my children		
k.	Where to take my children so they can have a nice time and learn		
l.	How to help my children retain their cultural heritage		
m.	How to use and develop the talents and skills that I know I have		
n.	How to refrain from hitting my child		
o.	How to guarantee that my child will succeed in school		
p.	How to talk to teachers		
q.	How to help my child learn a second language when I don't speak a second language		
r.	How to extend language learning		
s.	How to use my home environment as a learning experience for my children		

5. What is your opinion of preschool parents coming together at least once a month to talk and learn more about the areas to which you answered "yes"?
6. If you felt that this parent meeting is a good idea, how can we make sure that the meetings are worthwhile for parents?
7. Would you be willing to help organize the first parent meeting?
8. Are there other ways you might be willing to help with the parent meetings?
9. Name something special that you can do or make or that you know about that you would be willing to share with other parents.

Source: Mary Hohmann, Bernard Banet, and David P. Weikart, *Young Children in Action* (Ypsilanti, MI: High/Scope Press, 1979), pp. 328–329. Reprinted with permission of the publisher.

enough to warrant taking time from work; jealousy of teachers; teachers' lack of trust of parents; and a lack of activities to draw parents to school (Leitch and Tangri 1988).

Swick and McKnight (1989) found a cluster of characteristics in kindergarten teachers that strongly supported parent involvement, including belonging to a professional association and adhering to a developmentally oriented philosophy; they also found that administrative support for parent involvement was vital. Galinsky (1988) found that teachers who had more education and were parents themselves were more likely to have positive perceptions of parents. She explained that it is not being a parent per se that leads to positive perceptions but "the ability to put themselves in the parent's shoes and to be empathetic" (p. 8). If teachers feel that parental involvement is important, they will work to overcome the barriers that they perceive are keeping parents out of the school.

Every parent who wants to be involved should have the opportunity to do so. Teachers need to find out from parents how they would like to be involved. The most direct way of determining how parents feel and what they would like to do is to ask them—during a home visit or during a conference early in the year. Another way is to have them respond to a questionnaire. Figure 15.2 is an example of an interview form for teachers to use in determining the kind of involvement parents need or want.

In any case, teachers will want to have available lists of things that parents can become involved in and be accepting of their choices. Teachers might list a variety of things that parents can do at home and some that they can do at school. At home, for instance, parents might sew costumes for the dress-up area (teachers can supply the patterns and fabric), type a newsletter every two weeks, help collect materials needed for a project, tape record stories or poems for the children, and so on. At school, parents might supervise children during cooking, water play, or other activities that require extra supervision; read to individual children or small groups; talk to the class about their work; accompany the group on field trips; and so on.

Activities for Involving Parents

Many activities can be arranged to involve both parents who choose to be active and those who choose more passive roles. A number of levels of participation are possible:

1. Family reading, family math, or family science nights are evenings when the children and their families are invited to school and participate

in reading activities or math activities that are developmentally appropriate and that help parents understand why such activities are provided in school.

2. Potluck dinners offer a way to celebrate holidays by inviting families to share social evenings together. If the children can make part of the meal to share, so much the better.

3. Parent education workshops can range from sessions in which outside speakers talk about child development, discipline, or some other topic of general interest to meetings of small groups who want to discuss specific issues, such as sibling rivalry, with other parents.

4. Formal organizations of parents such as Parent-Teacher Associations can provide programs for parents and teachers.

5. Committees of parents can discuss school issues, including curriculum decisions, school policies, and hiring of staff.

6. Parents can become members of teams involved in making recommendations for children with special needs.

7. Parents and teachers can attend workshops in which they make instructional materials for use in the classroom.

8. Chapman (1991) suggests that parents can help produce videotapes that focus on lessons and explain the "whys" of the lesson (why certain materials, teaching strategies, responses to wrong answers are used) or that teach other parents specific techniques for helping their children, such as how to motivate them.

COMMUNICATION WITH PARENTS

It is the teacher's responsibility to keep the lines of communication with parents open. Communication with parents can be divided into two categories: communication *about the program* and communication *about the individual child* (Bundy 1991). The previous chapter discussed parent conferences, newsletters, and telephone calls. These are all avenues for communication, but they are used more to talk about an individual child than about the program. Home visits, parent visits to the school, school handbooks, letters and notes, and a teacher who is prepared with good written information about community resources will supplement the above-mentioned communication methods and keep parents informed about the school's program.

Cattermole and Robinson (1985) asked parents what they considered the most effective forms of communication they received from school. Their first choice was information they received from their children—followed by school newsletters, report cards, parent-teacher conferences, visits to school, notes or phone calls from teachers, and formal meetings and informal contacts with friends.

School Handbooks

School handbooks are especially useful for sharing basic information about programs. A handbook should include the school calendar; the hours of each session; school policies, such as procedures for getting refunds of tuition payments, celebrating birthdays at school, or handling sick children; a class list for each class; a list of the staff (with perhaps a short professional biography of each); and statements of the school's philosophy (Bundy 1991). The school handbook might also list the goals and objectives for the children, emergency procedures, bus routes, or other information useful to parents.

Home Visits

Although not as common as they once were, **home visits** are still an important means of establishing solid parent-teacher relationships. Some parents are much more comfortable in their own homes than at school. (However, teachers should be sensitive to the fact that some parents may find a home visit from the teacher uncomfortable or intrusive, for any number of reasons.) The information gained about the child, the parents, and the home environment are well worth the investment of time and energy required to complete home visits.

Home visit
A planned visit to a child's home by a school staff member, such as a teacher, counselor, or principal.

If a home visit can be arranged before school starts, the child and teacher can get to know each other individually before having to relate to each other in a group setting. Parents will also appreciate meeting the teacher before school begins and having a chance to ask questions about the program and discuss expectations for their child.

Home visits can be effective if teachers plan and prepare for them. The following suggestions may help in planning visits:

1. Schedule the visits well in advance. Send a written reminder of the visit. Let the parents know how long you expect the visit to last. Arrive and leave on time.
2. Make sure that parents know the purpose of the visit. Assure parents that they do not need to make any special preparations for your visit.

3. Be a gracious guest. If the parent offers something to eat or drink, accept it politely. Respect the parents and the home.
4. Do not make snap judgments about the home environment. If the physical surroundings do not match your image of a home, do not conclude that the home is not a good environment for the child.
5. Be prepared to talk about the program and your plans for the children in an informal manner. Listen, ask questions, and listen some more.

Often, teachers like to take something when they visit—materials for making a nametag for the child, a camera for photographing the child, a photograph album of activities from the previous year, a puppet, a wooden puzzle, a book that can be returned to the classroom later, or paper and crayons for drawing. Taking something can provide openings for sharing information and opportunities for observations.

It is also helpful for the teacher to take an information sheet for the parents that gives his name and phone number, a school calendar with holidays and special events marked, information about snacks if parents will be providing them, and a list of rules for celebrating birthdays and for bringing objects to share at school. The teacher might also take along a list of materials that he needs at school. Teachers in one school district hand out a list of "beautiful junk"—egg cartons, oatmeal boxes, assorted nuts and bolts, baby food jars, old paint brushes, wood scraps, bottle caps, used magazines, and the like—that most households accumulate and that even families of limited means can contribute.

During a home visit, the teacher may want to discuss the special needs and interests of the child, any allergies or health problems that the teacher needs to be aware of, and the expectations the parents have for the child in the program. If it seems appropriate, the teacher can also discuss how the parents would like to be involved in the program. Parents may also want to know about the teacher's background, training, and experience. He should be prepared to discuss the program, how decisions are made about what to study, and how he plans to deal with discipline problems.

If the teacher is unable to visit two or three parents at home, he might try inviting them to a special meeting at school, where he shares the information he would have shared in a home visit. Kieff (1990) found that parents of children labeled "at risk" by their school district preferred meeting in small groups with the teacher. These parents did not feel comfortable in large, formal parent meetings.

It is important that all parents understand how much they teach their children and how important they are in their children's education. Hohmann, Banet, and Weikart (1979) suggest that teachers help parents "realize that . . . parenting *is* teaching, . . . they already know a lot about child development in general and about their own children in particular, and . . . teachers are not purveyors of knowledge but rather people who wish to support and extend the learning that's already going on at home" (p. 20).

If parents cannot or will not come to school and the teacher cannot visit them at home, the teacher should try to contact them by phone or by letter to share the information. The teacher should make his contacts with them nonthreatening and nonjudgmental. It is vital that the teacher continue to reassure parents that he is interested in their child and will welcome their questions.

Parent Visits to School

Some parents can arrange to visit the school during school hours and should always be welcomed. Parents who come to observe the program and their children's participation in it should be invited to sit and watch or to join in activities, whichever they feel most comfortable in doing. Every parent who comes to observe should be invited to schedule a conference so that any questions or concerns can be discussed. One school sends special invitations to each parent to attend school on a given day, beginning a few weeks before regularly scheduled conferences. The invitations indicate that if parents cannot come on the stated day, they can come any time. With a little persistence, teachers in this school get almost 100 percent of the parents to visit the school, and conferences are much more successful after parents have seen the program in action.

Parents can be invited to participate in holiday celebrations that the children have planned or invited to visit when the children are involved in a group activity so that they can observe their child's behavior in a group setting. Rather than having children put on performances, it is advisable to ask parents to visit when the children are involved in normal classroom activities, such as singing, playing musical instruments, or dramatizing stories. These activities do not require practice by the children but do allow the parent to feel good about their children's abilities.

The teacher might want to prepare an observation guide for parents so that they can see some of the important aspects of the program during their visit. Figure 15.3 is an example of such a guide, which can be adapted to fit the teacher's own needs.

Sometimes, parents who cannot attend school during the day can be invited for an evening visit. The children can come, too, and get involved in some of their usual school activities, so the parents can learn more about what their children do at school.

FIGURE 15.3 Observation Guide for Parents

Welcome to XYZ School!

We are always pleased to have parents visit our programs. This sheet may serve as a guideline for observing your child as he or she interacts with others in school. We encourage you to schedule an appointment with the teacher to discuss your observations. You may use any part of this form or you may turn it over and write down some questions that you want to ask the teacher later. Please do whatever is most comfortable for you. Enjoy your visit!

Check or circle whatever items are appropriate.

Setting:
Indoors
Outdoors

Activity:
Choice time (individual)
Whole group
Small group directed by teacher

Social Interactions:
With other children
With adults

Materials, Equipment, or Activities Selected:
List here

Did your child use material or equipment as it was designed to be used? or did he or she use the material or equipment to make up a game?

Time Spent in Each Activity:
Estimate here

Types of Interactions:
Solitary activities (played alone)
Small group activities (joined or formed a small group)

A **parent place** in a corner of the classroom can help parents feel that they are important and needed. A table and a small bulletin board are all that is necessary to provide such a corner for parents. Parents can use the bulletin board to communicate with each other (notes about car pools, child care, and so on). The teacher can post photographs of parents working with the children or creating materials or games for the classroom, notices of special events of interest to families, lists of items that are needed in the classroom, and so on. The table can hold a small resource library for parents; copies of articles for parents, books that parents might find helpful, pamphlets, magazines, brochures such as those published by NAEYC on a variety of topics (see "References"), and other materials can become part of the library. Some larger schools provide "parent rooms" where parents can meet other parents, wait to pick up their children, or find information about parenting. Epstein (1991) lists making room (literally) for parents as an important component of parent involvement programs.

> **Parent place**
> A special area of the classroom or a room in the school set aside for parents.

When parents cannot visit school or stay long enough to observe, notes and photographs of their children engaged in activities help communicate what is going on in class. A videotape of a day in the class that parents can borrow may also help to communicate with some parents. The teacher in one class writes a daily log of activities, which is posted for parents to read as they pick up their child ("Prickly Problems" 1989).

Letters and Notes

Parents appreciate letters that give them information about school programs and their children, in particular. Instead of newsletters, some teachers like to send form letters that may include suggestions for things the parents could do at home to complement what the children are learning in school. Adding a personal note about the child at the bottom of each parent's letter makes this practice even more effective. Brief notes that communicate the child's progress are an important way of letting parents know that the teacher is aware of their child and her accomplishments.

Notes should always be positive. A note saying that "Sebastian succeeded in tying his shoes today" or that "Nancy read a complete book independently" will help parents feel that the teacher is staying in touch with them. Most teachers keep a list of parents and jot down the date when they send each parent a note. When all parents have been contacted, the teachers start over. Some schools even have notepaper printed with captions such as "Good News" or "Happygram."

D'Angelo and Adler (1991) suggest the following guidelines for preparing effective written communication for parents:

- *Keep sentences short. Try to keep sentences to ten or fewer words, and never allow them to include more than twenty words.*
- *Keep paragraphs short. Try to keep paragraphs to an average of six lines.*
- *Use easy words. Let the short, familiar words bear the main burden of getting your point across. Use big words or technical terms when only those words will express a message accurately.*
- *Get to the point. State the purpose of your message up front and omit irrelevant information.*
- *Write things in logical order. The newspaper formula of "who, what, where, when, why, and how" is helpful as an organizing device.*
- *Be definite. Don't hedge. Be careful with such words as* seems, may, perhaps, possibly, generally, usually, *and* apparently. *Give a clear picture of what you want to say.*
- *Be direct. Speak to each reader. Say "you should" or "please do" instead of "parents should."*
- *Use the active voice more often than the passive. Put the subject at the beginning of the sentence. For example, write "Please sign and return the consent slip if you want your child to go on the trip to the zoo," rather than, "A consent slip must be signed by the parent in order for the child to attend the field trip to the zoo."*
- *Know your audience. Ask yourself, For whom is the material being written, and how well does the audience read? If you aren't sure, test your materials on a few people representative of the target audience. When in doubt, assume that there are at least some poor readers in your audience.*
- *Know yourself. Be yourself. Write as you would talk, and write to express—not to impress.*
- *Write and rewrite. Write a draft, then read it over. How long are the sentences? How many long words have you used? Have you used the passive voice a great deal? Are there unexplained technical words? Have you used jargon or abbreviations that your audience may not know? Can you say the same thing more clearly, more succinctly, or more interestingly? Ask someone else to read what you've written. Then rewrite it. (p. 354)**

Telecommunication

Some centers use technology to make communication with parents quick and easy. Bauch (1990) reports that one center uses a computerized calling

---

*From Diane A. D'Angelo and C. Ralph Adler, "Chapter I: A Catalyst for Improving Parent Involvement," *Phi Delta Kappan* 72 (January 1991): 350–354. Reprinted with permission of the authors.

system to call parents and deliver messages about the program. These systems allow the calls to be placed at the times that are convenient for parents and in the language the parents prefer.

A similar use of current technology is to equip each teacher's room with an answering machine on which the teacher records a short message like the following, which any parent can hear by calling:

> *Today, we went to the zoo to look for patterns. We found patterns on the animals, in the enclosures, and in the pathways. You could help your child find patterns in your home. We printed patterns with junk items in art, and we read a patterned book,* Brown Bear, Brown Bear. *Your child has a copy of this book, and you could read it or let him or her read it to you. If you have a chance this weekend, encourage your child to look for patterns in numbers, such as the pattern of house or apartment numbers on your block.*

Parents of Children with Special Needs

Parents of children with special needs are by necessity more involved in their children's education than some parents because legal requirements specify that they be consulted and informed about decisions made about their children. (Please see the Epilogue for additional information about legal issues.) Meetings to plan educational programs for children with special needs must include the parents. Communication with these parents may take the same forms as it does with all other parents, but it may need to be more specific and more frequent. Teachers should check with their program administrators or principals about the legal requirements for communicating with parents of children with special needs.

In addition, parents of children with special needs may themselves need support from the teacher. Spidel (1987) notes that the parent of a child who is exceptional often expects the child's teacher to:

1. Understand his child's assets as well as his deficiencies
2. Appreciate his child's accomplishments whenever and however they appear
3. Help the parent (and the child) live without guilt or blame
4. Tell his child how it really is (the truth about himself may be difficult for a child who is learning disabled but not as difficult as the bewilderments and heartaches he experiences from half-truths and evasions)

Community Resources

Finally, many parents need information about resources available to them in the community. Teachers are not expected to be child psychologists or marriage counselors, but they can help by keeping on hand a supply of brochures that describe the services offered by various community agencies with contact and referral information.

VOLUNTEERS IN THE CLASSROOM

Volunteers
Parents or community members who help in the classroom without pay.

Volunteers in the classroom are very important, especially as resources continue to shrink and schools cannot afford to hire enough adults to maintain adequate adult-child ratios. Volunteers can be parents or others from the community. Community volunteers can be recruited from colleges, service groups, senior citizen groups, church groups, and the like. These volunteers often bring many skills and abilities to share with chil-

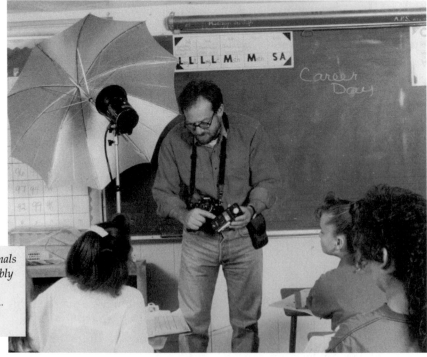

Parents and paraprofessionals can contribute immeasurably to school programs.

dren—talents in music, storytelling, woodworking, art, or other areas that can enhance the program. Many teachers are especially interested in recruiting older volunteers in order to promote the intergenerational contact that is so often missing in the lives of today's children.

Both community and parent volunteers must be screened and trained before working in the classroom. Some schools have volunteer coordinators who are responsible for interviewing prospective volunteers and determining their suitability for working with children. In other situations, teachers themselves interview volunteers. Whoever conducts the interviews should try to determine what the person has to offer the children, his expectations about volunteering, and his ability to communicate with and nurture children. If a volunteer seems unsuitable for working directly with the children, he can be asked to perform tasks that do not involve the children, such as typing materials, mounting artwork, placing the children's work in their portfolios, and so on.

Training for volunteers should clearly describe the philosophy of the program, goals for the children, activities that are appropriate for volunteers, discipline in school, and school policies and procedures. Such training is important, as every person who works in the classroom models behavior for the children and teaches by example.

Volunteers should always feel that the work they do is of real benefit to the children. They must perceive that the tasks they are asked to do in the classroom are a value added to the regular program. For example, if volunteers are asked to correct papers, they may see that task as something the teacher would do anyway and believe that they are not really adding to the quality of the program. It would be more appropriate to ask volunteers to do tasks that the teacher simply could not do without their help. Any special experience that can be added because the volunteer is available to help will make it clear to the parent or community volunteer that she is needed to provide this experience for the children.

Some examples of appropriate activities for mature and well-trained volunteers include:

1. Reading to children (individually or in small groups)
2. Supervising small groups in outdoor play
3. Taking a small group for a walk around the schoolgrounds (looking for signs of changing seasons, collecting natural materials, observing surface differences, and so on)
4. Supervising children in an area that could not be used without additional help (cooking, water, music, tumbling, sewing, and so on)

FIGURE 15.4 Instructions for the Art Area

➡ Children may choose to do art activities between 9:15 and 10:15.

➡ Choices available to the children: paint and easels, modeling clay, crayons or chalk and drawing paper, swatches of fabric for collage

➡ Any child who chooses easel painting should wear a painting smock. The smocks are on the hooks beside the sink. Children should be encouraged to get their own smocks and to replace them when finished. Completed paintings are placed on the drying rack to the left of the sink. All children should be encouraged to clean up and put away the materials they use when they have completed their work.

➡ We are emphasizing the concepts of texture. Please use texture words such as *rough, smooth, grainy, splintery, nubby, bumpy,* and so on when talking to the children about their work.

➡ Some children will need help labeling their work with their names. You can write their names and the date in one corner of their work. If they want you to write something about their work, please write exactly what they say.

Thank you so much for your help. We could not offer so many choices to the children without it.

---

5. Playing board games with children or helping them learn to play checkers, chess, or other such games

It is important to take the time to help volunteers understand what they can do in the classroom and how to do it most easily. Although many parent and community volunteers are quite able to work with one child at a time, they may not have especially good group-management abilities. Specific instructions allow those who are not specially trained in working with groups of young children to feel more secure. If a volunteer were going to supervise the art area, for example, the instructions shown in Figure 15.4 would be helpful. A planning sheet such as the one shown in Figure 15.5 would guide a volunteer in supervising a cooking experience. Another approach is to develop a file of cards listing suggestions for different activities and to laminate the cards for durability.

Teachers should always take the time to thank volunteers for their help. Immediate positive verbal feedback is important. Written thank-you notes are also invaluable in helping volunteers feel appreciated. These

FIGURE 15.5 Planning Sheet

COOKING PLANNING SHEET

Project _Fruit Salad_   **Date** _3/25_

Type: (Individual)   Small group

Purpose:

To help children learn about:

   (new foods)   similarities and differences in color

   other cultures   similarities and differences in size

   texture changes   similarities and differences in weight

   changes in smell   effects of heat

To develop:

   (small muscle skills)   eye-hand coordination

   other _____

Skills to be emphasized:

pouring	sorting	dipping	mixing	spreading
rolling	cracking	beating	juicing	grinding
slicing	grating	peeling	(cutting)	other _____

Ingredients needed:

apple   _walnut_ _____

orange _____ _____

banana _____ _____

pineapple _____ _____

Procedure:

1. _Prepare stations for each step of the recipe._
2. _Supervise children as needed as they complete_
   each step of the recipe.

_____

_____

_____

need not be expensive—a small note that the teacher can send home with a child for his parent or mail to a community volunteer is appropriate.

More elaborate displays of appreciation for volunteers are often planned once or twice a year. Some schools like to have a tea, a luncheon, or a breakfast to honor those who have contributed volunteer time. If teachers can get publicity in the local paper for special contributions by volunteers, they should do so—public praise is always welcome. Articles in newsletters that go out to all the parents can note the work that volunteers are doing at home and at school.

WORKING WITH PARAPROFESSIONALS

Paraprofessional
A paid assistant in the classroom.

Most classroom teachers are delighted to have **paraprofessionals,** or teacher aides, to work with in the classroom. Teacher aides can add immeasurably to the quality of the program; they can provide individual attention, increased supervision, scheduling flexibility, and assistance in instruction. (In most states, it is illegal for a teacher aide to *teach*, meaning that aides are not responsible for planning instruction and making instructional decisions.)

Paraprofessionals' levels of training and experience vary a great deal. Some will have completed programs of preparation to become paraprofessionals; others will have no training at all. In most schools, paraprofessionals must at least have high school diplomas and be eighteen or older. After the teacher knows about the background and experience of the aide, she can make plans for training or orientation.

Working successfully with an aide requires some planning on the teacher's part and some ability to communicate well with adults. The following guidelines will help:

1. Take the time to discuss your philosophy, the program, what you consider appropriate discipline, and other pertinent information with the aide. Even if the aide has training and experience, it is important that you agree on how the class should be handled.

2. If the aide lacks training, provide it. This is not always easy because the aide may be paid by the hour and may not be willing to stay longer or come earlier without extra pay. Try to arrange for your aide to be paid for the time spent in training. Provide written information, explain why you do things the way you do, and then model the behaviors that you expect in the classroom. Take a few minutes for discussion each day.

3. Do not assign the aide all the "dirty" chores in the classroom. No one wants to clean the gerbil cage and the painting area all the time and

never get a chance to do some of the more interesting classroom tasks, such as supervising a small group on a walk or in an art activity.

4. Provide positive feedback and praise for the work of the aide. It is important that he appreciate his contributions to the program.

5. Make sure that the children consider the aide as a teacher.

If the law states that aides are not to teach, what are they supposed to do? Generally, teacher aides can do almost everything that teachers do, with the exception of planning learning experiences and being responsible for assessment and reporting. However, aides can certainly contribute their observations of children or activities, which the teacher can communicate to parents and use in planning future activities. Assignments for aides should be determined by their level of skill and experience. A teacher could not expect an aide with no experience to work with the whole class during music time, for example.

Paraprofessionals can take on certain types of duties, including the following:

Instructional Duties
1. Reading to individual children or small groups or listening to children read
2. Providing individual help for children completing tasks
3. Providing small-group instruction that is planned by the teacher
4. Teaching children a song or a fingerplay
5. Working with a small group with manipulatives for mathematics or with materials for science investigations

Supervisory Duties
1. Supervising learning areas
2. Supervising outdoor play experiences (some states require one certified teacher on the playground during recess)
3. Supervising children on field trips
4. Supervising children as they move from one part of the building to another
5. Supervising the children as they complete routines (hanging up coats, using the toilet, and so on)

Classroom Maintenance Duties
1. Preparing classroom displays and bulletin boards
2. Setting up and helping serve snacks

<table>
<tr><td>

DEVELOPMENTALLY
APPROPRIATE
PRACTICE
....

</td><td>

Think about all you have learned about DAP and reflect on those principles when applied to working with parents and teacher aides. Adults should be treated in developmentally appropriate ways, just as children should be. For example, adults need choices about what and how they will learn, and they need to be able to apply what they know to new information. When thinking about DAP, consider the importance of volunteers and teacher aides in programs:

</td></tr>
</table>

- Are volunteers and aides given choices as much as possible?
- Are parents and teacher aides talked to and treated in ways that are respectful of their skills and abilities?
- Do the programs planned for parents allow choices and recognize the importance of parents as the first teachers of their children?

- Are parents' cultural and ethnic differences not only recognized but celebrated?
- Are the individual differences in parents considered when planning activities for parents?

3. Helping to keep the classroom and materials clean and ready for use
4. Setting up and running audiovisual equipment
5. Gathering materials from the library or other resources

As the teacher and aide work together, it is important that the teacher maintain good communication with the aide, discussing what needs to be done and the priorities for the day. The teacher should be sensitive to adults' need to be involved in making decisions and should plan to involve the aide in choosing tasks to be done. The teacher and aide must also evaluate the process as they work together: Is the aide learning new skills so that different activities are now appropriate? Does the aide feel appreciated? Is the aide comfortable with the tasks that he does routinely? Do the teacher and aide agree on most issues? Does the aide want to learn new techniques for working with the children? Are both the teacher and aide satisfied with the communication between them?

Working successfully with aides requires that teachers provide frequent positive feedback and praise for a job well done. Notes of appreciation to aides, notes to principals or administrators or in newsletters specifically commending aides, and any other special recognition that is deserved can make teacher-aide relationships more positive and assure that good work continues.

CHAPTER SUMMARY

- Parent-teacher relationships are very complex. Changing family structures, economic conditions, and isolation of the nuclear family all contribute to stresses on families that sometimes make parent involvement in the school difficult.
- A teacher must approach families with a non-judgmental attitude and be sensitive to the needs of children from many types of family structures.
- Family involvement is important for children's self-esteem and achievement. Parents may choose not to be involved, to be involved only passively, or to be actively involved in their children's education.
- Activities for involving families include family nights at school, potluck dinners, parent education programs, meetings of parent organizations, and committee meetings.
- Home visits by teachers can provide a wealth of information about children, their families, family interactions, and how children learn at home. Home visits must be carefully planned if they are to contribute to establishing good parent-teacher relationships.
- Inviting parents to visit and observe the program in action can open lines of communication

between parents and teachers. It is important to make arrangements for parents who cannot visit during the regular schoolday to visit at some other time and see how the program works.
- Setting aside a corner of the classroom for parents will communicate to them that teachers value their presence and believe that their involvement is important.
- Teachers should be prepared to offer assistance to parents who need help in meeting their basic needs; teacher must be informed about community resources, whom to contact for help, and the referral process.
- Parent or community volunteers in the classroom can enhance the program for children. Volunteers need to be screened and trained to be most effective and should be given tasks that benefit the children directly.
- Teacher aides can make vital contributions to programs for young children. Although they are not supposed to teach, aides can assume responsibilities for instruction, supervision, and classroom maintenance tasks. Teacher aides need carefully planned orientation and training.

WHAT WOULD YOU DO?

Reflect on your reading and your own experiences with young children as you think about the following situations:

1. A parent volunteers to help you in the classroom, but you don't believe he is well qualified to work with children. How would you respond to his offer?
2. You are a new teacher and have been assigned an aide who has been in the school a long time. The aide insists on treating the children in ways that you find unacceptable. How would you address this conflict?

3. You find that your new teacher aide only likes to do tasks such as cutting out letters for the bulletin board; she does not want to have any contact with the children. How would you approach her about her role as an aide?
4. The other teachers in your building use their parent volunteers to check papers and mount artwork and wonder why you do these things yourself. What would you tell them?

THEORY INTO PRACTICE

1. Interview several parents of young children about how they prefer to be involved in their children's education. Try to determine if their children's schools have offered them chances to be involved and how they feel about what has been offered.
2. Work with a small group of your classmates to plan a parent evening for math, reading, or science. Your plan should outline activities for the parents and children and include explanations of why these activities are important.
3. Interview several teachers of young children about how they involve parents in their pro-

grams. In their opinions, what are the most successful techniques?
4. Interview a teacher's aide to determine what she likes most and least about her work. Find out how she thinks her work situation could be improved.
5. Locate resources that might be needed by parents in the community where you hope to teach. Make sure that you know the procedures for referrals and whom to contact for each of these resources. Obtain copies of printed information that describes these resources and the services offered by each.

RECOMMENDED FOR FURTHER READING

Berger, Eugenia Hepworth. *Parents as Partners in Education: The School and Home Working Together.* 2d ed. Columbus, OH: Merrill, 1987.

Berger discusses the need for parent involvement in the schools and a variety of strategies for achieving the support of parents. The descriptions of school-based and home-based approaches to parent involvement are very thorough. Chapters that are especially helpful include those on working with parents of children who have been abused or who have special needs.

Cataldo, Christine Z. *Parent Education for Early Childhood: Child-Rearing Concepts and Program Content for the Student and Practicing Professional.* New York: Teachers College Press, 1987.

Thorough discussions of parent education and the relationship between schools and parent education programs are provided in this book. It is an especially valuable resource for those who are planning parent education programs or parent meetings. Several chapters discuss topics for parent education programs in detail.

Honig, Alice S. *Parent Involvement in Early Childhood Education.* Washington, DC: National Association for the Education of Young Children, 1975.

The author describes how parents can be involved in early childhood programs, why parent involvement

is important, and why getting parents involved is sometimes so difficult. Some of the resource lists are out of date, but the basic information in this publication is still very worthwhile.

Lightfoot, Sara Lawrence. *Worlds Apart: Relationships Between Families and Schools.* New York: Basic Books, 1978.

Lightfoot's work has been described as a classic study. It is an in-depth exploration of the sociocultural and historical factors that are integral to parent-school relationships. The book contains anecdotes by both teachers and parents that help to illustrate the points and help teachers translate the ideas to the real world of the school.

Stone, Jeannette Galambos. *Teacher-Parent Relationships.* Washington, DC: National Association for the Education of Young Children, 1987.

The author discusses in some detail how to work with parents on such issues as their child's anxiety at separation and suggests approaches to take in explaining policies on pickup time, toys from home, and other policies that influence parent-teacher relationships. The examples of language to use in communicating with parents illustrate the kinds of professional communication that all teachers would like to be able to employ in their teacher-parent interactions.

REFERENCES

Monographs for Parents from the International Reading Association

These inexpensive booklets can be ordered from the International Reading Association (P.O. Box 8139, 800 Barksdale Road, Newark, DE, 19711):

Chan, Julie M. T. *Why Read Aloud to Children?* #877.

Glazer, Susan Mandel. *How Can I Help My Child Build Positive Attitudes Toward Reading?* #879.

Rogers, Norma. *How Can I Help My Child Get Ready to Read?* #876.

Rogers, Norma. *What Books and Records Should I Get For My Preschooler?* #872.

Rogers, Norma. *What Is Reading Readiness?* #870.

These brochures for parents are available from NAEYC (see address in following section):

Keeping Healthy: Parents, Teachers and Children. #774, 1990.

Media Violence and Children: A Guide for Parents. #585, 1990.

Ready or Not . . . What Parents Should Know About School Readiness. #554, 1992.

Information about Parent Involvement

Further information may be obtained by writing or calling any of the following organizations:

National Congress of Parents and Teachers
700 Rush Street
Chicago, IL 60611
312-787-0977

National Coalition for Parent Involvement
in Education
National Education Association
1201 16th Street, NW, Room 810
Washington, DC 20036

NAEYC Information Service
1834 Connecticut Avenue, NW
Washington, DC 20009
202-232-8777 or 800-424-2460

General Sources

Bauch, Jerold P. "The TransParent School: A Partnership for Parent Involvement." *Educational Horizons* 68 (Summer 1990): 187–189.

Bundy, Blakely Fetridge. "Fostering Communication Between Parents and Preschools." *Young Children* 46 (January 1991): 12–17.

Cattermole, Juleen, and Norman Robinson. "Effective Home/School Communication—From the Parents' Perspective." *Phi Delta Kappan* 67 (September 1985): 48–50.

Chapman, Warren. "The Illinois Experience: State Grants to Improve Schools Through Parent Involvement." *Phi Delta Kappan* 72 (January 1991): 355–358.

Children's Defense Fund. *S.O.S. America! A Children's Defense Budget.* Washington, DC: CDF, 1990.

Children's Defense Fund. *The State of America's Children, 1992.* Washington, DC: CDF, 1992.

Cline, R. K. J. *Focus on Families: A Reference Handbook.* Santa Barbara, CA: ABC-CLIO, 1990.

D'Angelo, Diane A., and C. Ralph Adler. "Chapter I: A Catalyst for Improving Parent Involvement." *Phi Delta Kappan* 72 (January 1991): 350–354.

Epstein, Joyce L. "Paths to Partnership: What We Can Learn from Federal, State, District, and School Initiatives." *Phi Delta Kappan* 72 (January 1991): 344–349.

Epstein, Joyce L., and Susan L. Dauber. *Teachers' Attitudes and Practices of Parent Involvement in Inner-City Elementary and Middle Schools.* Baltimore, MD: Johns Hopkins University Center for Research on Elementary and Middle Schools, 1989 (as quoted in Olson 1990).

Galen, Harlene. "Increasing Parental Involvement in Elementary School: The Nitty-Gritty of One Successful Program." *Young Children* 46 (January 1991): 18–22.

Galinsky, Ellen. "Parents and Teacher-Caregivers: Sources of Tension, Sources of Support." *Young Children* 43 (March 1988): 4–12.

Greenberg, Polly. "Parents as Partners in Young Children's Development and Education: A New American Fad? Why Does It Matter?" *Young Children* 44 (May 1989): 61–75.

Halpern, Robert. "Major Social and Demographic Trends Affecting Young Families: Implications for

Early Childhood Care and Education." *Young Children* 42 (September 1987): 34–40.

Henderson, Anne T. "Parents Are a School's Best Friends." *Phi Delta Kappan* 70 (October 1988): 148–153 .

Hohmann, Mary, Bernard Banet, and David P. Weikart. *Young Children in Action.* Ypsilanti, MI: High/Scope Press, 1979.

Hranitz, John R., and E. Anne Eddowes. "Priorities: Parents and the Home." *Childhood Education* 63 (June 1987): 325–330.

Kagan, Sharon L. *When Parents and Schools Come Together: Differential Outcomes of Parent Involvement in Urban Schools.* ERIC Document Reproduction Service 281950. 1982.

Karr, Jo Ann, and Elizabeth Landerholm. *Reducing Staff Stress/Burnout by Changing Staff Expectations in Dealing with Parents.* ERIC Document Reproduction Service 351128. 1991.

Kieff, Judith. "Preferences of Mothers of At Risk and Peer Model Children for Parent Involvement Strategies." Doctoral dissertation, Oregon State University, 1990.

Leik, Robert K., and Mary Anne Chalkey. "Parent Involvement: What Is It That Works?" *Children Today* (May–June 1990): 34–37.

Leitch, M. Laurie, and Sandra S. Tangri. "Barriers to Home-School Collaboration." *Educational Horizons* 66 (Winter 1988): 70–74.

Lightfoot, Sara Lawrence. *Worlds Apart: Relationships Between Families and Schools.* New York: Basic Books, 1978.

Maryland State Department of Education. *The Early Childhood Model Parenting Program.* ERIC Document Reproduction Service 238526. Baltimore, MD: MSDE, Division of Compensatory, Urban, and Supplementary Programs, 1983.

Olson, Lynn. "Parents as Partners: Redefining the Social Contract Between Families and Schools." *Education Week* 9 (April 4 1990): 17–24.

"Prickly Problems #3: Parent Communications." *Child Care Information Exchange* 65 (February 1989): 15.

Spidel, Jo. "Working with Parents of the Exceptional Child." In *Parents as Partners in Education*, 2d ed., edited by Eugenia Hepworth Berger. Columbus, OH: Merrill, 1987.

Swick, Kevin J., and Shirley McKnight. "Characteristics of Kindergarten Teachers Who Promote Parent Involvement." *Early Childhood Research Quarterly* 4 (March 1989): 19–29.

Systems Development Corporation. *Effects of Different Head Start Program Approaches on Children of Different Characteristics: Report on Analysis of Data from 1968–69 National Evaluation.* Washington, DC: U.S. Office of Child Development, 1972.

· · · · · · · ·

Epilogue

In these final few pages, you will find information about the changing field of early childhood education and some issues that will concern you now and in the future. As an early childhood educator, you will face many of these issues and have to take a stand.

PROGRAM CHANGES OVER THE YEARS

The Child-Care Movement

The earliest **child care** was established in the settlement houses of big U.S. cities at the turn of the twentieth century "to provide a shelter for the children of mothers dependent on their own exertions for their daily bread; [but] also to rear useful citizens among the class represented by the children we reach" (Steinfels 1973, p. 29). Even though most working mothers worked because they had to for economic survival, the belief persisted that mothers should take care of their own children, so the availability of child care declined as the century progressed.

Other efforts at providing child care have been in response to national emergencies. During the Depression, the Works Progress Administration created nursery schools to provide teaching positions for unemployed teachers, and during World War II, the Lanham Act established nursery schools so that mothers could participate in the war effort. At the end of each of these periods, the federal funding ended, and so did the programs (Grubb 1989).

Child care
Care for children in a group, usually for the entire working day; the old term was *day care*.

During the 1970s, there were repeated efforts to pass legislation to support child care. Progress on child-care legislation stalled during the 1980s, but there is hope for the 1990s.

Head Start

The charity schools of the early 1800s (nursery schools supported by philanthropists to save children from poor families from disadvantaged environments) and the settlement house programs of the early 1900s shared the goal of trying to change the lives of young, poor children. Modern-day programs continue this effort.

Head Start
A program started in the 1960s to help young children who were disadvantaged prepare for success in school.

One component of the War on Poverty in the early 1960s was **Head Start,** a compensatory program that was a major feature of the plan to break the cycle of poverty in the United States. Head Start provides educational, social, medical, dental, nutritional, and mental health services to low-income preschool children. In 1990, Head Start celebrated its twenty-fifth anniversary, and although its funding is expected to increase, the program continues to be able to serve only a portion of the eligible children. Since the beginning of the Head Start program, over 11 million children and their families have been served (*Federal Register* 1990, p. 24838). Currently, 622,000 children are enrolled in Head Start programs, and the goal is full funding by 1996 (Collins 1993). Many different programs have been developed and evaluated as part of Head Start, and much research in early childhood education has been undertaken in Head Start programs. Thus, Head Start has been beneficial not only to the millions of children who have attended programs but also to the profession of early childhood education.

Because some of the positive effects of Head Start did not last once the children were in elementary school, Project Follow Through was developed. Follow Through attempts to maintain the gains made in Head Start by continuing family education and health care and by emphasizing success. Follow Through programs have never been as widespread as Head Start programs, however.

Programs for Children with Special Needs

The education of children with special needs has undergone radical changes in the last few decades. Early in the twentieth century, children with disabilities were often excluded from school experiences. Later, they were identified but segregated into special classes in schools. Often, all children with disabilities from a given school district were housed in a special school so that they had no contact with other children.

In 1975, Public Law (PL) 94-142, the Education for All Handicapped Children Act, was passed in the United States. This law is often called the "mainstreaming law," but it does not mention the word **mainstreaming.** What the law does say is that every child is entitled to an education in the **least restrictive environment (LRE).** Separate schools or classes are appropriate only when the "nature or severity of the handicap is such that education in regular classes with the use of supplementary aids and services cannot be achieved satisfactorily" (PL 94-142 20 U.S.C. 1412, 5, B).

Public Law 99-457, enacted in 1986, reauthorized PL 94-142 and extended its provisions to younger children. The intent of the original law had been to provide services to children with disabling conditions from birth to school age, but the law had been written so that states were not forced to provide services to children younger than school age. PL 99-457 extended the services to children from ages three to five and added incentives for states who served children from birth to age two, as well. Services can be provided by public or private agencies, but providers must demonstrate quality and integration. Key elements in PL 99-457 are its emphasis on the role of parents and its recognition of the importance of the family in the child's development.

Recognizing that labeling young children can be a very harmful practice, PL 99-457 does not require or emphasize categorical labels. Safford (1989) states the following reasons for avoiding labeling:

> *Young children's needs are difficult, if not impossible, to categorize with traditional labels.*
>
> *Especially during the early years, these needs change rapidly.*
>
> *Categorical labels have no utility for young children, since categorical programs may not be appropriate.*
>
> *Early labeling of children may limit and restrict them, since others may respond to these labels in limiting and restricting ways.*
>
> *Labels tend to follow the child, even after they are no longer applicable or appropriate. A label is a hard thing to lose!*
>
> *Least restrictive services for young children, required by P. L. 99:457, are intended to foster the interaction of handicapped and nonhandicapped children. Labels tend to impede that interaction. (p. 10)*

Federal law also requires that a minimum of 10 percent of the children enrolled in Head Start programs be children with disabilities and that services be provided to meet their special needs (Head Start, Economic

Mainstreaming
A placement approach in which children with disabling conditions are included in regular classrooms; inclusion.

Least restrictive environment (LRE)
The educational setting that is the least restrictive for an individual with given characteristics; the setting that provides the best educational opportunity for a child who is disabled.

Opportunity and Community Partnership Act of 1974, PL 93-644, 1974). To meet enrollment quotas, children who are disabled but not otherwise eligible for Head Start may be admitted (Safford 1989).

PL 94-142 was updated in 1990 and is now known as the Individuals with Disabilities Education Act (IDEA). IDEA expanded the categories of children eligible to receive special education services to include those with autism and traumatic brain injury. The new law continues to mandate parental involvement in educational decisions, education in the least restrictive environment, and individualized education programs (Hardman et al. 1993).

Kindergarten

The kindergarten movement began with Friedrich Froebel in Germany in 1837. The first kindergarten in the United States was opened in 1855 by Margaretha Schurz, and the first English-speaking kindergarten was opened by Elizabeth Peabody in 1860. The first publicly supported kindergarten was opened by Susan Blow in St. Louis in 1873 (Frost and Kissinger 1976).

Publicly supported kindergarten is available in almost all states, and many states now provide funding for public school programs for four-year-olds, especially those deemed at risk of failing in public school for any reason (Grubb 1989). In a few states, attendance in kindergarten is compulsory; that is, state law requires that parents send their children to school at five years of age. In most states, even though school districts are required to offer kindergarten, attendance is not mandated by law.

EARLY CHILDHOOD EDUCATION TODAY

Programs available for young children today include:

- Nonprofit and for-profit child care
- A variety of nursery schools, most of which enroll children at age three and many of which offer extended child care
- Public school programs for four-year-olds in many states
- Public school programs for three-year-olds with disabilities in many states
- Almost universal public school kindergarten programs

In addition to publicly sponsored programs, Jorde (1988) categorizes other types of programs.

- *Employer-sponsored programs*—It is not a new idea to offer child care in the workplace, but it is a growing trend. Some companies offer on-site care; others offer vouchers to help employees pay for child care and flexible work hours to make child care easier for their employees.
- *Church-sponsored programs*—Jorde (1988) estimates that 50 percent of the center-based care programs in the United States are housed on religious property. Most of these programs offer some religious instruction as part of the curriculum. According to Jorde, most churches offer child-care programs as a response to community need.
- *For-profit child care, both private and corporate*—For-profit child-care centers range from small, private operations to large chains that operate child-care centers in several states or regions. These centers offer services ranging from half-day nursery schools to twenty-four-hour-a-day child care for infants, toddlers, and preschoolers as well as after-school care for school-age children. The services they provide are as varied as their philosophies and program goals.
- *Programs sponsored by institutions of higher learning*—Although not many laboratory schools are left on college and university campuses, many schools today provide child-care centers for faculty and students. Most of these centers offer full-day programs of child care; some do not accept children younger than two or two-and-a-half years old.

CONTEMPORARY ISSUES IN EARLY CHILDHOOD EDUCATION

The issues presented here are not the only issues facing the profession of early childhood education. As you participate in reading, observing, thinking, and teaching, you will discover more issues and develop your own opinions on them. Your personal answers to the questions inherent in these issues will be important as you begin to make choices in your profession.

Entrance Age for School Programs

One of the issues that concerns educators is the age for entry into school programs. Most public schools now provide kindergarten for five-year-olds. Many public school systems now also provide programs for four-year-old children and programs for three-year-old children with special needs.

Some people believe that having such very young children in the public schools will result in a more academic approach to education of the young. They are worried that what was once the first-grade curriculum is being pushed into kindergarten and that the program once taught in kindergarten will soon be assigned to four-year-old children. Others argue that most young children are in some sort of group care, as more and more mothers join the workforce. They believe that the public schools can provide positive experiences for very young children because schools have control of teacher qualifications through state certification programs and are able to set standards for programs in the community.

Professionals in early childhood education are faced with many questions about programs for young children: Should very young children be in public school programs? Can programs for young children be incorporated into public schools without such programs becoming focused on academic learning? Who will teach young children in public school programs? Is there any danger that academic programs will be offered to younger and younger children? Who will pay for these programs?

You may have other questions about programs for young children, which you should ponder as you think about teaching.

Qualifications for Teachers of Young Children

What qualifications make a person a good teacher of young children? This question is difficult to answer to the satisfaction of the many groups concerned. Most people would say that "a love of children" and "patience" are personal qualities that are necessary for successful teaching. Beyond these personal characteristics, the answers vary considerably.

Some people believe that vocational programs at community colleges are adequate preparation for teaching young children; others believe that a four-year degree program is the minimum acceptable amount of preparation. In some states, additional coursework beyond an elementary teaching certificate is required of those who wish to teach in programs for young children; in other states, there are no special requirements beyond elementary certification. Generally, teachers in private schools are not required by law to have any formal preparation in teacher education; standards for preparation are left to the discretion of the employing school. In many states, teachers in child care are not required to meet any standards for preparation.

Two of the largest professional organizations for early childhood educators, the National Association for the Education of Young Children (NAEYC) and the Association for Childhood Education International (ACEI), have produced guidelines for teacher-preparation programs that include the following:

- Strong liberal arts education
- Knowledge of the foundations of early childhood education
- Knowledge of child growth and development
- Knowledge of curriculum
- Knowledge of the teaching-learning process
- Experience in working with young children in a supervised setting (NAEYC 1982; ACEI 1982)

Questions about what constitutes adequate preparation of teachers of young children are numerous: Is a combination of coursework and field experience the answer to better preparation of early childhood teachers? How should these components be balanced? If coursework is the answer, how much and what kind is ideal? What other alternatives might be acceptable? Should there be more regulations regarding the education and training of people who work with young children outside public school systems?

As you begin a program of studies on teaching young children, you will want to consider the answers to these questions proposed by various individuals or groups and try to analyze the rationales for their answers.

Decisions about Curriculum and Teaching Strategies

Curriculum experiences and teaching strategies are important issues. In some school settings, administrators believe that decisions concerning these issues are best made by a central administrator so that continuity and consistency are maintained—for instance, so that a child who transferred from one school to another would be presented with school experiences that would not vary much from those in his previous school. Children in all schools in a district would have similar experiences in school. Others argue that curriculum experiences must reflect the growth and development of individual children in specific classrooms and schools and address the interests and needs of those children.

The teacher is also an important variable in curriculum decisions. In some settings, the teacher has the freedom to choose program goals and learning experiences to meet those goals. In most situations, the teacher is provided with goals developed by committees of teachers; teachers and parents; or teachers, parents, and administrators but can choose the learning experiences to best meet those goals.

As you think about becoming a teacher of young children, you will want to consider your answers to the following questions: Who should determine the curriculum? If one approach to curriculum seems to be more appropriate, should it be legislated for all children? Who is responsible for evaluating the curriculum for young children?

These are complex questions that do not have simple answers. You may not feel that you can answer these questions adequately at this point, but as you become a professional teacher, you will no doubt form your own opinions and answers.

Changing Expectations of Young Children

Although the debate about what should be taught in kindergarten and preschool is not a new one, it has not yet been settled. For example, it was much less common twenty-five years ago to find programs of reading instruction in kindergarten than it is today. For many reasons, parents today seem to expect their children to achieve more academically at earlier ages. Some preschools teach what was once the common kindergarten curriculum; kindergartens teach what was once taught in first grade.

Many children's lives are also filled with a variety of lessons, from ballet and gymnastics to French—lessons that may be perceived differently by children and their parents. An elementary principal told of visiting a first-grade class on the first day of school. He observed a child putting on his jacket and asked him where he was going. The boy replied that he was going home. The principal said, "Oh, you don't want to go home. We're going to have lunch, then music and art and recess." The boy put his hands on his hips and replied, "Who in the _____ signed me up for all that?"

Some would encourage parents to teach infants to read and recognize numbers, claiming that infants learn more quickly than humans learn at any other time in their lives and that this ability should not be wasted. Many parents want their children to have a head start on other children in terms of achievement, and they invest time and money to make sure that their children can compete.

Debates in the popular press and in professional literature about education for young children have raised even more questions: Are higher expectations regarding achievement beneficial to children? Do today's children know more at an earlier age than children of previous generations? How can stress in the lives of young children be reduced?

As you continue your work to become a teacher of young children, consider your answers to these questions.

This is an exciting and challenging period in early childhood education. There is still much information to learn and much work to do to make life as good as it can be for children. The issues are important for children and for society.

Your answers are important, too. They will help you make decisions about where and how to teach, about political issues that affect the lives of children, and about your own education.

REFERENCES

Association for Childhood Education International. "Guidelines for the Preparation of Early Childhood Teachers." Working paper. Wheaton, MD: ACEI, 1982.

Collins, Raymond C. "Heat Start: Steps toward a Two-Generation Program Strategy." *Young Children* 48 (January 1993): 25–31, 72–73.

Federal Register, 18 June 1990, p. 24838.

Frost, Joe L., and Joan B. Kissinger. *The Young Child and the Educative Process.* New York: Holt, Rinehart and Winston, 1976.

Grubb, Norton. "Young Children Face the State: Issues and Options for Early Childhood Programs." *American Journal of Education* 97 (August 1989): 358–397.

Hardman, Michael L. et al. *Human Exceptionality: Society, School, and Family.* 4th ed. Boston: Allyn and Bacon, 1993.

Jorde, Paula. "Early Childhood Education: Issues and Trends." In *Early Childhood Education in the Schools,* edited by Jerold P. Bauch. Washington, DC: National Education Association, 1988.

National Association for the Education of Young Children. *Early Childhood Teacher Education Guidelines.* Position statement of the National Association for the Education of Young Children. Washington, DC: NAEYC, 1982.

Safford, Philip L. *Integrated Teaching in Early Childhood: Starting in the Mainstream.* White Plains, NY: Longman, 1989.

Steinfels, Margaret O'Brien. *Who's Minding the Children? The History and Politics of Day Care in America.* New York: Simon and Schuster, 1973 (as quoted in Grubb 1989).

Index

Note: A bold page number indicates that the topic is a key term and defined in a marginal note on that page.